The
MOFFATT
NEW TESTAMENT COMMENTARY
Based on *The New Translation* by the
REV. PROFESSOR JAMES MOFFATT, D.D.
and under his Editorship

THE REVELATION OF
ST. JOHN

The Moffatt
New Testament Commentary

THE REVELATION OF
ST. JOHN

BY

MARTIN KIDDLE
M.A.(Oxon)
Vicar of Christ Church, Harrogate
Lecturer of Leeds Parish Church

ASSISTED BY M. K. ROSS

HARPER AND BROTHERS PUBLISHERS
NEW YORK AND LONDON

EDITOR'S PREFACE

MOFFATT'S NEW TESTAMENT COMMENTARY

THE aim of this commentary is to bring out the religious meaning and message of the New Testament writings. To do this, it is needful to explain what they originally meant for the communities to which they were addressed in the first century, and this involves literary and historical criticism; otherwise, our reading becomes unintelligent. But the New Testament was the literature of the early Church, written out of faith and for faith, and no study of it is intelligent unless this aim is kept in mind. It is literature written for a religious purpose. ' These are written that ye might believe that Jesus is the Christ, the Son of God.' This is the real object of the New Testament, that Christians might believe it better, in the light of contemporary life with its intellectual and moral problems. So with any commentary upon it. Everything ought to be subordinated to the aim of elucidating the religious content, of showing how the faith was held in such and such a way by the first Christians, and of making clear what that faith was and is.

The idea of the commentary arose from a repeated demand to have my New Testament translation explained; which accounts for the fact that this translation has been adopted as a convenient basis for the commentary. But the contributors have been left free to take their own way. If they interpret the text differently, they have been at liberty to say so. Only, as a translation is in itself a partial commentary, it has often saved space to print the commentary and start from it.

As everyman has not Greek, the commentary has been written, as far as possible, for the Greekless. But it is based upon a first-hand study of the Greek original, and readers may rest assured that it represents a close reproduction of the original writers' meaning, or at any rate of what we consider that to have been. Our common aim has been to enable everyman to-day to sit where these first Christians sat, to feel the impetus and inspiration of the Christian faith as it dawned upon the minds of the communities in the first century, and thereby to realize more vividly how new and lasting is the message which prompted these New Testament writings to take shape as they did. Sometimes people inside as well as outside the Church make mistakes about the New Testament. They think it means this or that, whereas its words frequently mean something very different from what traditional associations suggest. The saving thing is to let the New Testament speak for itself. This is our desire and plan in the present commentary, to place each writing or group of writings in its original setting, and allow their words to come home thus to the imagination and conscience of everyman to-day.

The general form of the commentary is to provide a running comment on the text, instead of one broken up into separate verses. But within these limits, each contributor has been left free. Thus, to comment on a gospel requires a method which is not precisely the same as that necessitated by commenting on an epistle. Still, the variety of treatment ought not to interfere with the uniformity of aim and form. Our principle has been that nothing mattered, so long as the reader could understand what he was reading in the text of the New Testament.

JAMES MOFFATT.

PREFACE

When I told my friend Bishop Hensley Henson that Dr. Moffatt had invited me to write the commentary in this series on the Book of Revelation (following the untimely death of Sir Edwyn Hoskyns, to whom the task had been originally entrusted) he warned me of the magnitude of such an undertaking. ' Anyone who puts his hand to write a commentary on the Apocalypse is a bold man,' he said, and he warned me that the duties of the large parish to which I had been recently nominated as Vicar would leave all too little time for study. The Bishop's *caveat* was stated not less firmly by Dr. Moffatt. ' No one knows how difficult the task is until he has tried it for himself,' he wrote. But both were as generous in their encouragement as they were frank in their admonition. In one of his letters, Dr. Moffatt wrote as follows :

' The work of a parish is exactly the kind of preparation one needed for the commentary. My idea was and is to have it written by scholars who were in close touch with the actual life of Christian people, not from an outlook through college windows. One understands the New Testament, I think, best through contact with the plain difficulties and needs of life in the churches ; at least, that furnishes the Editor with an instinct for what doesn't need to be said ! '

I have tried to keep this wise counsel in mind during the three years spent in the preparation of the commentary. In my duties as Incumbent and Lecturer, it has been instructive to discuss the problems presented by the Apocalypse to the ordinary reader. The work has indeed been heavy, but singularly attractive, and was made lighter by the valuable help of my friend, Mr. M. K. Ross. His assistance has been close and extensive, and it gave me great pleasure when Dr. Moffatt and the publishers acceded to my request that our collaboration should be acknowledged on the title page of the commentary. I wish to thank also Miss Woodward, Librarian of Newnham College, Professor C. H. Dodd, and Dr. Vincent Taylor, all of whom have helped me in various ways. My indebtedness to the many eminent students of REVELATION is apparent from a reading of the commentary, and while it would be purposeless to burden this Preface with a long bibliography, I desire to express my gratitude.

One last acknowledgment is due. When Dr. Moffatt's suggestion that I should write the commentary reached me, I was on holiday with Professor Gilbert Murray at Rieder-furka, 5,000 feet above the Rhone Valley. We discussed the Apocalypse on our walks together, and I shall never forget the way my learned companion revealed its wonder and beauty. The grandeur of the scenery was a fitting setting for such tuition. For the first time I began to see REVELATION as John meant it to be seen ; and I should like to think I had succeeded in my attempt to impart to John's readers some of the inspiration I then had the privilege to enjoy.

MARTIN KIDDLE.

C/O THE WAR OFFICE.
1940.

CONTENTS

INTRODUCTION

COMMENTARY

CONTENTS

CONTENTS

CONTENTS

At the round earths imagin'd corners, blow
Your trumpets, Angells, and arise, arise
From death, you numberless infinities
Of souls, and to your scattred bodies goe,
All whom the flood did, and fire shall o'erthrow,
All whom warre, dearth, age, agues, tyrannies,
Despaire, law, chance, hath slaine, and you whose eyes,
Shall behold God, and never tast deaths woe.
But let them sleepe, Lord, and mee mourne a space,
For if above all these, my sinnes abound,
'Tis late to aske abundance of thy grace,
When wee are there ; here on this lowly ground,
Teach mee how to repent ; for that's as good
As if thou' hadst seal'd my pardon, with thy blood.

JOHN DONNE (*Holy Sonnets*).

INTRODUCTION

INTRODUCTION

I. The Modern Approach to Revelation

Of all the books of the New Testament, REVELATION is probably read least ; not, however, because it is the least interesting, for it has an exceptional fascination. The neglect is occasioned by its extreme difficulty. With some passages everyone is familiar, if only through hearing the superb extracts from the seventh and twenty-first chapters, which in modern times are commonly read at funeral services. But as soon as people attempt to read the book as a whole, they are perplexed by the obscurities which confront them in almost every verse. They may get as far as the end of the third chapter, though even in this first part they are baffled by many unusual details. As soon as they attempt to penetrate further, the book becomes so strange as to be meaningless. Then, if their interest is sufficiently active to encourage resort to a commentary, they find that the scholars are themselves acutely conscious of the uncertainties with which REVELATION appears to teem, and they are quickly lost in the maze of suggested reconstructions and interpretations. They may agree with Jerome that ' it has as many mysteries (i.e. symbols) as it has words,' but that will hardly convince them that it is therefore ' above all praise.'

Yet it is not unreasonable to attempt to design a commentary for the ordinary reader, because John undoubtedly wrote his book for ordinary people. Most of the difficulties are the legacy of time, not of the original writer's peculiar mind. This is not to deny that John had a taste for the mysterious, or that his visions are marked by that freedom of expression which distinguishes all psychic experiences. But the paramount condition of approaching REVELATION intelligently is to understand that the writer's interest was strictly pastoral, first and last; that he wrote to his fellow-Christians with the firm conviction that he had a special message whereby he could encourage and warn them in times of extreme urgency; and that nothing was further from his mind than to obscure that message for the sake of intrigue or impressiveness. It is indeed remarkable how consistently John adheres to his main pastoral purpose, and bends the apocalyptic medium to serve that purpose throughout the whole book. For this reason (apart from others), it is a mistake to suggest that the letters to the seven churches were originally circulated independently.[1] They are an essential part of the book, intended by John to point the practical moral of the apocalypse itself. But throughout the whole book, in vision as in exhortation, John is essentially practical. Repeatedly he reiterates his message that the time for God's great intervention in human affairs is near as the all-sufficient cause why the timorous should be emboldened, the weak fortified, the complacent warned, and the faithful assured. He is far too serious for any wish to stimulate or satisfy idle curiosity. So strong is our belief that John was constrained solely by his desire to inspire and explain that we hold the view that no obscurity which confronts the modern reader was either intended by him or caused through any uncertainty in his purpose. On the contrary, the solution of every difficulty, including the problem of judging rightly the horrors of the book which seem to offend modern morality, must be sought in the fact that originally John wrote only to help Christians, when times were too sorely pressing to justify indulgence in speculation or entertainment. Careful study proves that he fulfils the promise of the opening words of his book—*a revelation by Jesus Christ, which God granted him for his servants, to show them what must come to pass very soon.*

It is true that the revelation is mainly a series of visions which, on a superficial view, appear to be tinged by the incoherences to which products of ecstatic experiences are sometimes subject; true that the symbols John uses belong to

[1] See Ramsay, *Letters to the Seven Churches.*

heaven rather than to earth, or to this earth under abnormal circumstances. Still, it *is* a revelation which he sets out to give, an unfolding, an illumination, an explanation—not the opposite. Moreover, no matter how weird and unearthly the action of his great drama may appear, it is always related to the world of John's own day—the world in which Christians had to live, not merely to some domain of apocalyptic fantasy, thronged with imaginary beings which have no concern with mortal men. Although the action lies in the future, the purpose of describing that action is always to remove the mists of doubt and fear which obscured the Christian's outlook. Present and future are never divorced. In a word, John was honestly endeavouring to explain, not to obscure ; to guide, not to perplex ; to enlighten, not to darken. Whenever he thinks it necessary, he explains carefully and simply the significance of what he saw (e.g. i. 20, iv. 5, v. 6, vii. 13, xii. 17, xiii. 18, xvii. 7, xix. 8, etc.), and it is an instance of the irony of the misunderstanding to which REVELATION is still liable that modern commentators are often inclined to the opinion that such explanations must be the work of an early interpolator. Some are unwilling to allow John anything but a desire to frustrate an intelligent understanding of his own work.

Yet no one can suppress the wish that John had given more and clearer explanations. To many it seems extraordinary that so much of the book appears incapable of a reasonable explanation, and affords such unlimited opportunities for the various and even contradictory speculations of commentators. In no other book of the New Testament is the reader presented with such fantasies, such incoherent imaginations. Accustomed, as he is, to the (apparent) simplicity of the Gospels, and the straight-forwardness of the Epistles, it seems to him grotesque to look for any inspiration in a book where strange creatures worship, angels fly in mid-heaven or bestride the earth and sea, altars speak, and the earth is drenched in a succession of supernatural horrors. The ordinary enquirer must ask the same question as the Ethiopian eunuch : ' How can I possibly understand it, unless some one puts me on the right track ? ' And with that question he may reasonably add a protest that if John's purpose was pastoral, he might well have chosen a more intelligible medium. He will be inclined to agree with Luther, who, supposing that the obscurities of the book were the fault of the writer, esteemed it very lightly, and protested vigorously against the commands and threats which John makes about his book (xxii. 18–19), and the promise of blessedness to those who keep what is written in it (i. 3, xxii. 7) : 'when no one knows what that is, to say nothing of keeping it, and there are many nobler books to be kept.'

It must be clearly understood that what perplexes us presented fewer difficulties to the original readers for whom John wrote. The lack of explanations to which we have referred is testimony to the simplicity of the book, not to its obscurity, in the minds of the first-century Christians of Asia Minor. They understood it with comparative ease because they were versed in apocalyptic thought. To them, as to John, it was as natural as the air they breathed. It moulded and inspired the whole of their religious life. To what extent in the early Church this was the case there is insufficient evidence to determine, though Loisy thinks it was more widespread than is usually realized.[1] Certainly it was the normal habit of religious thought in the local churches with which John was familiar, for otherwise no one inspired by such a directly practical purpose would have used it. This does not mean that REVELATION presented no difficulties at all, even to its original readers. John did at least find it necessary to explain some points, and it cannot be claimed that his explanations are always as clear as we could wish. It is remarkable that his original meaning became a matter of conjecture at a very early date. For example, about eighty years after REVELATION was written, Irenæus could only guess what John meant when he said that the mark of the Beast was six hundred and sixty-six (xiii. 18) ; apparently he had no tradition to guide him. For that matter, we may fairly ask whether John himself, any more than other seers who were subject to ecstatic visions, was always quite certain about the interpretation of what he saw, even when

[1] *See* Loisy, *L'Apocalypse de Jean* (introduction).

guided by interpreting angels—to say nothing of the extreme difficulty of expressing those visions in words. Then, again, John did not expect his readers to understand his visions without effort. He expected them to be discerning, to pay careful attention, to ponder his message as he himself had done. Symbolism demands patient study, even from those trained in its uses. Nor must we overlook the probability that at times John had to be intentionally cryptic, because of the danger of his book getting into the hands of the Church's enemies. In dealing with matters involving reference to public affairs (especially to the emperor, and the emperor-cult, and the coming of Antichrist), the author was obliged to be cautious, to endeavour to be at once intelligible to the Elect, and highly unintelligible to outsiders.

All the same, these difficulties were few in number, dealing with special points. Nothing suggests that John thought his book as a whole would be obscure to his readers, as it so often is to us. He clearly intended that his message should be pastoral, a practical exhortation to ordinary folk ; and we know that, unlike ourselves, his original readers expected and enjoyed instruction through the apocalyptic medium. In fact, REVELATION was actually a revelation to those for whom it was first composed, because they had the master key which unlocked its mysteries. We have lost that key. It was lost at a very early date ; for although the apocalyptic temper can be detected in various phases throughout the history of the Christian Church, it was never the orthodox outlook of the Church as a whole—at least, not after the close of the first century—and the original meaning of apocalyptic symbolism was quickly forgotten. During the long centuries that followed, a succession of commentators have, with varying success, attempted to discover the lost key, and history records how unfortunate many of the results have been. ' Everyone thinks of the book whatever his spirit imparts,' says Luther, and it is truly unfortunate that REVELATION has proved such an attractive quarry for those whose enthusiasm exceeds their knowledge, and who approach it already convinced about what kind of religious or political systems it prophesies.

Modern knowledge, and the modern scientific approach to Bible study leave no excuse for any further repetition of such errors. We may safely claim to be in a better position for understanding the Apocalypse than was any other age since the first century. Many of the long-lost apocalyptic writings have been rediscovered, and the study of them has thrown much light on REVELATION, the greatest and grandest example of that class of literature.[1] We realize now that it is futile to attempt to manufacture a substitute key, as though the book must be made to reveal what we think it ought to reveal. Instead, we must attempt to get back into the mind of the writer, to appreciate his outlook, his reading of the times in which he lived, and his remedy for them. Only so can REVELATION become a revelation to us, as it was to John and his fellow-believers. Perhaps it is too much to expect that all the problems can be solved. The details are too intricate, the thought too subtle, to warrant the hope of achieving an exact and certain interpretation of every point. The longer one studies REVELATION, the less one is inclined to claim authority for one's own interpretation of its mysteries. The main message of the book can, however, be made intelligible to any reader who is prepared to give the matter careful thought ; and no important problem need be left unsolved.

II. JOHN'S OUTLOOK

We have observed that apocalyptic thought and expression were normal in the early Church. It would be outside the scope of this commentary to attempt an examination of apocalyptic literature as a whole.[2] It is enough for our present purposes to realize that the underlying belief which inspired apocalyptic thought and determined its particular mode of

---

[1] Cf. R. H. Charles, *Between the Old and the New Testaments.*

[2] Those who wish to study the subject should read Charles, *The Apocrypha and Pseudepigrapha of the Old Testament* ; Porter, *Messages of the Apocalyptic Writers* ; Burkitt, *Jewish and Christian Apocalypses.* A useful brief summary is also given by I. T. Beckwith, *The Apocalypse of John*, pp. 166–97.

expression was that God would shortly intervene catastrophically in human affairs, these having become so out of
hand, so irredeemably corrupt, that nothing less could dispel
the perplexities and vindicate the sufferings of the righteous.
In other words, the apocalyptists placed all their hopes in a
new age, which could come only when this world order had
passed away. It may well be that this eschatological emphasis
accounts for the absorbing interest in unearthly symbols which
distinguishes apocalyptic literature. When God's great Day
approached, and He began to execute His eternal purpose,
the natural order would be inevitably superseded. Thus the
apocalyptist, much more than the ancient prophet, was concerned with the future, or, rather, the future was contemplated
in order to explain the enigma of the present—a future which
would be essentially different from anything yet known, which
belonged to heaven rather than to earth; which would,
indeed, assert itself by sweeping away existing conditions.
That forward look is very marked in REVELATION. John was
chiefly desirous of preparing his fellow-Christians for the supernatural terrors which must come when Antichrist appeared,
and by his presence certified to the discerning that the
End was at hand. This alone is sufficient to explain the
unusual features of apocalyptic writings. When an attempt
is made to describe God and heaven and the future life, the
things of this world must be regarded as inadequate, if not
improper symbols. Then, too, the prophets who thus concentrated their attention on the last things, and received their
divine message in the form of visions, were necessarily released
from conformity to earthly patterns. The mental processes
of ecstatic experiences shared, to some extent, in the liberty
enjoyed by human imagination in dreams. When John tells
us that he was rapt in spirit, was granted visions, was carried
from earth to heaven, and saw heaven open wide, with its
innermost secrets laid bare, and conversed with angels and
even with Christ Himself, it is hardly surprising if, on a superficial reading, his book seems to abound in insoluble riddles.
One of the avowed purposes of the apocalyptists was to reveal
hidden secrets, and they were sufficiently conscious of the

obscurities of their visions to relate how they themselves needed explanations from heavenly interpreters (i. 20, vii. 13, xvii. 6–13).

Yet it would be a mistake to suppose that any Christian prophet regarded himself as free to let his imagination roam at will in unfettered ecstasy. Apocalyptic thought, like every other activity of the mind, had its origins, and in time created its own literary form. It grew out of prophecy, gradually, almost unconsciously, according to the needs of the times—we can trace the development in the Old Testament. The purpose and therefore the literary traditions of both were at first the same. In time apocalyptic thought progressed along its own independent lines, and to understand the visions it is often necessary to study the earlier ideas which the later writers used and developed. That is especially the case with REVELATION. Much of the book can be understood only by a careful study of John's use of certain books within and without the Scriptures. But this does not mean that John was nothing more than an editor, or that he necessarily obtained his ideas directly from other writings, or even that he was always conscious of his ' sources ' which we now attempt to trace for ourselves.

Here we touch upon a big difficulty, about which dogmatism would be specially unwise. Nowadays REVELATION is studied chiefly from a literary and a psychological point of view. In it we can now trace for ourselves, to some extent, John's devotional library, and also the trend of his thinking and meditation. By using the references in the Revised Version, for example, we can learn how very familiar he must have been with the books of the Old Testament. Moreover, in view of the large volume of apocalyptic writings outside the Scriptures, their widespread currency, and their popularity, we can reasonably suppose that he was familiar with these also, that he reverenced their message, and that he assumed a like attitude of mind in his readers. Yet we cannot for a moment believe that his chief function was that of a scribe editing a composition derived from older materials. A first-century Christian prophet who had suffered exile, who passionately

believed that the world was about to be drenched in supernatural terrors before its final dissolution, was unlikely to be
interested in literary research. This is where modern psycho-
logy can help. John's book gives abundant evidence that he
was the recipient of ecstatic experiences of a profoundly
emotional character, experiences which gave him the unshakable conviction that his message was divinely inspired
and of the most urgent importance for the Church. It would
be intolerable to argue that he adopted the convention of
visions as a convenient mode of transforming his literary
sources.

But then the question arises, Is it reasonable to conclude
that in his ecstasies John could have experienced visions so
rich in prophetic allusions, so fertile in literary interpretation? Would a vision, or a succession of visions, be distinguished by such careful symmetry, such clear development of
thought, such finished artistry? If John had reported his
visions exactly as he had seen them, would they not then have
appeared to be much more unintelligible than they do even
to us, 1,900 years later? Would John have been quite so
certain himself about their meaning? We cannot say. Only
those who have experienced the ecstatic state should attempt
to set limits to its possibilities—and they would be the last
to do so. In ecstatic experiences the mind is not numb
nor is the reason paralysed, as they often are in ordinary
dreams; nor is the memory blotted out—we know that the
materials of visions can be sometimes traced back to sources
previously acquired and stored in the sub-conscious mind,
though long since forgotten by the conscious memory. This
may well have been the case with John. Nor must we fail
to give full weight to the consideration that in REVELATION
we have a *report* of the original visions, not the visions themselves—a genuine report doubtless, an accurate report, John
would insist, but still a report in words of what was first seen
with the inward eye, and written after some lapse of time.
Then, too, it is not a cold, business-like report, it is in no way
similar to a Fleet Street production. Even as he wrote, John's
mind and heart must have been aglow with the memory of

the divine flame that had enthralled his whole being while he was 'in the Spirit.' Still, in the ordinary, quiet, objective frame of mind (for the body is inert during the trance), he had now to state in words what had been originally an experience. 'Write down your vision,' he was told. And he had to be practical, to make his book a pastoral exhortation for the faithful. There is little cause for surprise, then, if (perhaps quite unconsciously) he adapted his visions to the conventions of that class of literature to which he himself and his readers had been long accustomed.

Lastly, to understand John's thought, we must study his attitude to the ancient prophets, if only because the form of his visions was of necessity determined by his knowledge and study of their words. This is of paramount importance for an understanding of John's mind and method, and an appreciation of his unique contribution to religious thought. Like every other Christian prophet who sought for the divine solution to the crisis of the times, John turned to the authoritative utterances of the prophetic Scriptures. But he did not study them as examples of edifying literature. Still less did he search them for suitable materials for his own book. To regard him as one who merely 'adapted' the prophecies of the great writings in which his faith is saturated (especially Isaiah, Ezekiel, Daniel, and Zechariah) is to miss entirely his whole mental and religious genius. To him these were the inspired oracles of God, the infallible prophecies which must be fulfilled. But concerning whom were they predicted? When and how were they to be fulfilled? John, like all the leaders of the new faith, was certain that the Christian Church was the heir of the promises under the Old Covenant—it was no longer necessary even to argue the point as St. Paul had been obliged to do. The urgent problem was their fulfilment. By this time it was insufficient to concentrate attention on certain prophecies which served to confirm the Gospel message ; no longer enough to formulate the simple messianic hope which was to be fulfilled in the last days. That had sufficed in the early days of the Church's history, when faith was buoyant, and missionary expansion fostered an optimistic enthusiasm.

In John's day that cheerful hopefulness had passed. The dark shadow of impending persecution in a new form—determined, ruthless, organized, universal, inescapable—was about to burst upon the Church. What, then, of the ancient prophecies ? What was their message for the ' hour of trial which is coming upon the whole world to test the dwellers on earth ' ?

It was with this problem in mind that John turned to the ancient oracles, brooded over them, pondered them in the light of the conditions of the world in his own day, and then, in an ecstasy of inspiration, saw their message, and received the solemn conviction that God had commanded him to deliver it to the Church (see pp. 166ff., 174ff., 202ff., 302ff., 323ff., 359ff., 371ff., 387ff., 393ff., 437ff.). The prophecies are the unrefined gold now poured into the crucible of his soaring imagination and fashioned into his visions. '*This*,' says John in REVELATION, 'this is the vision from God Himself, given to me by Christ through His angel.' It is for us to study the prophecies as he had done, to read them with his eyes, so that we may the more fully share in the message which he has delivered.

III. The Literary Character of Revelation

In the foregoing section we have stressed John's creative genius as a visionary. That, however, does not alter the fact that we have to study his visions in literary form ; and we are bound to ask by what methods he actually wrote his book. Now, it would be useless to deny that the general impression of REVELATION suggests that, besides pondering Old Testament prophecy, John made use of other sources, either written or oral, outside the Bible. The distinct units which form the seals, trumpets and bowls series, and which, when we first examine them, seem to be only artificially connected with each other, point to this conclusion. But even if this difficult problem is studied from a literary point of view only, a hasty judgment would be ill-advised. What seems to be an awkward grafting of previously separate sources often proves, on closer study, to be an example of a skilful, and even subtle combination of visions which, for all we know, may have been the original creations of John's mind (cf. notes on viii. 1–5). It is by no means certain that REVELATION is (after chap. iii.), as some have argued, a compilation of sources that had been hitherto separate (as 1 Enoch in its present form undoubtedly is, and probably 4 Ezra). It is more likely that a prophet of John's temperament created an original work, though perhaps using, unconsciously rather than consciously, other material. Before we speak of John as an editor, we must acknowledge that we do not *know* that he used sources, either written or oral, outside the Old Testament. There are many possible—some would say probable—allusions to popular apocalyptic traditions, but no conclusive references, no definite quotations. The uncertainty about the date of many of the apocalyptic writings that have been discovered makes it just as plausible to assume their dependence upon REVELATION as to regard them as John's sources. As to the Old Testament, we have seen that the allusions appear to be the product of long-cherished memories, refashioned by ecstatic experiences, rather than conscious literary references. Would John not use non-Scriptural sources, if at all, in the same way? But in any case, since we have no exact information that he used any, is there much value in attempting to define the original form of sources the very existence of which is only conjectural? Is not the element of guesswork too great to allow any useful conclusions? At least it is well to bear in mind that the question of sources is only one of many literary problems in REVELATION, and that we are on surer and more profitable ground when we attempt to examine John's own literary plan and purpose, when we observe the way he so presents his visions that he succeeds completely in delivering the message that he had been commanded to transmit.

Such a study induces the conviction that John manifests a high degree of skill in the intricate and yet clearly defined narration of his successive visions. Although he had to deal with symbols which might have perplexed even those versed in apocalyptic thought, although he had to recall and report experiences no longer active except in the conscious memory, the presentation of his message is accomplished with consistent deftness and accuracy. Moreover, the book as a whole has about it that impression of finish and confidence which marks the work of one who is master of his material. Not only do certain passages reach loftiness of expression which ranks them among the greatest literary achievements ; there is a sustained grandeur and a successful endeavour to retain the reader's interest from the first verse to the last.

One of the many literary problems of the book is the relationship between the various visions. Are they successive episodes in one long narration, following a strict sequence in time until the End is finally reached ? Or are they contemporaneous, parallel to one another, complementary accounts of the numerous signs which would herald the last things ? The first alternative must be rejected, for we cannot suppose that John could repeatedly declare that the End has come at a certain fixed point of time, when, in fact, there are several accounts of that End, each followed by further detailed descriptions of the events leading to it (e.g. viii. 1 ; cf. x. 6–7, xi. 15–xii. 1 ; xv.–xvii. 1), some of which are evidently identical with incidents described in earlier visions. Nor must the supposed awkwardness of repetition be attributed to John's failure to assimilate sources which were originally independent—the bold freedom with which he reinterprets the Old Testament prophecies make such an explanation wholly unconvincing. The fact is that John can never be tied down to a strictly chronological scheme. He was a visionary, a prophet, a poet, and a literary artist, though one in whom reason had complete command over his soaring imagination. His literary scheme was the tool of his pastoral purpose. His mind was never the slave of his emotions. All the same, the fresh vigour of REVELATION suggests that even as he wrote his mind was still enflamed by the memory of his visions as he had first experienced them. Nothing could be further removed from automatic writing than REVELATION ; but so, too, nothing could be further from a prosaic literary scheme, mechanically planned and executed. This consideration is the key to John's literary method. It is misleading to argue that, since the visions are not strictly chronological, they must therefore be parallel and contemporaneous, for that suggests a mechanical mode of thought quite foreign to John's mind. It is clear enough that if the three main series of visions concerning the seven seals, the seven trumpets, and the seven bowls are put alongside each other in parallel columns, they cannot, by any ingenuity, be forced into an exact harmony, any more than they can be regarded as a chronological sequence. What does emerge quite definitely from such a comparison is the strictness with which John adheres to his purpose and gradually develops his message. An outstanding example is the way he enlarges in his successive visions, with almost wearisome repetition, on the destruction of the world when the End approaches. Thus he succeeds in doing exactly what he set out to do—that is, to impress on his readers the certainty and the horrors of the Judgment. The gigantic proportions and the completeness of the final ruin are indelibly imprinted on the imagination by the force of the combined accounts given in the visions ; and yet not only are the visions knit together in the main theme of the book, but there is a forward movement which holds the mind in suspense and gives the satisfaction also of at last reaching a grand climax.

We can see also that although the visions are parallel as to their purpose—warning concerning the events leading to the End, and the character of the End itself—they are complementary in scope and emphasis. John sees God's plan unfolded more and more clearly in vision after vision, each of which explains something not fully understood before, or which takes up some new detail connected with the common theme, and explains in greater detail its relationship with REVELATION as a whole. A very simple example occurs at the opening of the fifth seal (vi. 9–11), where John tells how he ' saw underneath the altar the souls of those who had been slain for adhering to God's word, and to the testimony which they bore.' Here, in these three verses, John refers quite briefly to a subject which for him is of fundamental importance —the role to be played by the martyrs in the great Distress. To that subject, therefore, he returns again and again, with ever-increasing emphasis, and always with additional information in his later visions. Indeed, the seven seals are in every way a brief introduction to the whole scheme of REVELATION concerning the final portents. Thus, the waiting of the souls beneath the altar, pleading for vengeance, is a preliminary indication of John's message that the martyrs will have an essential part in bringing about the final outpouring of God's wrath upon their persecutors in the last days. In other words, the significance of the events following the opening of the fifth seal is more fully explained, as John more fully understood it himself in subsequent visions (especially in chapters vii., viii., xi., xv.).

In this connexion, it is well to remember that when John begins his description of a vision with the words ' After this ' or ' Then,' he does not thereby intend to indicate that the vision happened at a particular point of time, or that it is related by time sequence with what he has described previously. Rather, this is his way of indicating a new phase in his visions or, sometimes, a new understanding of what he had seen previously. In fact, each new vision must be regarded as one of a whole series of visions, all interrelated, and all vouchsafed to John for the sake of the churches that they might the better understand what was about to happen. This is not to say that John attached no importance to time, for the movement of time towards Judgment meant everything to him. It was because he realized that all history was divinely planned and controlled, and that the intervening period during which Antichrist would be allowed to persecute the saints was strictly determined, that John could assure his fellow-Christians that God was in supreme authority over the world's destiny. But with the exact order of the events preceding the End he was not concerned. Many of the details which loom so largely and so vividly in his visions were derived either consciously or unconsciously from various conventional apocalyptic symbols, and he uses them freely to illuminate his teaching rather than to give a prophetic diary. Doubtless John believed passionately that the last days would be as he describes them. The strange and terrible ways in which destruction was to fall upon the natural world were most certainly more than picturesque details for John. He was convinced that God's punishment for the world's wickedness would be of this character. But only the shackles of a prosaic mind, enslaved by the modern notion of exact definition, can lead to the accusation that he is found to contradict himself when an attempt is made to square the details of his visions in each of the series ; or that the book is composed of disparate sources, badly patched together by an unskilful editor.

This warning is specially necessary when account is taken of the visions of the seven seals, the seven trumpets and the seven bowls. It is, of course, obvious that John attached great importance to numbers, and especially to the number 7, the sacred symbol of divine perfection. But it is pressing this fact too hard to insist that the whole literary structure of REVELATION is based on the number 7, and that all the material not included in one of the seven-fold series is an ' interlude,' or, alternatively, an interpolation. Frequently the so-called interludes are intended to be of the utmost importance (e.g. vii., xi., xii.) ; and can it be reasonably argued that chaps. xvii.–xxii. (following the completion of the vision of the seven bowls) are nothing more than an editorial appendix ?

These, and many other unhelpful and unnecessary theories, and the unconvincing attempts to mutilate the text which commonly accompany them, can be avoided when John's mind and purpose are correctly understood. He is not theoretical, but practical ; not a copyist, but a creative artist ; not an editor with a taste for literary research, but an inspired prophet—one, moreover, who exercised the freedom of expression essential to a prophet to whom visions of supreme significance concerning the last days had been exclusively entrusted for transmission to the Church. It follows, therefore, that if we wish to appreciate his literary scheme, we must study the religious convictions and the pastoral purpose which determined that scheme ; we must examine his singular reinterpretations of ancient prophecy ; we must observe his outstanding ability in describing the

symbols of his visions ; we must appreciate his power of focusing attention on one central theme in each successive development of his apocalypse ; we must recognize his gift of gradually enlarging the scope of his message, as each vision adds
more detail to the main subject ; and, most of all, we must
acknowledge the depths and the grandeur of his passionate
determination to transmit his own unshakable convictions to
the Church. These are some of the points we shall have in
mind, as we try to guide the reader's studies in the general
commentary. For special reference to John's literary method,
see pp. 65–78, 143–8, 161–3, 166–7, 207–8, 271–4, 296, 337.

IV. AUTHORSHIP

No subject of Biblical studies has provoked such elaborate
and prolonged discussion among scholars as that of the authorship of the five books of the New Testament which are traditionally ascribed to ' John ' (the Fourth Gospel, the three
Epistles of John, and REVELATION). And no discussion has
been so bewildering, disappointing, and unprofitable. The
student who attempts to follow the innumerable lines of
enquiry is soon caught in a maze of conflicting arguments
brought forward to support the rival theories, and invariably
finds himself unable to reach any definite conclusion concerning the authorship of at least some, if not all, of the books
concerned. In fact, it is quite impossible to determine the
authorship of any of these books from the available evidence.
The present writer has no intention of recapitulating the
arguments which are available elsewhere for those who desire
to examine them.[1] The reader can wander at will amidst a
wilderness of speculations, confronted at every turn by a tangle
of diverse and contradictory solutions. Was John, the writer

[1] A full discussion will be found in the following works : Beckwith,
The Apocalypse of John, pp. 343–93 ; Charles, *Revelation*, pp. xxxviii.–l. ;
Moffatt, *The Expositor's Greek Testament*, vol. v., pp. 320–7 ; cf. Martin
Dibelius, *A Fresh Approach to the New Testament and Early Christian
Literature*, pp. 105–10, 124–30. See also the sections on ' Authorship '
in the commentaries in this series on *St. John's Gospel* and the *Epistles
of St. John* (the latter in preparation).

of the Apocalypse, the same person as John the Apostle, the son of Zebedee, as Justin Martyr assumed ? Had he lived to extreme old age in Asia, as one tradition asserts ? What, then, of another tradition preserved by Papias and (apparently) supported by St. Mark x. 39 and some of the early calendars, that the Apostle suffered an early martyrdom ? Does Acts xii. 2 contradict this tradition ? Were there two Johns connected with Asia, of whom one was known as John the Presbyter (Papias, Irenæus, and Dionysius of Alexandria) ? Which John wrote the Fourth Gospel ? Could one and the same John have written the Gospel and the Apocalypse, in view of the contradictory evidence of vocabulary, grammar, style, and ideas, first observed by Dionysius of Alexandria (cf. Charles, Introduction, *I.C.C.*, pp. xxix.–xxxvii.), especially if the two books were written in the same decade ? Is it possible that linguistic difficulties can be accounted for by supposing that the Fourth Gospel was originally written in Aramaic and then translated into fluent Greek (Lohmeyer) ?

This exuberant but sterile enquiry has been stimulated by a desire to identify the various writers of the five books— exuberant because there are numerous hints in Christian traditions which seem to promise a clear solution ; sterile because closer examination proves that all these hints are too vague, too inconclusive, too tantalizingly ambiguous to support any indisputable decision. The remarks of Papias and Irenæus and the evidence of the early Church calendars are seductive enough to stimulate the dullest curiosity, but they are also sufficiently remote in time from the subjects with which they deal (to say nothing of the untrustworthiness of the transmission of these remarks) to render certainty as to their true meaning impossible. Argument has exhausted itself, and until some new and surer evidence is available the matter must remain an open question. Indeed, uncertainty marks all the available evidence outside the New Testament. For the authorship of the Book of REVELATION, at least, with which alone we are concerned here, our only sure guide is the book itself. There we learn from the writer that his name is John. Nothing in the book suggests that this is a pseudonym.

Apocalyptic literature was not always pseudonymous—the Shepherd of Hermas is not. John names himself without further explanation, evidently assuming that the local churches to whom his epistolary manifesto is addressed required nothing more for identification, just as he makes it plain that he is familiar with them. He calls himself a prophet (i. 3, xix. 10, xxii. 7, 9, 18), but he does not therefore claim any peculiar authority beyond that which his fellow-Christian prophets enjoyed, as those specially inspired by the Holy Spirit to give exhortation (cf. notes in this series on I Cor. xii.–xiv.; and the 'Didache'). There is no hint that he had any official status in the local churches, or that he had shared in the foundation or development of any one of them. Nowhere does he even hint at apostolic authority; and although his references to the apostles in xviii. 20 and xxi. 14 (see notes) do not in themselves rule out the possibility that he was an apostle (any more than that he was a prophet), there is, as Dr. Moffatt notes, a 'retrospective tinge' about them which makes it somewhat doubtful whether one of the Twelve would have thus expressed himself, and have made no reference to his having been an eye-witness of the early days in Galilee.

At the same time, it would be arbitrary to insist from such inconclusive evidence alone that the Apostle was not the writer of REVELATION. While it is reasonably clear on linguistic grounds, as well as those of subject matter, that the author is not the Fourth Evangelist (the fact that the books show a common familiarity with certain terms, though with a different usage, proves only a common local origin), there are arguments in favour of the Apostolic authorship of the Apocalypse not less convincing than some of those put forward to support that of the Gospel. Justin Martyr's testimony to the Apostolic authorship of REVELATION cannot be lightly dismissed— Dr. C. J. Cadoux has always protested at the summary way in which Dr. Charles relegated it to a footnote. Probably that testimony is as early as A.D. 136 (the time of the debate with Trypho), and if the Apostle did, in fact, survive to a very old age, who would presume to deny the possibility that the experience of the intervening years from the Crucifixion to the close of the century may have moulded the outlook reflected in the Apocalypse ? In literary criticism (especially criticism of the New Testament) nothing is more unsound than dogmatism about authorship.

Beyond this we cannot say without conjecture, and it seems that the authorship of REVELATION may prove the one mystery of the book which will be never revealed in this world. The supremely important point, which has been obscured by the barren speculations about this subject, is that John did not think it necessary for the authority and understanding of his message that more should be known about himself than what he has stated. Although writing in the first place under the form of an epistle to his own local churches, he makes it clear that his message is intended for the Catholic Church, to which, for the most part, he was completely unknown, and which nevertheless was now admonished to regard his words as having the supreme authority attributed to the Scriptures. This authority was not his, but that of the glorified Christ, who had received the vision from God and had sent it to John and his fellow-servants through His angel, and had directly commissioned him to write his ' vision of what is and what is to be hereafter.' No matter what further information may be gleaned concerning John in the future, it cannot add to or take away from the value of the message as he has delivered it.

V. DATE AND HISTORICAL SITUATION

There is no direct evidence in REVELATION itself to indicate any precise date for its composition. We have to ask instead what political circumstances might have constrained John to write as he did. REVELATION, like other apocalyptic literature, was written to meet a particular need ; the need was usually occasioned either by persecution or the threat of persecution. The faithful must be assured and strengthened to face the danger that might otherwise perplex and alarm them. Nothing in REVELATION is more apparent than the writer's conviction that a ruthless, universal persecution was about to burst upon the Church. Not less clear is the form that this persecution would take. The enemy of the Church (symbolized by a Beast) would be ' allowed to wage war on the saints and to conquer them ' (xiii. 7) ; this attack, moreover, would be made through the priests of the Imperial cult, who would demand universal worship of the Beast on pain of death, the detection of recusants being ensured by economic pressure (see chap. xiii., with notes, in the Commentary). Now, it would be useless to ask when such conditions actually prevailed, stimulating John to pen his book, for there was no persecution at all like it for severity and universality until the reign of Diocletian. Besides, John is plainly prophesying in chap. xiii. ; he is referring to the coming of Antichrist, an event connected with the expected return of Nero (see chaps. xiii. and xvii., with notes). Even the references to wholesale martyrdom in such passages as vi. 9–11, vii. 9–17, xvi. 6, xvii. 6, xviii. 24 are not to be regarded as testimony to the extent of martyrdom either in John's own day or in the Nero terror (though he may well have had the latter in mind) ; they are all prophetic, and a testimony to John's insight. That some had suffered for the faith we know from REVELATION, as well as from other sources : John himself had suffered banishment (i. 9), and Antipas, a well-known figure in the Church at Pergamum, had been actually martyred (ii. 13). We may reasonably believe that Antipas was not the only one who had died for the faith. External evidence suggests that there were other martyrs, though there is nothing to show that their number was great. The remarkable thing is the way John discerned from the small beginnings of opposition how fundamental was the principle involved, and how severe the persecution must inevitably become. ' From the position of matters he already argued the worst. The few cases of repressive interference and of martyrdom in Asia Minor (and elsewhere) were enough to warn him of the storm rolling up the sky, though as yet only one or two drops had actually fallen.'[1]

We must ask, then, at what period in the latter half of the first century were the conditions such as to provoke John's

[1] Moffatt, *Expositor's Greek Testament.*

sombre convictions concerning the future ? Nero's persecution doubtless brought home to thoughtful Christians what they must expect from the State whenever it deigned to notice them. Such a savage attack in the capital must have had wide repercussions throughout the Empire, although it was in itself an isolated, local affair, levelled, as Tacitus explains, through the whim of a tyrant, in order to divert suspicion from himself for the responsibility of burning Rome. Tertullian insists that the Neronic persecution resulted in what was, in effect, if not in law, the ' outlawry ' of Christianity. For a time, however, the crisis passed, and among the other pieces of internal evidence that point to a later date for REVELATION is the warning about the coming demand that everyone should pay divine homage to the Emperor. We have to enquire at what period insistence on the emperor-worship cult was sufficiently determined to disclose to a discerning mind that a real crisis was approaching.

Any loyal Jew or Jewish Christian was likely to be apprehensive of active hostility from the State when he recalled the desecration of the Temple by Antiochus Epiphanes in the middle of the second century B.C. It was that calamity which had occasioned the prophecy of Daniel over which John had brooded and sought for interpretation and fulfilment. There was not wanting good reason for such a fear in view of the increasing popularity of the custom (begun in the reign of Augustus) of attributing divine honours to the Emperor, even during his lifetime. Modern tendencies in certain States have made it easier to understand how intense patriotism encourages this idea. It was natural that the ' genius ' of the Empire should be thought of as closely associated with, and even dwelling in, the Emperor, its chief guardian ; and that the Emperor and his circle should encourage such an attitude of veneration—so valuable a guarantee of support ; natural, too, that the cult should flourish most vigorously in the provinces, where distance enveloped the Emperor with mystery. Nowhere was this tendency more marked than in Asia Minor (and perhaps in Egypt), where the general polytheism made it extremely simple for the pagan religions to include the Emperor as one of their gods. The chief towns vied with each other in thus demonstrating their patriotism ; some of them maintained shrines devoted exclusively to the emperor-cult, with their own altars and sacrifices and even choirs and priests.

All this, however, was not a menace to Christians (apart from causing an increasing suspicion on the part of officials that Christians were disloyal to the State, as their refusal to participate in the cult became more widely known) until an emperor was no longer content to accept and encourage the payment of these divine honours, but actually set out to demand them. Such an attempt was made by the half-demented Caligula (A.D. 37–41), who seriously determined to deify himself and to enforce universal adoration. The only subjects to whom acquiescence was unthinkable (because of their strict monotheism) were Jews and Christians—the two were at first undistinguishable to Roman officials. The strength of Caligula's determination can be measured by his decision to erect his statue in the Temple at Jerusalem. He actually prepared an army to enforce the desecration, and was prevented only by being murdered. The profound shock produced by this episode, and the memories of Daniel's prophecies that it evoked, can be easily imagined (probably there are echoes in the apocalyptic passages of the Gospels, cf. St. Mark, xiii. 14, St. Matt. xxiv. 15, and in 2 Thess. ii. 3–4). Caligula's immediate successors, however, did not take their divinity at all seriously, and there was no official attempt to enforce the cult until the latter part of the reign of Domitian (A.D. 81–96). Domitian was of a nature very different from that of Caligula —serious, suspicious, cunning, shrewdly aware of the value of the cult as a binding force in society, and relentless in his hostility to anything which even savoured of nonconformity to the Imperial policy. He insisted on being acknowledged as ' our Lord and God ' by State officials, and although there is no direct evidence that recognition of the title was enforced on the general populace, we may assume that this was done for him where patriotism was fanatical. There is reliable evidence that Christians were persecuted in his reign,[1] and although we are ill-informed about the Domitianic persecution in general, we do possess one piece of definite evidence about its history in Bithynia. When Pliny, the Governor of that province, wrote to the Emperor Trajan (*circa* A.D. 112) to ask his advice about dealing with Christians, he stated that there had been cases of apostasy in that province (pointing, in all probability, to a serious persecution), twenty years previously, that is, about A.D. 92. Altogether, the facts point to this period as confirming the earliest Christian tradition (Irenæus) that REVELATION was written then (cf. also the possible allusion to Domitian's decree against the cultivation of the vine in vi. 6. See note in Commentary).

It is noteworthy that in thus narrowing the conflict between Church and State to the simple issue of rival loyalties, John was in actual fact anticipating the correspondingly simple attitude taken by the State when official action became generalized. In the earlier spasmodic outbursts of persecution, Christians had been attacked on anti-social or criminal charges, as Tacitus confirms. Whether, after the Neronic persecution, Christians could be punished merely for acknowledging the name itself, is not certain. That is possible, and there may be a reference to it in I Pet. iv. 14 : ' If you are reproached for the name of Christ, blessed are ye ' (R.V.), though the writer may be implying nothing more than that Christians were liable to be ' denounced for the sake of Christ ' (so Dr. Moffatt translates the passage). The Epistle as a whole suggests that in any case the common method of obtaining convictions was by accusing Christians of criminal conduct (I Pet. iii. 16, iv. 15). Nor do the numerous references to ' the Name ' in REVELATION itself prove that by this time Christians as such were being convicted. But John nevertheless realized that this was very soon to be the simple issue. It would be enough to refuse to worship the Beast. And a few years later, when Pliny, the Governor of Bithynia (in the letter to which we have already referred), enquired of the Emperor Trajan what policy he should adopt towards accused

---

[1] Cf. Bishop Lightfoot's notes on the ' Epistle of Clement of Rome ' (*Apostolic Fathers*).

Christians, Trajan, probably referring to the practice of Domitian's reign, plainly indicated that anyone indicted as a Christian and persisting in his loyalty to the faith was liable to the extreme penalty.

In all this, John's profound insight concerning the issue at stake is not fully appreciated unless it is remembered that in REVELATION he is prophesying, anticipating the storm, and seeking to prepare his brethren before it breaks. As we have seen, it was not the severity of previous persecution which forewarned him; that was only evidence that the great Distress would shortly begin. The remarkable thing is the clearness with which John realized that the vast Imperial system, relying increasingly for its strength and support on the emperor-worship cult as a religious and moral force, was bound to be the mortal enemy of Christianity—a new religion which, as yet, it hardly noticed; or rather, as John would regard it, that the Christian Church must unflinchingly resist (by passive acceptance of martyrdom, xiii. 10) the challenge of a blasphemous claim to worship which belonged only to God. Professor E. F. Scott, in his valuable essay on ' The Opposition to Cæsar Worship,'[1] has pointed out that, although at first sight Christianity and Cæsar worship seem almost grotesquely different, they had, in fact, a number of affinities which ultimately rendered them competitors. Both endeavoured to promote a universal religion; both believed in an incarnation of the divine in human form; both were of recent origin, and had to compete not only with traditional cults, but still more with each other; both claimed to confer similar benefits on mankind and so to deserve their allegiance; above all, both found the centre of their systems in the adoration of one whom they hailed as ' Lord.' History has recorded the bitter struggle which ensued when the rivalry was acknowledged and fought out. But John saw what was at stake long before the State saw it. He realized that a crisis was imminent at a time when as yet the State officials were content to crush those whom they thought to be only members

[1] *Church History*, vol. ii., no. 2, published by the American Society of Church History.

of a fanatical and obscure sect, if these were brought to their notice.

Professor Scott makes the interesting suggestion that neither the State nor the Church really understood each other, and that this was the origin of their mutual hostility. ' The conflict with Cæsar worship may be said to have arisen out of a misunderstanding,' he writes. ' The Church, in its apocalyptic mood, mistook the secular power for the power of evil ; the government mistook the Christian ideals for a political programme. Yet, on a deeper view the ground of the conflict was well chosen. The imperial cult brought to its sharpest expression the inherent difference between Paganism and Christianity. Cæsar was the embodiment of all material forces —pride, wealth, the glory of this world. Were these things to be worshipped ? Were they to be regarded as the highest good ? The Church declared that Jesus was Lord. It understood His lordship in crude apocalyptic fashion, and so involved itself in a dangerous antagonism which might have been avoided. Yet at the heart of its confession there was a sense of those things which Jesus stood for. This was the real issue, and in the course of the struggle it became ever more explicit. By its resistance to Cæsar worship, the Church established, for all time to come, the Christian conception of life.'

These are illuminating words, but they provoke the question whether even the beginning of the conflict was due to mutual ignorance of each other's motives. Are we to believe that martyrs shed their blood because of a misunderstanding ? It is true that the State was, to some extent, mistaken in regarding the Christian Church as a dangerous, anti-social society, disloyal to the empire, and endeavouring to form a rival secular kingdom. But was the Church mistaken about the State's demand that the Emperor should be paid divine homage ? Was the State's claim fundamentally social rather than religious ? Origen thought otherwise : and when he distinguished between praying *for* the emperor and praying *to* him, he had little doubt why the State demanded what the Church could never allow. And indeed, we know that for the masses in the Roman provinces at least, the Imperial cult was a genuinely religious creed. When they offered sacrifice to the Emperor they were expressing something much more than loyalty. It was worship ; they were thus affirming their faith and hope in him as their Saviour. They venerated him as the one who was able, by his divine power, to save them from what they dreaded—civic disturbance, foreign invasion, social poverty ; and to give them what they valued—peace and plenty and security, the benefits that a dictator is often able to bestow. The Christian's conception of salvation was different, and his faith and hope were directed elsewhere. That was what John realized with true insight. That was the choice he put clearly and concisely and forcibly before the Church, in preparation for the crisis that he knew was bound to develop. Christians are still confronted with that same choice, and some are called to suffer martyrdom in their witness to the truth. They will find John's message as heart-searching and as bracing as it was in Domitian's reign.

VI. The Abiding Value of Revelation

It sometimes happens that the permanent value of a book proves to be of a character quite different from that which the writer originally intended. This is frequently the case in the books of the New Testament, for although many of the writers shared in the common belief that the end of the world was imminent, and therefore addressed themselves to their own generation only, their words have been of supreme value to every succeeding generation for nearly two thousand years. The worth of their message was not impaired by the narrow limits of their outlook. This is one of the proofs of the Bible's divine inspiration. God's message to men is unchanging ; unchanging, too, are the needs of humanity when fundamental principles are considered. In no case is this more apparent than in REVELATION. John wrote for the Church of his own day, convinced that history was about to be wound up, that God would shortly intervene in human affairs, and bring them to a close, that the End of all things was at hand. He wrote to show Christians everywhere ' what must come to pass very soon, for the time is near.' He was a prophet in the strict sense of the word. He undertook to predict the future. But it was the immediate future that absorbed his attention, for he believed that this was the only future left for the whole world. Inevitably, then, his message was shaped by the conditions of his own day. He dealt solely with the problems of the Church and the Empire and the world as he saw them. This focusing of interest is most apparent in the letters to the seven churches, but it can be clearly detected in the rest of the book as well. Even when he predicts the supernatural woes which were to precede the coming of Antichrist, he thinks and writes in terms of the immediate situation ; he makes use, for example, of the common belief about a Parthian invasion, and the legend that Nero would return to make a devastating attack on the Empire.

If these limitations of John's predictions had been more fully appreciated in the past, the Church would have been spared much mischief caused by the misguided enthusiasts, who have, in almost every age, endeavoured to prove that John's prophecies were directed to their own times. And yet such attempts have been not altogether unreasonable, nor completely useless. One excuse can always be made in their favour—the plain fact that John's prophecy has been unfulfilled. The world has not come to an end as he predicted. The Roman Empire did not collapse until more than three hundred years later, and then not in the way that John had foretold. The supernatural terrors did not burst upon the world. No single emperor, not even the worst of the Church's persecutors, can be identified with Antichrist. Unfortunately, however, though not unnaturally, students of REVELATION have been unwilling to admit that John was mistaken, mistaken in what he must have regarded as the central point of his prophecies. Anxious to vindicate this revered Christian writing, and eager to prove that they had been specially chosen to witness the end of the world, a long succession of John's interpreters have persuaded themselves that he had written exclusively for their own day. The dismal persistence of evil has encouraged their efforts.

History records how many persecutors of the Christian Church have provoked the conviction that they were exactly fulfilling John's prophecy of the Beast, and so pointing unmistakably to Harmagedon. And the futility of such conjectures has been repeatedly demonstrated by the inaccuracy of innumerable predictions concerning the End. All the same, by instinct, rather than by sound knowledge, these would-be prophets were on the track of a vital truth. For although John was mistaken in his prophecy about the shape of things to come, he was right in his penetrating discernment of the fundamental principles which would determine the issues at stake in the historical situation which confronted him. He was a true prophet also, inasmuch as history has proved that the principles he laid bare are eternal in their significance, and therefore are operative in every age. That is why it has always been so easy for ingenious misinterpreters of REVELATION to claim that John had prophesied about their own particular times. In disclosing the unseen spiritual forces at work in the world of his day, John pointed the only way to a satisfactory philosophy of all history.

What, then, was the situation as John visualized it ?

On the one hand he saw world power embodied in the Roman Empire, and he realized that it was essentially evil. In chaps. xi.–xviii. he gives a graphic description of Roman civilization through the eyes of an inspired Christian seer— wealthy, proud, boastful, self-confident, secular, material, vicious, crafty, irreligious, placing all its trust in physical might, demonstrating its satanic character unmistakably in its persecution of the Church.

Over against the world he saw the Christian Church, and he had no illusions about that either. He discerned that it was merely a handful of scattered communities, small, weak, despised, distracted, liable to be tainted by the world, susceptible to the very evils which were hastening the downfall of the world-empire. He saw the uncharity, the compromising with false teachers, the laxity towards immorality, and the spirit of worldliness—those grave imperfections so clearly exemplified in the churches of Asia Minor. And with real prophetic insight, reading the signs of the times, he foresaw that these two protagonists, the world and the Church, were shortly to be engaged in a life-and-death struggle, in which the whole weight of the State's power and authority was to be organized for the Church's destruction.

This sombre conviction serves to throw into high relief one of REVELATION'S greatest and most abiding contributions to religious thought—John's superb confidence that victory would be won by the Church. Never does he doubt that. Never for one moment does he falter in his assurance that the vast Imperial structure will speedily crash in irretrievable ruin. Never does he question the certainty that the Church would play the decisive part in accomplishing that defeat, and would inherit the promises of sovereignty made by the prophets to ancient Israel. John's urgent warnings against compromise and cowardice were not in the least due to any fear that the Church as a whole would fail. They are the natural expression of his pastoral care for his fellow-believers, to whom, as a prophet, he had been commissioned to address this special, final exhortation. The prospective martyrs are sealed and numbered already, each of them. It was for Christians to prove by their fidelity that they were among that number.

So we reach the source of John's faith, the secret springs of his unquestioning conviction—his visions of God and of Jesus Christ. How masterly and inspiring are his descriptions of God and the Lamb ! The Church is for ever indebted to him for the grandeur and richness of his visions of the Creator and the Redeemer. The dullest imagination is brightened, the coldest heart is warmed by the words which have encouraged countless saints and martyrs in their hour of trial ; have inspired some of the greatest achievements of religious art and poetry and music ; and will always have the power to constrain men everywhere to adoration. Conscious of the unique significance of his visions, John prefaces his letters to the seven churches with his first ecstatic experience on Patmos (chap. i.). That was the Christ with whom they had to reckon, vigilant, inescapable, strong to aid the faithful, terrible in His power to crush the craven. Similarly, he introduces his account of the final portents and of the End itself with his vision of God reigning in heaven and of the slain Lamb standing triumphant in the midst of the throne, both the Creator and the Redeemer being ceaselessly adored by the heavenly hosts and the whole creation. Thus does he begin his warnings and encouragement. Let Christians realize that the issue of the conflict awaiting them is in God's hand, that the Judgment is already determined, that the great work of redemption has in fact been already finished in Heaven, and that its consummation is about to be executed on earth.

And of what nature was the victory, thus acclaimed by heaven and earth? Not the punishment and destruction of the wicked. It is unjust to accuse John of taking pleasure in his description of the last plagues. Most of the colours with which he paints the world's overthrow have been borrowed from traditional apocalyptic symbolism, and even so are marked by a reticence unusual in apocalyptic literature. John does not gloat over the world's wreckage. There is a tragic splendour and even sorrow about the dirge over Babylon (chap. xviii.), not unworthy to be compared with Jeremiah's compassionate lament over his own nation, absolving John from the charge of cruelty and vindictiveness. Swift and complete and final, the judgment would surely be. Assuming John's conviction that the world was irredeemably corrupt, that attitude was inevitable. Part of the prophet's greatness consists in his insistence that the world was God's creation, and was therefore subject to God's moral laws, which could not be flaunted without judgment and penalty. Clearly, this belief was, and must always be, essential to the Christian faith, and requires emphatic reassertion in times of violence and persecution. For John, however, this was not the essence of God's victory; only one of its conditional circumstances. The victory was the vindication of the Church, redeemed, triumphant in heaven, secure for ever with the Lamb, who by His death and His conquest over it had won the victory for Himself and His Church. John never sees Jesus Christ alone, nor the Church alone. The two are always one, joined in the closest of ties, as Bridegroom and Bride.[1] The climax of the Apocalypse is the marriage-banquet of the Lamb (xix. 9). Here on earth the Church was shortly to suffer the severest affliction ; she must be tempted, persecuted, tortured, with the vilest cunning and cruelty. Let not that daunt Christian hearts, says John. He is realist enough to utter the bluntest warnings, but as a visionary, too, he is able to proclaim the strongest assurance. The Church as a whole would be protected during the allotted period of Antichrist's onslaught (xi. 1–6, xii. 6–14), thus ensuring the Christian witness in the evil days ; and by faithful endurance, that is, by the refusal to acknowledge the idolatrous claims of the world order (xiii. 15, xiv. 9)—faithful endurance if necessary even unto death (ii. 10)—the martyrs would share in Christ's victory over it, and in His triumph over all the powers of evil.

John's perception of the spiritual issues underlying the approaching crisis is the greatest and most abiding of the values inherited by the Church in REVELATION. These visions will always offer a message which Christians can never ignore without peril, or heed without enrichment. For what John thought would be the outcome of the future, albeit a future which was already pressing hard upon the present, we now recognize to be an eternal principle, always present, continually operative, and for ever true in every age. In the spiritual realm, which is for Christians the only reality, the evil which threatened the Christian Church at the close of the first century was much more than the worst and last mustering of Satan's powers. It is inherent in civilization itself ; it is a poison at the very heart of this world order ; but it is being eternally judged and condemned; and for Christians it matters not how long the time before God's sentence is executed. So too, the faith and endurance of Christ's followers through the power of His Death and Resurrection are being continually vindicated. This is not to say that the Church can ever abandon, or even minimize, John's teaching that there will be a winding-up of

---

[1] This point is made clearly in Dr. Porter's valuable article on ' Revelation ' in Hastings' *Dictionary of the Bible*, vol. iv.

this age, and a final judgment. That teaching can never be left out of account without mutilating the Gospel message, and disfiguring Christian morality. A thousand years with the Lord are but as yesterday, and one day as a thousand years, and John was mistaken only in so far as he narrowed too closely the focus of his gaze into the future. But his message is as valid and as vital for Christians to-day as it was for those who lived at the close of the first century.

The last words of this brief introduction have been written during the early days of another European war, and it has been difficult to avoid the temptation of mentioning what must be obvious to every thoughtful student of REVELATION—the remarkable relevance of its message to the Church in our own day. It is only one more example of the divine sanction, and the timeless significance of John's visions. Whenever there is a world crisis, whenever the State exalts itself and demands an allegiance which Christians know they cannot pay without abandoning their very souls, whenever the Church is threatened by destruction, and faith is dim and hearts are cold, then too REVELATION will admonish and exhort, uplift and encourage all who heed its message. Then also those who are called upon to suffer for their faith will turn eagerly to this greatest of all textbooks for martyrs, and will not turn in vain ; for through John's eyes they will see that unseen world where wickedness has been cast down, where the Lamb is guiding His own to fountains of living water, and where God wipes every tear from their eyes.

COMMENTARY

THE ORIGIN OF JOHN'S REVELATION
(i. 1–20)

i. 1–3 : THE SUPERSCRIPTION

A revelation by Jesus Christ, which God granted him for his 1
servants, to show them *what must come to pass* very soon;
he disclosed it by sending it through his angel to his servant
John, who now testifies to what is God's word and Jesus 2
Christ's testimony—to what he saw. Blessed is he who 3
reads aloud and blessed they who hear the words of this
prophecy and who lay to heart what is written in it ; for the
time is near.

To the tiny communities of Christians in the cities of Asia
Minor, no less than to every generation of Jews since the
Exile, an Apocalypse or **Revelation** was a trumpet call, a 1
martial summons to new resolution. Like us, they had every
reason to cry :

> Woe is me !
> Whence are we ? and why are we ? of what stage
> The actors or spectators ?

An apocalypse was a prophet's urgent reply to all such
perplexities. It was a glimpse into the meaning of the dark
and multitudinous affairs of a world which otherwise seemed to
assert a tragic denial of one or another of God's attributes.
God's word was made available to His servants, the prophets, 2
who in turn communicated it to the churches. The divine plan
working in the past and present was discovered, and the
reassured believer was stiffened against despondency or back-
sliding by the foreshadowing of **what must come to pass very
soon.**

3

It was only to be expected that John, using the method of a long apocalyptic tradition, familiar alike to Jew and Christian of his time, should also use traditional language and images. But though John speaks the same tongue as his predecessors, he sees with new eyes : he is an original spirit, vividly conscious of prophetic insight, aflame with desire to bring his interpretation of things to his fellow-Christians : **he testifies to what he saw.**

And the deep and solemn conviction with which he writes may be measured by his assertion that the truth of his visions rests upon the authority of **Jesus Christ** Himself.

For it is **Jesus Christ's testimony** about **God's word** which John claims to be reporting in his book. To John, as to all writers in the apocalyptic tradition, God dwelt far removed from men, in unapproachable majesty. The angels who swarmed in previous revelations, and the prophets to whom they spoke precious words of reassurance and illumination, were the only intermediaries between the ordinary man and his remote God. The angelic ambassadors and interpreters in John's book still bear witness to this feeling of need for intermediaries ; when they speak, however, it is always the voice of Christ which is being echoed. Accordingly, though John says that this revelation has been sent from God **through his angel,** he soon has direct vision of heaven's secrets, and Christ, **the first-born from the dead,** takes the place of the angel. John assumes that Christ's revelation of God's purposes by no means ceased with the Death and Resurrection. These were, it is true, the supreme events, upon which the whole structure of his faith was founded ; it is hardly too much to say that for John those events were the gospel. But it was equally true that the risen Christ still spoke to His servants, and that His words had the validity of the Gospel itself. This conviction makes John refer to the contents of his own book, to which he **now testifies,** as **God's word and Jesus Christ's testimony.** He uses this identical term to denote the original gospel tradition, for **adhering** to which he was banished to Patmos.

So confident is John of the divine origin of his revelation that 3 he assumes that it will be read **aloud** in public worship—like

4

the Old Testament books, and perhaps some of our New Testament literature. Indeed, he is inspired to **write down** his **vision in a book** expressly for that purpose, so that all worshippers may know of it. Hence, the first of the seven blessings (xiv. 13, xvi. 15, xix. 9, xx. 6, xxii. 7, 14) is pronounced on him **who reads aloud**, and on those **who hear the words of this prophecy and who lay to heart what is written in it.** John's motive for wishing his fellow-worshippers to share in this way what had been revealed to him is stated with dramatic brevity : **the time is short.** The events about which he is going to speak **must come to pass very soon.** His main purpose is not to satisfy curiosity by prediction, but to warn and fortify by thus showing God's determination to act almost immediately in this hour of final crisis.

i. 4-8 : THE PROLOGUE. GREETINGS

John to the seven churches in Asia: grace be to you and peace 4
from HE WHO IS AND WAS AND IS COMING, and from the seven Spirits before his throne, and from Jesus Christ 5
the faithful witness, the first-born **from the dead, and the** *prince over kings of earth ;* **to him who loves us and** *has loosed* **us** *from* **our** *sins* **by shedding his blood—he has made** 6
us *a realm of priests for* **his** *God* **and Father,—to him be glory and dominion for ever and ever: Amen.** *Lo, he is* 7
coming on the clouds, to be seen **by every eye, even by those** *who impaled* **him, and** *all the tribes of earth shall wail because of him :* **even so, Amen.** ' *I am* **the alpha and the** 8
omega,' saith *the Lord God, who is* **and was and is coming,** *the almighty.*

Why does John address himself to this group of **seven** 4
churches in Asia (compare verse 11) ? There were several flourishing communities other than those he names, and John must have known of them. Two conclusions may be gleaned from the manner of John's address. He assumes that the mention of his name alone is adequate identification for his

5

readers and their audiences ; and, even more significantly, he speaks with such simple authority that he must have held an accepted and honoured place in the life of the churches to which he writes. Now, as a prophet, John probably fulfilled as definite and separate a function in these early Christian communities as, let us say, an archdeacon in the modern Church ; he may have looked upon these churches as his special charge. Certainly his intimate knowledge of each church would lead us to suppose that he was no infrequent visitor, and it is hard to exclude the possibility that John, as an itinerant prophet, may have had special authority in a circuit which included these cities.

Whatever is the explanation of John's choice of this particular *group* of cities, his choice of the number **seven** was made for a very clear reason. He was making use of a convention which he employs freely throughout the book. For seven was a 'sacred' number in apocalyptic tradition : a symbol of divine completeness. Our consciousness of the artificiality of this device must not be allowed to hinder us from trying to appreciate its far-reaching significance for John and his readers. There can, for example, be little doubt that there existed in the prophet's mind a clear connexion between the seven churches which he specifically names, and the complete number of Christians, or of Christian churches. In fact, his letters to the seven churches form an ' open letter ' to all believers—to **anyone who has an ear**. But this is not all : the symbolism seems to have a meaning still nearer to John's purpose. Each of the seven letters contains an analysis of the life of the church addressed ; its essential faults and virtues are singled out, and warning or praise accordingly allotted. Two of the churches, the first and the last, are threatened with complete extinction, since each lacks qualities essential to the profession of the Christian faith. Unqualified praise is given to the second and sixth churches. The three central churches are complimented and castigated in varying degrees, for in each of them there exists a mixture of good and bad elements ; the faithful are promised rewards and the faithless are threatened with the severest punishments. The striking and

6

deliberate symmetry of this design strengthens the conclusion which is to be drawn from the whole picture of the life of the seven churches. They are intended to epitomize Christian life throughout the world. John's choice of this group of seven churches, rather than any other group of seven, was neither haphazard nor accidental : it was determined, not by the fact that the geographical position of the churches made them convenient centres from which his message might be widely circulated (Ramsay: *op. cit.*, pp. 180 ff.), but by the representative nature of their problems, their varying degrees of success in meeting those problems, and their aptness as illustrative details in a symbolical design.

Having thus addressed his letter to the seven churches, and hence to all Christians, John sends his greetings in words which he inherits from St. Paul. They are no mere formality : **grace**, that conscious state of communion with God's power and purpose, is the prerequisite of **peace** in the believer's heart. These blessings come from God, from the **seven spirits**, and from **Jesus Christ**. It is indicative of John's attitude towards God that he employs an ancient convention whereby the direct pronunciation of His name was avoided by the use of a paraphrase. Following usage, John points to the attribute of God which he wishes to stress : **HE WHO IS AND WAS AND IS COMING** : or, in other words, the Eternal, whose advent into the Empires of Time was so near. (The usual term had been : " He who is and was and *shall be*.') Similar though more curious testimony to John's extreme reverence for God is borne by the deliberately ungrammatical ' from He. . . .' Even a paraphrase of the name of the unchanging God must be preserved from declension !

The **throne** is an invariable symbol in REVELATION for the idea of ultimate power and authority in the universe (cf. iv. 3) and the **seven Spirits** who wait at God's behest **before the throne** are also inseparable from the prophet's conception of God's sovereignty. We may be sure that the traditional picture of heaven, of which they form an essential part, was commonly known to John's generation. Their history stretches back to the mythologies of Babylon and Persia, where the sun and moon and five planets were worshipped as the seven spirits of the sky. If we translate the picture of **the seven Spirits before the throne** into the abstract terms in which we habitually think, we shall think of them as symbols of divine majesty, power, and perfection. But though this is certainly the truth implicit in the scene, it is probably a mistake to imagine that John thought of them only as personifications of abstract qualities : they were living representatives, rather than fortuitous symbols of those divine qualities. Not only *through* these mighty beings, but **from** them, as from God and from Jesus Christ, could blessings be imparted to the churches. (See also p. 86.)

5   But it is **Jesus Christ** who stirs John from reverence and wonder to adoration. As he thinks of Christ, his heart over-flows with gratitude, joy, triumph, and solemn anticipation. The titles which he bestows are reminiscent of the earlier prophets' descriptions of a Messiah who was still to come. John's faith, more secure than theirs, could derive strength from three assured beliefs. The Messiah had come, and His death had proved Him an unswerving martyr—**the faithful witness,** whose example was before them in adversity, and whose unfolding of God's purposes must be true, in view of the resolute constancy which led to His Crucifixion. John's second article of faith was that Christ had risen, **the first-born from the dead,** and that His Resurrection guaranteed to believers continued communion in Heaven. Thirdly, the glorified Christ was the **prince over kings of earth**—as the earthly monarchs who persecuted Christians would soon have reason to know.

John's confession of faith does not end with this brief creed. As he thinks of the risen Christ, he utters what must always be for Christians the deepest of paradoxes : this **prince,** infinitely mightier and more glorious than any earthly prince, **loves us.** The **shedding** of **his blood** was more than an inspiring example of loyalty to conviction ; from it there flowed a consciousness of new freedom from crippling bonds. ' It is we,' cries the prophet exultantly, '*we* whom He has made 6 **a realm of priests.'** Jews had long dreamed of Israel

8

transformed at the Messiah's coming into a nation of ' prince-priests,' with a unique and final privilege—access to the very presence of God. And this dream was now fulfilled, John believed : not in the Jewish nation, however, but in the inheritors of the destiny rejected by them—in the Christian churches ; so great was the reward of those who were loyal to their God. That their responsibility was no less than their reward was one of the truths which John hoped to convey in his book.

In the greeting to the churches, we have a glimpse of the innermost impulse of John's faith. And when we ponder over the unfamiliar and sometimes even grotesque conventions which occur not infrequently in REVELATION, when we are confronted with the immeasurable agony and cosmic ruin which were to attend the last days, we shall do well to remember the almost breathless quality of John's adoration of Christ, and the tenderness and joy of his gratitude. Nor should we forget that for him, as we have seen, **grace** and **peace** were the distinctive marks of Christian life. If we add that grace must bear the fruit, not only of tranquillity, but also of alertness, we shall better understand the urgency with which John writes.

For it is noteworthy that the hymn of praise which speaks of Christ's unbounded love is followed inevitably by the thought of the terror and desolation of the Messiah's second appearance on earth, to vindicate His cause and punish all those who flout God's will. Those who had wilfully averted their eyes from goodness must be confronted by His actual presence, **to be seen by every eye,** a spectacle to inspire universal 7 remorse and dread. The Jews particularly, who **impaled him,** would be forcibly convicted of their unpardonable crime in rejecting Christ : not repentance, as the prophet Zechariah had hoped, but bitter remorse must be their lot. Nor were the Jews alone in their rejection of Christ. Every nation to which the gospel had been preached had shared in their crime : therefore, **all the tribes of earth shall wail because of him.** And John, realizing perhaps better than we the stern implications of the prophet's question, ' Can two walk together unless

9

they be agreed ? ' entertains no reluctance that these things should happen. **Even so, Amen,** is his prayer. The august sovereignty of God could admit of no trifling compromise. Judgment and retribution must necessarily fall on evil-doers, 8 when **the alpha and the omega,** the God of all-embracing power, displayed Himself on earth in the person of His Messiah.

i. 9–11 : John Falls into a Trance

9 I John, your brother and your companion in the distress and realm and patient endurance which Jesus brings, found myself in the island called Patmos, for adhering to God's word and the testimony of Jesus. On the Lord's day I found myself rapt in the Spirit, and I heard a loud voice behind me like a trumpet calling, ' Write your vision in a book, and send it to the seven churches, to Ephesus and Smyrna and Pergamum and Thyatira and Sardis and Philadelphia and Laodicea.'

Before speaking in detail about the contents of his first vision, John states as explicitly and deliberately as he can the authority upon which his words depend. It is not he who sits in judgment over his fellows ; he is still their **brother and** 9 **companion,** a sharer of a common heritage. It is Christ who utters the messages of praise and censure which he records, and it is at Christ's command that John, His prophet, communicates them to his brothers. Far from any spirit of self-exaltation, John professes himself one with the whole Christian family. He claims no privilege beyond that possessed by all—the privilege of living the life of a Christian : of suffering **distress ;** of sharing the glorious realm to be had only at the price of suffering ; of showing **patient endurance** in the face of persecution, on the one hand, and, on the other, delay in the coming hour of vindication. And John was no stranger to that part of the Christian life which involved distress. Indeed, had he not suffered banishment for his loyalty to **God's word and the testimony of Jesus ?** On these grounds, he is able to claim sympathetic attention.

The desolate **island called Patmos** was a place of exile under certain Emperors for political and religious offenders. It is clear, however, that in mentioning the place of his exile John was not concerned with authenticating his visions by creating a setting for them, like the pictures of the Babylonian Court in the Book of Daniel. He wishes only to establish a bond of sympathy with his readers. Similarly, in mentioning the time of his first vision, **the Lord's day,** John is once again quietly 10 emphasizing a common participation in the Christian life. A popular custom had arisen in Asia Minor of setting aside at regular intervals throughout the year certain days on which to celebrate the Emperor's birthday. And this, the first reference to the Lord's day in Christian literature, bears witness to the fact that the churches, no less than the devotees of the Cæsars, had their 'Imperial days,' set aside for the worship and contemplation of a heavenly king. Thus, John in Patmos was not totally severed from his brothers on the mainland. At a time when all Christians were united in prayer, their problems must have taken first place in his thoughts.

In these circumstances John **found** himself **rapt in the Spirit** : he fell into a trance, an ecstatic condition which in this messianic age was by no means rare. There flashed into his 11 consciousness an imperative conviction that God wished him to send certain messages to the churches in Asia Minor : messages of encouragement, warning, and rebuke. The **loud voice** which spoke to him was as clear and incisive as a **trumpet** note. It was the voice of Christ.

i. 12–20 : THE FIRST VISION

So I turned to see whose voice it was that spoke to me; and on 12
turning round I saw seven golden lampstands and in the 13
middle of the lampstands *One who resembled a human being,*
with a long robe, **and** *a belt of gold* round his breast ; his 14
head and hair were white as wool, **white** *as snow; his eyes*
flashed like fire, his feet glowed like finely burnished bronze, 15
his voice sounded like many waves, in his right hand he held 16

seven stars, a sharp sword with a double edge issued from
his mouth, and his face shone like *the sun in full strength.*
17 When I saw him, I fell at his feet like a dead man ; but he
laid his hand on me, saying, '*Be not afraid ; I am the First*
18 *and the Last,** I was dead and here am I alive for evermore,
19 holding the keys that unlock death and Hades. Write down
20 your vision of what is and *what is to be hereafter. As for
the secret symbol* of the seven stars which you have seen in
my right hand, and of the seven golden lampstands—the
seven stars are the angels of the seven churches, and the
seven lampstands are the seven churches.

* The words ' and the living One' (καὶ ὁ ζῶν) have been added as
a gloss from the next verse.

John's account of his first vision is dramatic and moving.
12 If it contained no more than his picture of the **seven lampstands,**
with Christ in their midst, it would give powerful expression
to a truth which the conflict of this world too easily obscures.
Doubtless the seer wishes his fellow-believers to be fully
aware that Christ is actually present among them, that He
is inseparable from His churches, that the light which they
diffuse to a darkened world is His light. So much is clear ;
but the symbol meant still more to John and his readers, who
would consciously associate the seven cressets with the
sevenfold lampstand which had been set before the holiest
place in the temple. For them there was in the picture the
implication that the Christian churches were now the embodiment of what for the Jews had been only a symbol, however
sacred. The temple at Jerusalem had been destroyed, and
the sacred lampstand was now lying extinguished in the
Temple of Peace in Rome. The Jews had been disowned and
disinherited by God, and the Christian communities had taken
their place.

In spite of its impressive and dramatic solemnity, however,
John's account may tend to leave the exacting reader of this
age a little mystified. Whether he regards the account of the
vision as the recollection of an actual episode, the ' lively
portraiture ' of ' some strange fantastic dream,' or whether he

thinks of it as allegory, the figurative expression of a mystic's communion with his God, he will perhaps feel that the narrative contains certain inconsistencies. He may consider that the Messiah's appearance, if visualized in all its detail, is unnecessarily strange. Possibly some details will appear inapt, and others obtrusive and scarcely conceivable. For instance, though it may seem trivial to advance such objections in the face of John's glowing enthusiasm, is it not inconsistent to say that from the mouth which held a **sword with a double edge** there also came a voice which **sounded like many waves** ? Or that the **right hand** which upheld the **seven stars** descended also upon the prophet to reassure him ? Was John really **testifying to what he saw** ? Or, alternatively, are not these artistic blemishes ? Again—and here a more serious difficulty occurs—in spite of the Messiah's explanation, the **secret symbol** of the **seven stars and the seven lampstands** seems in effect to be oddly confused. For though Christ tells John to write to the **angels** of the churches (the ' stars '), and though accordingly he does nominally write to the angels, the contents of his letter are applicable only to the churches themselves (the ' lampstands '), as bodies of men and women with human faults and virtues. What *is* the distinction, drawn by the Messiah Himself with such dramatic force ? And, finally, is it not strange that John, an earthly being, should be told to write letters, material things, to entirely spiritual beings like these angels—who in any case are very closely associated with Christ ?

These initial difficulties provide us with certain guiding principles which will help us to understand much of the profuse imagery elsewhere in REVELATION. In the first place, it seems clear that John did not necessarily ' see ' the pictures which his words evoke, in any visual sense. Perhaps he would even have been distressed to think that any such misunderstanding could arise. He did actually fall into a trance. He did emerge from that trance with certain convictions burning in his heart. He did credit his clear vision of these truths to the inspiration of Christ. And then, how was he to convey his newly sharpened perception of God's will to his fellow-

Christians ? Utterly convinced that God wished him to do so,
he had yet to find words adequate for so difficult a task. His
pen did not welcome abstractions, and yet some of the things
he had to say were subtle, out of the reach of ordinary experience and ordinary words. And so the truths which he saw
with a seer's keen and certain vision must resolve themselves
into a pictured language which is often magnificent, occasionally incongruous. For example, when we speak of guidance,
protection and reassurance, John speaks of the *hand* which
guides, protects and reassures—the right hand. The angels of
the churches are in the **right hand** of Christ : that is, he affords
them guidance and protection, as their Lord. Christ lays His
right hand on John, after he has fallen **like a dead man** : in
other words, He gives him reassurance.

John's portrait of Christ, awe-inspiring, mysterious, supernaturally bright, has for centuries been imprinted on the minds
of Christians. Until modern times worshippers have venerated
a mental picture of the risen Christ as depicted by John, rather
than Jesus of Nazareth, the teacher and healer. And yet John
was not primarily concerned with what we may term ' physical
portraiture.' He wished to say to the churches: ' These are
Christ's attributes. This is the character, and these the powers,
of the Messiah to whose name we adhere.' This statement
of the functions, character, and authority of Christ John
intended to form a prologue to the seven letters which follow.
To make his intention even more clear, and to press upon
each individual church the demands made upon it by the
Messiah whom he here describes in full, John prefaces each
letter with a statement of those attributes of Christ which
have peculiar reference to the needs of the church addressed.
For the most part these brief descriptions are drawn from this
initial picture.

When the seer turns to see **whose voice it was**, it is the
13 **lampstands** which first meet his eyes : and in the middle of the
lampstands is Christ. The churches are Christ's deepest
concern. His unremitting care of them is the more remarkable
because in His hands has been lodged unlimited power to
destroy the pagan nations and the evil powers of which, to

John's mind, they are the instruments. This Messiah, who watched over each small company of Christians struggling in the midst of the pagan cities, is endowed with the full splendour of God. The **long robe** and **the belt of gold around his breast** are emblems of royal dignity. The whiteness of His **head and hair** may well have been taken to represent wisdom— 14 the wisdom of one whose life was eternal , John takes the expression from Dan. vii. 9, where it is part of the description of God. The **eyes which flash like fire** indicate that Christ is all-seeing, ever vigilant over His churches, ' the searcher of the inmost heart.' The **feet** glowing **like finely burnished bronze** 15 symbolize power to crush evil and to punish unfaithfulness. The **sharp sword with a double edge** which issues from Christ's 16 **mouth** represents the Gospel in all its sternness : an instrument of retribution for those who ignored its stern precepts, a weapon to ' execute judgment upon the nations.' The **face, shining like the sun in full strength,** suggests the dazzling splendour of a heavenly Being.

A good illustration of the extent to which John depended on 17 literary reminiscence for the expression of his visionary experiences is afforded by reference to the Book of Daniel. ' I raised my eyes, and as I looked there I saw a man standing, robed in linen, with a girdle of fine gold from Ophir round his waist, his body gleaming like a topaz, his face like lightning, his eyes like lamps of fire, his arms and legs like the colour of burnished bronze, and the sound of his words like the noise of a crowd ! ' (Dan. x. 5, 6). Where John departs from Daniel's description, it is largely to emphasize Christ's divinity by ascribing to Him attributes previously associated with God. John acknowledges the same feeling of awe and terror in contemplating Christ as Daniel felt at the appearance of the heavenly Being. And he remembers his predecessor's expression of this feeling : ' But when I heard his voice I fell down in a dead faint, my face upon the ground. Then a hand touched me. . . .' Again for John it is the hand which symbolically brings reassurance. Such reminiscences, which abound in John's book, were doubtless recognized by many of his first-century readers ; they compel his readers of a later age to recognize the extent to which his narrative is allegorical.

But though so much of John's picture is derivative, it conveys a conception of the Messiah which is unique, for Christ is endowed with a splendour and authority which hitherto had been ascribed solely to God. John reserves to God the ultimate power in the universe : He alone is the **Almighty,** seated on the throne of heaven. But otherwise the Father has clothed His Son with every divine attribute. He is the **First and the Last,** all-embracing and eternal. His universal authority is exemplified most vividly in His power over death

18 itself. He holds **the keys that unlock death and Hades**—the abode where departed spirits awaited final judgment. And this authority He had won through His own death, from which He had arisen triumphantly, to be **alive for evermore.** In this assurance the Christian finds complete victory over all fear. Death is no longer a ' necessary end ' : martyrdom itself is merely the prelude to complete fellowship with Him who says, **Be not afraid.**

19 Moreover, in Christ the churches had not only one who had rid them of the final tyranny of death, but also a revealer of inspiriting truths. When, therefore, John reports the Messiah's

20 revelation of two **secret symbols,** the **lampstands** in the middle of which He stood, and the **stars** in His right hand, we are justified in seeking a truth of the highest importance to the believers ; a truth, moreover, with which hitherto they have been unfamiliar. We have already seen what a depth of meaning is contained in the symbol of the lampstands, and we have noted the difficulties connected with the symbol of the stars—the **angels** of the churches. Unless we understand that the angels themselves are symbolical, a metaphorical figure for some truth which has defied literal expression, we are left with a thought which does not warrant the great emphasis laid upon it by John. When Christ Himself moves amongst the churches, it is hardly an added inspiration to know that they had guardian angels ; nor is it of supreme religious value to learn that these heavenly creatures, somehow responsible for the destiny of the churches, should be addressed in John's

written messages. It is not unreasonable to suppose that John meant more than this. If the **lampstands** are to be taken as symbols for the communities as they exist on earth, is there not yet another aspect of their existence, not apparent to the worldly and unthinking ? Are they not also heavenly societies, living figuratively in the **right hand** of Christ, under His guidance and protection ? John sees in the churches more than merely temporal ' organizations ' ; he sees their divine character. Each earthly body of Christians has, as it were, a soul. And since it is John's purpose to make the churches conscious of their divine character, whether for the purpose of encouragement or rebuke, he addresses them, not as churches, but as angels.

LETTERS TO THE SEVEN CHURCHES
(ii.–iii.)

PREFACE TO THE SEVEN LETTERS

It is a natural impulse to wish to know more about the circumstances of the seven churches, and the cities and towns whose life they shared. Yet we need not regret that the satisfaction of such curiosity can at best be far from complete, since it is utterly foreign to the purpose of John's book to lay stress on the individual and native characteristics of the seven churches, or to *identify* them in any way with the fortunes of the cities themselves. Occasionally, it is true, John ' speaks in the dialect of the local situation,' using allusive language to convey certain ideas succinctly and forcefully ; to that extent it is necessary sometimes to enquire into local practices and institutions. The existence of incidental allusions of this kind, however, in no way justifies the attempt often made to detect elaborate analogies between the history and character of the cities and of the churches ;[1] we must

---

[1] See Ramsay, *op. cit.*

regard the churches as ' colonies of heaven,' ideally dissociated in every way from the life of the pagan cities (see chap. xii.). Moreover, the seven letters were not intended to be messages exclusively addressed to the churches named by John, as has often been assumed. Indeed, that is not even their primary purpose ; they form an address to the whole body of Christians.

The general conclusion to be drawn from the sevenfold design of the letters and from the careful symmetry of their arrangement has already been indicated (chap. i., p. 5). It follows without question that if the letters were intended to form a sevenfold discourse, at once an analysis of the whole Church and a message to the whole Church, they could not at any time have had separate circulation, as has been frequently suggested. In any case, the full cogency of the letters so much depends on a knowledge and understanding of the later chapters of the book that we must regard them solely as a preface. For John, REVELATION was more than a diocesan charge ; it was a prophetic encyclical. No narrower view does justice to John's conviction of the overwhelming importance of his book to the Christian community. For the ' hour of trial ' which he foresaw was about to confront all Christians ; the gathering-up of the forces of evil was to be a universal menace ; their final defeat was to be a prelude to the Messiah's reign. John's canvas is as wide as the earth and heavens, and the events depicted on it are for the eyes of every believer. Our chief concern, therefore, in approaching the seven letters must be not to reconstruct the *minutiæ* of local circumstances, but to appreciate the essential nature of the contribution made by each to John's sevenfold discourse.

We may, perhaps, allow ourselves to imagine that when John wrote the seven letters his thought ran somewhat as follows : ' God is about to assume His power and begin to reign (xi. 17), the Messiah is on the point of coming ; but first there must overtake the Church a trial of unparalleled severity, connected with the blasphemous determination of the

Emperor to compel all men to worship him. In what condition are the churches to meet this hour of trial ? In what condition are Christians to meet their Messiah ? ' And as he surveyed the churches, he saw that they could be divided into three groups : those who were completely healthy, those whose vigour was impaired but not destroyed by the existence in their midst of the false and disloyal, and those who displayed a marked lack of qualities indispensable to the profession of the Christian faith.

John addresses the first group of churches in the second and sixth letters, through the churches at Philadelphia and Smyrna. Already tempered by persecution from the Jews, these two communities demonstrated, not only their firmness and courage, but also their possession of a full measure of the essential Christian virtues. Hence they had proved their fitness for the more intense ordeal still before them. These two letters must therefore be read together, as complementary addresses to all loyal Christians, warning them of a future ordeal, praising their past conduct, and encouraging them to renewed constancy by the assurance that their heavenly reward was secure, no matter what their Satanic opponents might do.

The churches of the second group are addressed in the three central letters, those to Pergamum, Thyatira and Sardis. These three letters answer the question : To what extent has the Church severed herself from all compromise with pagan life, with its low morality, its idolatry and the supreme blasphemy of its emperor-worship ? In two of the letters, those to the churches at Pergamum and Thyatira, John addresses the faithful. He claims, however, that they are too tolerant of people holding unsound ' liberal ' beliefs, and leading a life which is summarily judged to be immoral. The prevalence of false teachers, disseminating a perversion of the Christian truth, was traditionally one of the signs of the End ; such men, John asserts, must be rigidly excluded from the churches. ' Nicolaitans ' or ' Balaamites,' and followers of false teachers like the ' Jezebel ' of Thyatira, must be treated with the utmost severity ; tolerance was at once an offence against the offenders, since it hindered repentance, and a danger to the churches, since tolerance of evil-doers might easily reduce the general abhorrence of the evil itself. In the letter to Sardis it is the unfaithful who are addressed. Nothing they have done is *complete* in God's eyes ; in other words, their devotion to the exclusive interests of the Christian faith and their severance from the pagan life around them are decidedly incomplete. Because they have clung in this way to a compromise, because they have ' soiled their garments ' by approaching too near to the defilement of pagan practices, their seemingly vigorous life is really so feeble as to be on the point of death. The letter to Sardis, like those to Pergamum and Thyatira, sketches a divided community, warns the unfaithful as sternly as possible, and encourages the loyal who exist by their side.

The churches of the third group addressed by John were in danger of losing their very claim to be called Christian through their lack either of a spirit of charity, or of zeal and true spirituality. The first and last of the seven letters are devoted to this problem—the problem of all those communities who were drifting towards rejection, through an incomplete grasp of the Christian faith. All three groups bore witness by their condition that the End was near ; as we see from the apocalyptic teaching of the Gospels, it was commonly expected that the Church must suffer both from external persecution and internal delinquency before the Messiah came (cf. St. Matt. xxiv. 9–13).

ii. 1–7 : THE LETTER TO THE CHURCH AT EPHESUS

1 To the angel of the church at Ephesus write thus:—These are the words of him who holds the seven stars in his right hand,
2 who moves among the seven golden lampstands : I know your doings, your hard work and your patient endurance ; I know that you cannot bear wicked men, and that you have tested those who style themselves apostles (no apostles
3 they!) and detected them to be liars ; I know that you are

enduring patiently and have borne up for my sake and have
not wearied. But I have this against you : you have given 4
up loving one another as you did at first. Now, remember 5
the height from which you have fallen; repent and act as
you did at first. If not, I will come to you very soon and
remove your lampstand, unless you repent. Still, you have 6
this in your favour: you hate the practices of the Nicolaitans, and I hate them too. Let anyone who has an ear 7
listen to what the Spirit says to the churches : ‘The
conqueror I will allow *to eat from the tree of Life* which is
within the paradise of God.’

The fifty years’ standing of the Ephesian church, and its
former intimate association with St. Paul, its founder, gave it
an importance which some have thought to be reflected in its
primary position among the seven churches addressed by John.
But it was not for this reason that the believers of Ephesus
were addressed first ; much less was it because Ephesus itself
held a position of primacy among the seven cities. The
Ephesian letter comes first in John’s admonitory discourse
because the warning it gave was of supreme importance ; and
this consideration also decided the emphatic final position of
the Laodicean letter. First and last, as it were, the churches
must guard against losing the essential qualities of their faith :
love and a fervent, unpresuming devotion.

John confronts the Ephesian church with the ever-present
Messiah of his vision, one **who is in the middle of the . . .
lampstands**, intimately aware of their condition, and actively
concerned with it. He reminds the Ephesians that it is to
Christ that they owe their continued existence and their hope
of future protection, for He holds **the seven stars in his right** 1
hand, *grasping* them firmly. His authority over them is
supreme. Both the privilege and the complete dependence of
their position demand of them much more than at present they
realize. Christ’s unfailing knowledge of their **doings** should be 2
for them a motive for rejoicing not unmixed with apprehension.
Nevertheless, though the unsatisfactory side of their life is
John’s chief concern in his letter, he acknowledges the good

ungrudgingly: both their hard work specified later as vigilance over the church's purity, and their patient endurance, a term of the highest praise, earned, no doubt, by their constancy in the face of the hostility of their pagan fellow-citizens. For whereas some Christian communities seem to have been on easy terms with their neighbours, the Ephesian church held it a cardinal point of their faith to keep themselves utterly free from the taint of such false teaching as might have brought them nearer to the beliefs and the immoral practices of pagan society. Nicolaitans (see pp. 32–4) and false apostles alike were rigidly excluded from their number. From the pagan point of view, they were no doubt a sect whose insignificance alone made it tolerable. They must have seemed disloyal, fanatically censorious, and, as the clamorous silversmith Demetrius had foreseen (Acts xix.), subversive to the interests vested in the local shrines. A faith so intransigent must undoubtedly have rendered hostility the more bitter.

The church at Ephesus had evidently taken to heart such counsel as that contained in the Pauline epistle which bears their name : ' Have nothing to do with the fruitless enterprises of darkness ; rather expose them.' Indeed, that seems to have become their preoccupation. The false apostles whose exposure and rejection John so applauds were tested according to precautions frequently urged in those days, as, for example, in 1 John : ' Do not believe every spirit, beloved, but test the spirits to see if they come from God.' Even in those days of hardship the growth of Christianity had attracted men of inferior character and belief. Emphasis is abundantly laid elsewhere in the literature of the period on the necessity of preserving the uncompromising nature of the Christian life. The generalization of 1 John again may well express the principle upon which the Ephesians acted : ' If any man love the world, the love of the Father is not in him.' The scrutiny which they directed on wicked men, particularly on self-attested prophets and teachers whose characters belied their large claims, is rewarded by unstinted praise.

Lest the Christians in Ephesus should be discouraged by the stern reprimand which is central in his message, John continues in this vein of praise. He once more does justice to their constancy and their courage ; Christ is ever conscious that they are still **enduring patiently,** loyal to the Name, that they 3 have **borne up** under recent persecution, and that their spirit is as vigorous as ever—they **have not wearied.**

Yet all their virtues were set at nought by their lack of **love** for one another. It is as if John had said : ' You have every praiseworthy quality except charity ; and lacking that, you have nothing.'

We are reminded of St. Paul's words to the church at Corinth : but the theme was, of course, familiar enough in early Christian writings. It is significant of the general temper of the cities of Asia Minor that the writer of the Epistle to the Ephesians should have found it necessary to confront the young Ephesian church with so formidable a list of vices bearing on the lack of a spirit of forbearance and charity. ' Bitter feeling and passion and anger and clamouring and insults, together with all malice '—all these were the insidious qualities of the pagan life which they were to set aside. In its pastoral aspect, the Epistle is largely an introduction to the *love* of the Christian life : the Ephesians must be ' fixed and founded in love,' and to that end the writer even assigns to each member of the family his duties and privileges, so that at least one source of strife may be avoided. When therefore we learn that the Ephesians had **given up loving one another** as 4 they **did at first,** we recognize that they had lapsed into a fault to which the ordinary life of a city of Asia Minor was subject to an extraordinary degree. Ephesus itself was a city where trade guilds, clubs, and the home all suffered from the diseases of fractiousness and rancour. The pagan philosopher, Apollonius of Tyana, speaking to the citizens of Ephesus not long after John addressed the Christian Church, found the same need to stress the importance of a spirit of amity.

The reason for the decline of the Ephesian church is not far to seek. In his farewell message to the Ephesians (Acts xx. 17 ff.) St. Paul is described as uttering forebodings of their future domestic troubles : 'fierce wolves will get in among you and they will not spare the flock ; yes, and men of your own number will arise with perversions of the truth.' These men had appeared, and the work of detecting and exposing them can have been carried on only at a great cost. An inquisitorial spirit must necessarily rob affection of its spontaneity, and reduce the forbearance and trust so necessary to the life of a small community. The condition of the church at Ephesus—and it can hardly have been unique—startlingly substantiated the prophecy of St. Matt. xxiv. 11 : ' Many false prophets will rise and mislead many. And in most of you love will grow cold by the increase of iniquity.' It was for that very reason that love had ' grown cold ' at Ephesus.

5   John tersely points to the remedy : **remember, repent, act.** There must first come an acute consciousness of the extent of their lapse. The proud memory of previous years must lead them to feel keenly the contrast of their present condition. The change of heart induced by such memories must result in a definite change of conduct : it must be expressed in deeds, not sentimental pretences ; in a reversion to their former life of harmony and love. John is expressing no new idea when he continues to tell the Ephesians that if they lack love they can no longer hold their present privileges and name. In fact, their fate must be no other than rejection : Christ will **come very soon and remove their lampstand.** The threat is vague : either the community will cease to exist as the earthly agent of the Messiah, or (more probably) it will be disowned, and hence lose the privilege of protection in the last days, to perish in the general cataclysm. But little depends on the alternative. The essential truth is that mistrust, quarrelsomeness, groundless suspicion, coldness of heart, and malice—in short, lack of love—must lead to spiritual death.

Yet the love which John commends to the Ephesians with such peremptory abruptness is not an undiscriminating amiability. Lest he should be misunderstood, he is at pains once more to make it quite clear that their intolerance of **wicked men** is wholly good. It is sealed with the approval of 6 Christ Himself, who, like the Ephesians, hates **the practices of the Nicolaitans** (see letter to Pergamum, p. 32 ff.). Love for their fellows must not reduce their hatred of falsity, of idolatrous and immoral behaviour—in fact, of any approach to the easy codes of the pagan world.

John's message to the church at Ephesus, as to the other six churches, is terse but comprehensive. The essential virtues and essential faults of the church are incisively stated ; praise, encouragement, rebuke, warning and exhortation are in turn presented with the outspoken vigour of one who is completely confident that he is commissioned to report the word of Christ. The solemn demand for attention with which he prefaces his words to the **conqueror** are cast in a formula sacred to the most impressive prophetic injunctions : **Let 7 anyone who has an ear listen to what the Spirit says to the churches.** The promise which ensues is sure of fulfilment, since it is made by the prophetic **Spirit** sent by Christ to illumine His followers. The reward set before all loyal Christians is no less than eternal life in the security of Heaven. Adam's forfeited heritage of bliss is once more available to the **conqueror** in the new Heaven (see xxii. 2) ; and the **conqueror** is he whose life bears the marks of purity and love, and whose faith triumphs over persecution (see note on the conqueror, p. 61).

ii. 8–11 : THE LETTER TO THE CHURCH AT SMYRNA

Then to the angel of the church at Smyrna write thus:—These 8 are the words of *the First and the Last,* who was dead and came to life: I know your* distress and your poverty (but 9 you are rich!) ; I know how you are being slandered by those who style themselves Jews (no Jews are they, but a mere synagogue of Satan!). Have no fear of what you 10 are to suffer. The devil indeed is going to put some of you in prison, *that you may be tested ;* you will have a distressful *ten days.* Be faithful, though you have to die for it, and I will give you the crown of Life. Let anyone who has an ear 11 listen to what the Spirit says to the churches : ' The conqueror shall not be injured by the second death.'

* Omitting, as in ver. 13, [τὰ ἔργα καί].

In the Christians of Smyrna John is speaking to men and women who lived under the double weight of persecution and poverty. Yet for them the one was the gateway to life ; the other a foil to the untold riches of faith. Only Christ, the faithful martyr, could inspire such constancy ; only a firm belief in the worth of His sacrifice, and faith in His triumph over death, could so transform their poverty and **distress.** To these 8 people John speaks in the name of one **who was dead and came to life** ; the Messiah, fully endowed with the all-embracing power of God, the **First and the Last.**

From this letter we can gain some idea of the unbounded fortitude of these early Christians. John assumes that the people of Smyrna (as typical of faithful Christians everywhere) share his own attitude to physical suffering : he speaks lightly of it, as one speaks of familiar things. Words so brief, spoken to men who might at any time go to their death, have in them a heroism which even now has power to stir the blood. In no way does John attempt to minimize their peril ; indeed, he soberly predicts that their troubles will be intensified. The trust in their constancy implied in John's simple frankness must have encouraged them. It is enough for them to know 9 that Christ is aware of their troubles : their **distress,** their poverty, and the fact that they were **being slandered** by false Jews. Clearly the unseen world, whose rewards they hoped in the future to receive, was much more real to them than the material hardships of the present.

They would take heart also from the scorn with which John mentions their powerful opponents, **those who style themselves Jews.** These men had lost the right to the name which signified the chosen people (see letter to Philadelphians, p. 48). No longer the instruments of God, they had become **a synagogue of Satan**—a congregation of men devoted to the dark Power who was the source of all persecution and trial. The proud name of Jew, with all its ancient associations, had become the prerogative of those who gave allegiance to the true Messiah.

No doubt the Christians of Smyrna, and of every other active and faithful community, aroused acrimony among the

Jews by the success of their missionary work, particularly among Gentile 'God-fearers' on the fringe of Judaism. Their vigorous polemic must also have given offence, since to the Jews the Christian position was sectarian and heterodox, its central doctrine nothing short of blasphemous. For we have seen (chap. i.) how Jesus, the obscure peasant of Galilee, who died a criminal's death, was worshipped as one endowed with the full splendour and authority of the Ancient of Days. The Jews' anxiety to dissociate themselves completely from such claims led them to be informers and persecutors. Hostility in the shape of contumelious taunts, excommunication, and execration failed to satisfy the more zealous of them ; powerless themselves to inflict more direct injury, they had recourse to the Roman administrators. And in cities like Smyrna, where the Imperial cult had been enthusiastically fostered for many years, it must have been an easy matter to urge the authorities to action. It was part of the Imperial policy to respect the religion of its subject nation, the Jews, who were legally excused from actual worship of the Emperor on condition that intercession was offered for him in synagogues. But Christians had no national name to protect them, and consequently no legal privileges. Once disowned by Judaism, of which to the casual eye of the pagan they might seem merely an eccentric and troublesome sect, they were at the mercy of the prejudices of local administrators. And certain Jews were not content with disowning and ridiculing their opponents ; there is reason to believe that they would on occasion traduce them, laying malicious accusations at their charge—accusations, for example, of disloyalty and positive sedition. In the account of the martyrdom of Polycarp, some years after John was writing, we have striking testimony of the lengths to which a malice bred of religious dogmatism could go. The Jews responsible for Polycarp's condemnation were among the most eager to heap faggots on the fire in which he perished.

John's prediction, **The devil indeed is going to put some 10 of you in prison** (cf. p. 251), is perhaps his reading of the trend of Jewish persecution. But however he arrived

at the idea, he intended it to convey a truth affecting not Smyrna alone, but the whole Church. It is a veiled foreboding of the events described more fully in the eleventh and thirteenth chapters—the great Distress (vii. 14) ' the hour of trial which is coming upon the whole world ' (iii. 10). The Imperial authorities, visible agents of the universal author of evil, are characteristically personified as the Devil himself ; or rather, their action as intermediaries is ascribed to the power ultimately responsible for it. (Satan, ' the old serpent,' and the Beast, the Imperial Power, are clearly distinguished till the very end ; cf. xx. 7–10, etc.) For the Christians of Smyrna, and of the faithful communities they were intended to exemplify, the future was indeed dark. But John does not seek to cast over it the rushlight of an evasive optimism. It is his purpose to reveal the worst. The churches must be **tested.** Their ordeal is also their opportunity, for those who fall in the great martyrdom will gain the conqueror's reward. And although all must be prepared to undergo the utmost rigours of persecution, even death itself, they need **have no fear,** for every loyal Christian, whether martyr or not, is spiritually protected : the malice of Satan cannot touch him (see note, xi. 1 and vii. 3). During this short period of intense persecution **(ten days :** as we should say, ' a week or so ') **some** are to be put **in prison,** and they doubtless are those who are to **die** (cf. xiii. 10*a* and context). These martyrs are addressed in the promise
11 **to the conqueror,** but the preliminary assurance is addressed to *all* the faithful. The victors in the games for which Smyrna was renowned were crowned with laurels ; but the Christian who remained loyal won an imperishable prize, **the crown of Life.** The crown, a customary symbol in Asia Minor for earthly honours, bestowed alike for civil merit and military or athletic prowess, was for Christians the sign of immortality. John's message to the believers of Smyrna is built upon this theme, that they must regard their sufferings with eyes lifted above the distressful present, towards a future guaranteed by one who Himself had triumphed over persecution. The conqueror, he who dies for his faith, more than anyone can be certain of this glorious future. What perils faced the soul in its

mysterious voyage after the first death, when it left the haven of the flesh ? For the disloyal, certain destruction ; or rather everlasting torture (xiv. 10–12). But the martyr need fear none of the terrors which haunted other men. He will rise in the ' first resurrection,' after the defeat of the powers of evil, to share Christ's power and judicial authority (xx. 4 ff.). ' Blessed and holy is he who shares in the first resurrection ; over such the second death has no power. . . .' **The second death** was the eternal damnation of the soul on the day of final judgment. The conqueror can face that day confidently, certain of his place in the new Jerusalem. To men who daily expected the bitterest persecution—and more, the dissolution of the earth and the advent of universal judgment—no assurance could have held greater joy.

ii. 12–17 : THE LETTER TO THE CHURCH AT PERGAMUM

Then to the angel of the church at Pergamum write thus :— 12 These are the words of him who wields the sharp sword with the double edge : I know where you dwell, where 13 Satan sits enthroned, and yet you adhere to my Name, you have not renounced your faith in me even during the days when my witness, my faithful Antipas, was martyred in your midst—where Satan dwells. But I have one or two 14 things against you: you have some adherents there of the tenets of *Balaam,* who taught Balak how to set a pitfall before *the sons of Israel by making them eat food which had been sacrificed to idols and give way to sexual vice.* So even 15 with you; you likewise have some adherents of the tenets of the Nicolaitans. Repent ; if not, I will very soon come 16 to you and make war upon them with the sword of my mouth. Let anyone who has an ear listen to what the 17 Spirit says to the churches : ' The conqueror *I will allow* to share the hidden *manna,* and I will give him a white stone inscribed with *a new name,* unknown to any except him who receives it.'

12   The two-edged **sword** with which John confronts the
believers of Pergamum proclaims a message both of terror
and joy : to those of their number whose carelessness and
lack of scruple were weakening the whole community it forms
a threat of the utmost severity ; to the faithful it is a reminder
that their Messiah had it in His power and purpose to overthrow the might of the pagan world around them. For the
sharp sword with the double edge (cf. xix. 15) was an instrument of punishment : the Word of God, ignored or lightly set
aside, was a ' sword to execute judgment ' on individuals as
well as on ' the nations.'

Pergamum was a stronger fortress of pagan life than any
other of the seven cities. To its temples and law court came
pilgrims and litigants from a wide district, which included
lesser cities like the neighbouring Thyatira. The ancient
capital of Asia, it had long been a stronghold of the Imperial
cult ; as early as 29 B.C. a temple had been erected there to the
' divine Augustus ' and the goddess Roma. This fact alone is
13 enough to explain John's phrase, **where Satan sits enthroned.** Yet
side by side with the devotees of Cæsar there were the votaries
of a god whose emblem was no other than the serpent—the
god of healing, Æsculapius. To the worshippers of this god, the
serpent was a symbol of renewal ; but to Christians it was the
unmistakable sign of Satan (cf. xx. 2). The worship of Æsculapius was neither formal nor perfunctory. His priests, who
held treasured medical secrets in their care, performed their
duties with true reverence and humanity, and their devotion
was reflected in the firm hold of Æsculapius on his followers.
Here, in opposition to Christianity, was a cult with a deep and
unusual religious appeal. But this was not all. Dominating
the city of Pergamum, high on the Acropolis, there had stood
for two centuries a great altar-platform, with huge figures
depicting the war of the gods on the giants—monsters with
serpentine tails instead of legs. This was the altar of Zeus
himself, the king of the gods, and therefore to John the lord of
evil. Well indeed might John exclaim, in the singleness of his
faith, that in Pergamum **Satan sits enthroned.**

The church at Pergamum had shown admirable constancy in

resisting such strong pagan influences, at once menacing and alluring. Confronted with an apparently recent outburst of persecution, during the days when the faithful Antipas was martyred, they had done well even to retain their faith in Christ. Once again we must refer to the martyrdom of Polycarp in order to appreciate the nature of the ordeal to which the Christians of Pergamum were probably subjected, and the nature of the submission demanded of them. ' And the magistrate pressed him hard, saying, " Swear the oath (by the genius of Cæsar) and I will release thee : curse the Christ." But Polycarp replied, " For eighty-six years I have served Him, and He has never injured me. How then can I blaspheme my King, who has saved me ? "' Polycarp's crime was simply his refusal to acknowledge Cæsar as the son of God : he was condemned purely for adherence to the Name. It is probable that Antipas also was accused of no offence other than his faith, and that the persecution in which he fell was interpreted by John to be an early sign of a more rigid application of the blasphemous claims made by the Imperial cult. Antipas seems to have been the first local martyr, perhaps the first in Asia Minor ; but he was not destined to be the last, John thought. All men eventually must ' worship the statue of the Beast ' or face death (xiii. 15).

John twice repeats his assurance that Christ is conscious of the supreme difficulties confronting His servants in a city where Satan dwells. They may be sure that their difficulties are weighed in the balance with their achievements. In this way he safeguards against the discouragement which might follow rebuke. Having clearly stated their merits and difficulties, he can define their fault with unmitigated force. The weakness of the church at Pergamum was the Ephesians' strength : it lay in a loose tolerance of men who compromised the purity of the faith.

In any pagan city, in Pergamum no less than in Corinth (cf. 1 Cor.), the conduct of Christians was beset with many acute problems. What were to be their relations with their pagan fellow-townsmen ? From what entertainments and clubs should they hold themselves aloof ? Was it justifiable to buy meat in the open market, knowing that it had been associated with sacrificial rites in the local temples? Into what enquiries about the source of food should scruples lead one? Where must cordiality and friendship end, and estrangement begin? To all such enquiries, the **Nicolaitan** party, condemned by John, had very easy answers ; for them there were few scruples. But for the stricter believers, who yet had no desire to set themselves apart as an exclusive community, there must have been many heart-searchings. As John so clearly saw, their daily intercourse was fraught with the subtlest and most insidious of dangers. There was no knowing where compromise in small matters might end. It would have been far from difficult for Christianity to have become yet another of the transitory cults of the Empire, undistinguished in its moral life from the rest. St. Paul's advice to the Corinthians on the subject of food was that they were to avoid rigorously any compromise on points of morality (for a close connexion existed in pagan cities between feasting and immorality), but that otherwise they must do what was expedient, without giving offence. Where no principle was involved, their care must be only to guard against misleading the weak, and to humour prejudice. But prejudice and principle were more difficult to separate in John's day, and expediency had become a dangerous guide.

At all events, John's puritan views leave him in no doubt.
14 **Food sacrificed to idols** was in itself repugnant from its association with ' Satan-worship,' and to eat it showed a lack of scruple which would tend to embrace the even more abhorrent sin of giving way to **sexual vice.** Hence, John does not hesitate to assert that the ' liberal ' believers of Pergamum, who lacked strict scruple in one way or another on points of food, clubs, entertainments and sexual relationships. held views worthy of a **Balaam,** whose story he briefly unfolds. The passing of time had not improved the Old Testament reputation of Balaam ; the legend quoted by John ignores his obedience to the angel and to the voice of God, and speaks only of his disastrous influence on the Israelites. Balaam had become the type of all sorcerers and corrupt teachers, whose **tenets** betrayed people

into idolatry and sensualism. It should be noted that John does not directly accuse the 'liberals' themselves of open immorality, but of holding treacherous and insidious doctrines which were liable to lead others into evil ways. John's purpose in drawing the analogy between these men and Balaam is apparently to reveal what is the intrinsic tendency of their teaching—a tendency which may well have been obscured by their high-sounding professions. It has even been argued that the **sexual vice** of which John speaks here and in the letter to the Thyatiran church is a metaphorical expression for idolatry. Such an interpretation is not impossible ; it is at least consistent with John's determination to reveal the stark choice before them, between Christ and the satanic power of Rome (chap. xiii.), and to show the disastrous folly of compromise. But whether or not we read John's words in their purely literal sense, the truth in them is plain enough ; pagan beliefs and immoral practices equally unfitted men for the service of Christ, and in any case the one often implied the other. Just as the Israelites had allowed themselves to be seduced by the craft of Balaam, so also the Christians of Pergamum were allowing the foundations of their faith to be undermined by men of unsound principle. To these ' Balaamites ' John gives the more explicit party name of **Nicolaitans**. 15

The Nicolaitans, according to patristic tradition, were the followers of Nikolaos, the ' proselyte from Antioch,' whose appointment is described in Acts vi. 1-6. Originally ' full of the holy spirit and wisdom,' he is said to have become antinomian through an extreme asceticism. Such a process, later reaching full development in teachers like Cerinthus, was one intrinsic tendency in early Christianity which, in clearing away the dusty lumber of unreal legal codes, reduced the force of some salutary restraints on conduct. The Church's path, like that of Christian, lay between two deadly giants : legalism on the one hand, with its exaltation of trivialities, its Pharisaical insistence on codes of rules—and on the other hand antinomianism, which often took its origin in a reliance on the strength of a devoted spirit, directly inspired by God and therefore freed from the tyranny of legal precepts and prohibitions. As an ascetic, Nikolaos may have been misled by his prepossession with the lofty affairs of the soul into a contempt for material things, and hence to a neglect of the laws which guide men in their use of them. Those who follow such a creed ' in love and truth where no misgiving is ' will do battle with the rebellious flesh ; others, holding that the satisfaction of physical craving is a matter altogether without significance, will stoop to sensualism without shame. Whatever their first state, by the time John was writing the followers of Nikolaos seem to have reached the latter condition ; at all events, their opponents, by a piece of popular etymology, had read into the Greek elements of the name Nikolaos the opprobrious meaning of ' Balaamite '—that is, one who ' confounds or destroys the people.'

The church at Pergamum is not accused of sharing the deplorable habits and views of the Nicolaitans. The fault of which she must repent lay in her laxity in giving free rein to the Nicolaitans, who thus hastened the faster to their destruction. Just as Balaam is related to have died by the sword, so the Nicolaitans will die by the sword of the Spirit, if they are 16 allowed to continue in their courses. Christ will **come among** the believers of Pergamum, and **make war** on the unfaithful in their midst, with the **sword** of his **mouth**. They will die no doubt like Ananias and Sapphira, stricken down by some mysterious pestilence ; for disease was commonly regarded as a visitation of God (cf. Acts v. 1–11, 1 Cor. xi. 30). Thus John brings into bold prominence the responsibility of the whole Church for the moral welfare of individuals. In her easy tolerance she had hitherto fallen far short of her duty. She must **repent,** thrust aside all leniency, and discipline the deluded Nicolaitans in hope of averting their destruction and recalling them to the true faith.

17 If he wishes to earn the title of **conqueror,** the believer at Pergamum must first cast off the indifference or fear which prompts his tolerance of the Nicolaitan tenets. He will then be recompensed for his abstention from the allurements of the pagan world by the twofold reward of privilege and security in the after-life. The **conqueror** is to eat heavenly food at the

messianic feast: the manna, which at the first fall of Jerusalem a prophet's solicitude had caused to be hidden lest it should share the general desecration, was to be restored with other lost glories of the Jewish people to faithful Christians. In the second and more mysterious promise John indicates that they were to be secure of admission to this heavenly society. A white stone in itself was precious to the ancient mind as a propitious charm and as a sign of admission to feasts. But it was to be inscribed like an amulet with a new name unknown to any except him who receives it. If this is held to be the new name of the individual Christian, granted on his inheritance of his heavenly reward where all things are made new (xxi. 5), John is here giving full expression to an idea rare in REVELA-TION, that the Christian will take his place among the heavenly hosts as a separate individual, not merely a nameless sharer in a general felicity. But it is perhaps more probable that the new name was intended to be that of Jesus (iii. 12, xix. 12), the name kept secret till the end from all but the conquerors (cf· xiv. 3 : only the martyrs can learn the ' new song '). The believer who possessed such a talisman—or rather, the power it symbolized—could not fail to be secure, protected as he was by the Name above all names. It was a general belief that only the knowledge of a god's name enabled men to worship him, to share his power or to avoid his anger. And since, as we see in the Philadelphian letter, Christ's new name was as yet unrevealed to men, the possession of it by the conqueror must necessarily be a privilege from which other men were excluded.

ii. 18–29 : THE LETTER TO THE CHURCH AT THYATIRA

Then to the angel of the church at Thyatira write thus :—These 18 are the words of the Son of God, *whose eyes* flash *like fire and whose feet glow like bronze.* I know your doings, your 19 love and loyalty and service and patient endurance ; I know you are doing more than you did at first. Still I have 20 this against you : you are tolerating that Jezebel of a woman who styles herself a prophetess and seduces my

21 servants by teaching them *to give way to sexual vice and to eat food which has been sacrificed to idols.* I have given her time to repent, but she refuses to repent of her sexual

22 vice. Lo, I will lay her on a sickbed, and bring her paramours into sore distress, if they do not repent of her prac-

23 tices ; her children I will exterminate. So shall all the churches know that I am *the searcher of the inmost heart ; I will requite each* of you *according to what you have done.*

24 But for the rest of you at Thyatira, for all who do not hold these tenets, for those who have not (in their phrase) 'fathomed the deep mysteries of Satan '—for you this is my

25 word : I impose no fresh burden on you ; only hold to
26 what you have, till such time as I come. 'And the conqueror, he who till the end lays to heart the duties I enjoin, *I will give him* authority *over the nations—*

27   *aye, he will shepherd them with an iron flail,*
       shattering them like a potter's jars—

28 as I myself have received authority from my Father ; also
29 I will grant him to see the Morning-star.' Let anyone who has an ear listen to what the Spirit says to the churches.

The letter to the Thyatiran believers gives us a vivid picture of the dangers and temptations besetting the Church in a small

18 provincial town. Life in **Thyatira** must have been much more intimate than in a bustling seaport like Smyrna, every aberration from normal conduct remarked on, every novelty spread by the tongue of gossip over the whole town. A creed which, if effective, necessarily withdrew men from the ordinary social life of such a town could scarcely fail to give offence. And where no citizen is a stranger, the penalties of ostracism and embargo (cf. xiii. 17) can easily be inflicted : a larger community marshals its punitive resources less readily and with less immediate effect. But although Thyatira was small, it was by no means insignificant. Its trade guilds were numerous, and if we can judge by the enterprise of the Thyatiran seller of purple who was so hospitable to St. Paul, some of them had commercial importance in the larger cities. Moreover, the

missionaries who first trod the high road between Sardis and Pergamum to bring the Thyatirans the news of Christ had gone in the steps of many pilgrims. For this was the seat of the Chaldean Sibyl, an oracle famous throughout Asia Minor.

The tutelary deity of the town was Apollo, the son of the most high Zeus. In the early days of the Imperial cult the Emperor had been acclaimed as Apollo incarnate, and hailed appropriately as the son of God—one of many similar adulatory titles. Such syncretism was a natural expression of patriotism, and doubtless still existed at the end of the first century. So when John delivers to the Thyatirans the words of the **Son of God,** he makes an allusion bearing a direct message to them. Christ is the true Son of God, not Apollo, nor the Emperor. A similar message is contained in the description of Christ as one **whose feet glow like bronze**— symbols of the punishment which was to crush both pagan oppressors, and stubborn wrongdoers in the Church. The extent of the allusion is uncertain. It is likely enough that the worshippers of Apollo Tyrimnaios trembled before a god whose character was often associated with punishment. But can we not say more about the feet which **glow like bronze ?** The word translated by **bronze** is met nowhere except in REVELATION. Was it a word which aimed directly at the bronze-smiths and modellers of Thyatira ? Or does the allusion carry us into the very temple of Apollo ? For it would have been strange indeed if Apollo Tyrimnaios had lacked a bronze statue in a town where the craft seems to have been highly developed—a town, moreover, specifically under his protection. Although we may suspect that the passing of time has robbed John's words of their allusive riches, we need not repine, for the general terms of his message are clear enough to us, as they were to the wider audience which he was addressing through the Thyatirans. In the introductory words of the letter, John makes a threefold assertion : that Christ is the true Son of God, the Messiah (for to Christians **Son of God** was almost a messianic title) ; that it is He, not the Emperor, who ultimately possesses the power to punish : and that He, scanning the innermost secrets of the heart with

37

eyes that flash like fire, knows unerringly when punishment is deserved.

He knows also when praise is deserved, however, and John does not hesitate to proclaim Christ's approval, based on 19 intimate knowledge, of their **doings,** of their **love and loyalty and service and patient endurance,** and finally of their progress. John judges by the fruits of the Christian life : it is a great thing that they **are doing more than** they **did at first.** These things remain true even though they tolerate disloyalty in their midst. For that was their fault. Whether out of regard for social benefits, deference to authority, anxiety for livelihood, genuine conviction or less creditable motives, a large party had gathered around a prophetess who preached new doctrines, doctrines apparently adding comfortable innovations to the exacting creed of John.

The situation at Thyatira is essentially the same as at Pergamum ; a sectarian party was unduly tolerated. But we must note in passing that while John accuses both churches of improper tolerance, only the believers of Pergamum are told to **repent.** This difference, however, is probably imposed on John largely by his preconceived design, whereby the first, third, fifth, and seventh churches are warned to repent. For it is the unfaithful, the Nicolaitans of Pergamum, who are really threatened. When John addresses the fifth church, another divided community, the unfaithful are in such a majority that he addresses them first, and recognizes the faithful minority only to give them an additional reassurance, almost duplicating the promise to the **conqueror** of that church. At Sardis, therefore, the injunction, ' Repent,' has its full force, since it is addressed to the real offenders. We must recognize that while John is anxious that each community should cut itself away from its dissident party, and regards tolerance as a fault, his anger is directed on the disloyal, not on those who merely tolerate.

Just as Balaam is the Old Testament prototype of the 20 Nicolaitans at Pergamum, so **Jezebel,** John urges, is the spiritual ancestor of this **woman who styles herself a prophetess.** John's language is not mere abuse. He evidently felt strongly that the churches did not fully realize the significance and tendency of such doctrines as those sponsored by the **prophetess.** Therefore her character must be painted in what he thought were its true colours. Jezebel had seduced Israel into Baal-worship, with its attendant immorality : this prophetess equally is leading people into **sexual vice.** By this 21 term John *may* mean primarily religious unfaithfulness (cf. Ezek. xvi. 15 ff., where the metaphor is elaborately worked out). But in any case such religious unfaithfulness would involve at least some acquiescence in the easy-going morality of the local cults. John denounces the carelessness of the prophetess's followers in the matter of **food** : he is probably speaking not only of food eaten at home, but of participation in the feasts held by guilds and clubs, at which the entertainments were often indecent. Presence at such feasts may not necessarily have involved licentious behaviour, but it could not fail to result in a serious betrayal of principle. For each guild had its tutelary god, and the clubs were at one in their acknowledgment of the Imperial deity ; to take part in their social life was inevitably to give at least formal acquiescence in their religious ideas. Harmless enough it may have seemed to be present at a feast where the grace before food formally acknowledged the Emperor as son of God ; harmless indeed if one's faith were truly enlightened. And this apparently was the presumption of the followers of the prophetess. They were enlightened. They had **fathomed the deep mysteries of Satan** : 24 that is, they had learned the precise limits of his power and the nature of his dominion over this world. They could therefore afford to be broad-minded. Their initiation into a secret knowledge protected them.

John naturally chose for emphasis the darker side of the prophetess's doctrines : those who enquire into the **mysteries of Satan,** he insinuates, must themselves be sinister and depraved. He was not, of course, accusing them of worshipping Satan. His charge conveys to us that they were exponents of a primitive gnosticism. The gnostics, whose tangled skeins of speculation contained threads from many different cults, believed that salvation was for a chosen few who were initiated into an esoteric knowledge. We can infer little about the beliefs of the Thyatiran gnostics from John's phrase beyond their assumption of superiority from the mere possession of such knowledge. But it is possible that they foreshadowed the speculations of later gnostics, who explained the existence of evil by assuming that the world had been given over to an inferior spirit, and was not directly ruled by God. John himself seems partly to share such a belief (cf. xi. 17, xiii. 4), as being an explanation of the apparent triumph of evil in his own day ; but he concludes from it that the Christian must maintain himself utterly apart from the evil forces loose in the world. It is here that he differs radically from the prophetess. She seems to have taught that, since Satan had sway in the world, it was only a part of wisdom to **fathom** his **deep mysteries.** The possession of a secret redemptive knowledge infallibly protected her followers against danger. Clothed with this magical security, they could without peril acknowledge the lesser divinities venerated by the pagan world, take part in their rites as convenience suggested, and even descend to immorality. We are not really justified, however, in supposing that licence was an object at Thyatira ; but we may well agree with John that anything like gnostic tenets, with their accommodation of the pagan gods in a generous theosophy, was well designed to rob Christianity of its distinctive claims.

In the letter to Thyatira, John's puritan temper is displayed in all its sternness : exacting and outspoken, he is vehemently indignant at practices which in our own generation might be passed over with a mere shrug. It may seem almost anomalous that a man capable of language so harsh could commend the Thyatiran believers for their charity, and reproach the Ephesians for their lack of it. But John's harshness is not wanton. He saw the sectarian activities of the liberals of his day as the first smouldering of a fire which might consume each small community. And in view of later events, we are justified in believing that it was largely the unyielding discipline enforced by men like John that preserved Christianity from ending in the dead ashes of a syncretistic paganism.

We need not reproach him, then, for the vigour of his threats against the **Jezebel** and her followers. The prophetess herself will be laid on a **sickbed :** she had been unfaithful to 22 Christ, and disease was generally held to be the reward for impurity. Her **paramours**—John seems to have had in mind certain definite persons, perhaps office-bearers in the church who gave her encouragement, and refused to cut her off from the life of the community—will be equally rewarded with **sore distress.** Those men who accepted her doctrine whole-heartedly and acted upon it—that is, her **children**—will be 23 **exterminated ;** they will suffer the fate of the seventy sons of Ahab. Sickness for the Jezebel, distress for her paramours, death for her children—an unequal punishment ? John was not concerned with degrees of punishment : the fact that he wished to press home was that disaster hung over them, a sudden and complete punishment which repentance alone could avert.

The plain truth is, John says, that Christ is not one to be content with formal observance, like the pagan gods. Nor is He concerned with the mere show of good conduct. Appearances may deceive men :

> In religion
> What damnéd error but some sober brow
> Will bless it and approve it with a text,
> Hiding the grossness with fair ornament ?

But Christ is the **searcher of the inmost heart.** The all-seeing God, **whose eyes flash like fire,** is able to reward and punish according to His knowledge of the most secret motives of conduct. Here certainly the unfaithful at Thyatira seem to be accused not of open and scandalous immorality, but of hiding vice beneath a cloak of respectability. In punishing them openly, Christ will reveal the hidden viciousness of their doctrines, so that the churches elsewhere may be thoroughly warned and put on their guard against such dangerous plausibility.

That John has previously discussed the whole matter with the Thyatirans is fairly clear. Probably he was referring to his own previous warning when he says : **I have given her**

time to repent but she refuses. . . . For the guidance of the faithful, he has recalled the decision of the Church at Jerusalem (Acts xv. 28, 29). To counter and discredit the prophetic authority at Thyatira, John appeals to apostolic tradition. This seems to be the bearing of the expression : **I impose no fresh burden on you.** John is reminding the faithful that the Christian freedom, nevertheless, has its limits,

25 not to be transgressed. **Only hold to what you have, till such time as I come.** The last phrase should be noted : the consciousness that the End was near made their present burden, no light one, at least tolerable. To forgo the social and material benefits of friendly intercourse with the pagan world demanded a deep conviction, and, perhaps, an immediate goal.

26 Even in his promise to the **conqueror** John continues to stress the necessity of moral rectitude in the present. He who fails to **lay to heart the duties** enjoined by Christ can never hope to achieve the glorious rewards of martyrdom. But those who steadfastly set their face against an unworthy alliance with the powers of this world will be endowed with a might infinitely greater than that of the Emperor himself. The Messiah had already been clothed in the splendour of punitive authority ; His martyrs were to be similarly honoured

27 —**as I myself have received authority from my Father** (cf. iii. 21). ' Ask of me and I will give thee the nations for thine inheritance, and the uttermost parts of the earth for thy possession ; thou shalt break them with a rod of iron. . . .' The vengeful dream of the Psalmist had been interpreted by generations of downtrodden Jews as a promise that their nation should have authority in the messianic kingdom to judge their Gentile oppressors. John does not flinch at the grimness of such a reward ; he claims it as a privilege of the Christian inheritors of the Jewish destiny, and sets it forth to the Thyatirans as an encouragement to greater strictness. Such prophecies, and the temper in which they were made, are distasteful to the sentiment of our own day. But we must understand the logic underlying them : the pagan world was, to John, utterly evil ; it must therefore be utterly destroyed

(cf. xiii. 10*b* and xvi. 6). Not otherwise could the pure reign of God be consummated. Hence, to be associated with the great ' reaping ' (xiv. 15) of the harvest of evil was the greatest of honours. The martyrs alone could claim it.

This first promise to the conqueror has reference to the reign of Christ on earth (xx. 4). As if to direct his eyes beyond his office of vengeance and to remind him of the ultimate bliss beyond it, John adds : **I will grant him to see the Morning-** 28 **star.** This has been taken to mean that the conqueror's path will not for ever lie through the dark night of oppression now encompassing him ; the dawn of a new day is to shine upon him ; he will soon see the Morning-star. But it seems more probable that the **Morning-star** is Christ (xxii. 16), the Bridegroom, to whom the redeemed community is to be ' married ' (chap. xxi.). In other words, the martyrs are told that they will not only ' reign on earth ' ; they will also achieve final happiness.

iii. 1–6 : THE LETTER TO THE CHURCH AT SARDIS

Then to the angel of the church at Sardis write thus:—These are 1 **the words of him who holds the seven Spirits of God and the seven stars: I know your doings, you have the name of being alive, but you are dead. Wake up, rally what is still** 2 **left to you, though it is on the very point of death ; for I find that nothing you have done is complete in the eyes of my God. Now remember what you received and heard,** 3 **hold to it and repent. If you will not wake up, I am coming like a thief ; you will not know at what hour I am coming upon you. Still, you have a few souls at Sardis who have** 4 **not soiled their raiment ; they shall walk beside me in white, for they deserve to. ' The conqueror shall be clad in** 5 **white raiment ; I will never *erase his name from the book of Life*, but will own him openly before my Father and before his angels.' Let anyone who has an ear listen to** 6 **what the Spirit says to the churches.**

In view of the similarity between the titles of Christ in the 1 letters to the churches at **Sardis** and Ephesus, and the vehement censure contained in both, it is at first tempting to infer that these two churches were intentionally associated in John's sevenfold scheme. A closer examination of the letter and its setting will, however, reveal more clearly the original symmetry of John's design. This letter is to be associated with the other two central letters—those to Pergamum and Thyatira. For whereas in the first and in the last communities addressed by John there exists no faithful party to mitigate the general threat of rejection, at Sardis a **few souls** still remain **who have not soiled their raiment.** In this the church resembles the ' divided ' communities of Pergamum and Thyatira. But its condition is much more perilous : at Sardis the great majority had failed, and to such an extent that it is they, the unfaithful, who must be addressed as representative of the church. At each of the two associated churches the faithful and loyal formed a nucleus which could be addressed as the more distinctive party ; the followers of Balaam and Jezebel are distinctly the sectarian groups. At Sardis the disloyal predominate ; and this fact has somewhat obscured the clarity of John's design and the implications which it contains (see Preface to the Seven Letters).

The church at Sardis had all the appearance of a thriving community, with a vigorous life ; but its activity was barren. John states the general fault with abrupt force : **You have the name of being alive, but you are dead**—that is, on the point of spiritual death. Desperate as their condition is, the deluded and unfruitful believers of Sardis must be recalled to the most profound truth of all, the truth which John had brought to the attention of the Ephesians, whose destruction was also imminent, though for a different reason. He reminds them that their very existence depends on Christ, who **holds** in His hand **the seven stars** (see note, i. 20). They are His to hold or to relinquish. The immeasurable privilege of their intimacy with Him is only equalled by the peril of a half-hearted service given in return. Nor may they presume to hope that their **name of being alive**, their swollen reputation among men, could ever mislead Christ. For He who had absolute authority over the churches had also at His command **the seven spirits,** and the seven spirits were His ' eyes ' (v. 6) (see notes on iv. 5, v. 6) ; they were ' sent out into all the earth,' to view the deeds of men. Whatever their reputation, Christ alone could truthfully say **I know your doings ;** He alone was competent to assess their true worth.

John's denunciation of the church at Sardis is most comprehensive : **nothing you have done is complete in the eyes of my** 2 **God.** When we remember what ' complete ' fulfilment of the Christian life meant to the Christians of Smyrna, and, indeed, at what bitter cost the Ephesian church won the praise which qualified the charges laid on her, we shall better understand what John demanded of the church at Sardis. Why was it that the malice of Jew and persecution of Roman remained quiescent there ? Can we not infer that the church at Sardis set herself the task of avoiding hardship, by pursuing a policy based on convenience and circumspection, rather than wholehearted zeal ? The accommodating temper of the pagan cults of Asia Minor found no difficulty in welcoming new religions if they could be absorbed into the Imperial scheme. A Christianity robbed of aggressiveness, enfeebled by looseness of thought and morals, its more distinctive claims subdued at the bidding of discretion—such a faith need arouse little opposition, either from Jew or Gentile. A policy of this sort was bound to leave its mark on the conduct of individual believers, and once again John makes the widest of charges, this time not of duties neglected but of sins committed. Only **a few** can be singled out, **who have not soiled their raiment.** 4 Not false beliefs, as at Pergamum and Thyatira, but spiritual poverty and complacency were leading them into moral error : the reason was different, but the results no doubt were very similar.

John's stern reprimand is softened by no words of encouragement ; the soldiers sleeping at their posts are aroused with a sharp cry : **Wake up ! rally what is still left to you, though** 2 **it is on the very point of death.** They must measure their present condition by remembering what they had originally

been taught about Christ and the kind of conduct He demanded
3 of His servants. **Hold to it and repent,** is the prophet's terse
advice. If memory alone is unable to spur them to repentance, let them also consider their peril. Belief in the imminence of Christ's coming had no doubt waned at Sardis ; we
may perhaps infer that, like the ' bad servant ' of St. Matt.
xxiv. 48, the unfaithful believer murmured : ' My lord and
master is long of coming,' and that he used this delay to
indulge himself unworthily. But he will come, John asserts,
when He is least expected ; secret, silent, hostile—**like a thief**
(cf. St. Matt. xxiv. 43). Those who are besotted by their sins
will be overtaken suddenly by the hour of judgment, in the
midst of their folly. Only immediate repentance can avert
destruction.

In appearance this threat is made to the whole community
at Sardis, as if the **angel of the church** has quite lost sight of
its true heavenly character. This, however, must be taken
to mean that the worthy minority at Sardis were too few in
number to be regarded as properly representative of the
church as a whole. At Pergamum some, at Thyatira many,
4 and at Sardis the majority have failed. To those **few souls**
at Sardis who remain loyal, a special promise is made : **they
shall walk beside me in white, for they deserve to.** And not
only at Sardis, but doubtless in many other communities there
existed small groups of believers who steadfastly refused to
follow a doubtful example set by their fellows. Their task
was doubly difficult, and their merit proportionately great.
They shall be rewarded, John asserts. Their righteousness on
earth will be recognized in heaven (cf. xix. 8), and they will
have fellowship with the Messiah.

All the faithful have before them this glorious destiny ; but
to one class of men it was assured without any shadow of
uncertainty—to those who proved their faithfulness by dying
5 the martyr's death. **The conqueror shall be clad in white
raiment** ; his inward integrity shall be allowed to shine in
visible glory (xix. 8), when, as one of the blessed company of
the redeemed, he enjoys full fellowship with the Messiah.
There is no question of *his* perishing in ' the second death '

(xx. 15), since his name is marked out for immortality. This promise, I will never erase his name from the book of Life, is made with a backward glance at the atrophied members of the church at Sardis. When a criminal's name was removed from the civic register of an Asiatic town, he lost his citizenship ; but it was citizenship of the heavenly society that the faithless were destined to lose. Lastly, the greatest reward of all, embracing all other rewards, is placed before the faithful. As conquerors, they will be acknowledged openly before the Father Himself, amidst the glory of the heavenly beings surrounding the throne, as faithful followers of the Messiah and therefore as sharers of His power and authority (cf. iii. 21).

iii. 7–13 : THE LETTER TO THE CHURCH AT PHILADELPHIA

Then to the angel of the church at Philadelphia write thus :— 7
These are the words of the true Holy One, who *holds the key of David, who opens and none shall shut, who shuts and none shall open.** Lo, I have set a door open before you which 8
no one is able to shut ; for though your strength is small, you have kept my word, you have not renounced my Name. Lo, I will make those who belong to that synagogue of 9
Satan, who style themselves Jews (no Jews are they, but liars!)—lo, I will have them *come and do homage before your feet* and learn that *I did love you.* Because you have 10
kept my call to patient endurance, I will keep you safe through the hour of trial which is coming upon the whole world to test the dwellers on earth. I am coming very 11
soon: hold to what you have, in case your crown is taken from you. ' As for the conqueror, I will make him a pillar 12
in the temple of my God (nevermore shall he leave it), and I will inscribe on him the name of my God, *the name of the city* of my God (the new Jerusalem which descends out of heaven from my God), and my own *new name.*' Let anyone 13
who has an ear listen to what the Spirit says to the churches.

* Omitting (with Primasius) οἶδά σου τὰ ἔργα, ' I know your doings,' a harmonistic gloss which interrupts the connexion of thought.

7 The letter to the **church at Philadelphia**, like that to the faithful of Smyrna, is designed to reassure and strengthen hearts already courageous, to confirm the faithfulness of minds already loyal. These two churches, at Philadelphia and Smyrna, represent in John's symbolical scheme of seven all completely faithful communities throughout the world. And the two letters, taken together, are intended to put before all loyal Christians the essential nature of their situation.

The similarity between the messages to Smyrna and Philadelphia is not confined to general approbation ; point for point, the letters cover the same ground. In the first place, the fundamental position of each church is the same. Each is confronted with slander and malice from those **who style themselves Jews** ; each has to face direct persecution from the Roman authorities for loyalty to the **Name** ; each is assured that the Jewish persecution, no less than the Roman, is Satanic, and implicitly that the Christian communities are now the true Israel.) To both churches the promise of spiritual security is made, as a reward for continued faithfulness (ii. 11, iii. 10), and in each instance this reward is associated with the crown of final victory. The church at Smyrna is poor, that at Philadelphia weak ; in each case their condition enhances the worth of their achievements.

These striking agreements assume their true importance only when we realize that the differences between the two letters are prompted not by any real difference in the local situation, nor in the quality of John's regard for each faithful community, but purely by their position in John's literary scheme. In short, the two letters are complementary. They are to be read side by side, the letter to the believers at Smyrna as a statement of the theme of faithfulness, the letter to the Philadelphians as an expansion of the same theme. The introductory verse of the former letter, for instance, makes the initial assertion that Jesus Christ, who rose from the dead, is the Messiah ; that He guarantees to His followers immunity from death ; that He is fully endowed with the authority and power of the all-embracing God. This assertion of the Christian belief about Christ contained an indirect challenge to the pagan authorities who ignored Him, and a direct, unmistakable challenge to the Jewish persecutors who denied Him. In the letter to the Philadelphians, the title of the Messiah confirms this assertion of Christ's full divinity, in a way which has clearer reference to Jewish taunts and recriminations. The Jews, furious at the appropriation to Christ of the Eternal's attributes, retorted that Christ, so far from being the First and the Last, was an impostor. John rejoins that Christ is indeed **the true Holy One**—'true' in the sense of *genuine*. How futile, therefore, that these false Jews should presume to excommunicate the loyal followers of the true Messiah! What folly to attempt to cut them off from the privileges of His future reign! For He alone held the **key of David** (Isa. xxii. 22)—only Christ could exclude people from the joys of the messianic kingdom; only He could admit men to these joys. He **opens and none shall shut ; He shuts and none shall open**—He, and no other. Even though the Jewish excommunication had the practical result of depriving the Christians of legal rights, even though they should therefore be faced with the dreadful alternatives of denying the **Name,** or death, the faithful believers need never fear. They were protected by Him **who opens.** The risen Christ held ' the keys that unlock death and Hades.'

It is clear, then, that the expression, **Lo, I have set a door** 8 **open before you which no one is able to shut,** is to be interpreted in the light of the description of Christ which precedes it. In spite of calumnious Jews and their excommunications, the loyal followers of Christ are promised their place in the new Jerusalem. As Isaiah said (xxvi. 2), the gates of Jerusalem shall be open ' for the upright ' (cf. xlv. 1). Indeed, the idea that the gates of God's community, the restored Jerusalem, shall be kept open for the upright is one which recurs in Isaiah ; it exists side by side with the idea that those who are at present weak and scorned shall eventually be made to triumph (cf. Isa. lx. 11 and 14). Thus, the **open door** means primarily access to God. It is not impossible, however, that the words have a further implication. St. Paul used the term ' open door ' to mean opportunity for spreading the gospel.

Now, even at this late hour, when John saw the sword of God's anger threatening unregenerate mankind with swift and awful doom, the churches still ' witnessed ' and ' prophesied ' before the world (see chap. xi. and notes). And John was convinced that the end of their period of prophecy should be for many Christians shame and death. Yet shame was to be changed into glory, death into life, in the sight of all. This great martyrdom was to be the final act of spreading the gospel ; those who fell in it—the conquerors—were sure of eternal life. It is therefore conceivable that John's readers would detect in the **door set open** before faithful Christians not only a promise of access to God, but also an indication of the surest way of attaining it—by the martyrdom which must follow fearless witness.

9 The denunciation of those **who style themselves Jews** once again amplifies a briefer statement of the theme in the letter to Smyrna. John repeats that these men have lost their right to the honourable title of Jew—**no Jews are they, but liars**— and implicitly claims it for Christians. In doing so he has in mind the privileges expected by the Jews in the messianic reign—the crowns, for example, of rabbinic legend (cf. iii. 11), once the possession of all Israelites until they were snatched away from them by hosts of dæmons, were finally to be restored to faithful Jews. But such royal privileges as these, John claims, had been forfeited by those who were Jews by virtue of birth and belief. They had become veritable instruments of **Satan**—the author of all slanderous accusation (cf. xii. 10) and persecution. In fact, they were as much to be identified with the purposes of the Devil as the Emperors and their servants, who seduced mankind from the worship of the true God (cf. chap. xiii.). Since they had completely abandoned true religion, their fate must be an ignominy hitherto assigned by them to the heathen oppressors of the Jewish nation. Isaiah had said of the pagan peoples : ' The sons of those who scorned and humbled you shall come to you, all bending low, and hail you as "The Eternal's own city" ' (lx. 14). And, again, kings and queens ' shall do homage to you, faces on the ground, and grovel in the dust

before your feet ' (xlix. 23). So to the statement of Jewish depravity in the letter to Smyrna there is added this prophecy of Jewish humiliation, in the hour when the **true Holy One** should demonstrate to the world that the persecuted churches were His people—that He **did love** them. In that hour Jews are to be no more privileged than the heathen nations. Their rejection is complete. And it should be remembered that John's words do not apply only to these two cities, Philadelphia and Smyrna. They form an analysis of the position of the Jews as a nation, an analysis comparable in scope with that of St. Paul in Rom. ix., though the conclusion it reaches is far different. *All* Jews who refused to acknowledge Christ as the **true Holy One,** and denied the authority of the Lord whom John called the First and the Last, must suffer the shame of rejection. Christians the world over, ' men from every tribe and tongue and people and nation ' (v. 9), though in contrast to the Jews their **strength** was **small,** now constituted the chosen people.

John, like other early Christian writers, found the weakness of the faithful communities rather a matter for rejoicing than commiseration. To assert that the small communities of Christians were actually the chosen people of God, those who were to be the objects of God's special favour in His work of judging and punishing ' all the dwellers of earth,' those who by their witness were to precipitate the flood of His avenging wrath (cf. chap. xi.)—this was to make a large claim; so large indeed as to seem paradoxical. So the despondent in the churches must have felt often enough. John records the apparent paradox : **Your strength is small :** yes, but that is of no significance. The essential thing is your loyalty : **You have kept my word, you have not renounced my Name.** The faithfulness under persecution here implied (cf. ii. 13 and note) is again recorded in the words : **you have kept my call to 10 patient endurance.** The Philadelphians (and we must remember that John was speaking through them to the faithful everywhere, whom they exemplified) had already shown their true quality in their obedience to the demands of the faith— Christ's **call** to unwavering and confident fortitude. They had proved their worth, and therefore they would be kept **safe through the hour of trial which is coming upon the whole world to test the dwellers on earth.**

What was this **hour of trial ?** The Christians of Smyrna had already been told that some of them were to be imprisoned, in order that they might be ' tested ' : a prophecy which, except for this more specific information in the Philadelphian letter, might wrongly be taken to forebode sporadic persecution, affecting only Smyrna and perhaps other individual communities here and there. But plainly John expects a universal intensification and expansion of the present distress. The prophecies to the faithful at Smyrna of prison (cf. ' captivity,' xiii. 10), and testing (cf. xiv. 12 and preceding verses), carry us forward to the events described in chaps. xi. and xiii.—the great Distress. This is the **hour of trial.** The simple grandeur of John's words becomes very clear when it is understood that the shadow of universal persecution hangs over them. Past loyalty shall have its reward in future protection : the faithful are to be kept **safe.** Were they then to understand that they would be preserved from death ? By no means : but whether they were to die, or whether they were to be preserved, the one supremely reassuring fact remained, that the Devil and his agents would have no power to seduce them from their loyalty and its reward. The parallel promise to the church at Smyrna anticipates John's later description (vii. 4, xi. 1, xii. 6 and 14–17 ; see notes) of what he means by this protection. ' Be faithful, *though you have to die for it*, and I will give you the crown of Life.' Clearly, some must die, and it is implicitly expected that others shall be allowed to survive. But *all* who are faithful shall be given immortality.

Finally, John adds a note of warning to his anthem of praise. This **hour of trial** is to be no light ordeal. There must be no relaxation of vigilance, with consequent loss of power to choose death rather than disloyalty. The loyal must firmly
11 hold to the faith which has nerved them to their present patient endurance, in order that their reward may not after all be lost. Here, in the letter to the Philadelphians, John speaks of the reward as if it were already in the possession of the

loyal ; whereas in the letter to Smyrna the **crown** is still to
be earned by the faithfulness which makes light of death. In a
sense John clearly thinks of both ideas as being true. As we
saw in the letter to Sardis (iii. 5) the names of Christians were
already written in the book of Life : no doubt John assumes
that they are marked out for the life to come, from their very
membership of the messianic community. But the name could
be erased. The crown could be lost, through unworthy
conduct. John's warning to the Philadelphians follows
logically from his reminder of the imminence of the Messiah's
coming. At all costs they must preserve their faith un-
weakened by any slackening of resolution. If the hour of trial
was at hand, so also was the Messiah, and the time of judgment
and retribution.

The assurance of spiritual safety in verse 10 differs only in
form from the promise to the **conqueror.** The additional 12
assurances in the second promise are implicit in the first.
Those whom Christ promises to **keep safe** naturally inherit all
the heavenly joys of the new Jerusalem. The only difference
is that the vision of the conqueror is directed more deliberately
to the final reward, which lay beyond the suffering of the
great Distress ; to the permanence, security and privileged
communion with God and Christ in ' the new heaven and the
new earth ' (chap. xxi.). As elsewhere, John speaks of the
conqueror in terms apt to the city which he addresses. Philadelphia had earlier in the century been devastated by great
earthquakes. By contrast the security of the heavenly life is
denoted in the expression : **I will make him a pillar in the
temple of my God.** It was a city of many temples, but these
were threatened by the unstable earth. From these temples
devotees had been forced in the past to flee in fear ; but the
conqueror **shall nevermore leave** the heavenly temple. And
when John speaks of the **temple of my God,** he is speaking
metaphorically of the very presence of God, since the heavenly
City has no temple : ' for its temple is the Lord God almighty
and the Lamb ' (xxi. 22). Perhaps we have some allusion
to the practice of the priest of the Imperial cult, who at the end
of his period of service erected his statue in the temple and

inscribed upon it his name, thus hoping to achieve prolonged communion with the power of the god. But the Christian is himself to be a **pillar** in the heavenly temple of God's presence : a metaphor which no doubt gained greater force for John's readers from the existence of pillars sculptured into human forms.

In the promise to the conqueror of the Philadelphian church John attempts to convey symbolically what is the ultimate and essential reward for the loyal : not merely to possess immortality, but to be ' a realm of priests,' perpetually in the presence of the supreme God. Four times the Spirit repeats the words, **of my God** : Christ's people shall share the majestic splendour of the heavenly scene no less than the angelic beings surrounding the throne of the Eternal. Such is the force of the inscription on the conqueror of the three names. To know the name of a deity was to share his power— to be enabled to invoke him successfully, to enjoy a consequent security and protection. The conqueror shall not only know **the name of my God** ; it shall be imprinted on him indelibly. Similarly he is assured of indubitable membership of the blessed society of the redeemed—the **new Jerusalem** (chap. xxi.) ; it is as one of the heavenly society that the conqueror belongs to God. And, finally, he is to belong manifestly and permanently to the Messiah, having full fellowship with Him (cf. iii. 21) in the knowledge of His **new name**, kept secret till the end (see xix. 12).

Although the description of the conqueror as a pillar in God's temple borrowed its aptness from the circumstances of Philadelphia, it would nevertheless be intelligible to the wider audience addressed by John. The *nuances* of local allusion may have been obscured by distance, just as to-day they are obscured by time. But many of John's readers, like John himself, were familiar enough with the later Isaiah to be reminded of a prophecy strikingly apposite to the circumstances of all loyal Christians, at present weak and scorned. but yet destined to triumphs (Isa. lvi. 3–5). ' Let not your foreigner say, " The Eternal will excommunicate me." Let not your eunuchs say, " Ah, we are but a barren tree."

For this is the Eternal's word . . . theirs is a monument within my temple . . . a memorial from myself that never shall be moved' (R.V., 'An everlasting name that shall not be cut off '). The ultimate triumph of the weak and oppressed, the 'lasting joy' that is to be theirs, the blessing of the Eternal's presence, the priestly privileges of the people so singled out for favour—may we not presume that John's language is even primarily designed to recall such Isaianic themes as these ? To make this assumption would be to recognize that the polemic note is once more sounded in the Philadelphian letter—sounded not only for the Philadelphians and those familiar with that city, but for the whole Church. For every true Christian was faced with Jewish contempt and excommunication, just as he was shortly to be faced with an intenser form of Imperial persecution. In either case he needed the reassurance that God's favour is for the weak and despised, and that a glorious destiny was available for him if he cared to secure it to himself.

iii. 14–22 : THE LETTER TO THE CHURCH AT LAODICEA

Then to the angel of the church at Laodicea write thus : These 14
are the words of the Amen, *the faithful* and true *witness,*
the origin of God's *creation.* I know your doings, you are 15
neither cold nor hot—would you were either cold or hot !
So, because you are lukewarm, neither hot nor cold, I am 16
about to spit you out of my mouth. You declare, ' I am 17
rich, *I am well off*, I lack nothing! '—not knowing you are
a miserable creature, pitiful, poor, blind, naked. I counsel 18
you to buy from me gold refined in the fire, that you may
be rich, white raiment to clothe you and prevent the shame
of your nakedness from being seen, and salve to rub on
your eyes, that you may see. *I reprove and discipline those* 19
whom I love; so be in warm earnest and repent. Lo, I stand 20
at the door and knock ; if anyone hears my voice and opens
the door, I will come in and sup with him, and he with me.
' The conqueror I will allow to sit beside me on my throne, 21

22 as I myself have conquered and sat down beside my Father on his throne.' Let anyone who has an ear listen to what the Spirit says to the churches.

Of all the seven churches, the Laodicean is the least satisfactory, and the rebuke administered to it is correspondingly the sharpest. It is therefore natural to expect that the introductory verse will bring before the Laodiceans those attributes of Christ which will most forcibly convict them of their lethargic and self-complacent feebleness, and arouse them to some comprehension of their perilous condition. And indeed, even though we do not seek any special allusion in the 14 words, the description of Christ as the **Amen, the faithful and true witness, the origin of God's creation** lacks nothing in solemnity. The **Amen** is the God whose word is unfailingly kept ; **the faithful and true witness** reminds the Laodiceans of a Messiah whose earthly testimony ended in death, whose heavenly testimony must always be trustworthy ; and this Messiah was to be associated with the unspeakable grandeur and power of the Creator, as the ' incipient cause ' of the universe and all in it. The particular aptness of this last description of Christ probably lay in the fact that both John and the Laodiceans knew St. Paul's letter to the neighbouring church of Colossæ. There (Col. i.) the thought of Christ's pre-existence, creative power, and supremacy alike over the angelic orders and the Church forms a prelude to the thought of His redemption of the Christians of Colossæ—a redemption available to all, if they play their part by adhering ' to the foundations and stability of the faith.' If this connexion between St. Paul's letter to the Colossians and John's letter to the Laodiceans is assumed, we see at once that John's association of Christ with the creative power of God carries with it, at least locally, a distinct moral challenge. But what of the wider audience—that lukewarm seventh (as it were) of the whole Church, which John was addressing through the representative church of Laodicea ? What memories would **the origin of God's creation** recall in them ? Allusion, used by a skilful artist, is perhaps the most powerful of literary weapons ;

and at the same time it is often the least susceptible of reconstruction. It is true that occasionally the context of one of John's quotations brilliantly illuminates his meaning. What he meant by the **Amen**, for instance, must almost certainly be understood from Isa. lxv. 12 ff. The God who disinherits those who refuse to listen when He calls, who punishes evildoers and rewards His true servants—this is the Amen. And the Amen not only punishes but forgives, forgets the past, and promises a glorious future to those who invoke Him. It is hard to resist the thought that when John calls Christ **the origin of God's creation** the minds of his readers would be irresistibly carried to the lessons taught by the prophets about the moral demands made on His creatures by the Creator. There can be no doubt that John was familiar with the lofty descriptions of the Creator-God in the later Isaiah, for REVELATION abounds in quotations from it. The exalted monotheism enunciated there always has unmistakable bearing on the moral and religious condition of the chosen people. Like REVELATION, its purpose is pastoral, not theological. Both Isaiah and John were passionately eager to awaken the minds of their fellows to the extent of the claims made on them by God. So Isaiah pleads with the exiled Jews to recognize that the God who formed the universe claimed undivided loyalty, and would utterly destroy the disloyal (Isa. xl.–lviii.) ; that He took the part of the poor and humble (lvii. 15) as opposed to the powerful and rich (xl. 23, xiv. 9) ; that He ' adds new strength to the weak ' (xl. 29) ; that repentance is a qualification for admittance to the new Jerusalem, which is the goal of creation ; and, above all, that He watched over His people with tender care, ' for your husband is your Maker' (liv. 5). (In REVELATION, of course, it is Christ who is the ' husband ' of the redeemed community.) So concerned was Israel's Maker for His people that He, the Majestic One, could actually *plead* with them : ' O Israel, you will not renounce me ? I have swept aside your ill deeds like a mist. . . . I have redeemed you ; oh, return to me ! ' Can we not assume that when John associates Christ with the God of creation, he is confronting the Laodiceans with a wealth of pleading and rebuke ? It is of less moment at this point to enquire about the theological import of John's phrase (cf. Col. i. 15) than to be aware of the moral challenge it was intended to convey. For the whole purpose of REVELATION is to stir men's hearts to the urgent need of discipline, courage and faith, in order that the great ' hour of trial ' should find them prepared and resolute.

The Ephesian church brought upon itself the threat of destruction through the very abundance of its zeal; but the Laodiceans completely lacked this quality, in itself so admirable. What was worse, they were quite unconscious of any deficiency. It is this complacency which so arouses John's concern. The harshness of the Messiah's rebuke is designed to pierce the stout armour of self-satisfaction.

15 ' **Would you were either cold or hot !** ' Far better to be completely untouched by the flame of religion than to have only smouldering embers, half choked in ashes. John repeats the accusation of lukewarmness with inescapable emphasis. The Messiah is nauseated with formal observance, feeble service and self-conceit. If this state of things should persist (the later part of the letter shows that rejection is still conditional on

16 failure to repent), the Laodicean church must perish : **I am about to spit you out of my mouth.**

Laodicea was a city of great commercial and financial importance, and it may well be that the Christian community in its midst had its share in the civic prosperity. It is sufficiently notorious that material riches often breed spiritual poverty. However that may be, John's attack is made, not directly on material riches, but on a false assumption of

17 spiritual well-being. The declaration, ' **I am rich . . . I lack nothing,**' is pharisaical and not to be endured, particularly at a time when the churches were about to be tested to the uttermost. The ' poor ' Christians of Smyrna, realizing the extent of their dependence on Christ, possessed all the riches of faith ; the Laodiceans, secure in their own approval and no doubt fortified in self-esteem by wealth, were spiritually bankrupt. We are reminded of Christ's condemnation of the Pharisee who stood afar off, of His praise of the humble and meek, and of His grave warnings about the effect of riches. How can the

poverty of these Laodiceans be relieved ? **Pitiful** and **poor** as they are, their only hope is to realize that none but Christ can supply their needs. The material riches of their city can avail them nothing ; they must buy **gold refined in the fire**—that is, 18 true gold, true religion, as opposed to counterfeit. It is from Christ that they must buy it (**from me** is emphatic) ; and He will accept only the coinage of humility and unstinted devotion. They have eyes, but see not : their blindness cannot be relieved by Phrygian powder, the eye salve prescribed by the oculists of the famous medical school at Laodicea. Only Christ could give them **salve** to lighten spiritual blindness. They were **naked** : but all the looms of their city could not weave cloth to cover their sins. Laodicea might supply the whole world with her tunics and clothing materials ; but righteousness was the **white raiment** which God demanded (cf. xix. 8), and this they must get from Christ. Nothing less could **prevent the shame** of their **nakedness from being seen** in the day of judgment, when ' the dead, high and low ' stood before the throne revealed for what they were, to be judged ' by what they had done' (xx. 12). In this vivid way John, following Isaiah (lv. 1–3), points to the Lord of the chosen people as the sole source of strength and renewal, and pours scorn on human self-reliance.

Lest the severity of the rebuke administered to them should leave them utterly despondent, thinking themselves already abandoned by Christ, John asserts emphatically that **the faithful and true witness** rebukes them in order that they may earn forgiveness. The Eternal, as the Book of Proverbs said (iii. 11), like a wise father, disciplined His sons for their own good. So with Christ : **I reprove and discipline those whom I** 19 **love.** The ' I ' is emphatic, and the whole sentence may be paraphrased thus : ' Others may be content to acquiesce in the misdemeanours of those whom they love, tolerant of evil by reason of their own imperfection, but I demand a change of conduct. My intolerance of my people's wrongdoing is part of my strong affection for them.' The invitation to be **in warm earnest and repent** briefly summarizes the underlying idea of the two preceding verses. All this rough rebuke is really a plea for a change of heart : this is Christ's love for them, that He

pleads with them on the very threshold of Judgment. For so
20 we must interpret the expression, **Lo, I stand at the door and knock,** with the subsequent promise of intimacy and privilege for him who **opens the door.** The parable in St. Luke of the servants who await the return of their master in the middle of the night, ' so as to open the door for him when he knocks,' forms a remarkable parallel. This is the last warning, the last chance to repent, for the Messiah is about to come into the world ' like a thief in the night.' He who rouses himself from lethargy to vigilance shall be rewarded. **I will come in and sup with him, and he with me** : in other words, he shall share in the messianic feast, one of the most general and ancient symbols for the bliss enjoyed by the loyal, when the reign of the Messiah is established (cf. xix. 9).

Perilous though the condition of the Laodicean church was, John certainly hoped that some at least would be moved by this final appeal. The least worthy of the churches might still provide some worthy of Christ in the ' hour of trial.' It has often been observed that the warmth of the promise to the
21 **conqueror** of the Laodicean church is in conflict with the severity of the rest of the letter. This, however, is to misunderstand the purpose of the seven promises to the conquerors in the churches. They are addressed to men designated for martyrdom (see note on the conqueror, p. 61), the most precious elements of the Christian community. That they should come from a substantially worthless church is distinctly to their credit rather than otherwise. To these potential martyrs of Laodicea, John addresses himself. They are to conquer even as Christ conquered (cf. xi. 12–13, 18, xiii. 7, xiv. 1). And just as Christ was rewarded with authority through His sacrificial death, so His martyrs will be allowed to share in this authority, in the ' rule of the saints ' which is to follow the great battle with the armies of evil (xix. 19, xx. 4). Christ's sharing of God's **throne** is, of course, simply a metaphorical expression for His sharing in God's power and authority. It is so with the martyrs. Theirs is the unique honour of sharing in the task of punishing the nations for their cruelty and wickedness (ii. 26), and in the judicial and

sovereign powers of Christ in His reign on earth (cf. v. 10), which is to precede the creation of ' the new heaven and the new earth.'

The Promises to the Conqueror

The esoteric flavour of the promises made to the seven churches must have had considerable appeal to believers of John's day. If the cults of the Emperor, Apollo, Æsculapius, and the rest had their mysteries, so also had the Christian faith, mysteries far grander, reaching out to a heavenly destiny. The general purpose of the seven promises is clear : it is to assert, with an emphasis which grows with reiteration, that the great crisis before the churches need cause them no fear, since the malice of Satanic persecution could never deprive the faithful Christian of immortality. For all that, there is in these pictures of the conqueror's ultimate bliss an element of mystery which is perhaps deliberate ; how much so it is impossible to say, since we cannot compute the extent to which John's audiences were familiar with the terms of the eschatological literature from which he draws. But we can be sure that they immediately saw allusions which to-day can be only partially uncovered after tedious excavation. To treat Revelation as a buried city of forgotten allusion is to abandon our primary task of tracing its main plan and appreciating its permanent contribution to the Christian faith. Besides, John himself has enabled us to appreciate the force of most of the seven promises. He seems to have written them after the main body of the book, after his description of the reign of the saints, of the day of Judgment, and of the heavenly City : or, at any rate, he composed them with those themes in mind. Hence, for all its mystery, the cumulative picture of the conqueror's heritage tells a story needing little comment beyond that provided by the last three chapters of Revelation.

We must, however, be quite clear about the meaning of the word *conqueror*. This term has a twofold significance. First, the conqueror must vanquish the temptations of this life, and demonstrate in action his possession of the Christian virtues.

This idea is implicit in all the promises to the conqueror. It is a necessary qualification of the second meaning of ' conqueror '—that is, he who wins a victory over persecution and death, the martyr. In other words, Christ is the prototype of the conqueror. His twofold triumph over temptation in His life, over death itself in His Resurrection and Ascension, inspires as it enables the martyr to win a similar victory. The conqueror of the Church must live as the ' faithful and true witness ' lived ; he must be loyal to the last, and die as Christ died (see notes on chap. xi.). His consequent reward will be to share Christ's power, just as Christ Himself, through His victory, had shared God's power (iii. 21).

Not all of the seven promises, taken individually, require us to think of the conqueror as the martyr. For example, at the day of Judgment (from which the martyrs are excluded, by virtue of their proved worthiness, cf. xx. 5–6) *all* whose names are found in the book of Life are admitted to the heavenly City, and to ' the Paradise of God,' where they may enjoy fruit from the tree of Life (ii. 7 and xxii. 2). The book of Life, as we see from the great Judgment scene, is by no means written only with the blood of the martyrs ; the names of all faithful Christians are there, all the righteous, pure, and true (cf. xxi. 27). And these men will escape the second death (ii. 11 and xx. 15), to form the blessed community which is to have intimate fellowship with Christ (ii. 28, iii. 12, and xxi. 2) no less than the martyrs themselves. Why, then, are these particular promises made to the martyr-conqueror, if they do not apply exclusively to him ? Their true significance is that the conqueror is *certain* of immortality, and of the bliss, security, privilege, and the like which the faithful are to enjoy. He has been fully proved ; even before the Judgment day his reward is secure, for he comes to life in the ' first resurrection,' to share in the Messiah's reign on earth. Therefore, unlike those who had not been fully proved, he need have no anxiety whatsoever about Judgment and the ' second death.' *His* name will never be erased from the book of Life (iii. 5). He is marked out, ' sealed ' with a sign of infallible recognition (vii. 3 ff.), for future life.

In two of the promises, however—those to Laodicea and Thyatira—the *conqueror* can be only the martyr : if in two, then in all. For John tells us in chap. xx. that the privilege of sharing Christ's power (iii. 21) in His reign on earth over the pagan nations (ii. 26–8) belongs only to the martyrs, who ' came to life and reigned along with Christ for a thousand years,' after the defeat of the Satanic powers at the great battle of Harmagedon.

The conqueror's unique security and privilege were not gained solely through his courage in dying for his faith ; on the contrary, his death is merely the last act of a life of devotion and service. The conqueror is ' he who till the end lays to heart the duties I enjoin ' (ii. 26). He is one who has ' washed his robes ' (vii. 14) and become pure and upright through the sacrifice of Christ. John emphasizes the divine source of their strength more than once ; to mention one example, the martyrs conquer Satan ' by the blood of the Lamb and by the word of their testimony ' (xii. 11).

The seven promises are put before all the faithful, in order that all might be ready to obey their destiny (cf. xii. 10)—to go courageously to their death, if that were to be their lot. It has been argued (cf. Charles) that by the time John came to write REVELATION he was convinced that no single loyal Christian could avoid martyrdom ; the whole Church was to be slain (xiii. 11 ff.) for refusing to worship the Emperor. Those parts of the seven letters which seem to express the idea that the churches were to survive, substantially unmolested, until the arrival of the Messiah, are explained by the theory that the seven letters were written at a previous date, and express John's earlier expectation. This view fails to take all the evidence into account. There are, it is true, two kinds of expectation about the fate of loyal Christians in REVELATION ; and these different expectations exist side by side in the seven letters. But it is a mistake to think that they are mutually exclusive. Some Christians were destined to die for their faith. They were the conquerors, and their story is told symbolically in chaps. xi. and xiii. Others, no less loyal, were to be preserved from the persecution which

affected all other men (xi. 1 and xii. 13 ff.), and were to survive the destruction of the pagan cities (cf. xviii. 4, 17 and
St. Matt. xxiv., etc.), until the Messiah's reign on earth
began. In this thousand years' reign they would no doubt
enjoy the benefits associated with the messianic kingdom on
earth by earlier prophets. According to Isaiah, for example,
longevity was to be one of the characteristics of this period
(see Isa. lxv. 20) : 'anyone dying under a hundred years
must be accursed by God.' But human beings must die, all
except the martyrs, whose resurrection (the 'first resurrection') guarantees their immunity from the final judgment.
They must die, and come to life again, some to be admitted to
immortality, some to be rejected and cast into the fiery lake.

With this scheme in mind, we can more easily explain the
rather curious duplication of promises in the letters to Smyrna,
Sardis, Philadelphia, and Laodicea : curious, because John is
otherwise so economical of words, and so tidy in his construction. The final promise of each letter is for the martyr-
designate : the promise which precedes it is for each loyal
Christian, whether or not he is destined for martyrdom. The
promises to Smyrna admirably illustrate this fact. 'Some of
you' are to be put in prison, i.e. put to death (cf. xiii. 10) :
but who ? The martyr's mark is not a visible one. All are
to be *prepared* to face death : 'Be faithful unto death '—or,
as Dr. Moffatt well translates : 'though you have to die for
it.' The reward of such *readiness to die* is immortality, the
crown of Life. To the conqueror John makes a more specific
promise : he will be secure from the second death. As we
have seen, this is an assurance peculiarly appropriate to the
martyr. Again, the promise to the Philadelphian church of
protection in the 'hour of trial' (iii. 10) is similarly addressed
to the whole body of the faithful, and equally implies that
loyalty secures immortality, whether or not the loyal suffer
martyrdom. The final assurance to the prospective martyr
is more·eloquent and specific only because it was John's main
purpose to nerve all men to the sternest ordeal by showing
them the full extent of its reward. The reason why John
makes two promises to each of these exemplary churches,

Smyrna and Philadelphia, is now clear : since all believers there were already unexceptionably loyal, it followed that all would be rewarded ; the only difference between the general promise and the particular is one of degree. The martyr's ordeal is greater ; his reward is more glorious and more certain. What, then, prompted John to make two promises to the churches of Sardis and Laodicea ? At Sardis John was concerned to make a complete distinction between the majority of disloyal and the minority of the faithful. All the faithful shall have their reward—though they are so few at Sardis : their desert shall be rewarded in its acknowledgment in heaven. The conqueror's reward is here described in similar terms. On the other hand, when John was addressing the church at Laodicea, all his concern was to induce repentance : the first of the two promises is a direct invitation to the Church to repent, in view of the imminence of the Messiah's advent. *All* who repent are to have their reward. But the more specific and glorious promise is reserved for him who so far succeeds in casting aside lukewarmness and unspiritual complacency as to die a martyr's death.

JOHN'S VISION OF HEAVEN
(iv.–v.)

INTRODUCTION TO CHAPTERS IV. AND V.

In the fourth and fifth chapters we peer with John through a door standing open in heaven ! The apocalypse, now fully addressed to the churches, takes for its first subject the exposition of those beliefs about God and Christ which have impelled the prophet to his task. We now learn the full meaning of his description of God as ' He who is and was and is coming ' (i. 4). We learn also why Christ is everywhere endowed with the Eternal's attributes. In fact, as we read the two chapters side by side, we find that the subject is the almost imponderable significance of Christ's sacrificial death in the scheme of creation.

This subject is woven into a storied tapestry, of glowing colour, of a design at once arresting and mysterious. Yet it is not as a literary artist that John claims our consideration. Nor even was it his primary concern to induce in his readers a spirit of worship, by his description of the heavenly praise and adoration. It is rather as a seer and prophet that he speaks. It is a prophetic message, intrinsically necessary to the whole of REVELATION, that we must seek in the two great visions (chaps. iv. and v.) of the heavenly scene. And this message is new and original. The language in which it is expressed, and the conceptions of heaven which accompany it, are largely derivative. But the central theme of the two chapters has no source but the prophet's own vivid and personal experience.

John recounts his visionary experience with great care and skill. It is of some importance to appreciate the simple plan on which chaps. iv. and v. are constructed. The fourth chapter describes the Creator-God, all-powerful, all-knowing, all-seeing. He is adored by the hosts of heaven (iv. 11):

' *Thou deservest*, our Lord and God, to receive glory and honour and power,
  for it was thou who didst create all things :
  by thy will they existed and they were created.'

But as he thinks of the remote splendour of the Creator-God, the prophet is filled with desolation. Mankind has no part in the heavenly scene : the Saviour does not appear before John's eyes in the first vision. So he thinks sorrowfully that the evil in which mankind is immersed is destined to continue. Never will the secret purposes of the Creator be revealed ; never will the hidden consummation of His divine plan be attained. None is found worthy to undertake so great a task. John's desolation and grief are banished, however, when he understands through his second vision that God's purposes cannot be frustrated. The evil oppressing Christians must inevitably be vanquished. For Christ, through His death, had **won the power** of revealing and putting into effect God's hidden purposes, and bringing history to its great consummation. The **seven Spirits** (that is, the Holy Spirit ; see p. 99), in the first vision associated with **the** power of the Creator, are now seen in the possession of Christ. The hosts who in the first vision worshipped the Creator **now** worship the Lamb (v. 9) :

> ' *Thou deservest* to take the scroll and open its seals, for thou wast slain and by shedding thy blood hast ransomed for God men from every tribe and tongue and people and nation ' (v. 9).

These two songs, deliberately associated by their identical introductory words, **Thou deservest**, are crowned by a third (v. 13), in which a sevenfold ascription of praise is offered jointly to **him who is seated on the throne and to the Lamb.**

The two chapters are, in short, altogether complementary. Their essential interest lies in three songs, one to the Creator (iv. 11), another to the Redeemer (v. 9) and the third to Father and Son, who together reign supreme (v. 13). The rest of John's description of the heavenly scene emphasizes and expands the story told in these three songs.

The general purport of chaps. iv. and v. is, then, clear enough. In chap. iv. the theme is that of the omnipotent Creator, reigning majestic and remote in a heaven from which man is excluded. The God whom John sees is the God whom Isaiah and Ezekiel saw. The heaven he sees is the heaven of the old dispensation. In chap. v. the focus of the seer's eyes changes, and with incomparable dramatic force he describes his vision of the Redeemer in whom lies every hope of man's salvation, every hope of a future kingdom of justice. So much is beyond question. But we cannot say that the details in the scenes before us are equally clear. We read about creatures who play no real part at all in our conception of God's presence —**four living Creatures** with fantastic shapes and an inconceivable multiplicity of **eyes** ; of objects which our knowledge of the universe denies—a **door** in the sky-ceiling of the world, through which heaven may be seen, and a **sea of glass resembling**

crystal stretched out before the throne. It is a heaven which the old ' optic glass ' removed from the vaulted skies. It belongs to a cosmology with which we are utterly unfamiliar ; and even when we grant that the cosmological background has infinitely less importance than the idea of God which is central in John's design, we are still likely to feel in alien realms of thought. For the details in these visions belong to a manner of thinking which even in Bunyan's day (if we may judge from the Author's Apology for his greatest book) did not appeal to everyone. Bunyan felt it necessary to claim Scriptural authority for his ' types, shadows and metaphors,' of which he protests :

> ' My dark and cloudy words, they do but hold
> The truth, as cabinets enclose the gold.'

In these days the Scriptural authority itself is questioned, and as we drift further and further away from the popular allegories of the Middle Ages, symbolism becomes less and less forceful in its appeal. A ' mystery ' was once something which was intended to proclaim a meaning beyond the power of literal expression : to-day, a mystery is something which withholds its meaning. Now, John actually *thought* in pictures. It was not that he conceived an idea as an abstraction, and then sought a convenient and traditional symbol to render it more vivid. It was probably in the shape of a symbol that an idea came into his mind, and it was certainly in this way that he was able to communicate it to his fellows. Modern readers have on their lips such phrases as creative energy, power to destroy, absolute authority, holiness and majesty—all abstractions which pass through the mind invisibly ; like a breeze over a field, with some sound and stir, but no lasting effect. We, for example, can contemplate *power* only in its result ; but John in his symbols could contemplate power itself. His visionary mind moved about in regions where *omnipotence* was recognized in a throne, where *omniscience* was indicated by innumerable eyes, where the very impulse to worship and pray found emblems in harps and bowls of incense. We find such a manner of thinking and speaking magnificent but sometimes obscure. The obscurity is the fault neither of John nor of his thoughtful reader: it is the fault of Time. John and his fellow-Christians dwelt by ancient streams of thought, many of which have long since ceased to flow ; their channel alone remains, and we can see nothing now of the currents and eddies once familiar to all. Things about which we are forced to argue precariously and prosily were then obvious almost beyond the need of comment (cf. notes on iv. 5 and v. 6). And we must bear that in mind as we examine the details of John's picture of the heavenly court. What is obscure to us was plain and illuminating to the intelligent reader of the first century.

Our greatest difficulty is fundamental, since it calls into question the very nature of John's visionary experience. Precisely what did he see through that open door ? If we examine chaps. iv. and v. detail by detail rather than as a whole we shall get the impression that John's vision amounted to little more than literary recollection. Ezek. i. seems to supply the basis ; there we read of the zoomorphic **Creatures,** the many **eyes,** the haloed **throne,** perhaps a suggestion of the **sea** like crystal. In Ezek. ii. we read that the prophet saw a **scroll** inscribed with ' laments and dirges and woes ' (John remembers this scroll again in chap. x.). And, indeed, the whole scene seems to have suggested to John the proper intro-duction to what was to be the last of all apocalypses. Other details seem to have been culled from similar visionary pictures of the Presence. Isa. vi. seems to have been in John's thought as he described the **six wings** of the living Creatures, and the words of their continuous worship. Dan. vii. is clearly echoed in the cry of praise to the Lamb. In fact, it could scarcely be held impossible that John was engaged in the purely literary task of conflating sources. Many critics have implied, and some have said outright, that this is indeed what he did. There is some warrant for such a view ; for apocalyptists often seem to appropriate to themselves the work of earlier writers, to attach to it their own interpretation. And John's claim of visionary illumination is the claim of every apoca-lyptist. It is true that John insists time and again that he is reporting purely ' what he saw,' and not what he has read, or what tradition has had to say ; he makes his claims with a solemnity, almost a vehemence, which is very hard to resist. But does not the evidence speak very plainly of considerable literary dependence ? And does not that deny at once the first-hand experience which John claims ? The alternative view is that John's mind has brooded so long over the story of prophet and apocalyptist that new visions have been brought to life—new visions, actually seen as John reports them and written down with a consciousness of divine help. The prophet sees what his meditations on the oracles of God in the past have taught him to expect ; and in recording what he sees, he is still conscious that he has witnessed afresh those eternal realities which others have known before him. Naturally, he recalls their words. He knows no other language for recounting what he has understood about God in his own ecstasy. He knows no better means of telling others about the new illumination of these eternal truths ; the language in which he writes is a language which all thoughtful Christians will understand. Clearly, the least we can do, if we believe in John's candour, is to acknowledge that his *understanding* of heavenly things has been illumined when he was ' rapt in the Spirit.' That is the least we can do—but at the same time we may be tempted to say that it is also the most. For when we try strenuously to visualize the scene described by John we find many details in it which are intellectually but not pictorially comprehensible. For example, it is obvious that the living Creatures are meant to convey amongst other things the idea of God's omniscience : but it is impossible to visualize ' eyes inside and out,' or to reconstruct a Creature with a face like a man, and yet with eyes all over. Or, to take another example, one of many : much arid speculation has been lavished on such questions as the distribution of the Lamb's **seven horns and seven eyes.** But were they ever visualized ? Did John see some weird original of that scene which the van Eycks have made immortal ? One may doubt it ; for how, let us ask, did a *Lamb* grasp the sealed scroll of the last days, and how did a *Lamb* break the seals which no other could break ? It would be a difficult feat, one for which the shape of a lamb is ill designed. It is in fact quite impossible to visualize, and we must therefore take it that John is using a metaphor so familiar that its pictorial quality does not appear. That is by no means true of all the scenes in John's book ; often enough his representation of some idea conjures up a magnificent picture, which tells as vivid a story to the eyes as to the mind (cf. vi. 1 ff.). But it is true of many ; and it will be found that the quality of dreamlike inconsequence which is often attributed to REVELATION, in order to explain *pictorial* inconsistencies or contradictions, is in reality an illusion of its later readers. For John uses symbols for their immediate intellectual appeal ; and when their immediate lesson has been delivered they vanish, or are subtly changed to present a new aspect of what the seer has understood about heavenly mysteries. We must illustrate this point, since it is much to the purpose in our study of this first vision of heaven.

The vision of chaps. iv.–v. depicts heaven as a royal court, dominated by a Throne, about which are grouped the angel courtiers. In succeeding chapters, however, a totally different scheme is displayed. The immediate presence of God is indicated by a temple (xi. 19, xiv. 15 ff., xv. 5 ff.) with an altar of incense (viii. 3, ix. 13, xvi. 7) and the ark of the covenant (xi. 19, xv. 5). Yet again, John implies that Mount Sion (xiv. 1), or the new Jerusalem which descends from heaven all ready like a bride arrayed for her husband (xxi. 2), exists in the heaven of his visions ; he tells us that the Lamb Himself, who shares the throne of God, is standing on this heavenly Sion after the great victory won by the martyrs.. And these martyrs, or rather all redeemed men, finally have two visionary titles : the Bride and the holy City : in chap. xxi. the two metaphors are actually united. Such apparent inconsistencies are held to illustrate that quality of dreamlike inconsequence of which we have spoken. But do they ? John at least seems conscious of some overriding purpose in his records of his visions of heaven. There is no sense of inconsistency in the two terms, the temple and the throne, for example : in xvi. 17 the two are mentioned in one breath— the last plagues come ' out of the temple of heaven from the

throne.' It becomes increasingly obvious, as we read REVELA-
TION, that the temple in heaven and all its furniture are neither
more nor less than *ideas*. Their disclosure represents (in our
terms) the disclosure of the very Being of God, His inviolable
holiness, the truth of His laws, His will to vindicate the righteous
and punish the wicked. The heavenly temple belongs to a
well-known tradition which had its roots in the Exile. Simultaneously with the restoration of the sacred people, a new
temple would arise in Jerusalem, the lost furniture of the old
temple would be found (for it was said that at the fall of
Jerusalem Jeremiah had hidden the sacred things of the
temple, safe from the sacrilegious hands of marauders) and
these things would be a sign that the God of righteousness
dwelt in full power among His righteous people. John knows
this tradition, but he speaks not of the finding of the earthly
symbols of God's holiness, but of the disclosure of heavenly
originals—in other words, the disclosure of the reality itself.
When the temple in heaven is opened in those last days, men
are to be conscious of the Being of the true holy One whom
they have denied. Thus it is not the sacred sign of God's
commandments, the ark of the covenant, which is to be found
again in these days : it is the reality of His wrath against sin
and His care for those who obey His commandments which becomes plain to all (see notes on xi. 19 and xiv. 6). The visible
shape of the symbol is a matter of small consequence beside
the idea which the symbol expresses : we can best realize how
predominantly intellectual is the message of the temple, when
we reach chap. xxi., and learn that John sees no temple in his
cubic city : that is, he sees no sign of God's separateness in
the new order. God dwells openly among men. The presence
of the pre-existent city in heaven is similarly ideal : we hear
of the heavenly Sion (xiv. 1) only at that point in John's
understanding of the course of the future when he is shown
that the true Israel, the Church, is to be vindicated and
preserved.

Why, then, is there no temple in John's first vision of heaven
—as there is none in his last vision of the new earth and the
new heaven ? We shall find the answer in examining the

occasions when John uses the two different symbols, throne and temple. It is apparently his view that the Presence of God may sometimes be better indicated by the one symbol, sometimes by the other. In chap. iv. there is no question of God's remoteness from the dwellers in heaven. They see the throne, and One seated on it ; they enjoy the beatific vision from which sinful men are excluded. The next occasion when heaven is seen as it is in chap. iv. is after the triumph of the martyrs. They rise from death to the presence of God ; by virtue of their proved holiness they are able to sing a new song before the living Creatures and the Presbyters (xiv. 1 ff.) : they are able to stand worshipping beside the crystal sea (xv. 2 f.). Next, we hear of all mankind before the throne (xx. 11) (the great white throne of Judgment). They are there to await the verdict. The unrighteous see the Holiest only that their impurity may be for ever rebuked by His purity. Finally, when all is over, redeemed man is to dwell for ever in the light of the throne : the righteous worship God in the full beatific vision. The temple, however, belongs to a different order of visions. It is only when John is speaking of the relations of God to the world which defies His laws that John speaks of the temple in heaven. God's punitive strokes come out of the temple (xi. 19, xiv. 14–20, xv. 6–8, xvi. 17–18) ; they come, in other words, from the presence of a God who is concealed from sinful men in the intensity of His holiness. Even when the temple is opened so that the last plagues may fall, God is not seen, for ' the temple was filled with smoke from the glory of God and from his might ' (xv. 8). It is very clear that there is a definite literary motive in John's different descriptions of the heavenly scene. If they are an account of ' dreams,' they are extraordinarily methodical dreams. We may well find that it is utterly pointless to argue about the disposition of the celestial objects which John describes, since the outward form of what is reported is of importance only as a vehicle of spiritual truths. Although frequently it is coloured by the splendour of its exalted subject, John's imagery has a strictly practical purpose. Even the description of angels, in whose literal existence John fervently believed, is designed to tell us things about the God who is to deal with mankind ; and it is with such a thought in mind, rather than with an inclination to admire without comprehension, that we should look upon them.

There is another extremely important stylistic matter which we must discuss before detailed comment on chaps. iv.–v., and that is John's use of allusion. No one can fail to see how widely John uses the language of the Old Testament in recording his visions ; we hear echoes from the prophetic books in particular at every turn. Why ? Is it because this is the normal idiom of a first-century Christian prophet, as it has been the idiom of many devotees since the Bible has been translated into the vernacular, and printed so that all may read ? Is it because such words naturally occur to the seer in the difficult task of communicating his ecstatic experiences ? Or because he was an artist, savouring the language of earlier artists for the archaic splendour in them ? We believe that primarily it is none of these things. We believe that John alludes in order to comment and interpret. REVELATION was to be the last great disclosure of God's purposes, for the time was short ; it was to lend meaning to all previous disclosures ; not to deny them, but to expound them, to show their express relevance to the Christian Church in the approaching crisis. It is hard for most Christians of to-day to appreciate John's attitude towards the Scriptures. The prophetic books were, he thought, the infallible words of God, oracles whose fulfilment must often necessarily still lie in the future (cf. xvii. 17). They were full of ' mysteries '—symbols and metaphors whose meaning it was the privilege of a later generation to discover. They were indeed like the sealed scroll in REVELATION ; their contents not to be understood until the approach of the End made them relevant. The writer of the Book of Daniel, in order to explain how it was that the visions he describes have been unknown to Jews during the long years between the Exile and Antiochus, relates that Daniel was told to ' shut up the words, and seal the book, even to the time of the end.' Twice this secrecy is insisted on : ' And I heard, but I understood not : then said I, O my lord, what shall be the issue of these things ? And he said, Go thy way, Daniel : for the words are shut up and sealed till the time of the end.' (John knew the passage from which these words are taken—he actually quotes from it in chap. x., just as he is about to explain what the angel in Daniel meant by the shattering of the sacred people (Dan. xii. 7).) How was *John* to understand the command to hold the book secret until the time of the end ? The Jews for whom the book was written believed that this command explained why nothing had been heard of Daniel's visions in the decades before the Greek tyrant came, and impiously challenged the power of the Almighty. For John there must be another explanation. The ' sealing ' must be metaphorical : not that the book was literally closed so that none might read, but that its *meaning* was concealed from men so that none might understand it until it was relevant, until the time of the End. John would attach a similar meaning to Isaiah's action in ' sealing up ' his prophecies (Isa. viii. 16). The prophets wrapped up their meaning in mysteries, because they had reference to a time in the far future, and were intended for the guidance of the pious in the last days. Such a view allowed John to interpret prophecy and apocalyptic with the greatest freedom. There could be no failures, no inconsistencies in oracles which came from God Himself. It was only a question of arriving at the right meaning. But this was impossible except through visionary enlightenment ; and John's claim to visionary enlightenment almost amounts to this : the End being at hand, God had told a Christian prophet how all things were to be interpreted ; He had broken the seals which held secret the meaning of all previous oracles. This must be illustrated, for in it lies much of the explanation of John's eagerness and exaltation. We have already seen that he applied the Old Testament titles of God to Him who ' is coming on the clouds, to be seen by every eye ' : we might say that, arguing from his premises, he was almost logically compelled to do so, by the evidence in prophetic books. Zechariah, for example, says that *God* shall descend upon the Mount of Olives, to do battle with His enemies. But it was an article of faith with John that the divine warrior was Christ

(xix. 11 ff.). Isaiah speaks of the First and the Last as the
'husband' of Israel: but, for John, it was Christ who redeemed and 'married' the Church—therefore Christ could be
called the First and the Last. Similarly, the pious remnant
of the Jews to which the prophets promised final vindication
becomes in REVELATION the Church : not a race, but a nation
of nations. Some prophets had said that the temple was to
be preserved : the temple measured for preservation must
therefore, in John's eyes, be the Church (chap. xi.). In the
prophetic books, Jerusalem is sometimes the holy City, sometimes the accursed City : but in REVELATION the name is
assimilated to that of Babylon the great, which means civilization. Jerusalem, Babylon, the Roman Empire—these mean
the city of earth which is defiled and must be destroyed
(xi. 7 ff., xvi. 19, xviii.) : the heavenly idea of Jerusalem shall
take its place (xxi.–xxii. 5). It is because he is anxious
to show the true meaning of the prophets, to interpret
them afresh in the light of God's revelation of what was
coming to pass very soon, that John quotes so often. And
it is for this very reason that he quotes in chaps. iv.–v.
the well-known passages in Isaiah, Ezekiel, and Daniel—as
they are remembered in the context of living apocalyptic
tradition.

Whether or not we hold that John's attitude towards the
Scriptures was misguided, we must at least concede that it
was thoughtful. And from his point of view there must have
been one very remarkable fact about such a vision as that in
Isa. vi. Elsewhere in the Book of Isaiah, John could discern
many references to the Messiah who was to save men ; but
in this first vision of the throne of God, the prophet sees
nothing of a Saviour. John can call Christ 'the origin of
God's creation ' ; but even among the glowing symbols and
figures of Ezekiel's vision there is still no sign of the Lamb.
This is the real point of chap. iv. of REVELATION. It is a
picture of the Presence as those earlier prophets saw it ; without Christ, and therefore without hope for man. *They* had
seen the wonder of the Creator, unutterably holy ; they had
felt the complete sufficiency of the heavenly choruses. But

what came out of these visions of the Presence? In each instance, the prophet was commissioned to prophesy destruction. 'Lord,' Isaiah had asked, 'for how long?' And the terrible reply came :

> ' Till they are ruined,
> till their towns are empty,
> and their houses uninhabited,
> and the land left desolate . . .' (Isa. vi. 11).

And Ezekiel, too, was told to prophesy the fall of Jerusalem and the dispersal and ruin of a stubborn and impious people. Must not these prophets have felt desolate as they saw the throne, even as John felt desolate, to see no sign there of swift redemption? But the Christian prophet saw more in the heavenly scene than his predecessors. He knew the meaning of Daniel's words : ' Then in my vision by night I saw a figure in human form coming with the clouds of heaven, coming up to the primæval Being, before whom he was brought and from whom he received dominion, glory, and a kingdom, that all nations, races and folk of every tongue, should serve him ; his dominion is a lasting dominion, never to pass away . . .' (Dan. vii. 13, 14). It was to this passage that Christians turned when they wished to illustrate the cosmic significance of Christ's sacrifice ; and it is Daniel's vision which John sees as an answer to the visions of other prophets, giving the indispensable clue to the understanding of God's creative purposes. John, indeed, sees more than Daniel—much more : he sees the Redeemer who **seemed to have been slain**, but yet bore the signs of deathless, all-powerful divinity. And the shout of jubilation raised by the heavenly hosts echoes, but transcends the words of Daniel ; it is a cry of tribute to Him who has become not only the Lord of the last days, but also the architect of a new Creation. Thus, briefly, in chap. v. John shows how Daniel's more hopeful picture of the heavenly scene transcends other prophetic pictures ; John says plainly what the prophets had left unsaid, and discloses finally what had not as yet been disclosed to them. This new understanding had come to him because the End, which Daniel saw far away in the remote future, was now at hand, and all must be known to the servants of God in the bitter ordeal before them.

This is a sort of inspired comment on the Scriptures. It is characteristic of the whole of REVELATION. John was casting a flood of light on the earlier revelation of God's purposes. He believed that the light which he as a prophet reflected on earlier prophets was a light from heaven. This is at least part of the truth behind John's claims to have *seen* through **a door standing open in heaven.**

iv. 1–11: THE ADORATION OF THE CREATOR BY HIS CREATION

1 After this I looked, and there was a door standing open in heaven ! And the first voice I had heard talking with me like a *trumpet* said, 'Come up here, and I will show you *what must come to*
2 *pass* after this.' At once I found myself rapt in the Spirit ; and lo a Throne stood in heaven with *One seated on the*
3 *throne*—the seated One resembled in appearance jasper and sardius—and *round the throne a rainbow* resembling
4 emerald in appearance ; also round the throne four and twenty thrones, and on these thrones four and twenty Presbyters seated, who were clad in white raiment with
5 golden crowns upon their heads. From the throne *issue flashes of lightning and loud blasts and peals of thunder.* And in front of the throne seven torches of fire burn (they
6 are the seven Spirits of God) ; also in front of the throne there is like a sea of glass, *resembling crystal. And on each side of the throne, all round it, four living Creatures full of*
7 *eyes* inside and outside ; *the first* living Creature resembling *a lion, the second* living Creature resembling *an ox, the third* living Creature with *a face like a man's, the fourth*
8 living Creature like *a flying eagle.* The four living Creatures, *each with six wings apiece, are full of eyes* all over their bodies and under their wings, and day and night they never cease the chant,

> 'Holy, holy, holy, is the Lord God almighty,
> who was and is and is coming.'

And whenever the living Creatures render glory and honour 9
and thanksgiving *to him who is seated on the throne, who
lives for ever and ever,* the four and twenty Presbyters fall 10
down before *him who is seated on the throne,* worshipping
him who lives for ever and ever, and casting their crowns
before the throne, with the cry,

' Thou deservest, our Lord and God,* to receive glory 11
 and honour and power,
 for it was thou who didst create all things :
 by thy will they existed and they were created.'

* Omitting [ὁ ἅγιος].

' The vase, wherein time's roots are plunged, thou see'st ;
Look elsewhere for the leaves.'
DANTE : *Paradiso.*

After this I looked, and there was a door standing open in 1
heaven ! In other words, after John had fully realized the
condition in which the Church stood to meet the great Distress
in front of her, to meet both Antichrist and beyond him Christ,
he beheld the majesty of God's dwelling, whence all the events
of the future must flow. The phrase **after this** commonly
introduces a new vision ; here plainly, elsewhere often less
plainly, its work is dramatic—it indicates John's gradually
increasing enlightenment about the realities of the present and
the future as vision succeeds vision. It is a phrase which
always refers to visionary sequence and not to chronological
sequence of events on earth. The **door standing open** (as we
have already remarked : iii. 8) had a metaphorical flavour for
early Christians, as it was used of opportunity for missionary
enterprise. We have no means of knowing precisely what
shape a Christian of the first century would ascribe to the
universe. We cannot tell to what extent he might accept as
literal or regard as figurative the details of the Semitic cosmos
sketched in Genesis and in hints throughout the Old Testament. It is best to look past this phrase, as John looked at
once beyond the open door ; for the truth is that, whether
or not there came into John's mind a picture of a sort of

trap-door leading to a bright Beyond, through the ceiling of a Mediterranean sky, his attention is not fixed on his initial awareness of heavenly vision, but on a **voice** which bids him see into the heart of all mysteries. We too must be alert, not to catch at curiosities, but to discern the accents of that voice, clear, thrilling, ominous **like a trumpet,** which said : **Come up here and I will show you what is to come to pass after this.** [Should ' after this ' come with the next sentence : ' After this I immediately found myself . . .' ?] These words seem at first sight strangely premature, for John does not hear for some time what is to come to pass in the future. Instead he sees a vision of the Presence, and then he sees a vision of heaven transformed by the triumphant appearance of the Lamb. Nevertheless, we must insist that these words of Christ form the title, as it were, for the whole of chaps. iv. and v., which are set down, not as an encouragement to worship, but as an introduction to the disclosures of the last days. It is the triumph of Christ which sets into motion the events of the last days ; that triumph is therefore the beginning of John's story. But its full wonder, its cosmic effect, cannot be realized until one thinks of the pre-messianic heaven. Therefore, like a true story-teller who has something of absorbing interest to relate, John holds his readers in suspense, while he paints an august but familiar picture of the heaven long known to apocalyptic tradition. In short, chap. iv. depicts the heaven of the old dispensation ; it is because there has been added to this heaven the figure of the Lamb that the approaching days of stress may be revealed to Christians, and indeed, that they may come to pass at all.

Though John's eyes are, as it were, already focused on heavenly things, and though his ear is already attuned to the voice of Christ the Revealer, a new rapture overtakes him as he becomes aware of the presence of the Most High. It 2 may be significant that John uses this phrase, **rapt in the Spirit,** whenever his mind goes on vast travels : when, for example, he is thinking of the churches throughout Asia (i. 10) ; when in a transport he is carried by an angel to survey the Roman Empire in its entirety (xvii. 3) ; when he

is carried by another angel to a huge mountain whence
he may see the great heavenly City of the future (xxi. 10) ;
or here, when his soul voyages to the far-away splendour of
heaven itself.

John sees in heaven for the most part what the older
prophets taught him to see—though we must remember that
their words were mediated for John by a long tradition of
comment and interpretation, so that what was a mere hint in
the prophets appeared to John as allusion to fully developed
doctrine.   There is, first of all, the **Throne,** a symbol for
absolute power, with rich associations in the devotional
literature which John knew so well.   It is a word which
is often used quite metaphorically, in REVELATION as elsewhere in the Old and New Testaments.   We have just read,
for example (iii. 21), that the Conqueror is to share Christ's
throne as his reward, just as Christ sat down beside His
Father on His throne : it would be obviously absurd to read this
otherwise than figuratively.   And here, too, we must beware
of visualizing the Throne (so to speak) as a piece of furniture.
It is the manifestation of God's absolute authority.   The
technical name for God the Father in REVELATION is **One
seated on the throne ;** one of the main notes of chap. iv. is
that God is the Ruler and Judge of all because He is Creator
(verse 11).

Like Ezekiel, John finds the appearance of God almost
beyond description : and that is how we should understand the
words : **the seated One resembled in appearance jasper and   3
sardius.**   There may be some secret significance in the stones,
but if there is it is lost to us, and we must not indulge in
guesses.   It is very clear, however, that it is more than the
single notion of splendour that John is attempting to convey
in these words.   The walls of the new Jerusalem shine with a
far greater splendour than these two semi-precious stones can
claim (xxi. 19 ff.).   Ezekiel (Ezek. i. 26–8) had seen ' on the
throne-like appearance . . . the *semblance of a human form.*'
But John's understanding of Ezekiel's words must have been
affected by the apocalyptic convention which spoke of a
celestial being as a **man,** or a **son of man** (see note on xiv. 14).

In other words, what Ezekiel saw according to this convention was something quite other than human—an appearance which emphasized the complete difference between God and man, as seems implicit in Ezekiel's own amplification of his description : ' from the waist upwards I saw something glowing like amber on fire, from the waist downwards there was something resembling fire. . . .' John's simile therefore probably means that God's appearance differed entirely from all earthly categories. The visionary appearance of his angelic mediaries, or of Christ Himself who was the Witness, carries with it certain symbolic messages to the seer. But God appears ' like Himself '—a Being celestial and indescribable.

The description of the Throne and its precincts has given rise to much purely speculative criticism ; John's mysteries unfortunately tempt the most sober judgments to a sort of guess-work which pays too little heed to the general bearing of the text, and to the interpretative capacity of first-century readers ; and, on the other hand, the very excesses of some critics have often driven others to deny the existence of symbolic implications in John's words, and to claim that on the whole he was depicting the heavenly scene of tradition, without much regard for any esoteric meaning which might lurk in the details of the picture. However, when we appreciate that the general idea of the chapter is to depict certain qualities of the Creator-God as He revealed Himself to the Hebrew prophets, the chief sources of error are swept aside ; we have a guiding principle in our interpretation. The **rainbow resembling emerald in appearance** is an example of one disputed point. It has been argued that this is purely an indication of the divine splendour—a reminiscence of Ezek. i. 28, and that no symbolical meaning must be sought in it. Now, it is certainly true that we can never be sure what John meant precisely by the simile, **resembling emerald.** It has been pointed out that the emerald had some talismanic significance in the ancient world, and John certainly seems to allude later in the book to ethnic beliefs attached to precious stones (cf. notes on xxi. 19 ff.). Where some precious stones have mysterious associations, all may be suspected. But our uncertainty about this is equalled by something like certainty about the rainbow itself. When Christians read of the rainbow in Ezekiel's vision, they assuredly thought of more than the prismatic splendour of light from the throne. It is a phenomenon which is too remarkable not to arouse memories of that familiar passage in Gen. ix. 12, 13 : ' " Here," said God, " is the symbol of the compact that I make with you and all the living creatures in your company for endless generations : in the clouds I set my rainbow, as a symbol of the compact between myself and the earth." ' Like the Egyptian plagues (cf. Rev. viii.–ix.) the Flood in which God embodied His wrath against an evil and adulterous generation came to have vivid eschatological interest for Christians. In St. Matthew and St. Luke the judgment falling on mankind is compared with the first great judgment ; just as terrible, just as unexpected and inescapable will be the judgment of men on Christ's return. We need not hesitate therefore in concluding that John's audiences read in the **rainbow** about the throne the sign that this was a God who had covenanted to withhold His wrath from mankind ; it is the symbol of God's long-suffering towards an earth which defied His laws. But later in REVELATION John shows how this sign has reference to the messianic community. It is they who are to be spared and preserved, as we learn when next we read of a rainbow (see x.–xi.).

There is an apparent lack of method in the way John recounts the appearance of the throne and all about it. He mingles description of celestial phenomena—the rainbow, the thunder and lightning, the sea of glass—with description of the angelic ministrants about the throne. The explanation of this is to be sought neither in literary awkwardness nor in visionary inconsequence, but rather in the fact that everything John mentions is primarily designed to indicate the qualities of the **One seated on the throne.** The rainbow had told us about His covenant with men ; now we hear of His royal authority in heaven ; we read that the throne is central amidst **four and twenty thrones,** and that the King of heaven is 4 attended by twenty-four celestial beings, regally appointed. The **four and twenty Presbyters,** each with his **white raiment** signifying celestial purity, his **golden crown** and **throne** signifying delegated sovereignty, minister to the idea of God's ultimate sovereignty. This we might infer from the first glimpse we have of them, but in verse 10 we actually see their obeisance to the King of heaven : they leave their thrones, **casting their crowns** before God, as they cry out their hymn of praise to the Lord of Creation. In the **Presbyters,** then, we must discern the second great truth about God which chap. iv. formulates : in spite of God's withholding His hand from destroying the evil-doers on earth, in spite of the appearance of evil's triumph on earth, God reigns supreme in heaven, His supremacy acknowledged and praised by beings far greater than the kings of earth who deny Him.

These **four and twenty Presbyters** have been the object of much speculative comment, which obscures their true bearing in John's scheme. An order of twenty-four angels is without precedent in Jewish literature, and this fact has tempted critics into the supposition that John is speaking of the twelve apostles and the twelve patriarchs united ; or of their angelic representatives, forming an ideal council about the throne. There is little doubt that the double twelve would appeal to John as having an aptness to be expected in the constitution of heaven (cf. xxi. 12–14). But this number is traditional ; we are forced to conclude that the twenty-four Presbyters were figures who appeared in the popular apocalyptic of John's day. Ultimately, their origin is probably to be sought in twenty-four star-gods worshipped by the Babylonians. Later apocalyptic adapted to its monotheistic creed such planetary gods, giving them the rank and nature of angels. In such a form they doubtless appeared in the living apocalyptic tradition known to John and his readers, who were probably familiar enough with a Scriptural passage suggestive to them of this council of angels—that is, Isa. xxiv. 23, where the triumphant reign of God among his ' ancients ' (the LXX. has ' presbyters ') is predicted for Jerusalem. In this feature, as in others, John was depicting a heavenly setting which any apocalyptist of his day might well have visualized. But consciously and skilfully he makes the setting bring out the truths which all acknowledged about the Creator.

We return now to a more direct intimation about the dread Being of God. We learn that **from the throne issue flashes of lightning and loud blasts and peals of thunder.** As in the instance of the Presbyters, we do not learn until later the full significance attached by John to this conventional theophany, with its reminiscence of Sinai. (The Exodus narrative was naturally remembered by Christians ; cf. the allusion in Heb. xii. 18. It was of particular interest to an apocalyptist, who assumed that the last plagues and the final deliverance would be like the first; cf. notes on viii.–ix.). This thunder, these loud blasts and flashes, represent on the one hand the theophany of the old dispensation—they should be contrasted with the voice out of the throne in xxi. 3 : ' Lo, God's dwelling-place is with men . . .' ; but they also represent the Creator's power to destroy the creation which denied His laws. It is of great importance to be aware of this later in REVELATION. Whenever John talks about the great climax of God's scourging of the world of evil-doers, the final deluge of destruction on a hopelessly incorrigible world, he speaks of the thunder, lightning, and loud blasts from the throne. When the seventh seal has been broken, when the seventh trumpet has been blown, when the seventh bowl of wrath has been poured on the earth (viii. 1 ff., xi. 15 ff., xvi. 17 ff.) we hear this refrain of doom, which indicates that heaven has been ' opened wide ' (cf. xix. 11) and God has disclosed Himself in wrath to a trembling world, no longer able to deny His omnipotence. It is the terrible ' eternal gospel ' which the angel in xiv. 6 cries out for every man on earth ; the revelation of all-powerful Truth which has been violated by mankind, and now, as the End comes, shines upon the world irresistibly in Judgment. On these three later occasions the portents of thunder and lightning and loud blasts are accompanied by others, showing the effect of the theophany on the world ; we read of an earthquake and a dreadful hailstorm. But here in chap. iv. we have the parent verse. John beholds the source of all the cataclysms which are to wrack the frame of civilization and nature ; he sees, but does not yet fully understand.

And in front of the throne seven torches of fire burn (they are the seven Spirits of God). These **seven Spirits**, in chap. v. called the seven horns and eyes of the Lamb, are different from the angel hosts in REVELATION, both in name and in function. We shall explain later (see v. 6) the reasons which make us see in this symbol of the **seven torches,** and the seven horns and eyes, a primitive formula for the Power whom we call the Holy Spirit. Meanwhile, it is important to understand the prophetic source of the symbols used to describe this Power. It is important, since it admirably shows how deeply John had considered the prophetic message for his age, and how radically his understanding of the prophets differed from our own. We must turn to the fourth chapter of Zechariah. There we read how an angel explains a strange vision which has come before Zechariah—a golden lampstand, with seven pipes to convey oil from a golden bowl in the centre to its seven lamps ; and on each side of this seven-branched lampstand, an olive tree. The angel tells the seer that the seven lamps are the eyes of God, which range over the whole earth, and that the two olive trees represent two servants of God, ' the sources of the oil of bliss, the two men who stand before the Lord of all the earth.' John has this passage in mind on three striking occasions : in this vision of heaven ; in the vision of the seven churches in i. 12, and in the vision of the great Distress in chap. xi. He sees in Zechariah's vision a suggestion, first of all, of the light-giving mission of the churches. There are, it is true, certain differences in detail between the picture of chap. i. and Zechariah's picture : for example, instead of a golden bowl (apparently a symbol for God Himself), Christ is in the midst of the seven lampstands ; and again, instead of a seven-branched lampstand, John sees seven separate single lamp-stands. But the relationship of this vision in chap. i with the passage in Zechariah is proved, in our opinion, by the cognate passage in chap. xi. where Zechariah's words are alluded to unmistakably. This time John is speaking of a proportion of the light-giving community ; he mentions two lampstands instead of seven ; and he speaks this time of the olive trees also, who represent the prophet among the Christian community, destined to martyrdom. Thus Zechariah's vision furnishes John with material to describe the situation of Christians on earth. But, equally, it still provides him with a term for two of God's attributes—the intense activity of His Being (the fire of the torches), and His omniscience (the eyes). For we know that the **seven torches of fire** are still the seven burning lamps in Zechariah's vision, as they are equated in chap. v. with the ' seven eyes,' which are the heritage of the Lamb. How are we to account for this twofold interpretation of a prophetic oracle ? How can John read in the one prophetic oracle a suggestion of a divine Power and a suggestion of a light-giving community, or particularly the prophetic members of that community ? The answer is to be found partly in a careful scrutiny of John's explanation of one of his own symbols, the Beast with seven heads : we read in chap. xvii. (where see note, xvii. 9-10) that the heads stand for seven kings and also for seven hills. Thus there was a certain elasticity in his symbols ; it is not that that particular symbol represents two quite different ideas, but that it conveys the whole of one complex idea—that is, the extent in time and place of the Beast's dominion. Now, having discovered this verbal trick of John's, we must apply it to the present problem. Are the seven Spirits and the seven churches in any way related ? Is it possible that one complex idea is involved ? When we acknowledge that the **seven** in each instance conveys the idea of unity and completeness, rather than diversity, so that we are to think of the Spirit and the Church rather than seven Spirits and seven churches, then we are in sight of a possible solution. We see a new significance in that very remarkable association of the seven Spirits and the seven stars, held in the hand of Him who speaks to the church at Sardis : they are the prophetic Spirit, and the celestial character of the Church, in whom the Spirit gives life. The association of the two is elsewhere often implied : in chap. v. we read that the seven Spirits dwell in the Lamb : they are part of his Being— his strength, his very eyes. But the Church is also united to

him in the closest of unions ; even on this earth she is the Bride
(xxii. 17). The fact is that John thought of the Church above
all as a prophetic community ; the seven Spirits are as
inseparable from the Church as they are from Christ. The
connexion between the seven Spirits and the prophetic Church
is best illustrated in the phrase met later in REVELATION :
' the Lord God of the spirits of the prophets' (xxii. 6). This
means the God who enables the prophets with His Spirit (see
ii. 7)—and thus gives them supernatural strength and insight.

Now, however, the **seven torches of fire** burn **in front of
the throne** : John does not see them burning in the hearts of
men, nor yet in the possession of the Lord of the churches.
His vision is like Zechariah's : full of wonder, a profound
mystery, but without the power of instant illumination. The
meaning of the mystery becomes clear later, after John has
finished speaking of the heavenly court as it appears without
the all-significant figure of the Lamb.

6 **The sea of glass resembling crystal** (and therefore clearly
transparent, unlike the earthly glass in the ancient world) is
like everything else seen by John, in that it is a more or less
conventional detail of the celestial court in apocalyptic. A
' sea ' in heaven is part of the ancient Semitic notion of the
cosmos, ultimately derived from the Babylonian creation
myth. It will be recalled, for example, that the flood which
fell on Noah's generation came through ' windows ' in the roof
of the world : the ' waters above the earth ' descended in
deluge upon the earth. Belief in the existence of a heavenly
sea, the waters above the earth, persisted in later cosmological
speculation, the fruits of which we not unnaturally find in
some of the apocalyptic writings between the Old and New
Testaments. The sea is there found in a heaven more intri-
cately arranged into seven spheres ; it is relegated to one of
the outer spheres. It will be at once noticed that John (though
he must have known these speculations about the seven
heavens and their properties) has no thought of dividing the
heavenly scene. The **sea** is **in front of the throne,** not in the
first or second of seven heavens. And it is worth remarking
here that it is invariably vain to seek the explanation of what

John sees in his visions purely by reference to Semitic theorizing, whether primitive or developed, about the structure of the universe. That will obviously help to explain the outward shape of John's symbols—as it does in this instance of the sea of glass ; but it will not explain the mystical significance which John attaches to what he sees. We are dealing with a mind which sought out essentials, which was occupied wholly with the relation of God with His creation, not with the mere shape of created things. We must insist that as John contemplated the traditional sea of heaven his first thought was : ' What is its *meaning* for men ? ' For, since its existence had been revealed to men through oracles of God, it must necessarily carry some message for them. In asking such a question, John was doing what many rabbis did, and the answer which he gave would be instantly understood by anyone familiar with the rabbinical interpretations of early Hebrew beliefs. In REVELATION the heavenly sea is at once a symbol of God's separateness—the burden of the trisagion in verse 8—and a threat against those who dishonour His creation and persecute His servants. There is a memory in it of the Flood which once destroyed a world given over to wickedness (cf. Jer. li. 42, where a *deluge* is figurative for the divinely ordered destruction of Babylon by an invading host) ; and there is also a memory in it of the Red Sea, which at first separated the Israelites from the Promised Land, and finally inundated those who attempted to destroy them. These allusions become clear only when we reach chap. xv., for it is not till then that John describes fully the cosmic results of the great martyrdom which he foresees for the Church. When he next sees the sea of glass it is ' mixed with fire '—the fire of God's wrath, which is at once to descend on an evil world, consuming civilization and all the enemies of right. But beside this terrible sea, safe from the malice of those who sought to shame and destroy them, the martyrs stand before the throne singing ' the song of Moses the servant of God and the song of the Lamb.' In chap. iv., however, the **sea of glass resembling crystal** stretches enigmatically before the throne, one of those many symbols of heavenly things which John believed to be mysteries sealed up until the last days. The last days were now at hand, and it had been given to him first of all men to understand its true meaning. He unfolds his new understanding of the sea at the appropriate point in his survey of the troubled future.

The **four living Creatures** are more obviously connected with the attributes of the One seated on the throne than is the sea of glass. The chief of all created beings in heaven, they mirror in their visionary appearance certain qualities in the God they adore, and their worship, too, conveys the supremacy of the Creator over all life. These four angelic attendants of the throne took their place in the heaven of an apocalyptist by virtue of an ancient tradition. They are ultimately connected with the four signs of the Zodiac, the bull, the archer, the lion, and the eagle ; their origin, in other words, is similar to that of the four and twenty Presbyters, and by a like process they were adapted to the Hebrew heaven, as servants of the one God. It is not with origins that we are concerned, however, so much as with the prophetic books in which John and his readers found the living Creatures. And it is at once obvious that Ezek. i. supplies the main traits of the four in John's vision, though Ezekiel's picture is modified in the seer's memory by recollections of other visionary descriptions of the Presence. The living Creatures are in some respects the most strange, other-worldly of all the actors in the heavenly scene ; but alien though they are to our own conceptions, their appearance in REVELATION is much less mysterious than it is in John's sources—as indeed one might expect, since REVELATION is intended to disclose what was previously wrapped in mystery. The reader may notice for himself the differences in detail between John's account of these angels of the Presence and that in Ezek. i. and Isa. vi. For the most part the differences mean little. In Ezekiel, for example, the four living Creatures have four faces each ; John sees the same faces, but each Creature in his vision has only one **face**. This change is insignificant, since it is clear that John saw in the four ' resemblances ' a representation of supremacy. It was a saying of the rabbis that there are four supreme orders in the world : among all created beings, mankind ; among birds, the eagle ; among domestic animals, the ox ; and among wild animals, the lion. In such words we must seek the significance of the shape ascribed to the four angels of the Presence. It is not that they represent, as some have supposed, the immanence of God in Nature, but that as the supreme angelic servants of God, the chief agents of His power, they represent the absolute authority of God over all the beings He has created (cf. the burden of verse 11 ; God's authority as Creator is uppermost in John's mind). Such differences in detail are to be expected, since John was freely quoting from memory, and consciously or unconsciously combining various features in different accounts, in order to give a comprehensive picture of the Presence as it was seen by earlier prophets. It is, however, of some importance to observe that John's understanding of the *function* of the living Creatures differs radically from what appears in Ezekiel. Whereas Ezekiel saw the living Creatures as *wheels*—supporters of a throne which moved throughout the universe—John sees them motionless, beside a motionless throne. Nor are they passive in his vision, as they are in Ezekiel's. They lead the heavenly hosts in worship ; and this trait, derived from Isaiah's vision, mingles with those supplied by Ezekiel to form a different conception, one which is essentially similar to the later apocalyptic description of the four angels of the Presence described in Enoch. What John saw in the appearance of these Creatures may be summarized briefly in our more abstract terms somewhat as follows : he saw beings who represented God's omnivision and omniscience—they are **full of eyes inside and outside** 8 **. . . all over their bodies and under their wings.** Eyes under wings !—the **wings** represent their power to act for Him who is seated on the throne, and no doubt the **eyes** in the wings indicate that their power to act springs out of perfect knowledge. He saw beings who represented God's supremacy in the creation—hence their strange shapes ; beings whose delegated might, greater than man may conceive, is laid aside in adoration as **they render glory and honour and thanksgiving to him** 9 **who is seated on the throne,** the living God who supplies their life. These things, John tells his readers in chap. iv., are implicit in what the prophets have said. But what has not yet been seen, or not yet been made explicit, is the connexion of these four with the events at once terrible and glorious of the last days. There is a hint even in chap. iv. of the eschatological emphasis which John is to place on them. Instead of crying out with Isaiah's seraphs :

> ' Holy, holy, holy, is the Lord of hosts,
> his majestic splendour fills the whole earth ! '

they chant the trisagion to a God whose majestic splendour is as yet deliberately withheld from the earth ; one who has deliberately limited His realm, so that He must be hymned as ' the coming One,' the Eternal, whose full sovereignty in the universe yet lies in the future : **he who is and was and is coming** (cf. note on i. 8). When John begins to paint his picture of the last days we find that it is the living Creatures who set in motion the destructive forces which disrupt the world of men (vi. 1) ; it is they who mediate the anger of God towards the world—they, finally, who deliver the bowl of wrath from God's temple to the seven angels with the last plagues (xv. 7). Incidentally, an interesting comment on John's brooding and reflective mind is his purely figurative interpretation of the *four winds* (vii. 1) ; they represent all the forces of destruction over which the living Creatures have control. Just as the ' winnowing wind ' in Jer. li. 2 represents an invading host to destroy Babylon, the four winds in REVELATION are equated with the forces of invasion, civil strife, famine, and death, summoned into action by the living Creatures. So these four angels of the Presence represent the overwhelming might of God to destroy the world ; and their hymn of praise bears witness to His *right* to destroy it. In their ' thrice holy ' they acknowledge the unapproachable purity of God's Being; but He is sovereign in a universe where righteous men sadly behold the apparent triumph of evil, and the living Creatures worship, as we have said, a God who is coming to put right all the wrongs permitted for a time by His inscrutable providence.

The chapter ends on a note of triumphant praise, with the antiphonal hymn of the Presbyters. No matter how thickly the clouds of evil overshadow the earth, no matter how impiously the kingship of the Creator is defied, He reigns in acknowledged, unchallenged supremacy in heaven. The living Creatures worship him **who lives for ever and ever.** And the Presbyters cast aside their royal insignia, **worshipping** him 10 **who lives for ever and ever.** This notably repeated designation of eternal life implies from its associations with Dan. iv. 34 (cf. Jer. x. 5 ff.) a contrast with the false and lifeless gods of idolators. It is a title of the Creator ; the Creator who is certain to bring His work to fruition (cf. Dan. xii. 7 and Rev. x. 6). And it is to the Creator-God that the Presbyters ascribe **glory and honour and power.** As they cry : 11

> ' it was thou who didst create all things :
> by thy will they existed and they were created,'

they voice the subjection of creation to the Creator. But in the mind of John and his readers there was inevitably the thought that most of mankind refused the obeisance which was due from them (cf. note on xiv. 6). And in the Presbyters' hymn they doubtless were reminded of the prophetic lesson, that the Creator's power to deal with mankind is as absolute as the potter's power and right to destroy the imperfect work of his hands. The hymn sums up what has been implicit in all the imagery of chap. iv. We may judge how suitable a preface it is to an account of the last days.

v. 1–5 : THE SCROLL

Then I saw, lying on the right hand of *him who was seated* 1 *on the throne, a scroll with writing on the back as well as inside, sealed* with seven seals. And I saw a strong angel, 2 proclaiming with a loud voice, ' Who is fit to open the scroll, to break the seals of it ? ' But no one was fit, either in 3 heaven or on earth or underneath the earth, to open the scroll or look into it. So I began to weep bitterly because 4 no one had been found fit to open the scroll or look into it ;

5   but one of the Presbyters told me, ' Weep not ; lo, *the Lion
of Judah's* tribe, *the Scion* of David, he has won the power
of opening the scroll and its seven seals.'

> ' Here is the Might
> And here the Wisdom that did open lay
> The path, that had been yearned so long,
> Between the Heaven and earth.'
>
> *Paradiso.*

Chap. v. is a continuation of chap. iv., and the two must not
be artificially separated. Either would be incomplete without
the other, inasmuch as fallen Creation is incomplete without
Redemption, and because in an apocalypse earth can be understood only in its relation to heaven. John realized that without chap. v. his vision would have given but little comfort to
the Church. When he was describing what he saw through
the door standing open in heaven he was not for a moment
unmindful of his readers. Through his eyes they too would
see the Presence of God Himself ; they too would hear the
ceaseless chant of praise from the celestial choir. But what
of themselves ? What part had they in the heavenly bliss,
what possibility of crossing the sea of glass, or of ever approaching the throne with its menacing flashes of lightning and loud
blasts and peals of thunder ? How could their poor voices
be joined to those of the glorious, sin-free living Creatures
and Presbyters, whose only delight was to obey and worship ?
Above all, what hope, if any, could be derived from such a
vision of awful, remote holiness concerning their own plight
in the dark days that were to fall upon them shortly ? It is
not easy to appreciate the depth of this passionate longing
that filled the hearts of Christians at the close of the first
century. Contentment with the world in modern times, in
spite of all its evils, has done a great disservice to many
Christian hymns which express a desire for heaven. The
obvious inability of congregations to sing them with any
semblance of sincerity has thrown them into almost complete
desuetude. In other times, when trust in this world was weak,
and faith in the unseen was strong, it was otherwise ; and if

94

we would recapture John's yearning for heaven's joys as he saw them in chap. iv., we must endeavour first to estimate the full weight of his sombre foreboding of the imminent fate of Christians on earth—the rigour of the peril that was to assault them in soul and body, the doubt that threatened to paralyse their faith. We must note also how with consummate skill John stirs his readers' deepest emotions in his description of the heavenly vision, in order to emphasize the wonder of the mystery that the Almighty, for all His remote holiness, was in the most intimate touch with earthly affairs. Since He is the Creator, therefore He also ordains and controls creation's destiny ; the world's fate was not merely known to Him—it was determined by Him. That is the significance of **the scroll** that John saw **lying on the right hand of him who** 1 **was seated on the throne.** That scroll contained the world's destiny (cf. Ezek. ii. 9, which is evidently the source of John's vision). On it was written God's plan for the immediate future—for all the future that was left, that short interval separating the present from the End itself. There was recorded God's inscrutable decisions, every phase of His will in such minute detail that there was **writing on the back as well as inside,** so full it was. There alone was the explanation of the perplexities now baffling the faithful, and which were to increase in number and oppressiveness a hundredfold when Antichrist appeared. We, however, can scan the scroll's contents by reading chaps. vi.–viii., like eager children who, too impatient to wait until they reach the story's end, skip the intervening pages. We can learn that the virulence of evil was to be a cause of reassurance rather than of doubt, since it was all part of God's purpose of punishing the wicked and testing the fitness of the faithful for their supreme reward. But so far all this was hidden from John and his fellow-Christians, fast-closed from sight by **seals,** of which there were **seven,** the perfect number. God's plan was secret, and the Church's fate was veiled in uncertainty. ' Who hath known the mind of the Lord ? ' asks St. Paul twice in his epistles, astonished at the wonder of Christ's redemption. John experienced a like marvel as he contemplated that God's innermost secrets, His schemes for dissolving this world-order, were enclosed in the scroll with the seven seals. The prophet's awe is deepened by the cry of the **strong angel,** challenging the whole creation to find some one **fit to open the scroll, to break the seals of it.** Only a strong angel, one of the celestial hierarchy, could appropriately convey a challenge of such supreme importance to the universe (cf. x. and xviii. 21). Moreover, John's emotion can be measured only when we take into account his perception of the moral and spiritual qualities necessary to disclose the scroll's mysteries. The destiny decreed for the world by its all-holy Creator, reigning in sublime isolation, adored by the heavenly hosts, was fast sealed against all who were part of that creation, subject as they must be to the corruption that was hastening its doom. The power that was to confuse Antichrist and his minions must be a divine power, wielded by someone fit for the task. That brings us to another consideration which is often over-looked. The strong angel's challenge to find some one worthy to open the scroll and to break its seals was much more than to ask for some one capable of *revealing* the world's fate. The demand was for one able not only to disclose God's plan, but to set it in motion, accomplish it, bring it to pass. Revelation must include the execution of what is revealed. This is clearly implied in the song of praise, when at last the Lamb accepts the challenge and takes the scroll. Here is an important interpretation of the Crucifixion not dealt with so explicitly and effectively elsewhere in the New Testament. By His death and exaltation, Christ does something infinitely greater than reveal the mind of God ; He is the divine Agent by whom alone the will of that mind is perfectly obeyed and brought to its appointed consummation. That is why John is careful to note in chaps. vi.–viii. that the enactment of the last things is performed through the Lamb. One by one, He opens the seals, and as each is broken, so God's plan is wrought. Always, throughout the Apocalypse, Christ is the power that controls the universe and determines its fate, even to the last great encounter with Antichrist when the divine Champion appears as the Logos of God (xix. 11–21).

Meanwhile, to indicate the immensity of the Lamb's achievement by His death, John stresses its unique character. **No one** else was **fit to open the scroll,** no one in the whole 3 universe—not the holiest and most exalted of all the angels **in heaven ;** not the purest and staunchest upholder of the faith **on earth ;** not the greatest prophet of the past now in the realm of departed spirits **under the earth.** And as he contemplates what life would be without Christ's Redemption, he begins to **weep bitterly ;** for in his distress he is mindful of 4 human hopelessness, bereft as men must then be of any glimmer of light to guide and uphold in the days of Antichrist, utterly helpless against the spirit-forces of evil.

Reassurance comes from **one of the Presbyters.** As it is the 5 function of the four living Creatures, nearest in the angelic circle to the Creator, to destroy the world's corruption (vi. 1, 3, 5, 7, xv. 7), so to the Presbyters and other interpreting angels belongs the gentler duty of explaining heaven's mysteries to the prophet (cf. vii. 13, xvii. 7, xix. 9, xxi. 9, xxii. 8). The strong angel's challenge is accepted by the only one worthy, and therefore able to do so ; and the wonder of this act, which moves first heaven and then the whole universe to ecstasy, is expressed in the titles ascribed to Him by the Presbyter. He is **the Lion of Judah's tribe** (cf. Gen. xlix. 9, 2 Esd. xii. 31, 32), **the Scion of David** (xxii. 16, Isa. xi. 1, 10). Briefly but effectively, John thus reminded his readers that Christ's death and victory had a threefold significance. Christ, not the Emperor who vaunted his power, was the mighty king, divine and victorious over death. Yet, secondly, that victory had been won (as they must win it through His power : xii. 11) in the flesh ; enthroned in heaven though He now was, they knew that He was one with humanity by His Incarnation, as by His persecution and martyrdom. Thirdly, it had been won as the fulfilment of prophecy, as these proud, historic titles reminded them—won by the true Messiah on behalf of the Church, the true Israel. It had been **won.** John never allows the Church to forget that. In this word is contained his ever-recurring insistence that Christ's conquest by death was the supreme spiritual victory, achieved against fearful odds (cf. St. Paul's emphasis on the same point, Col. ii. 14, 15). It was because John was acutely aware of the might of evil against which Christ and His followers had contended and must still contend—an enemy symbolized in chap. xii. by a huge red dragon and in chap. xiii. by the Beast—that he realized so clearly what Christ's conquest implied. REVELATION owes much of its moral force to that conviction, for by it John was able to fortify Christians with the knowledge that their strength was Christ's, and that His victory would be theirs (cf. especially iii. 21, xii. 11, xv. 2–3).

All this is defined with even greater emphasis in John's 6 vision of Christ as a **Lamb standing in the midst of the throne and the four living Creatures and the Presbyters.** To modern minds, the symbol of Christ as a **Lamb** is so familiar and appropriate that it might perhaps be thought that comment would be superfluous. Yet it would be easy to do John an injustice through failure to appreciate his peculiar contribution to Christian thought in this case, and to misunderstand what he originally intended to convey by the symbol. Nowadays the gentleness and meekness of Christ are the qualities usually associated with the Lamb, but John's use of the term here is different, though he too could write with exquisite taste of the Lamb's tenderness (vii. 17). From what we have already learned in this chapter, we may conclude that the Lamb is a symbol of power—power, moreover, which has been demonstrated in sacrifice. It is not much to the point to discuss the original conceptions from which John derived the symbol—to enquire whether he was referring to the paschal lamb in Exodus, or to the suffering lamb of Isa. liii. Probably both contributed to an idea which was rich in meaning, and must, as we know from other New Testament literature, have been familiar to the churches of John's day. Nor is its meaning affected by the often-noted fact that the Greek word for ' lamb ' in REVELATION is different from that used in the Fourth Gospel. In the one as in the other, the Lamb's death is the means of cleansing God's people from their sins (cf. Rev. v. 9 and i. 5 with St. John i. 29) ; and

John's chief concern is to emphasize the magnitude of Christ's death and its significance as the central event in history. He identifies the *Lamb* with the *Lion* of Judah's tribe, and in his vision he saw the Lamb, not lying lifeless, but **standing**, victorious over the death He had endured ; it is the exalted Christ whom he had seen in his first vision (i. 13 ff.), and who ' stands at the door ' to warn and encourage the churches (iii. 20). The same idea is manifested when John couples his statement, **it seemed to have been slain**, with the assurance, **but it had seven horns and seven eyes.** It is his way of saying, ' In your struggle against the world, remember that the Christ who shares the Father's throne has suffered the worst that earthly violence and wickedness can perpetrate ; but remember, too, that He has gloriously triumphed over it.' The **horn** was a common symbol of strength (cf. ix. 13), and the Lamb's **seven horns** therefore symbolized perfect strength, just as **seven eyes** symbolized fullness of knowledge and vigilance. John is also referring incidentally to an idea which, in accordance with his literary method, he intends to develop later—the contrast between the Lamb with His seven horns and His enemies the dragon and the Beast with their ten horns (xii. 3, xiii. 1). REVELATION is full of such contrasts, by which John successfully endeavours to bring home to Christians the choice they would shortly have to make (see also the notes on vi. 1).

When John says that the **seven eyes are the seven spirits of God sent out into all the earth** we may be sure that, as always when he adds an explanatory note, some important point is involved. It is meant to explain his previous rather enigmatic references to the seven spirits (i. 4, iii. 1, iv. 5 ; see notes). The original source of this verse is Zech. iv. 10, where the prophet refers to the seven eyes of the Lord which sweep all over the earth. We have here a typical example of the way John bestows on Christ the attributes which, in Old Testament prophecy, were reserved for God (cf. notes on i. 13–20). But a difficult theological question presents itself. John says that the seven eyes are **seven spirits**. Does that mean that they are seven distinct personal beings ? If so, are they divine or angelic ? Have we here a foreshadowing of the doctrine of the

Holy Spirit, and, more important still, part of the elementary thought from which ultimately it was derived ? If so, is there not more justification than is sometimes allowed for regarding the reference to the seven spirits in i. 5 as from John's pen (rather than a later addition), and an early example of what became a Trinitarian doctrine ? It seems simpler to regard the seven spirits as angelic beings who fulfil the Redeemer's will throughout the world, so that they can be aptly described as the seven eyes, just as they are symbolized by seven torches of fire, attendant before the throne in iv. 5. This view gains support from the reference in Tobit xii. 15 to the 'seven holy angels who present the prayers of the saints and go in before the Holy One.' Then these seven spirits belong to the angelic hierarchy, indeed, are its most exalted members, since in chap. iv. they seem to be even nearer the throne than the living Creatures and the Presbyters. But there is one serious obstacle to this argument. If the seven spirits are angels, why do they not worship, no matter how exalted their rank ? Yet even when John mentions in detail the adoration of the whole universe, whether in chap. iv. or v., he makes no reference to praise from the seven spirits.

The solution to the problem seems rather to be found in the sevenfold spirit which Isaiah foretold should be the Messiah's endowment in the very passage (Isa. xi. 1-2) which John certainly had in mind when, in verse 5, he calls Him the Scion of David : ' The spirit of the Lord shall rest upon him, the spirit of wisdom and understanding, the spirit of counsel and might, the spirit of knowledge and of the fear of the Lord ' (cf. also the sevenfold spirit in Enoch lxi. 11). This does not prove that John regarded the seven spirits as the Holy Spirit in the developed sense used in the Fourth Gospel. It is just as important to note that while the seven spirits do not offer worship, neither do they receive the worship ascribed to the Creator and Redeemer. John was merely painting in living thought-symbols what others regarded as abstract power— the complete, sevenfold power that belonged to the Messiah. All we can say is that the later doctrine of the Holy Spirit was rooted in the same necessity as that under which John laboured, of finding words to express the power exercised by the Creator and the Redeemer. John added his brief note to explain that the seven spirits are Christ's power of omnivision which enables Him to execute His omnipotence in all the earth. It was a distinct and precious contribution to the gradual formation of the doctrine of the Third Person of the Trinity.

v. 6–14 : THE ADORATION OF THE LAMB

Then I noticed *a Lamb* standing in the midst of the throne and 6 the four living Creatures and the Presbyters ; it seemed to have been *slain,* but it had seven horns and *seven eyes* (they are the seven Spirits of God sent out *into all the earth*), and 7 it went and took the scroll out of the right hand of *him who was seated on the throne.* And when it took the scroll, the 8 four living Creatures and the four and twenty Presbyters fell down before the Lamb, each with his harp and with golden bowls full of *incense* (that is, full of *the prayers* of the saints), *singing a new song :* 9

' Thou deservest to take the scroll and open its seals,

for thou wast slain and by shedding thy blood hast ransomed for God men from every tribe and tongue and people and nation ;

thou hast made them *kings* and *priests for* our *God,* 10 and they shall reign on earth.'

Then I looked, and I heard the voice of many angels round 11 the throne and of the living Creatures and of the Presbyters, numbering *myriads of myriads and thousands of thousands,* crying aloud, ' The *slain Lamb* deserves to receive power 12 and wealth and wisdom and might and honour and glory and blessing.' And I heard every creature in heaven and 13 on earth and under the earth and in the sea all crying, ' Blessing and honour and glory and dominion for ever and ever, to *him who is seated on the throne* and to the Lamb ! ' ' Amen,' said the four living Creatures, and the Presbyters 14 fell down and worshipped.

6　We must be careful lest the length of discussion necessary to ascertain the significance of John's brief but important point about the seven spirits should hide from us the unity of chap. v., and the close link between verses 5 and 6 which describe the Lamb and the following verses which relate His achievement. A breathless suspense pervades the scene as John, having told us the Lamb's attributes, proceeds to explain how the Lamb performs His great act of redemption. The world has waited for this moment. The long years have rolled their weary course to reach this critical event. This is the supreme act of history which kings and prophets and righteous
7　men had longed to witness. The Lamb **went and took the scroll out of the right hand of him who was seated on the throne** —a thought impossible to visualize, but magnificent as a symbol of the death of Christ and its results. In his own way, John is expressing the perfect harmony between the will of God and the will of Christ, elaborated in the Fourth Gospel and the Epistle to the Hebrews. Now God's plan for His creation is to be revealed and executed. Immediately, in two hymns which, with those in chap. iv., are unique in the New Testament, John describes the adoration of the Lamb, first by heaven, and then by the whole universe. Most remarkable is the skill with which he introduces, almost imperceptibly at first, what is for him the crowning glory of the Lamb's victory —the redemption of the Church. As soon as he refers to the worship offered by the Presbyters, he includes the divine
8　community on earth ; each of them was **with his harp and with golden bowls full of incense (that is, full of the prayers of the saints)**. The **bowls** were not mentioned in chap. iv., for John was not then ready to reveal the Church's share in the worship of God. Even now the reference is little more than incidental, but it will be expanded more than once as the revelation is unfolded. We shall hear, too, the music of the **harps** again, accompanying the martyrs' song in chap. xiv.,
9　and that **song** also will be new, for Christ's death has inaugurated a **new** era. We shall learn more about the **prayers of the saints** in viii. 3–5, where it is explained that they are not only acceptable to God, but powerful in effecting the divine

decrees of doom on the impenitent world. Thus the Lamb's achievement in opening the seals is linked with the Church's function made possible by that achievement. The full glory of the redemption is expressed in the song itself : ' **Thou deservest to take the scroll and open its seals, for thou wast slain.**' With that should be compared its earlier counterpart in iv. 11, ' **Thou deservest, our Lord and God, to receive glory and honour and power, for it was thou who didst create all things.**' In both it is divine merit which is acclaimed. ' Thou deservest . . .' Worship belongs rightfully to God as Creator and to the Lamb as Redeemer who brought back creation to its original perfection. But that is to speak abstractly when John's thought is essentially personal. That God's people have been redeemed is the great fact. The Church is central in his mind. By shedding His blood, the Lamb had **ransomed for God**—the God who had made them for His own glory— **men from every tribe and tongue and people and nation.** When the seven seals are opened we shall learn that wickedness is to increase ; earth's corruption is fast becoming so monstrous that only its destruction can be contemplated. Soon the wicked will be judged and punished. But not all will perish, not all God's creatures are beyond redemption. The prophets had foretold that a remnant should be saved ; and John, with inspired vision, sees that remnant in the tiny, scattered communities to which he was writing, drawn from every tribe and tongue and people and nation, many of them in sober fact slaves under Roman law, all of them liable to the frailties and sins that he had exposed so ruthlessly in his letters to the seven churches, but nevertheless **ransomed**, bought back by the Redeemer, catholic and united in this common bond of redemption. Soon we shall learn how the Church will share in Christ's sufferings as well as in His glory (chap. vii.) ; but consistently with his method of gradually unfolding his message in successive visions, he is content for the present to bid the Christian Church consider its heritage. Bought back from slavery in Satan's bonds, they were now made **kings and 10 priests** (cf. i. 6), sharing in God's own royal and spiritual kingdom ; they reigned with Him and worshipped Him. The boldness of such a claim must have been forcibly apparent to John's readers as they considered their plight in the world, despised and threatened by the Roman State, and persecuted in many instances by Judaism. What were the faithful at Smyrna and Philadelphia to think of John's assurance in the face of the Jews' bitter hatred and scorn ? St. Paul had been scarcely able to find words that could express his marvel at the thought that Gentiles should be allowed to share in the promises made under the Old Covenant. John asserts their inheritance in the most emphatic terms. The Church was the holy nation drawn from all the nations : the ancient promises of redemption to the chosen race had been fulfilled in the redemption of a new people of God. Moreover, in a very real sense, they were already enjoying their new privilege and dignity ; even in this world they had been made **kings and priests for our God.** But the present meant far less to John than the future. Existing conditions would be soon swept aside. The next thought is characteristically eschatological : **they shall reign on earth.** Prophets had said that the redeemed remnant should share the enjoyment of exercising sovereign sway over the Gentiles that had oppressed them, and Jesus had repeated the promise (in spiritual terms) to His own disciples (St. Matt. xix. 28 ; St. Luke xxii. 30) ; but John has in mind the actual situation in which God's judgment must be executed by reversing the world's harsh injustices. The martyrs who must suffer at the royal decree of kings of earth must be rewarded by the power to reign in the new age (see chap. xx.).

But these are themes which John intends to develop as he unfolds his visions ; now he alludes to them only suggestively. His main thought in chap. v. is the adoration ascribed by the whole universe to God and to the Lamb, both supreme in the redeemed creation. The splendour of the scene is reflected in 11 the vastness of the host that worships. The **many angels** who join their voices to those of the living Creatures and the Presbyters number **myriads of myriads and thousands of thousands.** In heaven as in the world the cry is taken up by every single creature. And all this because of what the Lamb

has achieved by His death. Nowhere else in the New Testa- 12
ment is Christ adored on such absolutely equal terms with
the Godhead. Redemption is equal in merit to creation, or,
rather, both are the realization of the divine purpose for men.
We see now the depth of meaning in John's words when he
vests Christ with the Eternal's attributes in chap. i., when he
speaks of Him as sharing the Father's throne in iii. 21. In
heaven itself the slain Lamb is in the midst of the throne
(v. 6), and He shares it eternally in the new heaven (xxii. 3).
It is fitting, then, that both should share the sevenfold ascription of praise which includes every blessing of power and
authority. And lest we should think that in his ecstasy John
exaggerates by including **every creature** in the worship—even 13
those in the sea—in view of the idolatry which is to be exposed
in succeeding chapters, we must observe that John believed
the day would come when even the impious would be compelled to fear God and give Him the glory that for a time they
tried to withhold (cf. notes on xi. 13 and xiv. 6 ff.). The
solemn liturgical **Amen**, preserved by the Church in the 14
original Aramaic from the lips of Jesus, now echoed by the
living Creatures and the Presbyters as they **fell down and
worshipped**, will conclude John's own prayers with which he
ends his book of visions (xxii. 20, 21).

THE LAMB OPENS THE SCROLL'S SEVEN SEALS
(vi. 1–viii. 1)

vi. 1–8 : THE FOUR HORSEMEN

Now when the Lamb opened one of the seven seals, I looked, 1
and I heard one of the four living Creatures calling like
thunder, ' Come.' So I looked, and there was *a white horse,* 2
its rider holding a bow ; he was given a crown, and away he
rode conquering and to conquer.

3 And when he opened the second seal, I heard the second living
4   Creature calling, ' Come.' And away went another *red
    horse ;* its rider was allowed to take peace from earth and
    to make men slay each other ; he was given a huge sword.
5 And when he opened the third seal, I heard the third living
    Creature calling, ' Come.' So I looked and there was *a
6   black horse ;* its rider held a pair of scales in his hand, and
    I heard like a voice in the midst of the four living Creatures
    saying, ' A shilling for a quart of wheat, a shilling for three
    quarts of barley ; but harm not oil and wine.'
7 And when he opened the fourth seal, I heard the voice of the
8   fourth living Creature calling, ' Come.' So I looked, and
    there was a livid horse ; its rider's name was *Death, and
    Hades* followed him. They were given power over the
    fourth part of the earth, *to kill men with sword and famine
    and plague and* by *wild beasts of the earth.*

> 'Devouring Famine, Plague and War,
> Each able to undo mankind,
> Death's servile emissaries are. . . .'
>   Shirley : *Cupid and Death.*

The Lamb opens the seals : a series of awe-inspiring portents
comes before the seer's eye, and the panorama of the future
is depicted, as seal after seal is broken. John sees and describes
at first only the bold outlines of the wide landscape before
him ; the warriors who range the darkened world—Invasion,
Civil War, Famine, Death—are sketched swiftly, without
distracting detail. And the glimpse we catch in verses 12–17
of comprehensive disorder in the very body of Nature is also
brief, for it is John's design to speak quite generally of the
graphic messages in the scroll of the last days. Indeed, the
modern reader may ask whether the churches to which John
addressed his apocalypse were not somewhat disappointed by
its contents. Was there anything very new and startling in
this disclosure after all ? Is John in sober fact revealing what
had till now been a fast-closed secret ? When the scroll that
Ezekiel saw stretched out to him by the Eternal was unrolled,
the prophet saw that ' it was written all over, outside as well

as inside, with laments and dirges and woes ' (Ezek. ii. 10).
No Old Testament prophet would have claimed that message
as a secret. It was the common burden of every man of God
that dire punishment would fall on evil-doers, and most
heavily on God's own people for their flagrant abuse of a
sacred trust. But is the message of John's scroll new, different,
unique ? Is it actually the unbaring of God's innermost
secrets ? Need John have wept bitterly for fear that they
should never be disclosed ? Are we constrained, on reading
them in chaps. vi.–ix., to join in the praises of the heavenly
choir ? At first sight we must confess surprise that so much
of the scroll's contents tells the same story as that of Ezekiel.
The main subject is the familiar one—' laments and dirges
and woes.' The four horsemen only announce the coming
destruction by war and faction and famine and death—an all
too familiar theme in those troubled times. It is very dramatic
as literature, but is it new ?

No, it is not new. What is said to issue from the sealed
scroll amounts in substance to little more than a brief re-
capitulation of the portents traditionally associated with the
last days : a survey in many points similar to those we find
in the synoptic apocalypses, and, like them, claiming the
authority of the faithful Witness. There is nothing really
new in the portents springing so vividly out of the scroll ;
apart from the epic grandeur of the imagery the story
unfolded seems to be one which was almost commonplace to a
reader familiar with Jewish eschatology. And we must therefore enquire how John could imagine that the revelation
granted him was something revolutionary, a disclosure at the
end of Time's unfathomed secret. The answer to this is of
fundamental importance to the student of REVELATION ;
without it he will miss the whole emphasis of the book.

The new thought is the message about the Church's fate
when these woes were to fall upon the world. That is the
secret which the reader must eagerly ponder. It is not on
the grim horsemen of the first four seals that his eyes must
be fixed, nor yet on the cosmic disorder sketched in verses
12–17 ; he must rather look to a passage which is often

referred to as 'an interlude' in the sequence of the seven 'seal' portents, but is much too important to be thus designated as though it were of minor significance, inasmuch as it gives meaning to the vision as a whole—chap. vii. The story there partially unfolded, and later told explicitly in its companion passage, chap. xi., casts a flood of light on the grim scenes of destruction traditionally held to proclaim the approach of the End. We are given a hint of John's leading thought in the portent following the breaking of the fifth seal : we learn then that the death of the martyrs has something to do with the consummation of God's purposes. We learn that the End is to come when a predetermined number of God's servants have suffered martyrdom. But it is in chap. vii. that the theme is avowedly taken up and developed. There we meet the first mysterious sketch of the destiny awaiting Christians in the last days. We are told that the distracted world of those evil times is a stage whereon the twelve tribes of the true Israel—the messianic people, the Church—must play the leading part. Later we are shown that the End itself, the last decisive stroke of God on a rejected world (viii. 5) is somehow connected, not only with the prayers of the saints, but with the presence in heaven of a host of triumphant martyrs. This is the secret of the scroll. For the Church as for the world, the last days would be a time of ' laments and dirges and woes,' but now Christians were to learn the truth of the assurance made by Jesus when He spoke of these things : ' There will be awful portents and great signs from heaven. . . . That will turn out an opportunity for you to bear witness. . . . Hold out stedfast and you win your souls.'

We must repeat, therefore, that it is not in the portents springing directly and avowedly out of the scroll that we must see the original feature of Christ's latest revelation to Christians, so much as in the all-important message in vi. 9–11, vii., and viii. 1–6 which is interwoven with them. It is clearly necessary to say this now, in order that we may see the true bearing of the four horses and their riders. But it is even more necessary to say it in order that we may understand

why the Revealer of these grim prophecies of woe is still
called **the Lamb**—the Redeemer.

It has been urged that when Christians used this title, the
Lamb, they had in mind not the notion of expiatory sacrifice,
but the notion of messianic leadership. A curious and
deliberately enigmatic convention arose in later Jewish
literature, whereby the human actors on the apocalyptic
scene were designated as animals. Thus, for example, 1 Enoch
calls the Maccabean leaders ' horned lambs,' a name which
the Testament of Joseph applied to one of the Maccabean
family (as Dr. Charles has inferred) with messianic significance.
If, as seems probable, this became a popular title for the
expected Messiah, Christians would inevitably have tended to
claim it for Jesus just as they claimed for Him other messianic
titles. Is it not natural, then, to assume that the **Lamb** opens
the seals, not because He is Redeemer, but because He is the
Messiah, the divinely empowered warrior (cf. xix. 11 ff.), who
defeats God's enemies and leads God's people to victory ?
There is little doubt that the term does contain messianic
associations : when we see the Lamb in xiv. 1, He is at the
head of His followers, a triumphant general, a messianic
figure. But even in chap. xiv. He is still regarded above all
as the Redeemer : for the host standing with Him are those
clad in white raiment, who in chap. vii. cry with a loud voice :
' Saved by our God who is seated on the throne and by the
Lamb '—saved, by the expiatory death of the Lamb, and
enabled to enter the heavenly scene because He has made
them pure and innocent (vii. 9–14, xiv. 4, 5). And equally
in chap. vi. He is the Redeemer : the Lamb who ' seemed to
have been slain.' It may appear to us a dreadful paradox
that the Redeemer of men, who through His sacrificial death
had won admittance to the Presence of God for His people,
should be so deliberately called the slayer of men : but that
is certainly implicit in John's account, and we must face it.
John's view of Christ's sacrificial death may be briefly stated
thus : by virtue of redeeming His people, purely by virtue of
that supreme task whereby the Church was created, a train of
cosmic destruction was released, ending only when all evildoers

on earth are destroyed. Most of this we learn explicitly from a later oracle—that in xii. 7–12. Meanwhile we are left with this startling implication : somehow, Christ's expiatory sacrifice is connected with the destruction of men ; from the Death on the Cross flow whelming tides of divine Wrath. The mystery of Redemption is, we say, as yet only partially disclosed. The great symphony of REVELATION has not yet reached the point when its main theme can be stated outright ; it is anticipated in these earlier chapters, as John speaks of the Lamb who is also the Lord of the last days. At present, therefore, we must be content with recognizing such anticipations, and giving them their proper value.

The Lamb, then, who has conquered that Last Conqueror, Death (i. 18), launches into the world both Death and all his ' servile emissaries ' : Invasion (the rider with the **bow**), Civil War (the rider with the **huge sword**), Famine (the rider with the **scales**), and **Death**, who requires no insignia—it is death by pestilence, appropriately accompanied by a personification of the dreaded **Hades,** the gloomy underworld where the dead awaited judgment. These four have ridden tempestuously through many prophetic books and apocalypses though not specifically grouped as John groups them. We have seen them in the synoptic apocalypses ; but their spectral figures were so familiar to the eyes of the devout Christian or Jew of New Testament times that it is almost beside the point to try to establish any but an indirect relationship between the synoptic apocalypses and that of John. It is as well, however, to be aware of the general reference of these portents. We have heard in chap. iv. of the covenant made by God with mankind : the rainbow about the throne brought it to our minds. We are now to realize that the covenant has been irreparably broken by mankind (for John believed that the Old Covenant, like the New, concerned the whole of mankind, not merely one nation). Since it has been broken, the decree of wrath pronounced on its breakers in Lev. xxvi. must be executed : God pronounces ' terrible woes ' on those who defy His laws, the condition of the compact He has made with men : consumption, fever, famine, defeat in war, and slavery.

'If even then you will not listen to me,' he continues, 'I will punish you *seven times more* for your sins. . . .' He threatens to break their prosperity and send more famines. And if that is unavailing, another seven strokes shall fall on them : this time wild beasts slaughter both cattle and men. Two more series of 'seven strokes' are threatened for the rebellious Covenant-breakers : we read of the sword of war, devastating pestilence, unprecedented famine, invasion, desolation—a punishment so terrible that the very sound of a leaf driven by the wind shall strike terror into men's hearts. This passage lies in the background of the various groups of seven of REVELATION, which portray the future chastisement of defiant and impious rebels, whose rejection of God's laws called down upon them the full measure of His wrath. The desolation on earth conveyed by the picture of the four horses and their riders grows out of the ancient priestly curse on the Covenant-breakers of Israel. But that is not to assume that the passage in Leviticus was laboriously followed by John as he composed his book : he carried his Old Testament in his mind—he had no bound book at his hand for reference. And other memories —memories of many grim prophetic warnings, wherein the cry of famine, pestilence and death becomes almost a fateful chorus —no doubt thronged in his mind, to drive home the lessons which Christians believed to have issued from the very lips of Christ. Indeed, so general in the Old Testament are the forebodings of the terrors which the horsemen of the first four seals personify, that we can name with certainty only one *specific* source, and that is a source which provides John not so much with the substance of what he has to say as with a convenient framework for it. Zechariah, a prophet whose mysterious and colourful symbols apparently exercised some fascination over John, saw a vision of four horses, chestnut, black, sorrel, and white in colour, with riders on them (Zech. i. 8 ff.). An angel tells the prophet that these four patrol the earth at God's command ; they are somehow connected with the seventy years of wrath which has fallen on the Jews. Predictions of destruction to be poured on the enemies of Israel follow this vision. Later Zechariah sees another vision :

' Once more I raised my eyes, and looked—there were
four chariots coming out between two mountains. . . . The
first chariot had chestnut horses, the second had black
horses, the third had white horses and the fourth had
dappled horses. Then I spoke to the angel who talked to
me ; I asked, " What are these, sir ? " The angel answered,
" They are going out to the four winds of heaven, after they
have presented themselves before the Lord of all the earth.
The black horses go to the north country, the white horses
go to the east, the dappled to the south, and the chestnuts
to the west country." They were eager to be off and patrol
the earth. . . . And they patrolled the earth. Then he called
to me, " Look, those who go to the north country will
satisfy my anger against the north country " ' (Zech. vi. 1-8).

The last words provide a clue for the meaning of this patrol
of the earth. John interpreted the four dire chargers in
Zechariah's first vision, and the four chariots with their
different coloured horses in the second vision, as symbols of
the wrath directed by God on the world. Their association
with the four winds is to be noted, as a point we must take
up later, when we reach vii. 1. But the really significant and
noteworthy thing about John's use of this passage from
Zechariah is not what he takes from it but what he makes of
it. It reveals a mind which is imaginative in the highest
degree, gifted with a certain intensity, a concentrative insight
which epitomizes many volumes of thought and emotion into
a few brief words : for it can be almost said that John has
brought to life every terror known to apocalyptic in these four
horses and their riders. What Carlyle said of Dante, he might
equally have said of John : ' His greatness has, in all senses,
concentred itself into fiery emphasis and depth. . . . There is
a brevity, an abrupt precision in him : Tacitus is not briefer,
more condensed ; and then in Dante it seems a natural con-
densation, spontaneous to the man. One smiting word ; and
then there is silence, nothing more said. His silence is more
eloquent than words.'

The first seal is opened, and one of the living Creatures cries,

'**Come !**' His voice resembles the thunder issuing from the throne; for the living Creatures mediate the will of the Creator and the Lamb to destroy those who have defiled the earth. Immediately John sees a portent of fearful import: **a white horse, its rider holding a bow.** This figure symbolizes 2 a host of invaders, an almost universal expectation of Jewish and early Christian eschatology (cf. notes on chap. xvi. 1–16). It is a personification of that host whom Isaiah, for example, foresaw despatched against Israel by God:

> ' He signals to a foreign power,
> whistling for them from the end of the earth;
> swiftly they come, speedily,
> none tired, none tripping,
> not a belt slack,
> not a shoe-string broken,
> arrows sharpened,
> bows all bent. . . .'
>
> (Isa. v. 26 ff.)

or, again, of the fierce armies whose attack on Babylon Jeremiah predicted, in an oracle which John often quotes: ' Set upon Babylon,' the prophet cries,

> ' Set upon Babylon, all round,
> all ye who bend the bow,
> spare not your arrows, shoot at her. . . .'
>
> (Jer. l. 14 ; cf. l. 26, etc.)

John adapted such prophetic oracles to his own day: or, rather, diverse though their details are, he believed them to have been uttered for his own times. He had little difficulty in seeing a fitness in the eschatological armies of other times to the circumstances of the Empire. For the bows, once symbolizing the fierceness of barbarian hosts named by the prophets, were now in the hands of the Parthians. And Parthian invasion had been a very real apprehension in the eastern provinces of the Empire, ever since the cavalry of this fierce people had demonstrated their martial qualities in A.D. 62. John is not, of course, alluding to past invasions; his eyes are turned upon the present and the future. (Perhaps the phrase **conquering and to conquer** could be pressed to yield an allusion to Parthian successes as John was writing:

more probably, since the whole oracle has reference to the future, it implies a continuous wave of invasion which encroaches on the civilized world until finally it is submerged (cf. xvii. 12–18). At any rate, whatever its initial stages, this is to be the last irresistible invasion predicted by prophets and apocalyptists, which must overturn the whole political structure of the Empire. It must not be thought that John was merely guessing at weak points in the Empire's defence : he did not think politically—his mind dwelt on God's oracles delivered through prophecy, and the certainty of their fulfilment.

It is worthy of note that when Christ is at last depicted as the warring Messiah (xix. 11 ff.), about to return to confront His enemies on earth, He bestrides a white horse, much like this personification of the Parthian invasion. **White** is emblematic of victory : and the horse, too, represents a conqueror's power, for dragoons were to that age what bombing aeroplanes are to our own. The resemblance between the first horseman and Christ arises out of the fact that the appearance of both is intended to convey the idea of victory. But Christ is to win the final victory, over all kings of earth and all powers of darkness : in His own right He wears many crowns—the first horseman is given a single **crown**, which signifies that divine Providence allows him to prevail in the last days. This is true of all four personifications in chap. vi. : they conquer as instruments of God ; they prevail because the living Creatures can cry, ' **Come !** ' And just as formerly the prophets conceived invading armies to be the agents of divine retribution, so the rider with the bow—though he represents forces which were the reverse of godly—is conceived to be the instrument of God and therefore irresistible. He rides away magnificently, fatefully, **conquering and to conquer.**

3–
4   The second ' **Come !** ' is answered by the portent of a **red horse,** to whose rider is given a **huge sword.** This apparently means internal dissensions, the bloodshed and ravages of civil war. The memory of turmoil and distress in the interval between the reigns of Nero and Vespasian doubtless coloured such anticipations appropriately. But, again, the theme of

prophecy fulfilled is primary (cf. St. Matt. xxiv. 15) and there is little to be gained from pressing the distinction between the kinds of war implied in the first and second portents. We might add, however, that a more detailed, but no less mysterious description of the kinds of eschatological warfare which John expected is given in xvi. 10–15 and xvii. 12 ff. It seems to be implied there that, just as Nero's subjects finally rose against him, so the subjects of the second Nero, the Antichrist, who at first welcomed him with fearful adulation (xiii. 4), would give him cause finally to turn and rend them : no doubt John expected history to repeat itself. However, the point is here that the End will be heralded by universal strife : the rider of the second horse is **allowed to take peace from earth and to make men slay each other.** The prediction is not intended to be specific. Rather than indulge in speculation about details, we should note the word **allowed** : everything is in God's hands (cf. ix. 3–5, xiii. 5–7). The worse the plight of men on earth, the surer the approach of the End : for warfare throughout the world was an infallible sign that God was at last hastening the time of His kingdom of righteousness on earth.

Invasion from without, civil war within—what could be the result on society ? What but famine, riding **a black horse 5 and holding a pair of scales in his hand ?** Here is a grim indication of the scarceness and costliness of food ; we recollect Ezekiel's forceful predictions of famine, which end with the words : ' Son of man, behold, I will break the staff of bread in Jerusalem : and they shall eat bread by weight, and with carefulness ' (Ezek. iv. 9 ff.) What seems **like a voice in the 6 midst of the four living Creatures**—presumably the voice of Christ, who is revealing these things to John ; who, moreover, is Lord of all the harvests of the last days, whether literal as here, or metaphorical, as in chap. xiv. 14–20—proclaims the scope of the famine. It will be severe, but not so severe as to usurp the lethal functions of other agents of wrath in the coming time of horror. A shilling (the approximate value of the denarius in the Greek text) was a day's wage for a labourer, and in Cicero's time would buy twelve quarts of wheat, twenty-four of barley. In Asia minor the relative value of barley was only a third that of wheat, as our text implies. In the time of famine predicted for the coming crisis, however, a shilling would buy only **a quart of wheat,** and **three quarts of barley.** The ' staff of bread ' was indeed to be broken, when the world's grain was reduced to a twelfth of the normal supply. The exception of **oil and wine** from the scope of this famine has a very mysterious appearance. An intriguing but perhaps too subtle explanation has been offered by some critics, who would paraphrase the command thus : ' Amidst famine of unparalleled severity, when solid food throughout the whole world is hardly sufficient to keep men alive, they will be mocked by a glut of unwanted luxury : there will be no shortage of wine and oil, but that will merely intensify the horror of the famine.' Such irony would perhaps miss its mark : John was writing for men who expected puzzles, but hardly of this sort. More recently an attempt has been made to show that it is an echo of a previous apocalyptic belief (Dr. Charles, *Comm.*, vol. i, p. 168) ; but this attempt fails, for it is ill-supported even by the tenuous evidence there offered in its favour. Dr. Beckwith has offered what seems the most convincing explanation (*The Apocalypse of John,* p. 521) : the term, ' oil, wine, and corn,' he says, is an Old Testament formula which means, comprehensively, human sustenance. When one of the three is attacked and diminished, and the other two spared, this means merely that part at least of the store of human food on earth will remain. He points out, furthermore, that it is true to nature and experience to talk of a famine affecting wheat and not other food : the vine and the olive are fed through roots deep enough to withstand droughts which damage the corn. Such a natural fact is certainly alluded to in ix. 5—the five-month season for locusts —and it seems almost certain that something like this explanation is the true one. John is predicting a **famine** of great severity, but not so severe as to be equal to the final plagues. It must be remembered that there are strictly two classes of plagues in REVELATION : those which are regarded as omens of the End and those which usher in the End of civilization ; the one class is partly admonitory and reformative (at least in intent ; cf. John's comment in ix. 20) ; the other is purely punitive—the verdict having been passed on evil-doers, the stroke of execution falls. The portent of famine is one of the preliminary portents, which traditionally proclaim the End to be at hand. It is therefore appropriate that the heavenly voice should set limits to the famine prophesied in the figure of the third rider.

It should be noted, incidentally, that certain critics believe that in the command **harm not oil and wine** we have an allusion to a Domitianic decree of A.D. 92. (See Dr. Moffatt's note in *Expositor's Greek Testament* p. 390.) The Emperor viewed with concern the disproportionate number of vineyards in Asia Minor, as compared with corn-producing land, and he decreed that many vineyards should be destroyed, and the land devoted to grain. An ensuing storm of protest led to the withdrawal of the decree. The inferences drawn by some critics from this are not altogether acceptable ; but we can at least see that the cryptic words of command would derive pointed significance from the Imperial anxiety about the supply of corn.

The last of this awful company of riders is **Death,** who strikes with many weapons, has many servants to do his will, but himself works through the torture of sickness and pestilence (cf. ix. 15–19). For the name of Death in Greek is also the name of pestilence : it is to be observed that the fourth rider is given power to kill by every means in that **fourth part** of the earth in his jurisdiction—even by **plague,** though that is a repetition of his very name. There is, however, no real confusion here, for the list in which the word ' plague ' occurs, **sword and famine and plague and wild beasts of the earth,** is merely an allusion to the eschatological threat in Ezek. xiv. 21, where God's ' four fatal judgments ' consist of precisely the same combination of horrors : such are the catastrophes which God allows in a fourth part of the earth. The limit thus formally indicated tells us that these are still preliminary warnings of the End: the last plagues (chap. xvi.) are universal in scope.

7–
8

Death carries no symbol to distinguish him. He is known by the corpse-like colour of his horse : a livid horse, bestridden by Death ! But an even subtler horror accompanies him ; in REVELATION, Death's boon companion is **Hades**. The two are inseparable, part of the one fearful fate awaiting mankind (i. 18, xx. 13, 14). The sufferer does not find peace as his tortured heart stops beating ; he must wait the final judgment in the cheerless underworld of the dead, full of unknown terrors. Only the Christian, perhaps only the martyr, could expect to be delivered from the miseries of Death and Hades, by the Lord who had conquered them (i. 18). For the rest of men, **the sword and famine and plague and . . . wild beasts of the earth** were calamities which opened gates into a dreadful vista of punishment.

vi. 9–11 : THE FIFTH SEAL : THE SOULS OF THE SLAIN

9 **And when he opened the fifth seal, I saw underneath the altar the souls of those who had been slain for adhering to God's**
10 **word and to the testimony which they bore; and they cried aloud, '** *O Sovereign Lord,* **holy and true,** *how long* **wilt thou refrain from** *charging and avenging* **our** *blood upon those*
11 *who dwell on earth ?* **' But they were each given a white robe and told to remain quiet for a little longer, until their number was completed by their fellow-servants and their brothers who were to be killed as they themselves had been.**

9 The opening of the **fifth seal** reveals a portent totally different in appearance from those which precede and follow it ; it is nevertheless related to them fundamentally. The picture which John sees of martyr-souls crying for vengeance conveys something of the motive behind the eschatological destruction which we see foreshadowed in the pageants of verses 1–8 and 12–17. For it was a general and long-established article of faith that the sufferings of the righteous must call down the wrath of God on persecutors ; indeed, there was a Jewish belief that the safety of the physical universe depended on the

well-being of the saints, without whose presence on earth the continued existence of the world would have no justification. John catches a glimpse of those whose martyrdom is already bearing fruit, in the scourging of the world which precedes and heralds the End. He sees **underneath the altar** (not actually in heaven, but in a place of privileged security, where they await the ' first resurrection ' ; xx. 4–6) **the souls of those who had been slain for adhering to God's word and to the testimony which they bore** : that is, he sees the martyrs from among the messianic people (xii. 17). Perhaps he means only Christian martyrs, like Antipas or the victims of Nero ; but more probably (since he does not use the specific term, **the testimony of Jesus**) he means all who died in God's service, whether in the Christian or pre-Christian dispensation ; ' all the just blood shed on earth ' (St. Matt. xxiii. 35) cries out for vengeance. So John assures the seven churches : the death of the martyr is not unavailing ; it will be one more count in the great indictment of ' the dwellers on earth ' (the technical term for unredeemed mankind in REVELATION ; see iii. 10, xi. 10, xiii. 8, 14) ; one more deed which helps them to fill up the measure of their fathers, the murderers of the prophets (St. Matt. xxiii. 31–6), and thus, brings nearer the Day of God, the hour when ' the great cup of the wine of the passion of his wrath ' shall be poured on civilization (xvi. 17 ff.). John hears the souls of the martyrs crying out a prayer that the hour of Justice may come soon ; it is a complaint in form, but a prayer in fact. The question ' **How long ?** ' had for centuries 10 been on the lips of apocalyptists (cf. Zech. i. 12 ; Dan. xii. 6), but it was always associated as it is in REVELATION with the cardinal belief, that He who was called **Sovereign Lord, holy and true** must sooner or later assert His power in a world which challenged His sovereignty, defiled what was holy, and hated what was true. The modern conscience is shocked at the passionate longing for vengeance breathed out by the martyrs, and, indeed, it is beyond doubt lower in tone than the lofty spirit of forbearance which distinguished the Christian Church in its earliest days. The change is a measure of the transformation wrought in the persecuted by persecution.

Nevertheless, censure is almost as pointless as it is easy. For John is here using the accepted ideas of his time, found alike in the Old Testament, apocalyptic—and even the Gospels in their present form. Perhaps the sufferings of both Jews and Christians in modern times, at the hands of secular powers inspired by motives not unlike those of the pagan world of the first century, will prevent us from too hasty a censure on this attempt to convince the future martyrs of the seven churches that the agony of their forerunners was not unregarded by God. In any case, we cannot grudge admiration for John's unwavering faith, which prompts him to such confidence that the triumph of righteousness is only a matter of time. To the martyrs' cry of **How long wilt thou refrain ?** comes the response that the time and season is in the hand of unfailing Providence. The *certainty* of the End is conveyed in the very sign of **the altar** under which the souls of the martyrs dwell. It was commonly held by pious Jews that the souls of the just (unlike those of other men) were gathered into ' treasuries ' to await the age to come (cf. the ' chambers ' in 2 Esdras iv. 35). But John tells us that they dwell beneath an altar. This is a very striking innovation, which cannot be lightly passed over. Many have seen in this altar a sign of sacrificial death. But it is more probably to be explained by reference to a common Jewish expectation, which plays a leading part in John's drama of heavenly portents (cf. Introduction to chaps. iv. and v., p. 72). A venerated Jewish tradition held that the furniture of the old temple at Jerusalem, once hidden by the prophet Jeremiah, and so lost to succeeding generations, would be revealed once more, and would once more be seen in the temple, in that Day when the people of God were vindicated in the eyes of all men. And here we see the heavenly original of that earthly altar ; we are to see it again soon, once more connected with the belief that the prayer of the saints availed in hastening the time of vindication and restoration (viii. 3–5). It is the heavenly original of the sacred symbol hidden by the prophet ; for the earthly shadows of heavenly realities are now no longer treasured in the hearts of Christians. What once symbolized a channel whereby prayer could ascend to God is now replaced by a reality : the voice of the martyrs rises unimpeded to the throne. And the altar is nothing more, nothing less, than a Sign.

But the assurance it gives is not allowed to remain implicit. The martyrs' cry is answered, in terms curiously remote from modern thought. They are first given a **white robe,** a pledge of 11 victory, of heavenly splendour and immortality, won through loyal service to God. They are **told to remain quiet for a little longer**—for the voice of their complaint is to be stilled. And then they hear why the End is not yet : **their number** is not yet **completed**—it must be made up by **their fellow-servants and their brothers** (cf. xix. 10 and xxii. 9 : the **servants** and **brothers** are Christian prophets ; see also xi. 3 ff.) **who were to be killed as they themselves had been.** To a mind so firm and loyal as John's, nothing is accidental. God's plan is fixed in its minutest details. We might profitably illustrate this article of the apocalyptic creed by a passage in 2 Esdras (iv. 33 ff.) : the visionary has asked ' How long ? ' ; he receives the reply :

' Thou dost not hasten more than the Most High : for thy haste is for thine own self, but he that is above hasteneth on behalf of many. Did not the souls of the righteous ask question of these things in their chambers, saying, How long are we here ? when cometh the fruit of the threshing time of our reward ? And unto them Jeremiel the archangel gave answer, and said, Even when the number is fulfilled of them that are like unto you. For he hath weighed the world in the balance ; and by measure hath he measured the times, and by number hath he numbered the seasons ; and he shall not move nor stir them until the said measure be fulfilled.'

A great martyrdom lies before the Church ; when it has been accomplished, the righteous shall rise to their reward.

vi. 12–17 : THE SIXTH SEAL : UNIVERSAL TERROR

12 And when he opened the sixth seal, I looked ; a great earthquake took place, *the sun* turned black as sackcloth, *the* full *moon*
13 turned like *blood, the stars of the sky dropped* to earth *as a*
14 *fig tree* shaken by a gale sheds her unripe figs, *the sky* was swept aside *like a scroll being folded up,* and every mountain
15 and island was moved out of its place. *Then the kings of the earth, the magnates,* the generals, the rich, the strong, slaves and freemen everyone of them, *hid in caves and*
16 *among the rocks* of the mountains, calling to the mountains and the rocks, '*Fall upon us* and *hide us* from the face of *him who is seated on the throne* and from the wrath of the
17 Lamb ; for *the great Day of* their *wrath* has come, *and who can stand it ?* '

After St. Matthew had recorded the predictions of wars, when ' nation will rise against nation and realm against realm', of invasion, when the stricken Jerusalem is to behold the worst of all horrors, in the defilement of the holy place ; of famines and earthquakes, and of the persecution of Christ's followers, he continued :

> ' Immediately after the misery of those days,
>   the sun will be darkened,
>   and the moon will not yield her light,
>   the stars will drop from heaven,
>   and the orbs of the heavens will be shaken.
> Then the Sign of the Son of man will appear in heaven.'
> (St. Matt. xxiv. 29–30.)

These are familiar words : they appear almost identically in the apocalypse of St. Mark (xiii. 24–6), and St. Luke alludes to them, only to add a vivid description of ' men swooning with panic and foreboding of what is to befall the universe ' (St. Luke xxi. 26). The tendency of most modern readers is to pass quickly over such mysterious predictions : their goal is the infinitely more precious narrative of the Passion. And in that they differ completely from the Christian of the first century, to whom the apocalyptic tradition preserved in the

Gospels must have conveyed messages of hope and fear almost beyond our powers of understanding. We have quoted the synoptic prediction of cosmic portents of the End, because it is essential to realize that the picture of a stricken universe sketched as the **sixth seal** is broken came before the eyes of 12 early Christians not as something strange, requiring explanation, but as a restatement of beliefs already held on supreme authority. What the faithful Witness at one time had said on earth, He now repeats from heaven. It seems to be John's deliberate purpose in verses 12–17 to paint a picture already very familiar—so that the minds of his readers will the more eagerly seek the meaning of the sealed scroll—will enquire wherein lay the secret so jealously guarded, demanding such merit of Him who would reveal it, and will seek it in the passage appended to these portents—the all-revealing comment on their significance for Christians (see notes on pp. 106–8).

We have said that all the catastrophic events described in verses 12–17 have a general and not specific relevance in John's survey of the future ; they are to testify to the nearness of the End, not to mark out the path to be trodden by Christians as the End approaches. It would be enough to say this and pass on quickly to chap. vii., if we to-day could hear the story of the rocking earth and disrupted heavens with the same eager reverence as did the early Christians. But the scene leaves most of us unmoved : we, alas ! expect portents of a different sort, which may perhaps forebode no less terribly the death of civilization ; and the vision of the sixth seal seems remote and unreal. But we must pause and listen. Here is the thunder of Yahweh, echoing out of Israel's past ; the voice of many prophets, crying aloud : 'The day of the Lord is great and terrible ; and who can abide it ? ' (Joel ii. 11). We catch once more the accents of Isaiah :

> ' The very sky shall roll up like a scroll,
>   and all the stars shall fade,
>   as leaves fade from a vine,
>   and foliage from a fig-tree.'
>
> (Isa. xxxiv. 4.)

We hear once again that terrible refrain sung over the doomed Israelites :

> ' Get into caves of the rocks,
> hide in holes of the ground,
> away from the terror of the Eternal,
> from his dread majesty.'
>
> (Isa. ii. 10–19.)

We recall the affliction of Jeremiah, weeping over the sins of a people who have stirred God to anger :

> ' I look out on earth—lo, all is chaos,
> I look at heaven—its light is gone,
> I look out on the mountains—they are reeling,
> and all the hills are swaying ! '
>
> (Jer. iv. 23–4.)

These forebodings of calamity darken the pages of most of the prophets. Nearly all raise their voices, like Joel, in the cry :

> ' The sun shall be turned into darkness
> the moon into blood,
> before the coming of the Eternal's day,
> that great and awful day.'
>
> (Joel ii. 31 ; cf. Isa. l. 3.)

But only when we recall that John read these prophecies with joy, as pledges that God's strong arm should establish on earth His kingdom of righteousness, shall we look on such memories through the eyes of the early Christians. Their confidence was without equal : in the very prevalence of evil on earth they saw, as it were, ' the Sign of the Son of man ' : the very swaying of the earth spoke to them of God's care for His people :

> ' Though mountains be removed,
> and hills be shaken,
> never shall my love leave you,
> my compact for your welfare shall stand firm.'
>
> (Isa. liv. 10.)

We need say little about the details of the far-reaching calamities described in the sixth ' seal ' vision. We have said enough to show that these portents are scions of the Christian apocalyptic tradition, and that their power to stir the heart was incalculably strengthened by memories of the prophets. A word of reservation might be added to this, however. The evidence of his book proves almost beyond question that John did allude consciously to certain striking prophetic books, or to particular passages within those books; it even seems to indicate that he expected his readers to be familiar with those passages. But while this is true, we cannot always assume that every echo of the Old Testament or of non-canonical apocalyptic amounts to a direct allusion. For example, John has no indisputable references to Hosea elsewhere in REVELATION; yet Hos. x. 8 clearly lies behind the cry of mankind as they flee **calling to the mountains and the rocks, 'Fall upon us and hide us. . . .'** This apparent allusion, and no doubt others, probably resounded in John's mind because he had heard them often quoted in the churches, as part of Christ's revelation of what was to come (see St. Luke xxiii. 30). Nevertheless, whether the associations of a particular phrase reach back to prophecy and pre-Christian apocalyptic, or whether they recall for Christians a message which they attributed to Christ Himself, the important fact remains that John's language does not give us bare formulæ, devoid of memories; its nakedness was clothed in brilliance of reflected light—a light which for us shines dimly across many centuries; mistily, across revolutions of thought.

Later in REVELATION, the events which in verses 12–17 John gathered together—to form a sweeping eschatological survey of portentous disturbances in Nature—are related to specific ideas or occasions. The **earthquake,** for example, a fit warning of the imminent downfall of all civilization (xvi. 18), is to take place as Christians ascend to heaven in the sight of their enemies (xi. 12). The portents in the heavens are specifically connected with the Egyptian plague of darkness in viii. 12. (The hyperbole in such quotations as **the stars of** 13 **the sky dropped to earth as a fig tree shaken by a gale sheds her unripe figs, the sky was swept aside like a scroll being folded** 14 **up** is too obvious to require laboured comment: we must, however, recognize that this is the language of hyperbole, and not imagine contradictions in less sweeping statements later in REVELATION; see note on viii. 12. The **sky,** for instance, which is here swept aside, does not in fact disappear until the Last Judgment; xx. 11.) The terror of unredeemed mankind

15 —the kings of the earth, the magnates, the generals, the rich, the strong, slaves and freemen (a characteristic division of men into seven classes)—and the eschatological implications of this terror, are specifically dealt with in two related passages: xi. 13 and xiv. 6 (cf. note on xvi. 11). At this point in his book, however, John merely notes the fact of this terror —the fact, assumed by apocalyptists, that the calamities of the last days must drive into men's hearts the realization that the God whose majesty they have provoked is omnipotent. Panic fear, not conscience, makes them long for the grave as a haven from the storm of unbearable wrath ; the

16 face of **him who is seated on the throne** is too terrible for sinful man to behold ; **the wrath of the Lamb** is not to be borne.

17 The cry of these terror-stricken men, ' **The day of their wrath has come . . .**' conveys to us that in this wide survey John has brought us to the verge of the End, when the sword of God is already about to fall for the last time. We see the lurid dawn of a Day for which the afflicted people of God have prayed for many centuries. What is to befall in this Day of wrath we do not hear until later. John breaks off his story, as we imagine he has reached his climax. But his next subject is more important for his readers than these familiar plagues and omens. They are to read, at first in mysterious hints, later in more explicit terms, what God expects of them in the last days, and what in return shall be their reward.

INTRODUCTION TO CHAPTERS VII. AND VIII. 1–5

The opening of the seals provides the literary structure for a series of prophetic descriptions of the unparalleled stress and turmoil of the last days. This series is the first of three. It is followed by another series of predictions, each heralded by a trumpet blast in heaven (chaps. viii. and ix.) and, after an interval, by still another series of seven, predicting the final plagues (chap. xvi.), when the ' bowls of the wrath of God ' are poured on the earth. All three cycles of prophecies are closely related, and the nature of their relationship will be discussed in greater detail at the appropriate points. It is, however, indispensable to the understanding of the 'seals' and 'trumpets' series to see at once how they are knit together, and what they are intended chiefly to convey. They should be studied side by side :

The Breaking of the Seals	*The Blowing of the Trumpets*
The first four seals broken :	The first four trumpets are blown.
(a) Warfare—invasion and international strife, famine and death come into the world.	(a) Great calamities fall upon the whole structure of nature.
(b) Fifth seal broken : souls of martyrs in heaven pray for the speedy coming of the End.	(b) Fifth trumpet blown : a plague of illness or disease inflicted on men by a host of dæmons.
(c) Sixth seal broken : great cosmic disturbances and destruction.	(c) Sixth trumpet blown : a plague of death, inflicted by dæmonic army.

After the breaking of the sixth seal and the blowing of the sixth trumpet two excursuses occur. The purpose of each is to show what is to be the lot of the faithful Christians. The second excursus (chaps. x. and xi.) amplifies the story of the first (chap. vii.).

Excursus (chap. vii.)	*Excursus (chaps. x. and xi.)*
Before the destruction of the last days the prospective martyrs will be 'sealed' with a mark which protects them against spiritual evil, and which guarantees recognition in heaven.	A gap in the information of chap. vii. is now filled up. How are these Christians to meet their death ? What will be their distinctive task in the last days ? How will they be rescued from the powers of wickedness after their martyrdom ? What will be the effect of their martyrdom ? All these questions are answered.
They are then depicted in heaven : such is the guarantee of the sealing.	

Each of these excursuses tells the same story, though from a different point of view : 'Before the End there must be a great martyrdom. It will accompany the final preaching of the gospel (the "witnessing" and "prophesying" in chap. xi.). Those who are killed will be sure of resurrection. Their death—the completion of the numbers of martyrs—*will be the signal for the End.*'

Following each excursus, John can say briefly that the End will assuredly come, after this great martyrdom.

The Breaking of the Seventh Seal	The Blowing of the Seventh Trumpet
(a) The seal is broken.	(a) The trumpet is blown :
(b) A pregnant *silence* follows : John reserves until later the revelation of the outcome of the martyrdom.	(b) ' *Loud voices* ' proclaim what was previously concealed. The martyrdom and resurrection of the faithful completed, the End can now come. The reign of God begins.
(c) ' There followed peals of thunder, loud blasts, flashes of lightning, and an earthquake.' The final portent (viii. 5).	(c) ' There were flashes of lightning, loud blasts, peals of thunder, an earthquake and a hailstorm ' (xi. 19).

(The prophet states in viii. 5 and xi. 19 that the End *will come* : but it is later that he describes the consequences on earth—xvi. 19. We learn then that the earthquake destroys all the pagan cities. The rule of the powers of evil has passed away.)

This tabular statement of the seals and trumpets series reveals the elaborate care with which John recounted his visions. If this literary scheme is kept in mind, the general bearing of the two series will be reasonably clear.

The *scroll* with the seven seals is, as it were, the book of the Future, as predetermined by God. When in his vision John sees this scroll gradually unfolded, he becomes aware that successive waves of disaster are to befall the world. These visitations of turmoil and ruin he depicts figuratively ; his pictures tell their own story to the discerning (and we should remember that John expects his readers to be ' discerning ' ; cf. xiii. 18, xvii. 9), but they are intended to be mysterious. We must understand that the prophet does not reveal in these vivid flashes of the future the exact course of events, neatly arranged in their chronological sequence. John is not in the least concerned with the construction of an accurate calendar of future events ; REVELATION has nothing in common with an astrological almanack. He is sketching out the general and essential characteristics of the last days. Three times he tells the story of the agony and turmoil of the future. All three accounts cover substantially the same ground, containing information which is often similar, and sometimes almost identical, and ending at the point when the rule of this world ends and the rule of God begins. But each of these series of predictions—the 'seals,' 'trumpets,' and 'bowls' series—has its own individual theme. The last days are described from three different points of view.

It remains only to say that the prophecies of disaster are regarded largely as a setting for a more positive story—a message of the utmost value for the churches. It is true that the mere assurance of an imminent punishment to fall on the pagan oppressor had its value in encouraging the faithful to continued resistance. It is also true that John's interpretation of natural calamities as the sure precursors of the final day of reckoning would satisfy an infinitely deeper need than idle curiosity in his readers. Yet John's main concern was with the message of redemption contained in the two excursuses (chap. vii. and chaps. x.–xi.). These two passages, which break so forcibly into the sevenfold pattern of their contexts, are focal points. John ceases there to utter general descriptions of the punishments and warnings to fall on the pagan world. He turns from the unrepentant and incorrigible pagan world to his fellow-Christians. What is to be *their* fate ?

vii. 1–8 : The Sealing of the Servants of God

After that I saw four angels standing *at the four corners of the* 1
earth, holding back *the four winds* of the world from blowing on the earth or on the sea or upon any tree. And 2
I saw another angel rise up from the east, with the seal of the living God ; he shouted aloud to the four angels who were allowed to injure the earth and the sea, ' Do no harm 3
to earth or sea or trees, until *we seal* the servants of our God *upon their foreheads.*' I heard what was the number of the 4
sealed—one hundred and forty-four thousand sealed from every tribe of the sons of Israel, twelve thousand sealed 5

7
8
6

from the tribe of Judah, twelve thousand from the tribe of Reuben, twelve thousand from the tribe of Simeon, twelve thousand from the tribe of Levi, twelve thousand from the tribe of Issachar, twelve thousand from the tribe of Zebulun, twelve thousand from the tribe of Joseph, twelve thousand from the tribe of Benjamin,* twelve thousand from the tribe of Gad, twelve thousand from the tribe of Asher, twelve thousand from the tribe of Naphtali, twelve thousand sealed from the tribe of Manasseh.

* The transposition of 5c–6 to a place after 8, as Dr. G. B. Gray points out (*Encyclopædia Biblica* 5209), yields a normal list of the tribes.

With the opening of the first six seals, John has brought us to the verge of the final revelation ; the scroll bearing record of God's predetermined plan for the future is now almost completely unrolled. The prophet now pauses in his relation of the catastrophic days before the End ; he has a truth of the highest importance to explain, and with the artistry of a skilful story-teller he explains it in such a way that his readers are kept in suspense about the culminating horror to be launched on the world, at the breaking of the seventh seal. They must learn something which affects them more closely than the spectacular portents of chap. vi.

It is easy to be totally mistaken about the real significance of chap. vii., if one fails to remember the meaning of the introductory words, **After this. . . .** John is reporting a new vision, the substance of which is chronologically quite independent of the events described in the previous chapter. A hasty reading of chap. vii. conveys the impression that after the portents of war, famine, pestilence, and cosmic disturbances had stricken and dismayed mankind, John expected a further disaster : **the four winds of the world** were to be unleashed—great hurricanes and tornadoes, to pile still more misery on a stubbornly unrepentant world. But this is far from John's meaning. If it had been his intention to describe yet another portent of the End, he would have done so within the framework of the ' seals ' allegory. No ; John is recording in chap. vii. a conviction which he intends to express in sharp and deliberate contrast to the tale of destruction in the previous chapter. We might convey the implication in the words, **after this,** as follows : ' Having received divine confirmation that inevitable destruction was to overtake the earth, having heard God's oracles of doom once again reiterated, I *then* understood. . . .' What ? What was this extraordinary flash of illumination, which turned a familiar story into something new and vital ?

We are soon to learn. But meanwhile John's allegory takes us back to a time before the horsemen were allowed to ride away on their grim mission—to a time when the destroying forces, licensed by God to punish the world, commissioned by Him to portend to all men the nearness of the End, were as yet restrained. This we must detect in John's striking picture of **four angels standing at the four corners of the earth, holding back the four winds of the world.** No doubt the winds have always provided a natural image for the destructive energy of God in the world : ' He blew, and they were scattered ' is a theme which did not die with the Psalmist. Jeremiah uses the term eschatologically, to denote terrible punishments which were to come upon Israel and destroy her :

> ' A hot blast blows from the desert
>   on my country-folk,
> no breeze to winnow and to cleanse,
>   but a wild, tearing wind ;
>   for now I sentence them.'
>
> (Jer. iv. 11-12.)

Later (li. 1-2), Babylon is threatened with a ' destroying wind '— a wind which will fan the ripe harvest of her wickedness : but this, like the hot blast from the desert, is no literal hurricane. It is invasion—more terrible than the fiercest of gales. In REVELATION, similarly, **the four winds** stand for the judgments which precede the End ; they are, in fact, alternative symbols for the four horsemen. We have noted the connexion of the four chariots and their horses in Zech. vi. 5 with the four winds ; and this connexion may have seemed to John even closer than Dr. Moffatt's rendering suggests. For the Hebrew text upon which our translations are based stands, without emendation, as follows : ' These [the chariots and horses] are the four winds of the earth ' (see R.V. *in loc.*). However that may be, John did find the two expressions closely associated in his source, and in his own mind he found it possible to identify them. He may have been assisted by some survival of an ancient association of the four winds with the angels of the Presence—the four living Creatures, who despatch the horsemen. He would find it easy to detect a symbolical flavour in the promise of Christ (St. Mark xiii. 27 ; cf. St. Matt. xxiv. 31) : ' Then he will despatch his angels and muster the elect from the four winds. . . .' John shows us **four angels** restraining all the forces of chaos and ruin in the last days ; and the **earth, sea,** and **trees** which they temporarily protect stand for the world of men (**any tree**—representative of living things in general. John uses the term consistently with the general image of the winds : trees are the first things to suffer from the violence of storms). This restraint exercised by the **four angels**, who, we are now expressly told, are plenipotentiaries of God in His design to **injure the earth and sea** in the last days, is of tremendous moment. John·emphasizes it by every means at his command. He uses the device of repetition, and this alone compels us to linger over the notion. But, more effectively, he casts the whole scene into a

2 dramatic mould. We see **another angel rise up from the east**—the region of light, the source of blessing (but see note on ix. 14 ff.). He comes from the Presence bearing a solemn, mysterious sign, **the seal of the living God.** His voice rings out with all the authority of a messenger from

3 God : **Do no harm to earth or sea or trees, until we seal the servants of our God upon their foreheads.** And the servants of God are sealed upon their foreheads—though John, with his wonted economy of words, does not actually recount

4 it. He hears the number of the sealed—**one hundred and forty-four thousand. . . .**

This is one of the most disputed passages in REVELATION, and the explanations of it offered by commentators are remarkably divergent, and often remarkably inconsistent with the plain evidence of the text. It is indisputably mysterious—

as John probably intended. The reader in his bewilderment at once demands, What is this ' seal ' ? Why must the servants of God bear a mark on their foreheads ? What is this mystic number, **one hundred and forty-four thousand** ? And why **' from every tribe of the sons of Israel '** ? In the interests of clarity, we shall answer these questions before we discuss the grounds for our conclusions about them. To take the last first : **the sons of Israel** represent the messianic community— the Church ; they are not Jews, but those who have inherited all the ancient promises of Judaism—Christians. More specifically still, they are Christian prophets ; so the term, **servants of our God,** implies. They are, in fact, the future martyrs from among the churches—those whom we have known hitherto as the conquerors. Their **number** is sym- bolical : it takes us back to vi. 11—it stands for that exact proportion of the Church for which God has destined martyrdom, before He brings to an end the earthly sway of evil. They bear a mark **upon their foreheads**—a sign visible to God and His agents alone—because they are under His protection, singled out from the impious on whom His judgments shall fall. And this mark is given to the martyrs, not to other Christians, because martyrs alone will need it.

The prophetic passage which lies behind all this is a colourful episode in the Book of Ezekiel. The prophet sees a vision of seven men (if we can call the portentous figures which he sees by that name—John certainly assumed that they were angels of revelation, like the ' men ' in the Book of Daniel). Six of these men are armed with battle-axes ; they represent invading hosts. The seventh is armed with a writer's ink- horn. After this, Ezekiel hears the voice of God :

' He called to the man in linen, with the writer's ink-horn, and said to him, " Go through the city of Jerusalem, and put a mark upon the foreheads of the men who bewail and bemoan all the detestable impieties that are being practised there." And I heard him say to the others, " Follow him through the city and strike, without mercy or pity, kill old men, young men, maidens, children, women—kill them, kill, but never touch anyone with the mark ; and begin at my sanctuary." '

(Ezek. ix. 1 ff.)

The servants of God in Jerusalem are thus marked, in order that they may be recognized and spared. Now, this notion of recognition is expressly attached to another ' seal ' which we are to meet in REVELATION. For when Antichrist comes into the world he also insists that all his servants shall be marked on their right hand or their forehead, ' so that no one can buy or sell unless he bears the mark—that is, the name of the Beast or the cipher of his name ' (xiii. 16–17). Those who do not bear this mark must, in short, face death. The two marks —that impressed on the foreheads of the one hundred and forty-four thousand by the **seal of the living God** and that enforced on unredeemed mankind by the Beast—must be considered together, since John intended a contrast. The one is a mark of eternal life, given by the **living** God, One who alone has the gift of life in His power (iv. 10–11). The other is the mark of eternal death—death which does not even hold the mercy of oblivion (xiv. 9 f.). But whatever blessings or curses issue from the possession of each of these marks, their immediate purpose is to ensure recognition, for the purpose of separating the believers and unbelievers of either party. This idea is, of course, implicit in the very restraint of the destroying forces of the last days, in order that God's servants may be marked : whatever plagues are to fall on the rest of men, they must be immune, for they have work to do for their God (cf. xi. 3 ff.).

We shall not be quite clear about the meaning of the seal on the forehead of these servants of God until we have learnt what actually is the distinctive work that they have to perform. For the Christian of John's audience there was probably no obscurity. The term, **servants of God,** alone was perhaps sufficient to show him that their function was prophetic (cf. notes on pp. 195, 449). The fact that the mark was placed **upon their foreheads** hinted that they must act prominently in God's service : for the mark is invisible to men, yet its possession is eventually to be recognized by all men. And this prominent service of God is certainly to be inferred in the passage from Ezekiel to which John has alluded. Those to be spared in Jerusalem are not simply men who live a holy life, but men who ' bewail and bemoan the detestable impieties ' of their countryfolk. So much is clear in chap. vii. But when we read on further in REVELATION, we are told specifically about the martyr's task (ch. xi.). He is to ' prophesy ' in the streets of Vanity Fair, the great city of civilization ; he is to preach the gospel of the End ; he is to be a ' witness,' as Christ was before him. And this he must do openly, in the sight of all. He will be protected from every attack of those who hate him by special powers given by God. He will be preserved alive, until the time comes when, like the faithful Witness whom he serves, he must die. But how shall he avoid the plagues which are sent from God to ravage the great City, the world of unredeemed men ? He is spared, because he bears the seal of the living God. The agents of destruction are not allowed to touch him (ix. 4) ; they are allowed to attack 'only such human beings as have not the seal of God on their foreheads.'

Now it has been inferred that John foresaw a universal martyrdom confronting the Church. No Christian was to be left on earth, to meet his Lord when he came ' like a thief ' (iii. 3). The **one hundred and forty-four thousand**, according to critics holding this view, represents the whole Church. This view is quite untenable, in view of the evidence (cf. notes on xi. 1-2, xii. 14, and xiii. 15 ff.). What John really believed was this : the Church as a whole would naturally be protected and preserved by God—that was to be assumed. They would not suffer the plagues which fell on the rest of mankind, the unredeemed, who are symbolized by John under the name of the great City (xi. 8), *because they were no part of the great City* They dwelt in the desert, like the Israelites of old. This is probably allegorical ; John probably means by the ' desert ' separation from the affairs of this world achieved by those who live in the quietness of a holy life. But whether allegorical or not, their dwelling in the desert enables them to escape the plagues falling on the great City. The martyrs, on the other hand, by virtue of their function, were necessarily 'within' the City of Destruction. Therefore they had to be distinguished from other men by the mark of the seal of God.

Much of this is anticipatory ; but it must be said for two reasons : first, because the identity of the host of the sealed has been so widely misunderstood, and, secondly, because the reader will naturally wish to be reassured that the preliminary judgments of God on the world are conceived to distinguish between good and evil men. The distinction is certainly clear in John's mind. He does not stress it more at the present juncture because he is now concerned supremely with one single thought : ' What is to happen to the martyrs who must fall in God's service ? What part are they to play in the imminent crisis which is to come upon the world ? '

John describes the character of those who are sealed with great deliberation ; the servants of God belong to **the twelve tribes of the sons of Israel.** In other words, John makes what amounts to a twelvefold assertion that the Christian churches are the chosen people, complete heirs to the ancient Jewish heritage (cf. Jas. i. 1 ; 1 Pet. i. 1) ; it was as the elect nation that they must both suffer persecution and enjoy vindication. 5- The detailed and almost painfully deliberate list of the twelve 8 tribes, each of which was to supply its due number of martyrs, should be compared with verse 9, where the triumphant martyrs from the Christian churches no longer have a figurative Jewish nationality ascribed to them, but are spoken of as ' a great host, from every nation and tribe and people and tongue.' Theirs are all the glories foreshadowed for the loyal Jews in prophecy and apocalyptic. First, certain of their number must be martyred : nevertheless, every individual amongst them shall rise from death into immortality.

The number, **one hundred and forty-four thousand,** and its components, **twelve thousand** from each tribe, are purely formal ; each represents that proportion of Christians who in the book of destiny are inscribed as martyrs. It has sometimes been asserted that Christians of the first century had little notion of the Church ; all they knew were ' the churches '—

scattered communities, each a distinct and separate 'colony of heaven.' But it is clear that John had no such narrow view. The division of Christendom into the twelve tribes of the chosen people, the messianic nation, can only mean that John saw in its diversity an essential unity : that all its outward divisions, linguistic, national and racial, could not conceal its essential spiritual oneness. This thought will help us to identify the **one hundred and forty-four thousand** when next we see them—and we are to see them again very soon.

vii. 9–17 : THE SEQUEL : A VISION OF THE MARTYRS IN HEAVEN

After that I looked, and there was a great host whom no one 9 could count, from every nation and tribe and people and tongue, standing before the throne and before the Lamb, clad in white robes, with palm-branches in their hands ; and they cried with a loud voice, ' Saved by our God *who is* 10 *seated on the throne,* and by the Lamb!' And all the angels 11 surrounded the throne and the Presbyters and the four living Creatures, and fell on their faces before the throne, worshipping God and crying, 'Even so! Blessing and glory 12 and wisdom and thanksgiving and honour and power and might be to our God for ever and ever : Amen!'
Then one of the Presbyters addressed me, saying, 'Who are 13 these, clad in white robes? where have they come from ? ' I said to him, 'You know, my lord.' So he told me, 14 'These are the people who have come out of *the* great *Distress, who have washed their robes* and made them white *in the blood* of the Lamb.

Therefore they are now before the throne of God, 15
serving him day and night within his temple,
and *he who is seated on the throne* shall overshadow
them with his care.
Never again *will they be hungry, never* again *athirst,* 16
never shall the sun strike them, nor any *scorching heat* ;

17   for the Lamb in the midst of the throne *will be their
      shepherd,*
        guiding them to fountains of living water ;
        and God shall wipe ever tear from their *eyes.'*

The next vision recorded by John has an immediate *logical*
connexion with what precedes it, but once again it is not intended to convey immediate chronological sequence. Having
said that every martyr is infallibly protected by God, John
shows his audience what is the reward promised to those who
faithfully perform the martyr's service. Between the sealing
of the one hundred and forty-four thousand and their appear-
9 ance in heaven as **a great host,** clad in white, there is an
interval. In this interval the agents of ruin ravage the earth
at God's command ; but the martyrs are secured from the
plagues which they bring into the world by the mystic mark of
God's seal. An important part in this drama of ruin is to be
played by the Imperial authorities, the chief agents of the
Devil (see chaps. xiii. and xvii.) ; from their malice, too, the
martyrs are for long protected (xi. 5–6). But we learn later
that, ' when they have finished their testimony, the Beast that
ascends from the abyss will make war on them and conquer
them and kill them ' (xi. 7). This is the event which fills the
interval between the sealing of the one hundred and forty-four
thousand and their appearance in heaven. We are told this
in verse 14. For the present, John deliberately holds us in
suspense, as he depicts a scene of transcendent joy. New
voices have been added to the celestial choirs whom we have
heard worshipping the Creator and the Lamb (chap v.). *Men*
have gained access to the throne. A new era in the history of
creation has begun.

But, it may be objected, how is it possible to identify this
great host whom no one could count with the carefully enumer-
ated one hundred and forty-four thousand of the previous
vision ? Does not this show us that the two hosts are quite
different ? Must we not wait to see the triumph of the first of
the two hosts until later in REVELATION (xiv. 1), when John
recognizes a hundred and forty-four thousand, standing along

with the Lamb on the heavenly Sion ? Many have decided that in these three passages, two in chap. vii. and one in chap. xiv., John has described two quite distinct hosts. But this is far from the true meaning. Our first instinct is to see a logical connexion between the host of verses 4-8, who are numbered, and the host whom no one could count of verses 9 ff. Literary consistency demands this connexion, and it is certainly there. The point is this : John saw in the vision of the angel with the seal of God that *all* martyrs could count on protection from the plagues of the last days : he therefore tells us this, and in order to convey the sense of *all* martyrs, he uses the symbolical figure of twelve times twelve thousand. But he has not yet seen that *all* these servants of God have been slain ; he has not seen that every one of them reaches heaven—and that therefore the number of those who have been 'killed for adhering to God's word and to the testimony which they bore' has at last reached the limits laid down by Providence (vi. 9-11). When he is able to proclaim this knowledge, he is able to say that he has seen into a secret which generations had longed to know. The End will come when the complete number of martyrs are to be found in heaven. At this point John does not see the martyr host as that complete and fateful number. He sees them as a host whom no one could count—no one, for God alone knows the hour of the End, and He alone could determine how many of the martyrs must fall before the cup of wickedness on earth was filled. But in the later vision, in xiv. 1 ff., John sees the number completed. And after that vision he is at last able to describe the execution of the last plagues. It could be held that this represented the course taken by John's gradually increasing visionary insight into future events. At first he sees vaguely, then more clearly. Undoubtedly this is the plan he follows in his book. But no doubt there will be those who see in this gradual unfolding of a theme a very deliberate literary scheme, which gives to all of John's visions the character of literary device. Whichever view we take, there is no denying that John felt behind these vivid scenes in heaven and earth the authority of a divine revealer, whose hand was visibly at work in the trances which came over him, and whose power to illuminate a prophet's mind was testified in a new apprehension of how the oracles of the last days were at last to be fulfilled.

The glory of martyrs—but not specifically of that mystic number of martyrs—is John's immediate theme. They are shown **standing** confident and unashamed in the presence of God and Christ. They are **clad in white robes** (cf. iii. 4–5), and **white**, as we have seen, is the colour of victory : they are the 'conquerors,' victorious in life, victorious in death. But we must remember the source of their triumphant strength. One of the Presbyters shows expressly that their robes are **white** because they have **washed** them and **made them white in the blood of the Lamb**. (It should be observed how little John thinks of the metaphorical character of the term **the blood of the Lamb** : the figurative incongruity (blood making robes white), so marked to a reader not familiarized by hymns with this metaphor for redemption, argues that the term was known and commonly used among the Christians for whom John wrote : cf. vii. 17, where John says that 'the Lamb . . . will be their shepherd.') John insists, with much emphasis, that it is righteous conduct which gives value to the martyr's death : only the stainless, he tells us, are fit to be a sacrifice to God (xiv. 5). But ' the righteous conduct of the saints ' (xix. 8), of which their white robes are fitting symbols, has been made possible by Christ's sacrificial death. The victory belongs to God and Christ ; and that is why, as they stand **with palm-branches in their hands** (an ethnic symbol of victory), they ascribe the victory, not to themselves, but to **God** who created them and **the Lamb** who redeemed them. They
10 are **saved!** Saved from the taint of evil ; saved from the devil's endeavour to make them submit to his Imperial agents ; saved once and for all from all the perils and darkness amongst which their earthly life was cast ; saved—and they alone can yet say so—from the Judgment and the second death (xx. 6).
11 The choruses of praise sung by all the **angels** about the throne, and **the Presbyters and the four living Creatures** ring out once
12 more ; this time the sevenfold ascription of praise is sung to

God (cf. v. 12), whose creative purposes have at last reached their goal, in the triumph of the redeemed.

As in chap. v., when John was confronted with the sealed scroll which none was worthy to open, **one of the Presbyters 13** addresses him to explain the significance of this mighty host, whose voice has stirred the heavenly choruses into a hymn of adoration—a hymn which must henceforth be raised **for ever and ever.** It is a moment of immeasurable solemnity ; a new age has dawned upon creation, and the ' sons of the morning ' are now not angels but men. **' Who are these, clad in white robes ? where have they come from ? '** They are martyrs, John is told. **' These are the people who have come out of the 14 great Distress, who washed their robes and made them white in the blood of the Lamb.'**

The great Distress—we have heard ominous anticipations of this event : in the letter to the church of Smyrna, John mentioned ' a distressful ten days ' which the faithful must endure (ii. 10) ; and the warning was repeated in the letter to the Philadelphian Christians, who were told of a universal ' hour of trial ' in which all men were to be tested (iii. 10). We must wait until chaps. x.–xi., however, before we shall know fully what is meant by the great Distress ; there, in a passage which is in every respect the complement of chap. vii., we learn the details which are at present withheld.

One cannot but shrink from attempting to comment on a passage of such beauty and tenderness as John's description of the martyrs' heavenly bliss. It opens the door into that secret chamber where the prophet has prayed alone, and contemplated in rapture the blessings stored up by the Father for His loyal sons (cf. xxi. 1–7). It is in this passage and in the description of the new Jerusalem (xxi.–xxii. 5), much more than in John's descriptions of desolation and terror, that we feel most clearly aware of a mind which has brooded long and devoutly over God's ancient promises to His people ; the echoes that we hear of psalmist and prophet tell us that John had read their oracles as one who hears the Most High pledging His word. He listened, and remembered ; what he had read became his own—and that is why we can read REVELATION as an original, astonishing work of art, not as a stiff mosaic of quotations. When John quoted or alluded, it was as if he had voiced his secret devotions. He had thought deeply and ingeniously over those words of God which puzzled him by their apparent contradictions (cf. notes on xxi. 24–7, xxii. 1–5), and elsewhere in REVELATION he is often concerned to show how by divine guidance he has seen the essential truth which disperses all such difficulties. But here he has nothing to explain, no puzzles to resolve. His purpose is to direct the eyes of future martyrs towards the eternal bliss which followed the brief pangs of their suffering.

Much of the language of these verses is reminiscent of the promises made to ' the conqueror ' in each of the seven churches. To stand in God's Presence, to be owned there by the Lamb, was the privilege promised to the loyal at Sardis 15 (iii. 5) : here we see these loyal souls **before the throne of God.** The conqueror in the church at Philadelphia was told that he would be made a pillar in the temple of God (iii. 12) ; and here we learn that the martyr shall serve **him day and night within his temple.** Those who are known as the servants of God (cf. xv. 3) on earth do not lose the peculiar honour of such service when they take their place among the resplendent hosts of heaven. They will be seen **serving him** in heaven, priests in the very presence of God (for this is the meaning of the word **temple** : cf. xxi. 22 and notes on p. 289). Worship and praise is their delight ; they can then adore God **day and night**, without any interruption from the forces of evil on earth. 16 **Never again will they be hungry**, because they will ' eat from the tree of Life ' (ii. 7) and ' share the hidden manna ' (ii. 17) ; **never again athirst**, since all their longing for God is now assuaged in the joy of communion with Him. The **shepherd** 17 who guides them to this **living water** is the Redeemer—**the Lamb in the midst of the throne** : we see with what joy, at once fervent and thoughtful, John lingered over such songs of faith as Ps. xxiii., such exalted oracles as Isa. xlix. 10. But it is not altogether easy for us, who seldom know the sufferings of **scorching heat,** for example, to appreciate the aptness and force of the images of psalmists and prophets (e.g. Ps. cxxi. 6)

as John did. But even familiarity cannot rob the last promise
of its wonder, for all are acquainted with sorrow : **God shall
wipe every tear from their eyes.** The God, from whose throne
issued flashes of lightning and loud blasts and peals of thunder,
whose sword of Judgment beats upon mankind with stern, unsparing blows, consoles His children tenderly, like a father. In
His presence their bitter suffering, their long, weary vigils,
their yearning for deliverance from the hands of evil-doers—all
that distressed and afflicted them is forgotten. The martyrs
inherit at once all the bliss which other loyal souls, who have
not been marked out for martyrdom, will finally enjoy in the
new order, after the great Day of Judgment (xx. 6, and
xxi). That is why we read in chap. vii. the promises which
John repeats later in his description of the new Jerusalem ; as
soon as they arise from death at the bidding of the voice who
cries ' Come up here ' (xi. 11–12), they are secure in the possession of every blessing.

viii. 1–5 : THE SEVENTH SEAL IS OPENED : THE END

When he opened the seventh seal, silence reigned in heaven for 1
about half-an-hour. Then I saw seven trumpets being 2
given to the seven angels who stand before God. And 3
another angel went and *stood at the altar* with a golden
censer ; he was given abundant *incense,* to be laid *with the
prayers* of all the saints upon the golden altar in front of the
throne ; and the smoke *of the incense with the prayers* of all 4
the saints rose up from the angel's hand before God. Then 5
the angel took *the censer, filled it with fire from the altar,*
and poured it on the earth ; there followed *peals of
thunder, loud blasts, flashes of lightning,* and an earthquake.

Chap. viii. affords an example of the necessity of understanding John's literary method before his pastoral purpose
can be fully appreciated. Otherwise, it appears confused and
disjointed, an unsuccessful attempt to insert the vision of the

seven trumpets into that of the seven seals, these two, it has been suggested, being originally current as two separate sources. An anticlimax seems evident in the first two verses.

1 When the **seventh seal** is opened, we naturally expect to read that the End has come ; and the expectation becomes acute in the breathless pause that follows, the dramatic **silence** that **reigned in heaven for about half an hour.** Hushed are the praises of the angelic hosts for this ominous period, the silent herald that all is over. It is a brilliant device for deepening the suspense. But the End, it seems, does not come. Instead,

2 John proceeds to relate his next vision of the **seven trumpets** series. Perhaps, it may be thought, this was the only way he could weave the two sources into his Apocalypse ; but the seam in the tapestry of his visions obtrudes more awkwardly than we should expect to find in the finished work of a skilful artist.

The difficulty proves imaginary when we understand John's method and purpose. The student of REVELATION must never tire of learning the lesson which John teaches untiringly throughout the book—the lesson of reiteration. Yet John is never monotonous. When he reiterates he never merely repeats. His thought grows. Important points are referred to again and again, but always with added detail and increased emphasis, as he himself understood God's message more clearly in the successive visions, and as he anticipated that his readers' grasp of that message was becoming stronger. No better illustration could be desired than the beginning of chap. viii. When the seventh seal is opened, we expect the End, and we may be quite certain that John means us to understand that it would be the End. But for the present he is content to state the bare fact ; indeed, he does not even state it except by implication, but proceeds with a new thought. He will do the same thing more than once as his theme develops. Time after time he will bring us to the edge of final doom, but each time he will tell us more about it ; always some new and important detail will be added to our knowledge about that supreme event. For consider his next description of the End in chap. xi. When the seventh angel sounds his blast, we are given an account of the final catastrophe in considerable detail. Now we learn that after the silence ' loud voices followed in heaven,' proclaiming Christ's victory ; that the nations are to be punished ; that the dead are to be judged ; that the prophets and saints are to be rewarded; and that those who destroy God's creation are themselves to be destroyed (xi. 15–18)—all of which will be again expanded in subsequent chapters. In other words, we are shown that the End is not a momentary event, accomplished, so to speak, like a flash of lightning. It is a solemn performance of God's final decrees, involving ethical and spiritual principles. If this is duly considered, it will be seen that chap. viii. is in no way an anticlimax. The events announced and ushered in by the seven trumpets are precisely those which ancient prophecy and apocalyptic tradition had foretold, and give us a closer view of the final drama than could be enacted in the introductory series of the seven seals.

But most of all, John uses his literary power of expansion in order to stress his special theme—the work and destiny of the Christian Church in the last days. In the seals series he could do little more than touch the subject incidentally (vi. 9–11) and show that the martyrs would be ultimately saved (chap. vii.) ; but he has much more to explain, particularly in chaps. x. and xi., between the sixth and seventh trumpet blasts. This, it may be suggested, is the key to the intricate verses, viii. 1–6. Surprise is sometimes expressed that John should first relate how he saw the **seven trumpets being given to the seven angels who stand before God,** and then, before they sound their blasts, insert his account of the offering of **prayers of all the saints upon the golden altar.** 3 It would have been in accordance with apocalyptic tradition to assign the offering of the prayers to the seven angels in verse 2. Thus, in the well-known passage, Tobit xii. 15, we read, ' I am Raphael, one of the seven holy angels which present the prayers of the saints, and go in before the Holy One.' But having reserved the seven angels for the heralding of the new series of woes, John is obliged to introduce **another angel** for the offering of the prayers. We may be sure, however, that the arrangement, for all its apparent awkwardness, is made deliberately as part of a carefully conceived plan. This is John's method of insisting on a truth of vital interest to the Church. The End will not, indeed, cannot come until the prayers of the saints have been offered. Not only does God hear them, not only do they reach the Presence itself 4 (here symbolized by the **smoke of the incense,** which in the old dispensation was the visual token of divine acceptance) ; those prayers are the actual means whereby the End is brought to pass. That is why John now thinks of heaven as a temple, symbolized by the **altar** at which worship is centralized, as well as a royal court with a **throne** ; for he can freely interchange or combine his symbols according to his purpose. Frequently when he describes the last terrible punishment meted out to the ungodly, he indicates its divine sanction by using the time-honoured ideas associated with the pre-Christian temple (cf. especially xi. 19, xiv. 17, xv. 5–8). So it 5 is much more than an incidental detail that **the angel took the** *same* **censer** previously used to lay the prayers of all the saints upon the golden altar, and **then filled it with fire from the altar, and poured it on the earth.** In vi. 9–11 John assured the martyrs that they had not died in vain, that their blood would be avenged when their number was completed. Now he teaches a lesson as important in life as in death ; no prayer was futile. The prayers of all the saints (and perhaps John is here including the yearnings of all the faithful in every age till his own) were the very means of encompassing the doom of the ungodly that oppressed them. Clearly it never occurs to him that this could be in the least out of harmony with God's character. The time had come when heaven and hell, righteousness and wickedness, the Church and the world, stood over against each other in complete antithesis. God's holiness could be vindicated in one way only—the punishment of the wicked and the rewarding of the faithful. That, in fact, is brought to pass. The **fire from the altar**—that same altar where the prayers had been presented—now poured on the earth, inflicts utter destruction ; the prayers are answered. Now we know why the seven angels were given their trumpets, but did not sound them until another angel had performed his essential preliminary task. Dr. Beckwith has well expressed John's thought (*The Apocalypse of John*, p. 550) : ' The angels receive the trumpets at the opening of the scene, but they stay the use of them till the tokens in the earth (verse 5) show that the prayers of the saints have been graciously received.' It may be suggested that we can say more—that the seven angels do not sound the trumpets until now because John knows full well the established apocalyptic tradition that a trumpet would announce the End, and because, in his view, the acceptance of the prayers of all the saints brings, in actual fact, the End. All things considered, there is no anticlimax in viii. 1, for the End does not occur there, but in verse 5. The **peals of thunder, loud blasts, flashes of lightning, and an earthquake** are John's formula, as it were, for the world's dissolution ; we shall read it again in xi. 13–19, only with further details, especially about the earthquake, the significance of which is at last fully explained in the account of the shattering of the great City which includes all the cities of the nations (xvi. 19). Then, because the End has come, **the seven angels with the seven trumpets prepared to blow their blasts,** and so we learn fresh information about it. 6

It may be asked why John makes no reference to a belief which, by the time he was writing, must have been firmly established in the Church through Christian tradition alone, quite apart from its earlier origins—the belief that the last trumpet would be the signal for the resurrection of the faithful (cf. especially St. Matt. xxiv. 31 ; 1 Thess. iv. 16 ; 1 Cor. xv. 52, 53). John does not forget or ignore this belief either. There are seven trumpet blasts, and, as always in his literary scheme, the last of the seven is of outstanding importance. In xi. 15–18 we read that when the seventh angel blows, the angelic choir thanks God that

> ' the time has come for the dead to be judged,
> the time for rewarding thy servants the prophets,
> and the saints who reverence thy name, both low and high.'

How was that to be accomplished ? By a resurrection. Just

as the two witnesses heard a loud voice (cf. ' the loud summons,' 1 Thess. iv. 16) from heaven telling them, ' Come up
here ' (xi. 12), so (later) we are told of the ' first resurrection '
for the saints who share in the millennium (xx. 6).

THE SEVEN TRUMPETS
(viii. 6–xi. 19)

viii. 6–13 : Four Angels blow their Trumpets : Partial Destruction of the World

6 The seven angels with the seven trumpets prepared to blow
7   their blasts. The first blew, and *there came hail and fire*
    mixed *with blood*, falling *on the earth* ; a third of the earth
    was burnt up, a third of the trees were burnt up, and all the
8   green grass was burnt up. The second angel blew, and
    what looked like a huge *mountain on fire* was hurled into
    the sea ; a third of the sea *turned blood*, a third of the
9   creatures in the sea—the living creatures—perished, and a
10   third of the ships were destroyed. The third angel blew,
    and *a* huge *star* blazing like a torch *dropped out of the sky*,
11   dropped on a third of the rivers and on the fountains (the
    name of the star is Wormwood) ; a third of the waters
    became wormwood, and many people died of the waters,
12   because they had turned bitter. The fourth angel blew ;
    and a stroke fell on a third of the sun, a third of the moon,
    and a third of the stars, so as to darken one third of them,
    withdrawing light from a third of the day and likewise of
    the night.
13 Then I looked, and I heard an eagle flying in mid-heaven with a
    loud cry, 'Woe, woe, woe to the dwellers on earth, for the
    rest of the trumpet-blasts that the three angels are about
    to blow ! '

John's practical purpose in this passage can be easily over-looked. Since the symbolism can be more readily visualized than in many of his other visions, there is a tendency to con-centrate attention on the pictorial details. The results have been often unfortunate. For example, the plagues have been subjected to a close scrutiny, as though John were giving a scientific treatise on the last things. Commentators have claimed to discover inconsistencies and contradictions ; they point out that in verse 7 John declares that **all the green grass was burnt up,** and yet in ix. 4 the locusts are told not to harm the grass. Again, in viii. 12 **a third of the stars** are darkened, although the whole sky had been already denuded of stars at the opening of the sixth seal (vi. 13). Was John forgetful, or so independent as to ignore such inconsistencies, or, finally, has the text been tampered with ? The difficulties are largely imaginary, even if we consider John's tempestuous imagery from the cold, scientific point of view adopted by the critics. Dr. Beckwith has explained (*Apocalypse of John*, p. 556) that when John says that *all* the grass was burnt up, he means all the grass in that third of the earth subjected to the hail of fire. Similarly, it could be argued that for all his sweeping generalization in vi. 13, John does not say precisely that every single star dropped to earth ; or, again, that in any case, although the trumpets and seals series are complementary, it does not follow that the results of the opening of the sixth seal and the first trumpet blast are parallel incidents—a third of the stars may have fallen in an earlier catastrophe, the whole sky being denuded later. But such arguments are beside the point, and to subject John to petty fault-finding as though he were writing an *Old Moore's Almanack* is to show a failure to understand his purpose and method. The fact is that John was not in the least concerned with unimportant details. It was not the bare events that he wished his readers to consider, magnificent and terrible as they are when re-created by his fertile mind. What they *signified* absorbed his attention—what message they conveyed to the Church. Much of the imagery in these plagues is borrowed from Old Testa-ment prophecy and apocalyptic traditions. It was a common belief that the Messiah's coming would be preceded by disasters in the natural world. But what comfort or assurance did John expect Christians to receive from this account of destruction ? He never slavishly repeats traditional ideas without good reason, without some thought of strengthening his pastoral message. Yet it is clear that none of these woes inflicted at the sounding of the first six of the seven trumpet blasts concerned the Church *directly*. There is nothing about the persecution of the faithful by the ungodly in these woes ; that will be described in chaps. xi.–xiii. Indeed, Christians are not mentioned at all from viii. 6 to the end of chap. ix. The explanation is that John is here giving God's indictment of humanity in general, quite apart from the Church. REVELATION is, in large part, an account of the world's punishment and destruction ; and the writer is at pains to make clear that the world deserves this terrible fate because of its inherent wickedness. It is true that he regards its hostility to Christ and His witnesses as its crowning infamy ; but he is aware of the not less important fact that moral corruption is the cause of that hostility. The whole passage is John's equivalent to St. Paul's indictment of the world in Rom. i. 18–32 ; and the underlying principle is that God the Creator destroys His handiwork in order to demonstrate His sovereignty to those who depend on Him for their existence and yet refuse to acknowledge Him.

6 John thus describes in the first four trumpet blasts how the woes fall on God's creation in its fourfold aspect (cf. especially xiv. 7) of earth (7) and sea (8–9) and fresh waters (10–11) and sky (12). The earth is devastated by a storm of **hail** : it was popularly supposed that the second deliverance of God's people would be preceded like the first, from Egypt, by a series of similar plagues ; but now there would be added horrors—

7 **hail and fire mixed with blood,** by which the **earth** (soil) and **trees** and **grass** (common types representing all vegetation) would be **burnt up** over **a third** of the earth's surface. **A third** was the conventional term for a large but not the greater part (cf. note on verse 11) ; and by this John means to explain that these terrible afflictions would not be universal—for then could

no flesh be saved—and their sole purpose is to give those who escape them warnings of so forcible a character that no vestige of excuse for refusal to repent would be left. The thought of ix. 20 is the burden of all the six plagues alike, and is a testimony to John's conception of God as long-suffering with those who oppose Him—a testimony which is sometimes forgotten when the severity of his justice seems to offend. Admittedly, John appears to entertain no hope that the ungodly would repent (cf. xvi. 11), but at least he was certain that no opportunity of inducing them to do so would be neglected. He would have agreed heartily with Amos' description of God's tragic fourfold protest over His rebellious people whom punishment would not correct : ' And yet, says the Eternal, yet you would not come back to me. So now I will deal with you ' (Amos iv. 1–13).

The result of the **second** trumpet blast is again a combina- 8 tion of an Egyptian plague with later apocalyptic beliefs. Ideas similar to that of the **huge mountain on fire** are found in Enoch xviii. 13, ' I saw there seven stars like great burning mountains,' and in the Sibylline Oracles v. 158, ' Then shall come a great star from heaven into the divine sea' (see also p. 334). It is a picturesque way of explaining that these disasters are of heavenly origin, that the God who punishes creation is its Creator. The horror of the result is striking—a large part of the sea **turned blood,** destroying a corresponding proportion 9 of fish and shipping. It has been pointed out that in living memory, as well as in past history including John's own lifetime, volcanic action has had effects similar to the second woe. Burning coals have fallen from great heights into the sea, giving it the appearance of blood. In certain instances fish have been poisoned by the chemical action. Such research is valuable in suggesting actual experiences which may account psychologically for the material of John's visions ; but it is essential to remember that for John his symbols were not picturesque details added for effect. He believed that a large part of the sea would, quite literally, turn to blood, as it did before the first deliverance in Egypt. Blood seems to have had a peculiar horror for John ; this reference, and that of xvi. 2–7, suggest that he considered such a punishment fitting for those who had so callously shed the blood of the innocent (vi. 10).

10 After the sea, the fresh water is attacked ; **a third of the waters became wormwood,** with the result that **many people died (many people** is John's own definition of **a third).** This, too, is probably an echo of the **bitter** waters forced upon the 11 rebellious Israelites in the wilderness. **Wormwood** was believed by the ancient world to be poisonous because of its taste (cf. Jer. ix. 15, xxiii. 15; Lam. iii. 15, 19) and it is named quite simply from its effects (cf. ix. 11). Like the other plagues, John sees this to have divine sanction ; the poison falls in the form of a **huge star, blazing like a torch dropped out of the sky :** the vision is quite natural to John because of his belief in angels, good and evil, and that angels often appeared as stars (cf. i. 20, and especially ix. 1, below, where he refers quite simply to the star as ' he '). It is not impossible that John selects the rivers and fountains for special punishment because of the widespread pagan worship of the spirits that were believed to inhabit and control them (cf. the reference to dæmon-worship in ix. 21) : but it is more likely that his purpose is to punish men for their ungodliness rather than to punish the spirits they worshipped. He tells of the plague mainly to point to its results on humanity—**many people died of the waters ;** in the parallel passage, xvi. 5, he evidently conceives that the angel of the waters is in harmony with his Creator, for the same angel announces his approval of the punishment on the wicked.

The fourth angel heralds the partial darkening of the normal 12 **light** of the heavenly bodies by day and by night. As in the rest of the passage, John's words must not be subjected to minute scrutiny. His method is to give the general impression of the horror of darkness similar to that of the ninth Egyptian plague, and in fulfilment of a common prophecy that the last days would be accompanied by this terror (e.g. Amos v. 18 ; Joel ii. 1, 2 ; St. Mark xiii. 24, etc.). Each of the first four woes is restricted in scope to ensure that their reformative purpose is brought home to the rest of mankind. Moreover, they are but the beginning of travail—the other three plagues are to be much worse. In each of the three series of the seals, trumpets, and bowls, John's plan is to divide them into groups of four and three, or, rather, four and two and one, the seventh being always separated from the rest to emphasize its supreme importance. So now he indicates the greater dreadfulness of the rest of the remaining three plagues by assigning their dramatic proclamation to an **eagle flying in mid-heaven.** 13 Here is an excellent example of the working of John's mind, and its spontaneous fertility in producing symbols. The emphasis which we have just mentioned so coldly and abstractly, John expresses warmly and concretely in the **loud cry** of the eagle. This is not to say that John mechanically invented the symbol. His mind was such that he would certainly see the eagle ; that is how such an idea naturally formed itself in his consciousness. An **eagle** was a bird of ill-omen, in the Scriptures as well as in common superstition—a suitable harbinger of the three **woes** about to fall upon the world. It was **flying in mid-heaven**—that is, in the open sky (cf. xiv. 6), because the disasters it announced were to fall not on a part of the earth only, as in the case of the first four woes, but on all **the dwellers on earth,** the heathen gentiles as distinct from the Church (xi. 1) : by this phrase John always means the whole wide world (cf. xiii. 8, 14). Although in ix. 18 we learn that even in the fifth and sixth woes not everyone is killed, it is plain that everyone is affected by them, everyone, that is, except the sealed—and this is an indication of their special character already heralded by the eagle's cry.

ix. 1-11 : The Fifth Woe : a Plague of Dæmon Locusts

The fifth angel blew, and I saw a Star which had dropped from   1
    heaven to earth ; he was given the key of the pit of the
    abyss, and he opened the pit of the abyss, *till smoke poured* 2
    out of the pit, *like the smoke of a* huge *furnace, till the sun*
    and the air were *darkened* by the smoke from the pit. And 3
    out of the smoke came *locusts on the earth ;* they were granted

4   power like the power wielded by scorpions on earth, but they were told not to harm *the grass* on earth *nor any green thing nor any tree,* only such human beings as had not *the*

5   *seal* of God *upon their foreheads ;* these they were allowed, not to kill but to torture, for five months—and their torture was like the torture of a scorpion when it stings a man.

6   In those days *men will seek death,*
        and not find it :
    they will long to die,
        but death flies from them.

7 *The appearance* of the locusts *resembled horses* armed *for battle ;*
8   on their heads were sort of crowns like gold ; their faces were like human faces, their hair like women's hair, and
9   *their teeth like lions' fangs ;* they had scales like iron coats of mail ; the whirring of their wings was *like the noise of*
10   *many chariots* charging into battle ; their tails and their stings were like scorpions', and their power of hurting men
11   for five months lay in their tails ; they had a king over them, the angel of the abyss—his Hebrew name is Abaddon, but in Greek he is called Apollyon.

    The first and second of the last three woes announced by
1 the **fifth angel** are different from the four preceding woes not only in their severity, not only in affecting all humanity except the sealed (whereas the previous plagues fell on only a third), but still more in being inflicted directly by dæmonic agents. The greater seriousness of these two disasters, heralded by the eagle's loud cry to the whole world, is indicated also by the more elaborate measures by which they are set in motion. When the fifth angel blew, John saw **a Star which had dropped from heaven to earth.** We saw that the star in viii. 10 was probably an angel—apocalyptists, like the pagan world in general, assumed that all stars were celestial spirits, some good and some evil ; but in the third woe John was content to describe the result quite briefly. Greater detail is necessary for these greater plagues. It is shown that their origin and character prove that they are due to evil spirits, controlled and

commissioned by God. This, in itself, was food for thought for Christians, dismayed by the power of wickedness in the last days. Time after time John explains that iniquity is multiplied only because the pent-up forces have been unleashed by divine sanction to fulfil God's will against the ungodly (cf. vi., vii. 1–3, ix. 13–15). That **the Star** of ix. 1 is an evil spirit is proved by its origin—it **had dropped from heaven,** an expression equivalent to ' thrown down ' (cf. xii. 9 and St. Luke x. 18), as well as by its special function—**he opened the pit of the abyss.** 2 The underworld, the gloomy region beneath the earth, supposed in Old Testament times to be the realm of all departed spirits, beyond God's rule, was for John **an abyss,** confined to evil spirits only (the martyrs were beneath the altar, vi. 9). In accordance with apocalyptic tradition, which teemed with angels in their various degrees, certain angels were entrusted with the guardianship of important places (cf. xx. 1), or of special destructive powers (cf. vii. 1–3), or of companies of their own number (cf. ix. 14–15). The firmness of John's faith that everything, whether good or evil, was in God's hands—a faith indispensable to the Church of his day, perplexed by persecution—is as noteworthy in his almost unconscious allusions to that divine sovereignty as in his deliberate arguments : the angel-Star **was given the key** that set in motion the fifth woe, just as the locusts **were granted** 3 **power** to torture men (cf. the way the Beast ' was allowed ' to blaspheme, and given authority over the world, xiii. 5–7) ; they **were told** to limit their destructive activity, and **were allowed** to exercise it only for the strictly limited period of five months. As the successive visions were unfolded, so the readers of REVELATION learned more and more about the significance of God's rule described in chaps. i., iv., and v.

For his description of the locust plague, John depended mainly on two Old Testament passages—Exod. x. 12–20 and Joel i.-ii. As he gazed at the **smoke** that **poured out of the pit** (an idea naturally associated with the abyss by those who in that region often saw volcanic vapours issuing from underground caverns), so dense that **the sun and the air were darkened,** his visionary mind would probably recollect Joel's striking account of a locust plague that had devastated the neighbourhood of Jerusalem :

> ' Sun and moon are dark,
> The stars have ceased to shine.'

Or he thought of the swarm sent to punish Pharaoh that ' covered the face of the whole land, till the country was black with them.' Of that plague, the writer of Exodus said it was ' such as never had been before, such as never will be again,' and John had no intention of falsifying the statement by predicting even thicker swarms in the last days. Indeed, in the last three woes he is no longer concerned with destructive action against Nature ; that was the theme of viii. 6–12. Now his thought is different. He is elucidating what we should call the *ethical* significance of the coming troubles, the *spiritual* values that were being determined by the last plagues. That is why he ingeniously asserts that these locusts were expressly told not to commit the destructive mischief in the natural world that they would perpetrate under normal conditions :
4 they were told not to harm the grass or earth or any green thing nor any tree. Plainly we are meant to regard this woe as being essentially different in character from the four previous plagues. Why does John furnish the dæmon locusts with such 5 hideous powers to inflict pain like the torture of a scorpion when it stings a man ? It has been suggested that this was a refinement of cruelty, devised by John to compensate in advance those Christians whom pagan humanity was soon to subject to inhuman treatment ; that he was forewarning them that the death to be inflicted on the martyrs would be later coveted in vain by their murderers, as a release from their torment :

6
> In those days men will seek death,
> and not find it :
> they will long to die,
> but death flies from them.

The suggestion is not convincing. Not that John is incapable of insisting on the direst punishment his mind can devise to justify God's holiness and to vindicate the martyrs' sufferings (cf. xiv. 10–12). But in chap. ix. the Church hardly comes into the picture, though, needless to say, every word is written for the sake of the Church. His object, for the moment, is to vindicate God's righteousness in itself, for its own sake and by its own standards. He wishes to prove that God gives the ungodly every possible chance to reform; that He shirks no measure, however drastic, that might conceivably persuade them to avoid the ultimate doom of the impenitent. The death that comes catastrophically to a large part of men at the blast of the first four trumpets gives the victims no opportunity to repent ; the lesson could be learnt only by those who escaped and witnessed the sudden destruction of their fellow-men. The remorse of the doomed is too late for penitence (xi. 13). But the fifth plague comes to all—that is, to all such human beings as had not the seal of God upon their foreheads—and it comes in this world, while there is still time for amendment. Nor is the torture a momentary experience : it lasts for five months, a period sufficient to test its results (the destructive power of locusts is limited to the five dry summer months).

It is tempting to suggest that in view of the peculiar character of this woe, its dæmonic origin and agency, the forceful transference of the normal power of locusts against Nature to the causing of human affliction, the restriction of the plague to the pagan world as distinct from the Church for a limited period—that, in view of all this, John had in mind the torturing of the pagan *conscience*. Certainly he visualized the time when the ungodly would experience remorse (i. 7, xi. 13, etc.) ; and the avowed purpose of the woes is to bring their victims to repentance (ix. 20). But it is doubtful if John considered that the wicked had sufficient capacity for reformation, enough good to enable them to respond to anything but physical pain. He is convinced beforehand that even the locusts' torture, even the hideous punishment of the sixth woe, will not have the desired result. One consideration only is in John's mind as he predicts the misery inflicted by the Creator on His creatures—God's character : by exhausting every attempt to bring them to a better mind, God demonstrates His sovereignty, vindicates His holiness, and justifies His final sentence of doom. This same principle constrains the prophet to describe in detail the stark terror of the locust plague. It is the kind of passage in which John is able to use his superb imagination to the full. Joel had described the locust plague with telling effect :

> ' A host has invaded our land,
> powerful and numberless,
> their teeth the teeth of a lion
> with the fangs of a lioness ;

> ' They look like horses,
> they run like war-horses,
> as chariots rattle,
> they leap on the hilltops,
> like flames that crackle, consuming the straw,
> like a vast army in battle-array.'
>
> (Joel i. 6–7, ii. 4–5.)

Many of John's readers would remember Joel's words ; now they were to learn that the dæmonic locusts would be equally ruthless in their attack on the ungodly. In the vision their 7 appearance, too, resembled horses armed for battle—in shape the insect is not unlike a horse. The sort of crowns like gold on their heads, a feature added by John, signified their inescapable power to fulfil their mission (cf. vi. 2). For the rest of his description, he may have depended on the similes used by Arabian poets (see Moffatt, *Expositor's Greek Testament*, p. 407), though for the teeth like lion's fangs, and the whirring of their wings . . . like the noise of many chariots charging into battle, he had to seek no further than Joel's prophecy. The actual appearance of locusts is sufficient to 8 account for the likening of their long antennæ to women's 9 hair, and their scales to iron coats of mail. In any case, John's account is so straightforward and vivid that comment is superfluous. His sole purpose is to stress the severity of the plague, and the impossibility of escaping from it, and the fact that it was to be an evil instrument, executing God's decree, and under His control. Being dæmons, the locusts were inevitably associated in John's mind with serpents (cf. ix. 19), so that he carefully explains that **their power of hurting men for** 10 **five months lay in their tails,** not, as in the case of ordinary locusts, in their voracious jaws. And with typical determination to make his point clear beyond shadow of doubt, he ends the fifth plague as he began it by indicating its dæmonic character : here was no accidental calamity—**they had a king** 11 **over them, the angel of the abyss,** the Star-angel referred to in ix. 1, divinely controlled and directed.

But why should John trouble to give the angel's name, in both **Hebrew** and **Greek** ? Not, as in viii. 11, merely to signify the effect of the plague. There the name was necessary because of the prophet's extreme brevity in a relatively unimportant passage, whereas eleven verses have been devoted to the fifth plague—twice as many as to all the first four plagues. Some have suggested that John was making a gibe against the heathen god Apollo, whom the pagan world venerated, and one of whose symbols was a locust. It would be effective sarcasm, especially as Caligula and Nero, both notorious for their blasphemy and persecution, were devoted to that deity, as Antiochus Epiphanes, their prototype, had been before them. But his main thought was probably associated with the Hebrew personification of Death and Hell as the place of destruction, under his title **Abaddon.** In ix. 6 we saw how the tortured heathen ' will seek death and not find it ' ; but that will be for only a limited period, the five months allotted to the dæmon locusts. Death and Hell awaited the impenitent after this opportunity of repentance. In both the Hebrew and the Greek name John's readers would see the symbol of the impending destruction that awaited the ungodly at ' the time for destroying the destroyers of the earth ' (xi. 18).

ix. 12–21 : THE SIXTH WOE : INVASION OF TWO HUNDRED MILLION CAVALRY

The first woe has passed : 12
two woes are still to come.

13 Then the sixth angel blew ; and I heard a voice from the four
14   horns of the golden altar before God, telling the sixth angel
    with the trumpet, 'Let loose the four angels who are bound
15   at *the great river Euphrates.*' So the four angels were
    unloosed, who had been kept ready for that hour and day
16   and month and year, to kill the third of men. And the
    number of the troops of their cavalry was two hundred
17   millions (I heard what was their number). And this is how
    the horses and their riders looked in my vision : they wore
    coats of mail red as fire, dark-blue as jacinth and yellow as
    smoke ; the horses' heads were like lions' heads, and
    from their mouths poured fire and smoke and brimstone.
18 By these three plagues the third of men were killed, by the
    fire, the smoke, and the brimstone, that poured out of their
19   mouths ; for the power of the horses lies in their mouths
    —and also in their tails (their tails are like serpents, they
    have heads, and it is with their heads that they hurt).
20 Yet the rest of mankind, who were not killed by these
    plagues, did not repent of *the works of their hands* and give
    up worshipping *daemons* and *idols of gold and silver and*
    brass and stone and wood, which cannot see nor hear nor
21   *stir ;* nor did they repent of their murders, *their magic*
    spells, their sexual vice, their thefts.

12   John reminds us that only two woes are still to come ; in
viii. 13 the eagle heralded the last three, and in xi. 14 the last
of these three woes is announced. It is his way of persistently
warning his readers that the woes become worse as the End
draws near, and also of heightening the dramatic effect of the
final dissolution. The sixth woe, like the other two in this
last series of three, is described in much greater detail than
the previous four ; and its importance is stressed in the
elaborate preparation by which it is brought into action. The
heralding angel is told to loose the four angels who restrain
the vast army of cavalry that executes this penultimate
chastisement. Once again John alludes incidentally but
effectively to the Church's share in the execution of God's
monitory plagues : the command to the sixth trumpeter is given

by a voice from the four horns of the golden altar before God. 13
The phrase is a sermon in itself to ' the discerning ' (xiii. 18,
xvii. 9), to ' anyone who has an ear ' (ii. 7, etc.). They will
recall John's earlier reference to ' the golden altar in front of
the throne ' (viii. 1–6)—that is, as now stated, before God ;
they will know that the four horns (i.e. the four corners) of
the altar, signify strength, God's strength, His almighty power
expressed in action ; they will recognize that four (like seven)
represents *complete* power ; and, finally, when they remember
how the angel had offered the prayers of the saints upon that
altar, they will be assured that those prayers have been
accepted and will be answered in the coming demonstration
of righteous indignation against the ungodly. But how
clumsily and prosily we are obliged to think and speak about
truths which John visualized briefly and clearly in symbols
radiant with meaning !

Commentators are agreed that the four angels who are 14
bound at the great river Euphrates are not the same as the
four angels in vii. 1. These are ' at the four corners of the
earth,' those in chap. ix. are located in one place ; these are
told not to inflict their destructive powers, the others are
unloosed for that very purpose. But is the argument decisive ?
Is it certain that two distinct groups of angels are intended ?
At least the similarity is such that it is found necessary to
disprove their identity. Now John, for all the subtlety of his
mind, and his freedom in using the symbols with which it
teems, is usually lucid and consistent. No one can justly
accuse him of confusion or carelessness. Seldom does he give
even simple minds an excuse for misinterpreting his message
—and probably no one knew better than he how simple were
many of the faithful to whom he wrote ! For this reason alone
we may doubt whether he would have called attention to two
similar but separate groups of angels without making their
identity clear ; whereas if, as we hope to show, they are
identical, elaborate definition was unnecessary. Not that the
point we are now discussing is of vital consequence, but it is
arguable that here we have an interesting example of the way
John recapitulates his message in successive visions, and yet

expands it at the same time. In so doing, he succeeds in giving the impression of a continuous forward development towards the End which has been repeatedly demonstrated in its various phases. The significance of the command to the four angels in vii. 1 is to restrain their destructive mission. But why, and for how long ? The commanding angel gives the reason explicitly—the martyrs have not yet been sealed ; they must first be protected by the divine token, just as God's people were distinguished to protect them from the destroying angel in the last great Egyptian plague. The restraint was imposed only until that safeguard had been made. But in chap. ix. the sealing *has been done* ; John immediately described it and its results in chap. vii., and he refers to it again plainly in chap. ix. where he tells us that the dæmonic locusts were allowed power against ' such human beings as had not the seal of God upon their foreheads ' (ix. 4). If this is the case in the fifth woe, why should it be otherwise in the sixth ? It is because the martyrs are sealed that the bound angels can be **let loose.** It is for this only that they had been stayed. Nothing else warranted the postponement of God's almost desperate attempts to reform mankind : they had been 15 **kept ready** for that exact date, **that hour and day and month and year,** so perfect was the divine control over creation's destiny.

But, it may be argued, this does not answer the other difficulty—the difference of locality : the four angels in vii. 1 are ' at the four corners of the earth,' those in ix. 14 are ' at the great river Euphrates.' The difficulty is more apparent than real. John is always careful to explain real problems, but he is never pedantically precise. His mind is not the slave of the symbols it creates. In vii. 1 his purpose is to give the impression of impending destruction over the whole wide world. What better symbol could he use than that of the four winds, restrained by four angels, acting under divine orders, ready at a given signal to belch their fury ? In chap. ix., also, John is describing destructive woes that are universal in scope, but now he adds a new thought. The sixth woe has its origin at the great river Euphrates. Why ? Because, both in prophecy (cf. Isa. vii. 20, viii. 7, Jer. xlvi. 10) and through the bitter experience of history, the terror of world invasion was expected to break from that neighbourhood, the Empire's eastern boundary. May not this be one of the reasons why John, with his usual forward glance, tells us in chap. vii. that he saw the angel, who commands the four destructive winds to restrain temporarily their mission, 'rise up from the east' —that is, the locality where the restraint was to be withdrawn as soon as the sealing has been completed (cf. xvi. 12)? May not this also explain why there are still **four** angels in ix. 14, although, as far as the plague is concerned, the number is of no significance (as it is in vii. 1), for they do not command the cavalry they had restrained? And, finally, may not this be the reason why John refers quite simply to **the** four angels, assuming that their identity will be recognized as being the same as in chap. vii.? The question, however, hardly deserves the attention we have given it, except as an illustration of John's allusiveness ; and with that, an example of the futility of trying to confine him to precise definitions.

The reader should be excused if for a moment he forgets John's pastoral purpose in describing the sixth plague, and, instead, lingers in wonder at its spectacle. Indeed, John intends to impress and terrify, and succeeds marvellously. It is a triumph of literary art. The general effect of his pen picture is as magnificent as anything in REVELATION. The invading army's vastness and horror alternately fascinate and paralyse the imagination. The four angels, tearing frantically at their restraint, are at last **unloosed,** and as they leap forward are quickly blotted from sight by the cavalry that follow. **Two hundred millions** of them charged to the attack. **I heard** 16 **what was their number,** John says, meaning that the information was given to him by an angel, since he could not possibly count such a host (cf. vii. 1). Their appearance was as frightful as their number was overwhelming. The **coats of mail** pro- 17 tecting the horses and their riders were coloured like the poisonous fumes that poured from their mouths, glowing with a combination of **red** like **fire, dark-blue as jacinth** corresponding with the **smoke,** and **yellow** like the sulphurous vapours of the brimstone. What seems a weird fairy tale to us was a dreaded reality to John's readers. Fire-spouting monsters were common figures in mythology ; and the three destructive 18 plagues by which **the third of men were killed** were all associated in popular superstition with the hellish underworld, whence, in the natural world, volcanoes belched their fury, and to which the damned were sent for punishment. In fact, the cavalry were giving the wicked a foretaste in this world of what was to be their everlasting torment in the next (cf. xiv. 10, xix. 20, xxi. 8). Such dire chastisement must inevitably cause widespread mortality ; the cavalry **had been kept ready . . . to kill the third of men.** The slain, however, are not John's main concern. As in the first four previous plagues, his thought is still the impenitence of the ungodly survivors. They see a great part of their fellow-men meet a violent death, but they are unmoved. Not even though they themselves suffer torture by the dæmonic locusts and the cavalry can they be brought to a better mind. This is the thought underlying John's some- 19 what awkward explanation that **the power of the horses lies in their mouths—and also in their tails.** He has the torture of the dæmon locusts in mind (ix. 10) ; the sixth plague is an intensification of the fifth.

It is of small consequence whether John's vision here depended on his knowledge of the Parthian custom of the binding of their horses tails so as to make them **like serpents,** or whether he was alluding to the snaky creatures on the great pagan altar at Pergamum (ii. 12) ; dæmons were commonly given serpent-like tails in ancient sculpture. All John wishes to express is their devilish origin, in anticipation of themes he intends to expand more than once in later visions—that the ungodly would be attacked by the same evil forces as those with which they have afflicted the Church ; and that in the last days the whole world would be ravaged by the destructive fury of wickedness, unloosed by God for this very purpose, until the time had come for the devil's agents themselves to be destroyed (cf. xvi. 12–16, xix. 11–21).

Constantly, however, when reading the account of the plagues, we must remind ourselves that John was not writing for the sake of the ungodly, not even to warn **the rest of mankind** 20 **who were not killed by these plagues.** Not a ray of hope that they might repent illumines the darkness of an evil world fit only for annihilation. Still, after this sixfold warning, they would be worshipping dæmons, those same evil spirits commissioned by God to torment them. Still they would be worshipping **the works of their hands . . . idols of gold and silver and brass and stone and wood, which cannot see nor hear nor stir.** John had in mind the innumerable pagan shrines of Asia Minor, where the false priests and prophets persuaded the idolatrous to bow down before the figures claimed to be the dwelling-places of the gods they represented. He thought of the increasing number of temples devoted partly or exclusively to the emperor-cult. He thought, too, of the abominable moral corruption (always associated with idolatry by the Old Testament prophets and the early Church) that disfigured society—the general disregard for the cardinal principles of the moral code inherited by the Church from the old dispensation. Neither would the heathen repent of these—**their** 21 **murders . . . their sexual vice, their thefts**—all of which the Christian was pledged to abhor ; nor yet of **their magic spells,** that love of sorcery by which the dwellers on earth were being seduced (cf. xiii. 13, 14, xxi. 8, xxii. 15 ; Gal. v. 20), and which invariably led to sexual vice. No, they would still cling to their old ways, says John. Nothing will make them **repent.** The last warning is unheeded ; the final opportunity is spurned. Why, then, does he write about them ? Because in this world of impenitence was the Church. In this world it must live and suffer temptation and persecution. Here, too, the faithful must witness and the martyrs must die, before the End could come. John will recount the Church's fate in his next visions (cf. chaps. x.–xiii.), but meanwhile he has done what he can to leave his readers under no delusion about the world in which they must await the approaching storm.

Introduction to Chapters X. and XI.

To understand John's purpose fully at this point, we must note carefully not only that he uses Dan. xii. as his chief source, but that he reinterprets it (cf. p. 74). Indeed, since he obviously assumes that his readers will be aware that he is referring to the earlier prophecy, he must have intended that they should recognize also that he was explaining how Daniel's prophecy was to be fulfilled in the near future. Daniel had been told to keep his prophecy hidden from the world : ' And now, O Daniel, keep all this a close secret, and keep the book shut as a secret, till the crisis at the end ' (Dan. xii. 4). Now, *we* know that the writer of Daniel was using a device common in apocalyptic writings. Since it was believed that prophecy had ceased, the only means of ensuring the acceptance of a new contribution was to attribute it to some ancient prophet. In Dan. xii. 4 the writer is explaining why this prophecy had been so long unknown : Daniel had been told to hide it until the crisis for which it had been written was at hand. But this is a discovery of modern scholarship. John and his readers would have no reason to doubt that Daniel had written the book. What, then, were they to make of the injunction to secrecy ? It could not refer to the book itself, for it had been long known to the faithful. There was only one explanation. Daniel's message had been secreted in symbols which had never been understood before, but were now revealed to John for the Church, the faithful who were willing to lay to heart what was written. The crisis of which Daniel had been fore-warned was at the very doors. The symbolic three years and a half which must elapse before ' the power of him who shattered the sacred people shall be over ' (Dan. xii. 7) was about to begin. The faithless would not understand : ' none of the evil shall understand things, it is the pious who understand.' To them, to those who could keep themselves stainless and loyal, the secrets of Daniel were at last to be disclosed. For them the strong angel offered to John a small scroll that was no longer shut but open.

We may be sure, then, that chaps. x. and xi., which intrude so forcibly and, at first sight, so awkwardly, in the trumpet series, have a very special message for the Church. It will be remembered that after describing how unparalleled disorders shook the frame of the universe at the opening of the sixth seal, John deliberately turned aside to set before the eyes of the faithful two pictures : first, the sealing of the hundred and forty-four thousand—the Elect, the prospective martyrs ; and, secondly (the outcome of the sealing), martyrs in possession of their heavenly reward. He was told by a Presbyter that the event which intervened between these two occasions was 'the great Distress.' At that point John revealed nothing more about the ordeal before the martyrs. Now, however, he has arrived at the point when he wishes to say more about the great Distress. He chooses the most dramatic moment of his story for the telling of his most important news. The sixth trumpet has blown ; its woe has followed. We are waiting for the strident music of the last trumpet—the music which is to 'untune the sky.' At this moment John chooses to hold us in suspense, as he did when we were waiting for the opening of the seventh seal. The episode which separates the sixth and seventh trumpet blasts so significantly is, in fact, not merely parallel to the episode which separates the portents of the sixth seal from those of the seventh ; it is in all ways complementary. What is left untold in one is told in the other. Nothing but the most compelling of reasons could have induced the seer to thrust these episodes into his septiform literary scheme. In no sense is he digressing. The events predicted in both passages form an essential prelude to the End : hence their place in REVELATION, immediately before the first two brief descriptions (viii. 5 and xi. 19) of the portents of the End. The gospel must be published in every part of the earth before the End can come. John shows how the Church performs her task, how her most loyal and devoted sons are martyred. This is the burden of the two chapters, which tell one continuous story, the first forming a solemn introduction to the second.

X. 1–7 : PREFACE TO THE ACCOUNT OF THE GREAT DISTRESS : THE VISION OF THE ANGEL WITH THE SMALL SCROLL

1 Then I saw another strong angel descend from heaven; he was clad in a cloud, with a rainbow over his head, his face like the sun, his limbs like columns of fire, and a small scroll open
2 in his hand.   He set his right foot on the sea, his left upon
3 the earth, and shouted aloud like a lion roaring ; and at his shout the seven thunders gave voice.   After the seven thunders had spoken, I was going to write it down ; but I heard a voice from heaven saying, ' *Seal up* what the seven
5 thunders have said, do not write it.'   Then the angel I saw standing on the sea and the earth *raised his right hand to*
6 *heaven and swore by Him who lives for ever and ever, who created the heaven and what is in it, the earth and what is*
7 *in it, and the sea and what is in it,* ' There shall be no more delay ; in the days of the seventh angel's voice, when he now blows his blast, then shall *the secret purpose of God* be fulfilled, as he assured *his servants the prophets.'*

1 The prophet sees another strong angel descend from heaven,
2 holding a small scroll open in his hand.   The first ' strong angel ' appeared in John's second vision of the heavenly court (v. 2) : he proclaimed in a loud voice the impotence of all created beings to open the sealed scroll of destiny.   This strong angel now bears an open scroll : the future enactment of God's decrees can now be revealed.   The small scroll is a special revelation, of spiritual necessity to the faithful.   It contains the record of those who were to die ' for adhering to God's word and to the testimony which they bore ' (vi. 9).

As befitted a messenger with tidings so important, the angel's appearance is unusually impressive.   We are reminded for a brief moment of the description of Christ (i. 13–16) ; but the two pictures are different in kind.   Almost every detail in the picture of Christ is symbolical, whereas the picture of the angel is on the whole boldly impressionist in style.   We see a being of dazzling, portentous brilliance—one whose glory can be conveyed only in terms of light : the diffused light of the cloud, the reflected colours of the **rainbow,** the direct rays of the **sun,** the unearthly glow of great **columns of fire**—all details associated in the Old Testament with divine mystery and splendour. Only the last of these details, **the columns of fire,** seems designed to speak to the discerning mind more than to the reverent eye. John's recollections of the story of Exodus have been discussed elsewhere (see viii. 6 ff. ; xi. 8 ; xii. 14) ; the theme of Egypt and the Israelites plays an important part in the central chapters of REVELATION, and we may therefore conclude that the description of the angel's limbs forms a conscious and significant allusion. The Israelites in the desert were guided at night by a column of fire. Christians also dissociated from the life and fortunes of the cities of this world— and therefore spiritually ' in the desert ' (cf. xii. 14)—are likewise given guidance in the night of their troubles. That is the angel's mission.

' He doth bestride the narrow world like a Colossus,' **his** **right foot on the sea, his left upon the earth :** in other words, 3 his message is to be heard over the whole world—it concerns the destiny of all men. So also we conclude from the loudness of his cry : he shouted aloud **like a lion roaring ; and at his** **shout the seven thunders gave voice.** In the ancient world thunder was regarded as the voice of the Eternal—a voice that some could interpret (cf. St. John xii. 27–33). John himself associates ' flashes of lightning, loud blasts and peals of thunder ' with the outpouring of God's avenging wrath. Hence the solemnity of the angel's shout : it is a celestial portent. The thunderous sound shatters the skies in one overwhelming broadside, and then, as it is echoed and re-echoed, John detects in it the intelligible accents of divine wrath. To catch the spirit of John's vision we must read Psalm xxix. ; it is quite possible that this exultant ode on the irresistible power of the Eternal, whose voice is seven-fold thunder, may have suggested directly or indirectly the seven thunders of REVELATION. Clearly the prophet wishes to convey that at the sound of the angel's shout he becomes conscious of the nature of fresh ' woes ' or ' plagues ' to fall on the earth—another series, like those associated with the seven seals and trumpets. The psalm, with its seven thunders, may well have suggested to John a framework for another series of predictions about the last days. It has, on the other hand, been suggested by commentators that John's use of the definite article (' the seven thunders ') compels the presumption that he is referring to a cycle of eschatological predictions already known to his readers. This argument is hardly convincing. In view of what follows in the text, it is more natural to suppose that John expected his readers to understand by **the seven thunders** simply *the audible or intelligible expression of the divine will* for the days of terror before the End. For the seer is told by a voice from heaven that he must 4 not divulge the secrets of the seven thunders : **seal up what the seven thunders have said, do not write it.** If we are to suppose that John wrote in good faith and knew the meaning of words, this injunction of secrecy can mean only one thing : that he is deliberately withholding from his readers certain predictions about the last days—predictions unknown to them. To regard the divine command as a device whereby John asserted an authoritative reason for failing to include familiar eschatological predictions into his book is to give too little weight to the prophet's remarkable originality : he reinterprets much of the eschatological material provided for him by tradition, and is everywhere patently conscious that his story is the fruit of his own inspiration. Moreover, John's words, taken at their face value, almost forbid such an idea. And, on the other hand, to imagine as some have done that the seer was concealing things too sacred for utterance (like St. Paul's secrets, 2 Cor. xii. 4) is to ignore the extent of the revelation already given : we have looked through ' a door standing open in heaven,' we have seen the Throne, and the Lamb, we have witnessed the opening of the scroll of destiny itself. Why then does John record the mere fact of his hearing the seven thunders and the command to keep secret what they have uttered ? His intention becomes perfectly clear if we survey the whole of chap. xi.

As the seven seals are opened, as the seven trumpets are

blown, we witness something of the terrible ordeal which is to overtake mankind in general. We are intended to conclude that the seven thunders told the seer a similar story, probably in a somewhat different way ; again the theme was to be the affliction of the world and unrepentant humanity. But to unfold this new version of the story before the eyes of Christians was unnecessary. Enough has been disclosed already about the punishment and warning of evil-doers. To say more would be to pander to curiosity. Now at last the all-important moment has arrived to answer the question : ' What is to happen to the Church, amidst all the terrors of the last days ? ' John's subject is now, not mankind in general, but Christians. So a voice from heaven forbids the record of further woes (the plagues of chap. xv. are the ' final ' plagues —not a new revelation, but the completion of the process already begun, and described in chaps. viii.–ix.) : the faith of Christians must be content with the assurance that the End *shall* come, and come without delay. This assurance is given by the angel with the utmost solemnity. Thus the ' sealing ' of the thunders is the first part of a statement which the angel's oath concludes.

Like his precursor in the Book of Daniel (xii. 5 ff.) the strong 5– angel in REVELATION swears by him who lives for ever and 6 ever—the Eternal, the Lord of life. But in REVELATION we have an even greater solemnity. The angel swears by the Creator of the universe : of the heaven and what is in it, of the earth and what is in it, and of the sea and what is in it. We are intended to conclude that the promised immediate fulfilment of the secret purpose of God is the consummation of His creative activity ; no new development, forced on God through the present assaults of His enemies, but an intrinsic feature of eternal providence. We are reminded that for John Christ is not only the messianic ' King of kings and Lord of lords ' (xix. 16) but also the ' Logos of God ' (xix. 13), ' the origin of God's creation ' (iii. 14). The angel swears by the eternal Creator partly because He is all-powerful, but more because the last days, no less than the first, are in His hands. He who made the earth may justly destroy the earth. He alone can replace what He destroys, with the 'new heaven and new earth.' He who created the chosen people will preserve them and vindicate them in His new creation. This last, and for Christians most important, element in the Creator's 'secret purposes' is best understood by reference to the later Isaiah (cf. Isa. xliv. 24 ff.).

The angel's oath is an echo of Dan. xii. 7. It fulfils a similar purpose. Both passages are an answer to the question : ' How long ? ' The angel in the Book of Daniel replies that ' it would be three years and half a year ' (a conventional expression for a limited time of distress : see notes below, xi. 2), and that ' when the power of him who shattered the sacred people should be over, then the end of all should arrive.' The reply given by the angel in REVELATION follows the passage in Daniel more closely than at first sight appears. We must first note John's conviction that the End will come as a fulfilment 7 of prophecy : **then shall the secret purpose of God be fulfilled, as he assured his servants the prophets.** As we shall see in chap. xi., John believes that the ' sacred people '—that is, the Christian churches—are actually to be ' shattered ' as Daniel foretold ; at any rate, the most loyal and devoted of Christians are to be martyred. And after their death the seventh trumpet heralds the end of this order, and the beginning of the rule of God in the world (xi. 15 ff.). Again, the angel of REVELATION purports to be speaking to the seer actually at a point in the future : between the blowing of the sixth and seventh trumpets. He says, **in the days of the seventh angel's voice when he now blows his blast.** The ' now ' is proleptic, and follows from the context : in reality, the angel is speaking of precisely the same period as that mentioned in Daniel, the ominous ' three and a half years.' This, John is told (xi. 2) is to be the time of Gentile domination ; and the greater part of this period is to be the duration of the martyrs' witnessing (xi. 3). We gather from the angel's ' **now** ' a complete certainty that the End will come, as it is morally bound to; this is more important than the mere matter of time. As soon as the preliminary conditions are fulfilled, *then* **there shall be no more delay.** As soon as the complete number of the martyrs have died, *then* the seventh angel's voice shall be heard. In face of such an assurance, what need is there for the faithful to know what the seven thunders communicated to John ?

x. 8-11 : THE PROPHET RECEIVES A NEW COMMISSION

Then the voice I had heard from heaven again talked to me, 8 saying, ' Go and take the small scroll which lies open in the hand of the angel who is standing on the sea and on the earth.' So I went to the angel, saying, 'Give me *the small* 9 *scroll.*' ' Take it,' *said he, ' and swallow it ;* it will *taste* sweet as honey, but it will be bitter to *digest.*' I took *the* 10 *small scroll* from the hand of the angel *and swallowed it ; it did taste sweet, like honey,* but when I had eaten, it was bitter to digest. Then I was told, '*You must prophesy* 11 *again of many peoples and nations and languages and kings.*'

The heavenly **voice** which had ordered the prophet to leave 8 the message of the seven thunders unwritten now commands him to take the angel's scroll. It should be noticed that John emphasizes by repetition the fact that the scroll is **open** and that the angel stands **on the sea and on the earth** (see above, notes on verses 2 and 3).

Like Ezekiel (Ezek. ii. 8 ff.) the prophet must **swallow** the 9 scroll : that is, he must thoroughly assimilate its contents. And again like Ezekiel he accepts it eagerly, at first finding its taste **sweet, like honey.** The first prophet is required to utter ' laments and dirges and woes ' on the old Israel ; he has no regret in accepting the commission to herald the rejection of ' a rebellious folk . . . defiant and stubborn.' John, however, soon finds the scroll **bitter to digest.** His message is 10 to the true Israel, the Christian Church : and though it ends with the triumph of God's people, it speaks also of a formidable ordeal which must precede their vindication. This new bittersweet knowledge he must broadcast to the churches in all

11 lands. He must **prophesy** of their fate at the hands of **the
many peoples and nations** amongst whom they dwelt. His
message is the reverse of local, and this we must bear in mind
in reading chap. xi. We must give full weight to his words :
**you must prophesy again of many peoples and nations and
languages and kings.**

INTRODUCTION TO CHAPTER XI.

Chap. xi. is at once the most difficult and the most important
in the whole book of REVELATION. Its difficulty has been
generally recognized—so clearly, indeed, that the failure to
find a solution has induced most commentators to assume
that it is of relative unimportance, that here John was making
use of a source, or, more probably, several sources, which he
was unable to adapt successfully to his theme. The whole
chapter is often described as ' an interlude,' ' a proleptic
digression ' in which the author has turned aside for the
moment from his main theme,[1] a meaningless intrusion which
mars the symmetry of the Apocalypse. To challenge such
seemingly established opinions, and to assert that in many
respects this chapter is the key to John's central theme must
therefore put our claim that his purpose is consistently pastoral
and practical to a crucial test. We shall also endeavour
to prove that even if the conjecture (for it can be nothing
more) that John has made use of sources be accepted, his
own version is nevertheless entirely unified and sustained in
its development.

The reason for supposing that one or more sources can be
detected is patent enough. Taken literally, the passage would
be meaningless even to the Christians to whom John originally
wrote at the close of the first century. But, it is argued, it
would be quite appropriate to devout Jews shut up in the
temple during the siege of Jerusalem in A.D. 70. An unknown
prophet was assuring those holding out against the Roman

[1] Charles, *I.C.C.*, vol. i, p. 274.

invader that they would be divinely protected, though Jerusalem itself would be destroyed. Now, commentators are agreed that this would mean nothing either to Jews or to Christians nearly thirty years later, long after the temple had, in fact, been completely desecrated. Can we then believe that John was so far removed from reality as to insert a meaningless passage into his Apocalypse ? Surely not. He was writing for Christians in days of extreme urgency, when every word was precious. Dr. Charles rightly insists that in xi. 1–2 we have a notable instance of reinterpretation on the part of our author. ' The Temple of God,' he says, ' is here the spiritual temple of which all the faithful are constituent parts ; the outer court is the body of unbelievers who are given over to the sway of Antichrist.'[1] Unfortunately, Dr. Charles, like most of the great commentators, failed to recognize that John freely used his power of reinterpretation throughout the whole chapter, as elsewhere in REVELATION. The stumbling-block has been the following verses, 3–13, relating to the Two Witnesses, of which no convincing explanation has been offered, and which are usually (though quite wrongly) separated from what precedes and follows. (The passage is continuous : John connects verse 3 with verse 2 by the Greek *kai*, which might be better translated ' And ' rather than ' But.') While allowing that John attached symbolical significance to the temple, many critics assume that his reference to the witnesses must be interpreted literally, and therefore regard it as being almost meaningless. So, too, ' the holy city ' in verse 2 is assumed to be one certain, or, rather, uncertain city, for it is a matter of dispute whether John intended Jerusalem or Rome to be understood.

What message, if any, do these verses convey if taken literally ? That the two witnesses are Christian prophets (whatever their character in the original source) is generally agreed. Two men will be allowed to prophesy for an allotted period, divinely protected by a consuming fire from their mouths against any attempt by their enemies to inflict physical harm. They have power also to prevent rain from falling, to

---

[1] *Op. cit.*, pp. 273–4.

turn water into blood, and to inflict plagues, all of which is
clearly reminiscent of the powers possessed by Moses and
Elijah. The strangest feature of this strange story, however,
is their death and what follows it at the close of the allotted
period. We are told that ' the Beast that ascends from the
abyss will make war on them and kill them, and their corpses
will lie in the streets of that great City whose mystical name
is Sodom and Egypt—where their Lord also was crucified.'
What a strange phrase to use of the death of two individuals,
though they have been divinely protected—' make war on
them and kill them ' (a phrase which is quite natural and
appropriate in the similar and, as we hope to show, parallel
passage in xiii. 7, where the Beast ' wages war ' on the saints
in general). Stranger still is what happens after their death.
This was no parochial affair, of interest only to the small circle
of those who had been obliged to listen to their unpleasant
prophecy, or had witnessed their slaying by the Beast ; no
ordinary event calculated to attract the attention of their own
local city. It was nothing less than universal in its significance. The whole world was moved—John stresses the fact
three times over : ' For three days and a half men from all
peoples and tribes and tongues and nations look at their
corpses, refusing to let their corpses be buried ; and the
dwellers on earth will gloat over them and rejoice, sending
presents to congratulate one another—for these two prophets
were a torment to the dwellers on earth.' The whole world
is concerned, the whole world gazes at their bodies (though
John says nothing to suggest that they come to the City to
do so—that would be awkward indeed !) ; and every single
person congratulates each other in turn at this welcome relief
from two prophets who, in some unknown manner, have
succeeded in arousing the enmity of all mankind. Then is
related their ascension, followed by a disastrous earthquake
in which a tenth of the City (i.e. presumably the particular
town where they had prophesied and had been killed) was
destroyed, and the rest were constrained to ' give glory to
the God of heaven.'

Regarded in this literal way it is small surprise that the

section is considered an awkward intrusion, scarcely connected, if at all, with the first two verses, and altogether divorced from the central theme of REVELATION ; nor that doubt should be expressed whether even John could have had any definite meaning in his own mind as he penned such an incoherent passage. Twice Dr. Charles expresses his doubt on this point, and adds : ' For the moment the steady progressive current of our author's thought has been checked, and he has here turned aside into a backwater.' The only constructive suggestion put forward to justify John as having had any reasonable purpose at this stage in his Apocalypse, is that he wished thus to indicate his belief that the Jewish nation as a whole would be converted in the last days, this theme linking verses 3–13 in a loose sort of way with the verses 1–2. The divine community, assured of protection, included certain Jews, who, in accordance with the hope expressed by St. Paul in Rom. xi. and elsewhere in the New Testament (cf. Beckwith, *op. cit.*, pp. 584 ff.) would be at last persuaded of the truth of the faith they had so long rejected. In view of what we have said already (e.g. note on iii. 9), it is unnecessary to repeat our conviction that John's attitude to the Jews (' no Jews are they, but liars . . . a synagogue of Satan ') rules out the possibility that he would express any expectation that they would be converted. Certainly there is not a word in the passage now under consideration to support such an idea. Nothing indicates that the two witnesses preached to the Jews. In any case they were in the world outside the temple which John expressly states was ' given over to the Gentiles.' There is no suggestion of Jews in the great City of verse 8, even though it is identified (though wrongly so, in our view) with the earthly Jerusalem. Nor is it necessary to argue whether John would be likely to describe the result of the conversion of Jews as that ' they gave glory to the God of heaven ' ; surely ' conversion ' is an inappropriate term for the acknowledgment wrung by sheer terror from the wretched enemies of the two witnesses when it was too late. Is this not rather an exact parallel to the fearful demand for fear and worship made by the angel with the eternal gospel for the inhabitants of earth in xiv. 6 ? John could hardly make it plainer that all humanity, without distinction, was concerned with the witnesses' message and the results of its rejection.

The real test, however, of the literal explanation of the passage is made by asking the simple question : Of what value would it be if so interpreted to the Christian Church in John's day ? And the answer is obvious—none. That must always be the criterion in every attempt to rediscover John's message. If as we believe, he was writing in a time of supreme and urgent crisis, if he was passionately convinced that the Church was about to face the great Distress of ruthless persecution, if he was anxiously warning his fellow-Christians that the End of all things was at hand and that nothing remained but to fortify the faithful, can we really accept the view that after his vision of the strong angel and his acceptance of the message of the small scroll, he would turn aside into a ' backwater,' and indulge in academic speculation far removed from the life and witness of the Church ?

So we approach the problem of this chapter afresh with this principle as the basis of all our attempts to define what John originally intended by it—that he was writing a direct message to the Christian Church about its own problems in the immediate future, and that every verse is essentially connected with that one theme of REVELATION from which he never for a moment departs. What would be the fate of the Church in the dreadful days that were coming ? That is John's sole concern. And it is with this question in mind that we must now consider the three most important symbols in chap. xi. : the temple, the two witnesses, and the great City.

We have observed that John's reference to **the temple** is commonly admitted to be symbolical, that he is here reinter-preting an earlier prophecy. When John wrote, the temple at Jerusalem had been in ruin for a round score of years. Wherever a Jewish colony existed, in whatever part of the Empire, the noise of its fall had been accompanied with lamentation. It had echoed also in every scattered Christian community ; the fall of Jerusalem and the desecration of the temple were eschatological events (cf. the apocalyptic passages in the synoptic Gospels). But years slipped past, and the End did not come. Why? What Jewish Christian could refrain from asking this question, and asking it earnestly, repeatedly? That the temple was ruined can have been no other than a notorious, incalculable fact in the mind of John's readers. When they were told that the temple was to be 'measured' for preservation (see note) they must inevitably have perceived an allegorical sense. Taken literally, the words were meaningless. And after all, John had given his readers every reason for peering below the surface of his words. He has shown how the sacred institutions and privileges, formerly part of the Jewish heritage, are now the unique possessions of the Christian churches. He has given the churches a variety of names to indicate their assumption of the ancient Jewish right to be called the people of God : they are the twelve tribes, the seven golden lampstands, a realm of priests ; they are to be the new Jerusalem, the Bride of the Messiah. In fact, a common assumption underlies a great part of the literary allusion in REVELATION : it is clear almost beyond the need of demonstration that whatever the prophets and apocalyptists of the past had promised for the 'faithful remnant' of the Jews, John takes to have reference to loyal Christians, and to them exclusively. If the readers of REVELATION did not share this assumption already, the first few chapters can have left them in no doubt. It would be natural in them, therefore, to seek in the opening sentences of chap. xi. a meaning which concerned themselves. Nor was it in any way difficult for them to understand the temple metaphorically. The same figurative language comes easily to the mind of St. Paul (cf. 1 Cor. iii. 16 ; 2 Cor. vi. 16). But John's interest, unlike St. Paul's, is wholly eschatological. He is showing (if only incidentally) how the earlier expectations about the End are to be fulfilled. Was it once believed that the temple in Jerusalem would be preserved until the very End? Yes, so the prophets had foretold. But they had spoken in symbols. Their predictions would indeed be borne out ' until the words of God are fulfilled ' (xvii. 17). They *would* be fulfilled—but not as people had imagined. Not the temple at Jerusalem, but the living temple of faithful Christians—this was the object of God's solicitude. St. Paul calls Christians ' God's temple ' in order to impress on them their responsibilities : John uses the same metaphor allusively, in order to assure the churches that God will look after His own. Even though the whole world is to be under the power of Satan, as represented by the Imperial rulers of the Gentiles, loyal Christians (not the half-hearted or temporizing—those who remain in the outer courts of the Faith) will be protected from harm. The holy City will be under the heel of the Gentiles, but the temple will be protected : the world, God's creation, and therefore once holy, will remain in Satan's power, but the Church is in the hand of God.

But this assurance of protection provoked an even more urgent question : How would the Gospel be preached to the whole world as fore-ordained before the End if the world was to be under the heel of the Gentiles? Indeed, loyal Christians might well protest that protection was not enough. Protection for what ? That was essential for only one purpose—the bearing of witness. Protection from martyrdom was not desired. Was not that the sure way—Christ's way—of over-coming evil and securing the joy of heaven ? It is because he realises this problem, and knows that those who receive his message will be aware of it likewise, that John adds his state-ment, ' And I will allow my two witnesses to prophesy.' By that he means to say : ' Be reassured. Although the world in which you must live will be subjected to the rule of the un-godly, the Church itself will be divinely protected, and so I shall ensure that the Gospel is preached, that the Christian witness is maintained.' But how ? By **my two witnesses.** Here is the crux of the whole matter. On our right under-standing of the witnesses depends the satisfactory explanation of chap. xi.

First and foremost, then, we must note that the two wit-nesses are symbols. It is illogical to admit that John is speak-ing symbolically, figuratively, eschatologically in his reference to the temple, and to deny that he is doing so in his account of the two witnesses. To regard them as individuals is to throw his message into meaningless confusion. Every word that describes them and their function shows that he is writing allusively, that he is referring to traditions well established in Christian apocalyptic thought, that as usual he is reinterpreting, and that in his view a little careful explanation (verse 4) will make his meaning clear.

Now, when John's readers understood that in verses 1–2 the prophet was showing them the true interpretation of a familiar eschatological theme, they assuredly did not approach the rest of the chapter with the puzzled thought of Jerusalem or of the Jews in their minds. They had heard something which closely concerned themselves: they naturally expected the sequel also to concern them, for the first word of verse 3 asserts a logical connexion. 'And I will allow my two witnesses to prophesy for twelve hundred and sixty days '—that is, for the period of Gentile domination,. the three and a half years of verse 2. Even so, John may not have expected his readers to understand at once who the two witnesses were, since he takes the trouble to explain (or at any rate to retain and probably expand the explanation in his source) ; ' they are the two olive trees and the two lampstands which stand before the Lord of the earth.' We have heard nothing hitherto about olive trees, but we have heard a great deal about lampstands. John explained with care and emphasis that ' the seven lampstands are the seven churches ' (i. 20). And we drew the further conclusion that those seven churches represented the whole Church. Why, in view of this previous passage, did John describe his *witnesses* as lampstands ? Was he here guilty of a piece of clumsy writing ? For while it is natural—indeed, inevitable—to use a variety of symbols to express one complex idea, it is a defiance of common sense to use the same distinctive symbol for two different ideas, within the compass of one book. The problem becomes more acute when we remember that there was not the slightest need for John to define the witnesses in these terms. Even though we take the view (an unlikely one) that the words in question were taken over from the hypothetical source of A.D. 70, we do not thereby explain why the prophet should retain for two *individuals* the term used earlier in his book so forcibly and repeatedly for *churches*. In Zechariah (a book with which John was evidently familiar) the two witnesses are less elaborately described. Zechariah (Zech. iv. 1–14) sees a lampstand, a seven-branched lampstand, not a single cresset like those of Rev. xi. 4 and i. 13. This lampstand is symbolical of God's omnipresence and completeness of vision. On either side of it stands an olive tree, and these two olive trees are prophets. Observe how the story is altered in REVELATION. John's witnesses stand, not beside a symbolical seven-branched lampstand, but before the Lord of the earth. John's witnesses are not merely olive trees, but lampstands—that is, single cressets. It seems highly probable that John deliberately omitted the most distinctive feature of Zechariah's symbol. The reason for his omission is not far to seek. In Zechariah, the seven-branched candlestick is, in effect, the symbolical equivalent of his .phrase, ' the Lord of all the earth.' But in REVELATION the seven-branched lampstand of the temple has already supplied the symbol for the churches. John avoids using the same, or a very similar symbol in two different senses ; but why should he make the further change, calling the witnesses lampstands, as well as olive trees ? Only one answer is convincing. The change is a deliberate reminder of the earlier collocation of lampstands and churches.

This argument is, of course, less cogent if we suppose that it was not John who altered Zechariah's text, but the writer of the hypothetical source of A.D. 70. We take the view that John altered it, since he had a very good reason for doing so, whereas it is difficult to imagine the earlier scribe being confronted with any adequate reason for the twofold change. But even though John did not alter Zechariah's story, at the very least he endorsed the alteration, with almost certain knowledge of the original prophet's text. And he can hardly have been unconscious of the fact that after the explanation of i. 20 the word lampstand was irrevocably associated in his book with a body of Christians.

But what is the precise nature of this association, if in xi. 3

it is made deliberately ? In what relation do the two lamp-stands stand to the seven in chap. i. ? We have seen that whereas seven lampstands represent all Christian communities, only two of the seven represent the completely faithful communities. This is at first sight suggestive ; but we must be wary of drawing the plain conclusion that the two witnesses represent merely the completely loyal communities exemplified by the churches of Smyrna and Philadelphia. John expected each community, even the Laodicean, to supply loyal souls, stout enough to face martyrdom : the promises to the conqueror are made to men drawn from all seven churches. The utmost we can say is that the two witnesses stand for that proportion of the sevenfold Church which must suffer martyr-dom. In other words, John did not imagine that certain communities would be massacred and some spared ; but that out of each community there would fall a certain number of martyrs—the stainless (xiv. 4–5) and fearless, who openly pro-claimed the Gospel under the stress of the Spirit of Christ. For this is the work of the witnesses. They prophesy : and, as John tells us, ' the testimony borne by Jesus is the breath of all prophecy ' (xix. 10 ; see also notes on xi. 3). Their task is no less than the universal publication of the Gospel, an essential prerequisite of the End in the Christian traditions preserved by the synoptists (cf. note on xiv. 6).

So in the two witnesses we have a brilliant reinterpretation of another familiar apocalyptic theme. Elijah was to return before the End, to preach repentance to the Gentiles—some said Elijah and Moses, others Elijah and Enoch. John, know-ing the vastness of the Gentile world (far too great a parish for any two individual prophets, however great, and however en-dowed with supernatural powers), and conscious also of the more urgent Christian tradition that all men on earth should be confronted with the Gospel before the reign of God could begin, sees a new meaning in the older expectation. He does not abandon it ; he shows how it is to be properly understood. The martyrs, John believes, will be endowed with a spirit of prophecy no less powerfully than the greatest prophets of old. The opposition they must face will be equally fierce—it will come from the same source. Their need for supernatural protection will be equally great. Therefore they shall be equipped with the same powers as Moses and Elijah (see notes, below, on verses 4 and 5).

When we understand that by the witnesses John means the militant among the Christian churches, two rather baffling expressions become startlingly clear. ' Men from all peoples and tribes and tongues and nations look at their corpses ' (xi. 9). How ? Does the world come to Palestine ? John does not say that this host of men come to look at the bodies of the witnesses. They have no need to ; the witnesses are slain in their midst, for the churches are scattered throughout all the cities of the world. In all parts of the world there will be Christians. Everywhere the faithful will bear witness. Everywhere their enemies will regard them as a torment— these upholders of the truth whose very existence is an irritating rebuke (cf. Wisdom ii. 14–16). Again, ' the dwellers on earth will gloat over them . . . for these two prophets were a torment to the dwellers on earth ' (xi. 10). John does not say that these enemies will actually *come* to the great City for this purpose—there will be no need to do so, for every city will have its victims. Have we not been already told that the martyrs form ' a great host whom no one could count, from every nation and tribe and people and tongue ' (vii. 9) ? They will ' gloat over them.' We understand now why all mankind has so keen an interest in the fate of the witnesses. It is another way of saying : ' You will be hated of all men on account of my name ' (St. Mark xiii. 13 ; St. Matt. xxiv. 9 ; St. Luke xxi. 17).

But, it will be objected, the crucial difficulty has been scouted. What is to be made of verse 8, **the great City whose mystical name is Sodom and Egypt—where their Lord also was crucified** ? Is not this unquestionably Jerusalem ? Briefly, it is not. **The great City** is neither Jerusalem nor Rome—and yet, in a sense it is both Jerusalem and Rome. It is the city of this world order, the Earthly City, which included all peoples and tribes and tongues and nations. It is, so to say, the city of civilization, utterly alien to the will of God.

Here we have another example of John's great breadth of vision, as well as of the staunchness of his faith. Prophets had predicted with untiring energy that Jerusalem would fall ; and with the growth of apocalyptic thought the anticipation of her fall in the first century was accompanied with the belief that such a gigantic event would inevitably prove the signal for the End of the world itself—we can hear the echoes of that lively conviction in the synoptic Gospels. Then, in A.D. 70 the holy City was devastated, and the temple itself was defiled and destroyed. But the End did not come. The confident words of the prophets, Jewish and Christian alike, were unfulfilled. Were they actually falsified ? ' No,' says John, ' the teaching of the prophets has been misread. The words of God *must* be fulfilled (cf. xvii. 17). The prophets spoke in symbols. When they spoke of Jerusalem they meant all cities.'

Let us pause for a moment to remind ourselves of what John meant when he drew his picture of the heavenly City. The new Jerusalem (chap. xxi.) is the heavenly community of the loyal followers of Christ. It is to be a complete antithesis—of what ? Of the earthly Jerusalem ? Much more : it is to be the antithesis of the whole of civilization, of Vanity Fair, the pomp and pride of this earth. Bunyan's story is, in fact, the best comment on chap. xi. Vanity Fair lay on the road to the Celestial City, and through this Fair, with its rows of nations, its booths of merchants, its corrupt courts, its folly and cruelty and vice, the two pilgrims must pass—the two pilgrims who were representative of all Christians. There they were persecuted, and Faithful took the shortest road to the Celestial City ; he was martyred, and like the faithful Christians in REVELATION, was brought to life and ascended to heaven.

We have called this earthly city Vanity Fair. John, in a later chapter (xvii. 5) called it ' Babylon the great, the mother of harlots.' Of this earthly city he could just as appropriately say, ' where their Lord also was crucified ' (xi. 8), as ' in her was found the blood of prophets and saints, of all who were slain upon earth ' (xviii. 24). The ironical words of Christ should be compared with this indictment : ' it would never do for a prophet to perish except in Jerusalem ' (St. Luke xiii. 33). Whereas in the reproaches of so many earlier teachers Jerusalem itself had been the exemplar of earthly depravity and cruelty, John now tells us that her viciousness is shared by the whole of civilization. Babylon the great is the enemy of the saints : ' the woman was drunk with the blood of the saints and the blood of the witnesses of Jesus ' (xvii. 6). The double title given to the great City, the ' mystical name ' of ' Sodom and Egypt ' is also instructive. The first name, Sodom, had been associated previously in prophetic writings with Jerusalem : the second is John's own addition. It recalls to us the fact that the woes of the trumpet series, coloured as they are by the Egyptian plagues of Exodus, fall on the whole world (cf. chap. viii. ix). But in general the double title means simply a city doomed to utter destruction —a city from which the saints will flee, to avoid sharing its punishment. In St. Matt. xxiv. 16 the Elect are counselled to flee from Judæa to the hills. But the Elect are now dispersed through the wide world. And it is from Babylon the great that they must now flee. ' Come out of her, O my people, that you share not her sins, that you partake not of her plagues ' (xviii. 4). Finally, John even preserves and reinterprets the tradition that great armies must gather round Jerusalem immediately before the End. ' But when you see Jerusalem surrounded by armies, then be sure her desolation is not far away,' wrote St. Luke (St. Luke xxi. 20). These armies, partly human, partly dæmonic, appear in REVELATION at the mysterious Harmagedon (xvi. 12–16). Their congregation is the signal for the final plague, when the earthquake overturns the earthly City,' the cities of the nations ' (xvi. 19).

It will not be inappropriate to anticipate chap. xvii. while we are commenting on the great City in chap. xi., inasmuch as John plainly identifies the community among which the two witnesses meet their fate with the great harlot seated on the Beast. It should be observed then that we do not identify the great City in either chapter or elsewhere with Rome, not though John calls her 'Babylon the great, the mother of harlots and of all abominations on earth.' This is not to deny that many of the colours of John's picture of the Earthly City were supplied by Rome, since Roman power was dominant and ubiquitous. The seven cities of REVELATION, like every other city of the civilized world, were in his eyes almost suburbs of Rome. They were at all events essentially at one with her in spirit. Distance had no power to diminish the fervour with which the divine Emperor was worshipped ; indeed, it lent him enchantment. Rome, as much as Jerusalem, was in John's mind when he spoke of the great City. But when we examine chap. xvii. carefully, we see that no single city is intended in the symbol of the ' great harlot.' The ' seven hills on which the woman is seated ' are not merely the seven hills of Rome : they represent the whole world (as the seven churches represented the whole Church). We are told so outright in xvii. 15. The harlot is also seated on 'many waters,' and these many waters are ' peoples and hosts, nations and tongues.' Just as the strong angel bestrode the whole world when he placed one foot on the sea and the other on the earth, so the harlot, Babylon the great, is seated on all seas and all lands—on the whole world. In short, Babylon the great is to be identified with Rome only in so far as she is the dominant force in all cities, in so far as all cities, all rulers, all peoples partook of her character and shared her life (cf. xvii. 2–3). In chap. xviii. Babylon the great appears as the doomed city, Sodom and Egypt, the antithesis of the eternal heavenly City. And when John says of her in xi. 8, ' where their Lord also was crucified,' he has attained in his own way the universality of the Fourth Gospel : ' He came into the world, and the world was made by him, and the world knew him not.' Not merely Jerusalem, not only Rome, but the wide earth itself was a realm of corruption (Sodom), where the Church was persecuted (Egypt). Not merely Jerusalem, but the world at large had shared in the sins which had crucified their Lord (cf. i. 7).

Thus, if John's power of reinterpretation is recognized, if we read the symbols of chap. xi. as bearing a universal and timeless significance, we shall realize why it was that after John had swallowed and digested the small scroll handed to him by the strong angel (x. 11), he was told that his next message must refer to the world at large: 'Then I was told, "You must prophesy again of many peoples and nations and languages and kings." ' (Note that Dr. Moffatt rightly makes no break between the end of chap. x. and the beginning of chap. xi.)

xi. 1–2 : THE CHURCH IS PROMISED PROTECTION

1   And I was given *a reed* like a rod, and told, ' Rise up and measure the temple of God and the altar, numbering the
2   worshippers ; but omit the court outside the temple, do not measure that, for it has been given over *to the Gentiles ;* and the holy city will be *under their heel* for two and forty months.

We shall interpret this chapter in accordance with the conclusions reached in the foregoing introduction, in which it has been argued that **the temple of God** is an allegorical expression whereby (as in verse 4, where he calls the witnesses ' lampstands ') John alludes to his cherished conviction that the Church is the true Israel, and therefore as such will be divinely protected while fulfilling its mission in the evil days.

The prophet tells us that in his vision he was given **a reed like a rod** (the Greek word *kalamos* signified a regular unit of measure) and commanded to **measure the temple of God and the altar, numbering the worshippers.** Later we are told that the City of God (where there is no temple) is to be similarly measured, only then, as is fitting in the new heaven, with a golden wand. In each case the measurement is a sign of immunity from harm (cf. xxi. 15–17). The measurement of an object was a figurative way of indicating either its protection, or its impending destruction : its dimensions taken, God had

it totally in his power. Here, as in Ezek. xl. 3 ff. and Zech. ii.
1 ff., the intention is plainly preservation. John would see the
fulfilment of these two prophecies in the protection of the
faithful from the world's hostility. The Christian Church only
was worthy of God's solicitude on earth. The Church would be
protected ; but only the true and devoted of its members.
People like the adherents of Balaam at Pergamum or of the
Jezebel at Thyatira, loveless people like those at Ephesus,
formal, insincere people like those at Sardis, smug and self-
satisfied people like those at Laodicea—these were no true
Christians. Without repentance they could hope for no
protection. If they remained in **the court outside the temple,** 2
they must be **given over** like the rest of the world to the rule of
the **Gentiles.** In the old Israel, the heathen who were on the
fringe of Judaism had been allowed to enter the outer court
of the temple at Jerusalem, but in these urgent, killing times,
such half-heartedness could not be tolerated. There was no
reason, save spiritual perversity, why anyone should remain
on the fringe of Christianity. The waverers will suffer the
fate of all those who are under the sway of the Beast (xiii. 5 ff.)
both in this life (xvii. 15 ff.) and the next (xiv. 9 ff.), and they
will have no protection from the plagues sent on the world by
God to warn and to punish.

The significance of the period **two and forty months** set for
Gentile domination (and therefore for the protection of the
temple) may be ascertained by noting, first, that it is equivalent
to the ' twelve hundred and sixty days ' allotted to the two
witnesses in the next verse, and also to ' a Time, two Times,
and half a Time ' (i.e. three and a half years), the conventional
period during which evil is allowed free rein (cf. xiii. 5 ; Dan.
vii. 25, xii. 7) ; and, secondly, that it is for this same period
that the woman clad in the sun in chap. xii. is preserved in the
desert (xii. 14), while the Beast is allowed to utter blasphemies,
and to exert authority (xiii. 5). These two passages in chap.
xi. and chaps. xii.–xiii. are plainly parallel. The protection
described in the one is the same as the preservation in the
other. The Gentile dominion in the first is the same as the
activity of the Beast in the second. And we shall find that the

fate of the witnesses in xi. 3–13 is the fate of those who ' keep God's commandments and hold the testimony of Jesus ' (xii. 17) described in chap. xiii.

In fact, the second passage throws necessary light on the first. In what sense is the Church to be preserved if her most loyal members are to be martyred ? John makes his meaning quite clear in xii. 14–xiii. 1–18. The messianic community is to be protected ' in the desert '—that is, in her spiritual detachment from the affairs of the world, dominated by the Beast. The ' huge red dragon ' of chap. xii. (that is, Satan) finds his attack on her of no avail. So he directs his venom against ' the rest of her offspring.' The first of her children was Christ ; the messianic community still gives birth to martyrs, and it is they whom the Beast conquers (xiii. 7). She herself remains unharmed until the end of this order of things— until the reign of God on earth is established. This seems to be the meaning of the preservation of the temple. As a community, the Church of Christ is to remain, unharmed by the assaults of evil. Nevertheless, it is ordained that many of her sons shall perish, and of this we are told in the next ten verses.

It is noteworthy that John was told to measure the **altar**, as well as the temple ; and that he here refers to the divinely protected Church as a body of **worshippers**. These terms are, of course, specially appropriate, since the faithful are regarded as within the temple of God. But we may be sure that John would also thus remind his readers that their final destiny is to worship God. From first to last, REVELATION breathes a spirit of adoration. No higher reward of fidelity is conceivable than to worship. That will be the unspeakable joy of the loyal in the next world (cf. v. 6–14, vii. 9–16, xi. 15–19, xv. 1–4). That is why on earth they are the exact antithesis of the Beast's worshippers (chap. xiii.). We should observe, too, how John alludes to the personal character of his faith—he is told to **number the worshippers**, the numbering being equivalent to the measuring. Not less than St. Stephen and St. Paul, John is aware that God's temple consists, not in stones, but in individual human beings, each of whom is known to God, each being one of that exact number that can count on His almighty protection ; it is the same thought as in chaps. vii. and xiv.

But in what sense can the world which is to be under the heel of the Gentiles be called the **holy city** ? The reason for John's use of this particular term is to be sought in the denunciation poured on Jerusalem by the prophets ; John applied this oracle of doom to all mankind, just as he interpreted Jeremiah's oracle on Babylon to the whole world. If we ask why the epithet **holy** is still retained, we must recall John's emphasis on God's lordship over His creation : the world was made according to the perfect pattern of His thought ; since He made it, it was holy (cf. chap. iv.). But it had been defiled by sin, and consequently the Gentiles (that is, in John's own language, the ' worshippers of the Beast ') were allowed to have dominion over it. The new Jerusalem is the perfect embodiment of God's creative thought, and that is the eternal holy City.

xi. 3–6 : The Story of the Martyrs

But I will allow my two witnesses to prophesy for twelve 3
hundred and sixty days, clad in sackcloth (they are *the two* 4
olive-trees and the two *lampstands which stand before the
Lord of the earth*) :

> whoever tries to harm them, 5
>> *fire shall issue from* their *mouth and consume their*
>> *enemies ;*
> whoever would try to harm them,
> so must he be killed.'

They have power to shut up the sky, *so that no rain falls* during 6
the days when they are prophesying ; and they have power
over *the waters, to turn* them *into blood, and* also *to smite* the
earth *with all manner of plagues* as often as they choose.

The prophet Zechariah recounts (Zech. iv.) how in a vision 3–
he saw **two olive trees** standing beside a septiform lampstand, 4
whose lights, he was told, symbolized ' the eyes of the Eternal '

which ' sweep all over the earth.' The olive trees represented
two prophets : ' these are the sources of the oil of bliss, the two
men who stand before the Lord of all the earth.' In popular
tradition, until John reinterpreted the passage, the two witnesses were identified with the forerunners of the Messiah who
were to perform the function ascribed by Christians to John the
Baptist. Some said that Elijah would return to be the
Messiah's herald—Elijah alone (cf. St. Mark ix. 9–14) ; others
(for it was a speculative topic) said Elijah and Moses (cf. St.
Mark ix. 4) ; and some, apparently, Elijah and Enoch. It is
not strange that such beliefs should find nourishment and the
soil for hardy growth in non-Christian eschatological schemes.
But are they not an intrusion in REVELATION ? What need
had the risen Christ of supernaturally resurrected harbingers
to proclaim His return ? Had He not His own prophets,
utterly devoted to His cause, demonstrably possessed and
transformed into His likeness by the Spirit ? It is to
such Christian prophets that REVELATION is dedicated (cf.
xxii. 6, 7). Moreover, the messianic glory had already
appeared before men, when ' the woman clad in the sun ' (the
messianic people) ' gave birth to a son, a male child . . .'
(xii. 1, 5). And the Fourth Gospel confirms what we gather
from the three synoptic Gospels—that Christians saw the
fulfilment of the prophetic teaching about the Messiah's herald
and path-leveller in John the Baptist : in him Elijah had
already returned—or, rather (as the Fourth Gospel is careful
to insist), not Elijah, but one who performed the work assigned
to him by prophetic tradition. The Messiah had come to earth
and won His victory : it remained with His followers to
demonstrate it before mankind ; and they alone had the
power to proclaim everywhere His ' eternal gospel ' to ' the
inhabitants of earth ' (xiv. 6). The advent of the two older
prophets into the world-conflict of REVELATION certainly
seems strangely inapposite. If we take them literally, we
must confess that their appearance is irrelevant from both
the religious and literary points of view, and that their
task is wrapped in needless mystery (see Introduction above,
pp. 174–88).

John has baffled his later commentators, it seems, much more than his original readers. Of one thing we may be quite certain ; John had not the slightest intention of including in his book curious apocalyptic material with no bearing on the central problem in contemporary affairs. His first and last concern was with the churches ; REVELATION was a life and death message to the faithful. There is no room in it for matters of speculative or merely academic interest. There is hardly room for the reassurance of the ' ordinary ' faithful Christian. John was writing to those about to die for their faith ; to the hundred and forty-four thousand servants of God, who bore the divine seal on their foreheads, and who were to pass through the great Distress to their heavenly bliss. He wrote, in fact, to answer what was for Christians the great question of the times : ' What will happen, when the menacing sword of Imperial persecution descends on the Church ? '

John's first readers had more reason than many of their successors to seek in REVELATION an answer to this question. And whoever the **two witnesses** proved to be, those who surveyed the contemporary scene as John did would be predisposed to find that their appearance had some bearing on the matter of supreme importance. Let us try to read with a little of their prejudice. John has just announced that the Church is to be preserved—the Church as a whole. He adds to this statement ; for the conjunction **But** (or ' And ') asserts that the third verse is connected with the preceding passage, and has similar importance. This connexion may be rendered alternatively : it may be that John means, ' In spite of the Gentile domination of the world, I will allow my two witnesses to prophesy ' ; or, ' Although the Church as a whole will be preserved inviolate during the Gentile domination of the world, the two witnesses will suffer a different fate.' In view of the later parallel passage of xii. 17, the second of these interpretations is preferable—the conjunction dividing two distinct but related statements, and referring to the whole of the section which it introduces (xi. 3-13). In either case this one word brings verses 3-13 into close relationship with the two preceding verses. This decided, we must deduce the identity of the two witnesses from John's brief explanation of them. They are **the two olive trees and the two lampstands which stand before the Lord of the earth.** We note that this explanation owes something to Zechariah ; but we note also that it was not Zechariah who described his prophets as **lampstands.** And we shall remember that the symbol of the *seven* lampstands, which plays so dramatic a part in the first chapter of REVELATION was one which John himself found it advisable to explain with care, since, evidently, as he used it, it was something new. They represented the visible associations of Christians on earth. Have not **the two lampstands** logically something of the same meaning—*bodies* of Christians who diffused the light of Christ in this world ? The two lampstands are, in fact, the **conquerors** of the seven churches. It is they who stand most intimately in God's presence— **before the Lord of the earth :** they, the ' stainless,' on whose ' lips no lie was ever detected,' whom Christ fills with the spirit of prophecy. It is they whose death releases the final outpouring of wrath (cf. vi. 9–11) : they, therefore, who are for Christians the **two olive trees**—' sources of the oil of bliss ' (Zech. iv. 14). Above all, they alone in their numbers can perform the task of the two messianic forerunners of the Zechariah tradition, in preaching a world-wide gospel of repentance to the Gentiles, before the Day of Wrath—they will be clad in **sack-cloth,** appropriate garb for the evil times, and for the sombre tidings of judgment with which the world must be confronted.

This conclusion is in agreement with their character and function. The Greek word for witnesses, *martures,* has a certain grim flavour which is lost in the English word. The same root supplies the word translated as ' testimony ' (*marturia*) : John was banished to Patmos ' for adhering to God's word and the *testimony of Jesus* ' (i. 9) ; the martyrs under the altar of God (vi. 10) ' had been slain for adhering to God's word and the *testimony which they bore.*' The prospective martyrs of xii. 17 are distinguished from the rest of the messianic people by the description : ' those who keep God's commandments and *hold the testimony of Jesus.*' The first part of this description is explained by the formidable assertion of xiv. 5 : the martyrs are completely ' stainless '—they keep God's commandments to the letter. The second expression, ' who . . . *hold the testimony of Jesus,*' can only mean that they bore active witness—openly proclaimed the Gospel. While the weaker member of the Church would be enabled to live an uninterrupted and retired life of virtue, compatible with his smaller store of spiritual strength, the completely devoted Christian must speak his faith boldly, and hence suffer inevitable martyrdom. This was the character of the **witnesses**.

Finally, they **prophesy**. An interesting comment on the nature of their prophecy is to be found in two later passages, xix. 10 and xxii. 6. In both passages an angel is disclaiming worship which John is inclined at first to offer him. In the first the angel says : ' I am but a servant like yourself and your brothers *who hold the testimony of Jesus.*' Now, the word ' servant,' as applied to mortals, is almost a technical expression in REVELATION for a prophet ; and that the *brothers* mentioned by the angel are John's fellow-prophets is shown conclusively by the parallel passage in xxii. 6 : ' I am but a servant like yourself and *your brothers the prophets.*' The truth is that John thinks of REVELATION as a prophetic book, written for prophets : ' The Lord God of the spirits of the prophets has sent his angel to show his *servants* [i.e. the prophets] what must come to pass very soon.' For a prophet was one who ' held the testimony of Jesus ' openly, at the bidding of the Spirit, and in defiance of peril. Prophecy could be concerned with nothing other than the Gospel of Christ : ' The testimony borne by Jesus is the breath of all prophecy.' Such was the task of the **witnesses**—to affirm, at the bidding of the Spirit, the ' testimony borne by Jesus.' These men were the active, fearless, utterly devoted Christians who invited the attentions of the Imperial inquisitors by their zeal in proclaiming the Gospel. The tradition of the synoptic Gospels is reproduced in allegorical form. There we hear that before the End the Gospel must be published to all nations (St. Matt. xxiv. 14 ; St. Mark xiii. 10 ; cf. St. Luke xxi.

12–15). We hear that as it is proclaimed, some Christians will be persecuted and martyred (St. Matt. xxiv. 9 ; St. Mark xiii. 9 ; St. Luke xxi. 12). And we are told by St. Mark (xiii. 11 ; cf. St. Luke xxi. 15) that in the hour of adversity the Holy Spirit will inform the speech of the persecuted Christian.

5 The Gospel must be preached to all nations, and the witnesses will be inspired and sustained by the Holy Spirit. But how, in view of the intenser Imperial hostility against Christians, are the prophetic witnesses to survive long enough for the fulfilment of their task ? Will not they be slain at once ?

John was convinced that they would survive to perform their task, but only by reason of God's intervention. They would be supernaturally protected against Satan's power in its modern Imperial guise, as Moses and Elijah had been protected and armed against his malice in former days. It is at this point (verses 5 and 6) that the narrative commends itself least to the reader of to-day. The witnesses seem to become mere magicians. We must try to do justice to John's point of view, however. The powers to be given to the witnesses were the only guarantee, in John's eyes, that the Gospel should ever be universally broadcast, so that the End might come ; the servants of the Devil must not be allowed to frustrate Eternal Providence, and therefore the witnesses must be adequately armed against their satanic onslaughts. Moreover, it was not as individuals that the witnesses were to be so fearfully equipped with power to destroy. As men they were ready enough to die, when their work was done. They were to be supernaturally armed as representatives of all that was most precious and holy in the Christian faith ; as the necessary heralds, moreover, of the approaching liquidation of the bankrupt and fraudulent world-order. Moses and Elijah together represented the Law and the Prophets ; the witnesses stood for a faith which included and transcended the Law and the Prophets, and this faith demanded the protection afforded in earlier times to the chosen people and their heritage. John was concerned in verses 5 and 6 purely with the necessity and inevitability of this protection. The means described in these verses were suggested by tradition, and their form merely emphasizes John's belief that, as ever before, God would take care of His own people.

Elijah had possessed the power to **shut up the skies** as a 6 punitive gesture (cf. 1 Kings xvii. 1). Moses had had power **over the waters to turn them into blood, and also to smite the earth with all manner of plagues.** But the witnesses, unlike 'Amram's son,' had no 'potent rod' wherewith to work spectacular magic. The fire which **shall issue from their mouths and consume their enemies** is figurative, like the sword issuing from Christ's mouth in chap. i. It is the 'fire·' of God's anger—the fire from the altar. God has already passed sentence on those who try to harm His witnesses ; the 'fire' is His swift, invisible executioner (cf. St. Luke ix. 54, R.V., margin). Similarly, the **plagues** at the command of the witnesses are simply the expression of His anger, the performance of judgment already passed on wickedness. The contemners and assailants of the witnesses stood self-indicted and condemned by God, not by His servants. The witnesses, it is true, were concerned in their punishment. They prayed that evil should be scourged, and their prayers were answered in the descent of plagues (see viii. 3 and notes). The character of these plagues suggests that they were definitely connected in John's mind with the plagues of the trumpet blasts (chaps. viii.–ix.). This fact is deeply significant of John's confident belief that the part played by Christian prayer and witness during this climacteric of the old world's existence was decisive (cf. viii. 3 ; also xii. 10–11). So far from being tragic, defenceless victims of Imperial despotism—a despotism which took note of such insignificant mortals only to brush them violently aside as troublesome insects—Christians were the embattled army of God. And the ultimate foe was far more deadly than any earthly enemy. The terms in which John writes of the **witnesses** and their **power** bear their own strange testimony to his lively sense of the great unseen, spiritual conflict enjoined on the saints.

xi. 7–10: THE GREAT DISTRESS

7   But, when they have finished their testimony, *the Beast that ascends from the abyss will make war on* them *and conquer*
8   *them* and kill them, and their corpses will lie in the streets of that great City whose mystical name is *Sodom* and Egypt—
9   where their Lord also was crucified. For three days and a half men from all peoples and tribes and tongues and nations look at their corpses, refusing to let their corpses be buried;
10   and the dwellers on earth will gloat over them and *rejoice*, sending presents to congratulate one another—for these two prophets were a torment to the dwellers on earth.

The supernatural protection afforded to the witnesses is
7 withdrawn **when they have finished their testimony**; when, that is, they have broadcast to all nations on earth their gospel of repentance and their warnings of the approach of universal judgment. The gist of their **testimony** may be gathered from xiv. 7 and xiv. 9 f.: ' Fear God and give him glory, for the hour of his judgment has come; worship him who made heaven and earth, the sea and the fountains of water.' ' Whoever worships the Beast and his statue . . . he shall drink the wine of God's passion, poured out untempered in the cup of his anger.' John probably had little hope that many would heed the cry of the witnesses. Justice demanded, however, that all men must be enabled to choose deliberately under which king they would serve, and the protracted mission of the Christian prophets served this purpose.

Their message pronounced, the witnesses must suffer as **their Lord** had suffered; they must demonstrate by death their complete devotion to His cause. Christ was the first ' child ' of the messianic community (xii. 5); but the martyrs were likewise her children—' the rest of her offspring ' (xii. 17) —and their fate was to be like His. As we shall see more clearly in chap. xii., John had a very simple philosophy of history. He viewed the past course of events as essentially a conflict between God and Satan. And the enemy who now assails the witnesses is the same as the enemy who stood ready to devour Christ as soon as He was born (xii. 4), and who later was prevented by God from exterminating the messianic community (xii. 17). This enemy, acting through his incarnate ministers of evil, the Roman Emperors (xiii. 2), is now ' allowed to wage war on the saints and to conquer them ' (xiii. 7). That the Emperors are, collectively, called ' the Beast ' (a Beast having the same allegorical shape as the great Dragon himself ; see chap. xiii.) is sufficient indication that the expected assault on the loyal servants of God is to be Satanic in origin —no mere political aberration. John's readers, familiar with similar expressions in previous apocalypses, would at once catch the general idea behind John's words ; he defers his full definition and explanation of the Beast until chap. xvii., when he can devote his attention solely to the one topic.

The enemy who is to **kill** and **conquer** the saints is still ultimately the author of all evil ; nor, in the eyes of the truly discerning, has the scene of the conflict changed. For the saints are killed in **that great City . . . where also their Lord was crucified.** This is not to say, in Jerusalem ; John is speaking of the allegorical (**mystical**) city of vice and cruelty —the Earthly City, as opposed to the Heavenly City— typified once by Jerusalem, now by all civilization, where the Satanic power of Rome was dominant. Bunyan gives this city two names—the City of Destruction and Vanity Fair. And John's two **mystical** or allegorical names convey much the same ideas. The city is called **Sodom,** as Jerusalem had been (cf. Isa. i. 10) because it is given over to wickedness and destined to annihilation. It is called **Egypt** because in it—in all earthly cities—the saints are oppressed. These two terms are not merely invective—they are intended to clarify the allegorical meaning.

So by the statement, **their corpses will lie in the streets of** 8 **that great City,** we are to understand that the witnesses lie dishonoured in death in every town and city in the world— wherever they ' hold the word of their testimony.' Mankind will indulge its lustful hatred of the witnesses by inflicting on them the last contumely known to Oriental malice, the refusal

9 **to let their corpses be buried**—a grim anticipation of the actual
fate of at least one Christian martyr (cf. martyrdom of Polycarp). Perhaps it is too much to charge all mankind with
this refusal. John says, **men from all peoples and tribes and
tongues and nations ;** he is speaking of the worshippers of
Antichrist. But they certainly form the greater part of mankind, as we read in chap. xiii. : ' The whole earth went after
the Beast in wonder, worshipping the dragon [Satan] for having
given authority to the Beast, and worshipping the Beast.'
This is hyperbolical. A few, John expected, whose names
were ' written from the foundation of the world in the book of
Life,' would abstain from the general rejoicing at the death of
God's servants. But the majority in this dark hour would
identify themselves openly and irretrievably with the will of
Satan and his agents. In this way will most men answer the
testimony of the witnesses. Too wilfully blind to see that the
men who were a **torment** to them were heralds of salvation, too
10 wilfully wicked to acknowledge righteousness and truth, **the
dwellers on earth** acclaim the Imperial act of persecution.
They **gloat over** the corpses of their denouncers, **and rejoice,**
evincing their satisfaction in characteristic Oriental manner
by **sending presents to congratulate one another.** We are
reminded of the synoptic apocalypses : ' You will be hated by
all the Gentiles on account of my name ' (St. Matt. xxiv. 9 ;
cf. St. Mark xiii. 13 ; St. Luke xxi. 17). By thus acquiescing
in the slaughter of the saints, by showing joyful approval of
the great Distress inflicted by the Beast on the witnesses, the
great part of mankind assumed the guilt of the act itself.
They are now beyond redemption : ' whoever kills with the
sword, by the sword must he be killed ' (xiii. 10*b*).

xi. 11–13 : The Martyrs are raised from the Dead and
ascend into Heaven

11 But after three days and a half *the breath of life* from God *entered
them ; they stood on their feet* (*terror fell on* those **who saw**
12 **them) and heard a loud voice from heaven telling them,**

' Come up here.' So up *to heaven* they went in a cloud, before the eyes of their enemies. At that hour *a great* 13 *earthquake* took place, a tenth of the City *was destroyed,* and seven thousand souls perished in the earthquake : the rest were awe-struck, and gave glory to *the God of heaven.*

The sun of righteousness has sunk ; night has fallen. For a short time of horror, represented symbolically by the sinister three days and a half, the Devil's victory seems complete. But 11 God does not desert His servants. The dawn of His reign breaks suddenly and miraculously, and soon the daystar ' shines in the forehead of the morning sky ' with undimmed brilliance. For the witnesses are summoned into heaven by a loud voice ; their resurrection and ascension are witnessed 12 by their enemies, by those men from all peoples and tribes and tongues and nations who had forbidden their burial, by the dwellers on earth who gloated over their corpses. Little wonder that mankind is stricken with terror (cf. St. Matt. xxvii. 54).

One can only marvel at the sobriety with which John tells his story of how the witnesses die like their Lord, and like Him rise from death and ascend to heaven. His restraint certainly has its reward. The simple words of his narrative are charged with an incalculable force of emotion, more especially for those who had brooded over the prophetic consolations of the oppressed people of God, and had trustfully taken to themselves the promises of providential rescue and vindication. We too must recall some of these glowing words—those of Isaiah, for example :

> ' A message from the Eternal
> from Israel's deliverer, Israel's Majesty,
> to one scorned openly, whom nations loathe,
> whom tyrants hold in thrall :
> Kings shall start up at the sight of you,
> kings and princes shall do homage . . .
> For when the favouring hour comes I will answer you
> and aid you when the day for rescue dawns.'
> (Isa. xlix. 7 ff.)

What were John and his fellow-Christians to think of such

promises as these ? Was the Church, the true Israel, to be thus rescued in her darkest hour by Israel's deliverer ? Impious to doubt it !

It is hardly possible to overstress the importance of the influence exercised over John's thought (perhaps one should rather say, over his visionary mind) by certain of the great prophetic books. His debts are manifold. He owes more to the prophets than a wealth of imagery ; directly or indirectly he owes much of the seed from which his own thought springs. He read with a mind at once simple and ingenious. What was written must be fulfilled, he thought (cf. xvii. 17)—and this firm belief in the truth of the many apparently conflicting elements in prophetic conceptions of the last days is responsible for some of the more puzzling things in REVELATION. This simple attitude of mind could persist only by the exercise of great ingenuity. Conflicting expectations must somehow be reconciled. Prophetic oracles about the Jewish nation must be adapted to the changed circumstances of the Church ; or, rather, as John would have said, the ciphers and symbols in which the prophets wrote must be properly read, as God had really intended. To some extent he was helped by the prophets themselves, who sternly distinguished between the faithful remnant of God's people, and the Jewish nation as a whole. What was spoken to the ' faithful remnant ' in the prophetic books, John takes to be intended for the Christian Church ; the reproaches and execrations heaped on the ' stiff-necked and uncircumcised in heart and ears ' he assigns to the false Israel, who denied Christ, or the disloyal Christian, perhaps, who deserted Him. This was, of course, a natural and common process among early Christian writers ; only the extraordinary allusiveness and idiosyncrasies in John's book make it necessary to associate it distinctively with him. The resurrection of the martyrs, for example, is described in terms which probably hold a remarkable implication. The words, **the breath of life entered into them ; they stood on their feet,** and also some of the suggestions in their context, are recollected from Ezekiel's famous prophecy about the valley of dry bones (Ezek. xxxvii.). Ezekiel is granted a

vision of the spiritual regeneration and the rehabilitation of
the Jewish people. As he prophesies, the ' dry bones ' of his
countrymen are covered with flesh, and into their ' corpses '
new life stirs. ' I prophesied as I was told, and *the breath did
enter into them* ; they came to life and *stood upon their feet,*
a mighty host of them.' Ezekiel explained that he was speaking of his people ; but for John this ' mighty host ' was formed
of the loyal servants of Christ, the witnesses, the 'great host'
(vii. 9) of those who had been sealed. But what process of interpretation is involved in this allusion ? For we must insist that it
represents more than any literary recollection. We to-day
look back over the long vistas of history through the tele-
scopes of research, we see Ezekiel in the setting of his age, and
we attempt to understand the meaning which he himself
attached to his words. For John, however, such a prophecy
was an oracle, spoken beforehand for present guidance, and
valid detail by detail for contemporary circumstances. Axio-
matically, the oracle contained a divine truth. But what was
it ? There could be no question of its reference to the Jews as
a people, since the Christian churches had supplanted them ;
they alone were now the true Israel, as John points out with
inescapable emphasis in chap. vii. Nor was there any need
for the spiritual regeneration of the true Church of Christ—
communities like those at Smyrna and Philadelphia. As to
the disloyal among the Christian churches, they received their
warning, and were free to repent or to stay condemned.
Ezekiel's prophecy to the ' whole community of Israel '
assuredly had no reference to them. How then was it to be
understood ? The answer was a startling one. It was to be
understood literally ! As John became certain that a great
persecution was to overtake the Church, he saw a new and
astonishing significance in Ezekiel's words. The ' stainless '
followers of Christ would be martyred, and the Spirit would
literally recall them to life ; they would literally rise to their
feet—all that ' mighty host.' And when the Eternal promised
that they were to be restored to their own land (Ezek. xxxvii.
14)—where was this land ? Where, but **heaven ?**

So up to heaven they went, in a cloud. This is the ' first resurrection ' (xx. 4 and 5) ; the martyrs have gone to their reward, secure of bliss and eternal life. The seven trumpet blasts, we now see, have been signals, not only for the destruction of the earth, but also for the preservation of the Elect. The **loud voice telling them, 'Come up here,'** represents the trumpet calls of resurrection and ascension. We shall not now make the mistake of objecting that the seventh trumpet has not yet been heard, for we can now see the true logical and chronological relationship of the episodes of chap. vii. and chaps. x.–xi. to their context. We can now see that both passages are surveys of the fortunes of the Elect from the beginning of intense persecution to the beginning of God's reign. In fact, each episode is practically co-terminous with its septiform series of predictions about the world in general. The presence of the Elect in heaven is the sign that God's reign on earth has actually begun ; simultaneously with the completion of the number of the martyrs in heaven, the blood of the righteous is avenged on those who dwell on earth (vi. 9–11). And this dreadful time is described in REVELATION on the breaking of the seventh seal, the blowing of the seventh trumpet, and the emptying of the seventh bowl of the wrath of God.

The ascension of the witnesses reminds us that the Christian prophets who in life resembled Moses and Elijah, performing as they did the functions assigned to them by tradition, are like them favoured in their departure from this earthly scene (cf. 2 Kings ii. 11 and the Assumption of Moses) ; and, again, that the resemblance between the careers of the witnesses and their Lord is now brought to its glorious conclusion (cf. notes on xii. 6 and xii. 17). The ascension of Christ demonstrated the powerlessness of the ' dragon ' to frustrate God's purposes ; the ascension of the martyrs demonstrates the dragon's final defeat. Mankind are now forced to recognize that God is all-powerful ; hence their **terror.** It is more than a natural shrinking at a supernatural spectacle ; it is the dread of men who at last recognize in this spectacle, and in the havoc of the accompanying **earthquake,** the omnipotence of the righteous God, whose cause they have flouted, whose servants they have killed, whose enemies they have deified (St. Matt. xxvii. 52).

At this point John's vision is once again coloured in a remarkable, almost perverse way by prophetic tradition. It was thought by certain pious psalmists and prophets that ultimately the pagan nations would acknowledge the unique power, splendour, and holiness of God. In Isaiah's words (Isa. xlv. 23) :

> ' As I am God and God alone,
> I swear by myself,
> I swear a true word,
> never to be recalled,
> that every knee shall bow to me
> and every tongue swear loyalty.'

In Isa. lii. 13-15 this ' conversion ' of the nations is associated with the exaltation of Israel, as the result of some signal act of God's favour : ' For they shall see what they were never told, a sight unheard of.' Ps. lxxxvi. 8-10 (cf. Ps. xxii. 27-31 ; Ps. lxv. 2, 5-8) expresses this belief in a more general way : ' There is no God like thee, O Lord, there are no deeds like thine ; all nations thou hast made shall come and bow down before thee, glorifying thee, O Lord, for thou art great, thou workest wonders, thou, only thou, art God.' John was naturally conscious of this expectation. He actually quotes from Ps. lxxvi. : ' Yea, all nations shall come and worship before thee ' (xv. 4)—and this quotation occurs in the ' Song of Moses and of the Lamb ' sung by the martyrs in heaven. It is this thought which is expressed allegorically in the statement of xi. 13. The **City, one tenth** of which is **destroyed,** is the world, as we have seen above (verses 2 and 8), and **the seven thousand souls** who perished in the **earthquake** represent a like proportion of mankind. The **seven** indicates that the calamity falls universally. Mankind in general is represented by the number seventy thousand ; just as the host of conquerors (the hundred and forty-four thousand) is represented by the *two* witnesses. After so many of mankind have been slain, **the rest were awe-struck, and gave glory to the God of heaven.** In other words, the prophecies of Isaiah and the psalmists have been fulfilled. The nations have seen ' what they were never told, a sight unheard of ': they have witnessed the miraculous vindication of God's servants; it is impossible that they should any longer blind themselves to the eternal might of God. They must perforce give Him **glory.** But this is not what it seems; John does not share the optimism of Isaiah and the psalmists. In fact, he knows that the great mass of mankind will have committed the unpardonable crime of deifying evil. They will have pledged themselves to the cause of Satan, and damned themselves eternally (xiii. 8, 14, xiv. 9–11). In these circumstances, there is no question of any general ' conversion ' of mankind in the last days. Men give **glory to the God of heaven** when it is too late for their own salvation—when they are compelled by overriding terror to recognize that the true Lord is Christ and not Antichrist. Remorse and not repentance is their condition. The scene should be compared with that in vi. 15–17, where the terror of men is equally an acknowledgment that at last they have understood God's omnipotence and the approach of inexorable judgment.

The **great earthquake** is the first shock of the final upheaval referred to in viii. 5 and xi. 19, and described in greater detail in xvi. 18–19. John speaks of the initial destruction of only a part (a **tenth**) of civilization, in order to make room for his picture of terror-stricken and remorseful humanity. It is as if to say, as soon as God reveals His irresistible strength, the heathen nations who now deny Him will be blinded into involuntary homage.

xi. 14–19 : THE SEVENTH TRUMPETER HERALDS THE END

14 The second woe has passed :
the third woe soon is coming.
15 Then the seventh angel blew ; and loud voices followed in heaven, crying, '*The rule* of the world has passed to our *Lord and his Christ,* and *he shall reign for ever and ever.*'
16   Then the four and twenty Presbyters who are seated on their thrones before God, fell on their faces and worshipped
17   God, saying,

'We thank thee, *Lord God almighty, who art* and wast,
that thou hast assumed thy great power and *begun to
reign ;*
the nations were enraged,   18
but thy *wrath* has come,
the time has come for the dead to be judged,
the time for rewarding *thy servants the prophets*
and the saints *who reverence* thy name, *both low and high,*
the time for destroying the destroyers of the earth.'
Then the temple of God in heaven was thrown open, and *the ark* 19
of his covenant was seen *inside his temple ;* there were
flashes of lightning, loud blasts, peals of thunder, an
earthquake, and a *hailstorm.*

The climax of the trumpet series of plagues has been 14
suspended during the long interlude of chaps. x.–xi. 13.
Verse 14 now marks the resumption of the series ; we are
taken back to the eagle's cry in viii. 13, which introduces the
three ' woes ' announced by the last three trumpeters. These
woes are direct scourges of mankind. The last is decisive.

The **loud voices** following the seventh trumpet blast pro- 15
claim what was formerly concealed in the **silence** after the
breaking of the seventh seal (viii. 1) : ' **The rule of the world
has passed to our Lord and his Christ, and he shall reign for
ever and ever.** John can be more explicit now about this
fact, for he has told his readers the story of the great Distress,
the event which he believed to be the necessary prelude to
the End. At the conclusion of both series of predictions, of
those associated with the breaking of the seals and those
announced by the blowing of trumpets, we have arrived at
the end of civilization, the end of temporal anomalies, of the
apotheosis of evil ; we have arrived at the beginning of God's
everlasting reign of justice. Whereas this fact is left to inference after the breaking of the seventh seal, John now chooses
to announce it quite plainly.

If these literary tactics puzzle us, we must remember that
John claims to be reporting his own gradual enlightenment
about the course of the future. Through vision after vision,

the mists of the present disperse ; little by little, the shape of the future, and the principles underlying the trend of events, become clear. It is not only that he is finally able to scrutinize the furthermost limits of his landscape, to see there the pinnacles of the Eternal City ; more to the point, he is able to see nearer objects increasingly stripped of obscurity and distortion. At the seventh trumpet blast he can distinguish what the straining vision of Christians had so long sought—the beginning of God's universal reign. And John has at this point eyes for nothing else. Later he will describe what he sees at this stage in greater detail ; nor has he yet finished his sketch of the foreground, stained as it is with the blood of martyrs and the crimes of their enemies, and illumined with the lightning flashes of God's wrath.

16 The song of the **four and twenty Presbyters** (see note on iv. 4) takes up the theme announced by the **loud voices.** These angelic beings cast aside their royal state to pay homage to
17 the **Lord God almighty,** who has **begun to reign.** No longer is He the Lord 'who is and was and *is coming'* (i. 8, iv. 8); He *has come,* and the Presbyters now cry : ' Lord God almighty, **who art and wast.** . . .' To John's mind the present rifeness of evil in the world could be explained in one way only ; in order to 'test the dwellers on earth' (iii. 10; cf. ii. 10), God had allowed the Devil and his agents to exercise authority in the world, an authority with the widest of boundaries (chap. xiii.). Until this time of testing was over, and men had shown themselves true or false, God's **rule** was incomplete. His indeed was always the final authority ; John makes it quite clear that the Devil reigns on earth by God's permission, to serve divine purposes. At this stage, however, God exercises immediate authority : ' **Thou hast assumed thy great power and begun to reign.'** (The R.V. translation of the Greek *ebasileusas,* ' didst reign,' is literal, and misses the idiomatic force indicated in this translation.) The defiant rage of Satan (cf. xii. 12 and 17) and his servants, which causes them to oppress God's people, is now at last met with the full force of **divine** punishment ; their last opposition is vanquished
18 (cf. xix. 17 ff.) : **the nations were enraged, but thy wrath has**

come. This is a reminiscence of Ps. ii., previously cited by John (ii. 26-7) to indicate that the *conquerors* of the seven churches will be rewarded by a share in the infliction of punishment on ' the nations '—that is, the pagan nations, devotees of the Imperial Antichrist. No doubt the quotation of xi. 17 retains the flavour of its original context, for the judicial and royal authority to be wielded by the Elect in the messianic reign has a prominent place in John's mind (cf. ii. 26-27, iii. 21, v. 10, xx. 4). It is of this reign and these privileges that John is speaking in verse 18 : ' **the time has come for rewarding thy servants the prophets and the saints who reverence thy name, both low and high.'** The **prophets** are they who died in the great Distress or previous martyrdoms (cf. note on xi. 3 ; ' witnesses ')—who come to life in the ' first resurrection.' **The saints, both low and high,** whose service of God consists in reverencing His name rather than in proclaiming His Gospel, in worship rather than in prophecy— these are they who are preserved both spiritually and physically until the reign of peace begins (cf. xi. 1-2, xii. 13-17). They too must be rewarded. They cannot enjoy the martyrs' ' thrones ' nor immunity from the pangs of death and the ordeal of Judgment, since all but the martyrs must rise on the second resurrection, on the day of reckoning (xx. 4 ff.) ; nevertheless, although John does not go into any detail, he expects that all loyal Christians will have favoured places in the messianic kingdom on earth. The nature of their rewards may be gathered from those passages in the prophetic books which describe the blessings of the Davidic reign. The time for **destroying the destroyers of the earth** (for this phrase, see notes on xvii. 15-18) is an event which must precede the final establishment of this kingdom. We read of this event in xix. 17-21, where the hosts of Satan are defeated and the Imperial powers, with the supporters of their blasphemous claims, are consigned to ' the lake of fire that blazes with brimstone.' The punishment of the living for their impiety, the reward of the martyrs and saints for their fortitude and loyalty, the destruction of their persecutors—these are the immediate issues of God's assumption of His **great power.** The reference to the judgment of the **dead** is anticipatory ; the dead are judged after the reign of the thousand years (xx. 5, 11). This need give rise to no perplexity, however, for when the Presbyters sing, ' **The time has come,**' they are merely asserting that an era has begun, in which all wrongs are to be righted, and all evil-doers punished, even beyond death. From this beginning flows the whole course of God's reversals of the terrestrial order.

After the Presbyters have finished their song, John sees in his vision the portents of the End. Here again he tells us more than in viii. 5, after the breaking of the seventh seal. He tells 19 us first that **the temple of God in heaven was thrown open and the ark of his covenant was seen inside his temple.** In other words, John is able to see in the holiest place, in the very presence of God, the sign that the Elect have been gathered to their celestial home. The Ark of the Covenant had been lost long ago ; according to rabbinic tradition it had been hidden with other sacred objects (the altar of incense, for example ; cf. viii. 3 ; and the pot of manna contained in the ark ; cf. ii. 17) lest it should share the destruction of the temple. And for centuries the Jews had believed that at the restoration of the chosen people the holy things of the temple would be disclosed at last, and the shame of their loss wiped out (cf. Jer. iii. 16 ; 2 Esdras x. 22). John, however, is less concerned with the earthly shape of holy things than with their heavenly originals. It is the heavenly **temple** which is **thrown open** (and cf. note on xxi. 22), and the **ark** is a heavenly sign that God's compact with His people had been fulfilled. Nothing now delays the outpouring of His wrath on the world : **there were flashes of lightning, loud blasts, peals of thunder, an earthquake, and a hailstorm.** These are the portents of the End, described as in viii. 5 formally and briefly. The thunder and lightning are traditional symbols of divine anger ; the earthquake is the last earthquake, of which we hear more when the ' seventh bowl ' of the wrath of God is poured on the earth (xvi. 18 ff.) and the hailstorm, an addition to the details of viii. 5, also appears at the end of the final series of plagues, where its terrible effect on men is announced.

SEVEN ORACLES CONCERNING THE LAST DAYS

INTRODUCTION TO CHAPTERS XII.–XIV.

The method of narration and the terms employed in chaps. xii.–xiv. are so different from anything we have hitherto encountered that we must at once consider what is the relation of this section with the two cycles of predictions preceding it.

At the end of the eleventh chapter John has brought his readers once again to the end of his tale of destruction, to the Day of Wrath, when the kingdoms of this world receive their final defeat at God's hands. Against that lurid background of general havoc he has shown us the spectacle of the martyrs— their spiritual protection, their witnessing, their death, resurrection, and ascension, and their ultimate reward in heaven. It should be noted that the two septiform surveys of destruction, with their all-important excursuses, have been concerned with the ominous period between the first portents of the End and the End itself—in other words, with the ' three and a half years ' of Antichrist's dominion ; but the new survey contained in chaps. xii.–xiv., however, covers the whole messianic period, and its material lies partly in the past (xii. 1–5) and partly in the ominous period of the future (xii. 6–xiv.). This difference is symptomatic of a change in method. Previously John has spoken of the future objectively. He has said : ' You must expect these things to happen ; these events are a necessary prelude of the End.' Now he pauses to lay bare the inner truth of the conflict and turmoil of the earth's climacteric years. He explains his prophetic picture of what is to come by a prophetic picture of the past. Whatever others might think of the disasters which were to overtake the world, of the sinister powers enthroned in it, of the future holocaust of the unblemished witnesses of God, the devout reader of John's apocalypse was armed against all disheartenment or doubt. Undiscerning believers might think of their persecutors as mere flesh and blood ; they might see no essential principle lending unity to the bewildering sequence of events. But John tells them that the ordeal will come as a climax to a continuous struggle, ultimately prompted, not by the brutality of men, but by the malice and fury of Satan. He is of one mind with St. Paul : ' For we have to struggle, not with blood and flesh, but with the angelic Rulers, the angelic Authorities, the potentates of the dark present, the spirit-forces of evil in the heavenly sphere' (Eph. vi. 12). The prince of these unseen adversaries John depicts as a huge red dragon : the incarnate ministers of evil, known to the world as Emperors, are described in the symbol of the Beast which bears the shape of the dragon himself. As to the shape of future events in a world so governed, could there be any astonishment at persecution, any dismay at the ubiquity of evil, any consternation at the advent of world-wide plagues and portents of God's wrath ? No, these things were inevitable ; they were intrinsic in the mighty battle between good and evil—between the servants of God and the servants of Satan. It is this conflict which forms the subject of chaps. xii.–xiv. John's desire is to show the martyrs of the future that their part in the battle will be decisive, as it had been in the past. From the messianic people came the Child who eventually was to crush Satan and his ministers. And the messianic people must supply those who would finish the task of earlier martyrs, and raise the flood-gates of divine wrath. The whole section is pastoral in purpose, and its moral is stated outright in chap. xiv.: let no Christian shrink from the destined battle—the final issue is assured, and the fruits of victory are shown to be ineffably sweet ; but the penalties of insincerity, compromise, feebleness and cowardice are horrible, almost beyond contemplation.

If this is indeed the burden of John's story, has he not found needlessly obscure terms in which to convey it ? So the schoolboy complains as he wrestles with his annotated Milton ; and if we in turn quarrel with John's symbols, the schoolboy has the juster grievance. We should have no difficulty in following the patriotic moralist who spoke of Britain as a crusading warrior vanquishing a fiery dragon, and rescuing the innocent from oppression. Whatever international event inspired such a patriotic encomium, whatever the new circumstances dictating the shape of the dragon, the mode of battle, the character of the distressed maiden, and whatever interpolations these circumstances cast into the original dragon story, we should still recognise the lineaments of that legendary conflict which gave us our patron saint. The allegory of xii.–xiv. 5 is similarly allusive : the reason why it is so strange to modern readers is that they are not as spontaneously aware as were John's contemporaries of the allusions to myth and legend which helped to determine its form.

It will be of some help in appreciating the character of John's narrative if we observe that there is every evidence, here once again, of a septiform arrangement. The main survey of these chapters, ending at xiv. 5, contains seven distinct oracles. With one exception they are arranged to tell a continuous story in chronological sequence, but there is, nevertheless, an occasional detail which overlaps. The first oracle states the theme of the **woman clad in the sun** (the messianic community), who gives birth to **a son**, the Messiah ; the Messiah is threatened by the lord of evil, depicted as a **huge red dragon**, but through His ascension is delivered from the hostility of the evil one. The second oracle proclaims the ejection from heaven of Satan, and the consequent intensification of his activity on earth ; it contains an allusion to the heroic constancy of Christian martyrs, whose death has been the signal for Satan's ejection. The next theme is the sharpening of Satan's hostility against the messianic people. The ' woman ' flees from the dragon and her flight is supernaturally assisted. The dragon's attacks are of no avail ; the woman is preserved in the desert. The fourth oracle takes us into the future, and shows us how Antichrist emerges into the world (**the Beast rising out of the sea**). Antichrist emerges into the world endowed with the attributes and authority of Satan. He seduces most of mankind to his worship. In the fifth oracle we are told of his execution of the witnesses of God—**the rest of the** offspring of the messianic community (the first 'child' was Christ); although the community as a whole will be preserved, her most devoted sons are destined to martyrdom. This prediction tells in a different way the story of chap. xi.; with the accomplishment of the great Distress we know that the End is to follow immediately. But John has still more to say about the character of Antichrist's dominion over the earth, so in his sixth oracle he tells how the first Beast's will is to be enforced by a second Beast—symbolizing the religious institutions devoted to the cult of Antichrist. Thus, the inquisition is to cast its fine-meshed net over the whole world. Finally, John describes the martyrs in possession of their reward. Their suffering is to be no light one—but how infinitely glorious the prize ! Here is the conclusion of the story which, John found, ' did taste sweet, like honey, but when I had eaten, it was bitter to digest ' (x. 10).

A woman clad in the sun ; a grotesque, hydra-like dragon spouting floods of water ; an eagle like Sindbad's roc to help the woman in her flight to some mysterious desert ; a Beast incarnate in the dragon's shape ascending into the world of men ; another Beast with a Lamb's horns and a dragon's voice—strange intruders in a handbook for Christian martyrs ! The reader who plunged into the maze of REVELATION in the brave hope of finding his way unhelped must now at last call for a guide—doubtless with the irritated feeling that the way out of his perplexities is all the time very simple and almost within sight. There are many guides, however, and the adventurous reader will too often find himself in new mazes of speculation and exegesis. He is, in fact, put to much needless trouble. For most of the difficulties rising out of chaps. xii.-xiv. have been born of three mistakes. First, there has been a failure to realize fully that these chapters form a single unity with one focal point ; the strife which culminates in the great martyrdom. Secondly, many vain attempts have been made to interpret details without close reference to that subject—such details, for example, as the birth and ascension of the child, and the dragon's ejection from heaven. Thirdly, it has been assumed that the author

of REVELATION was often content to be little more than a re-
dactor, a purveyor of second-hand visions, so lacking in
literary deftness that he has been unable to trim his old wares
to suit their new setting. The evidence of the seven letters
alone should be enough to guide us past those errors. There
we see a prophet who had a consuming purpose ; who was
artist enough to express his purpose in a form demanding the
strictest literary discipline—the rigid exclusion of all but
essential material, the careful co-ordination of every considered and significant detail with a symbolical design ; who,
finally, was convinced beyond question that he had seen something of priceless worth, something new and indispensable,
and was bound to testify to what he saw. Nor are those
qualities lacking in the rest of REVELATION. ' Sources ' John
may have had—and so had Shakespeare. How many sources
can we not trace in the great Doom Song of chap. xviii., and
the picture of the new Jerusalem in chap. xxi. ? But these
sources are treated with something like Shakespearian freedom ; in his use of recollected material John displays both
subtlety and originality. It would be more than strange if in
that part of the book which deals with the great Distress—
the supremely important event of the future, the ' only
begetter ' of REVELATION—John found himself wholly reliant
on a source for the framework of his story. It would be still
stranger if he had not striven with all his powers to make every
detail of his story effective.

Essentially, the story of xii.–xiv. 5 is one of supernatural
conflict between the forces of light and darkness, of good and
evil—a theme forming a constant substratum in all mythologies. Doubtless the story was told in many forms in Asia
Minor ; as with popular religions, the traits of native myths
could mingle easily with the foreign. If we assume that
xii.–xiv. 5 is an original composition, for some reason containing certain clear allusions to a well-known myth, we are
not therefore under any necessity to seek precedents for every
small detail. All we need do is to find the particular mythical
theme to which John was alluding. And it seems almost
certain that this theme is to be recognized in a myth known to

be popular in Asia Minor—that of Leto, Apollo, and Python. Leto, a goddess with child by Zeus, is attacked by the dragon, Python. She flees, and is helped to an island refuge by Boreas. Shortly after his birth, Apollo pursues the dragon and slays it.

Now there are, admittedly, several points in John's story which find no place in the myth ; but what of that ? John was not modelling his story to form a Christian replica of a pagan myth ; he was alluding to the characters in a mythical conflict. Naturally there are large discrepancies between the details of the myth and those of John's narrative. He was free to let his own story take its proper course, and to show the actors in it as he himself saw them. Consider the dragon alone ; here is a more fearsome creature than the mud-born Python. Yet, none the less, he bears some kinship to this serpentine creature of the myth : Python's hostility to Apollo arose out of a prophecy that the sun-god would be his slayer. Here is the familiar monster of Hebrew folk-lore, the spirit of the hostile and chaotic ocean—Leviathan, Behemoth, Rahab ; the serpent who is the subtle tempter and seducer of mankind ; the angelic ' prosecuting counsel ' of later Jewish fancy—the sinister being who used the privilege of access to the Seat of Judgment to slander the righteous before God. And what Hydra-like creature of Babylonian mythology suggested the seven heads ? His very colour, a menacing red, seems to be suggested by the Egyptian monster Typhon, the persecutor of the sun-goddess, Osiris. In fact, John's picture of the Evil One is as syncretistic as the pagan religions of Asia Minor.

Are we then to be so bold as to say that a Christian apocalyptist of the first century could freely speak of the messianic people in terms appropriate to a sun-goddess, and in one breath associate Christ and Apollo ? Whether John was composing freely or not, it is absurd to imagine that he was unaware of the implications of so colourful a picture as he gives in xii.–xiv. 5. We must accept his words for what they are, and try to find the motives prompting them.

We need not seek far. The mythical colours of chap. xii. are an elaboration of the process of polemical allusion already noted in some of the seven letters. In two at least of the introductions to the letters we detect an implicit contrast of the true claims of Christ with the false claims of the Imperial power. Christ, not the Emperor, possesses the symbolical sword of power, and the feet glowing like bronze, strong to punish. Christ, not the Emperor, is *dei filius*. This last Imperial claim, which links the Emperors with Apollo of our myth, is reflected in John's picture of the Satanic being who was to be at once the last of the Emperors and the complete embodiment of the evil power hitherto only partially revealed in the individual members of the Imperial line. The first Beast of chap. xiii. has 'blasphemies' written on his heads; and indeed his whole character is the infernal counterpart of Christ (see notes). John did not see the Emperors of the past and the fierce monster of the future as political personages ; they were beings who arrogated to themselves the worship due to Christ, and who claimed His unique relationship with the Eternal God. When, therefore, he uses the title ' Son of God ' for Christ he is asserting a truth and incidentally challenging a falsity. It is so with the whole story of chap. xii. John tells the true story of the conflict between good and evil, and incidentally denies the false one. It is not that he is eking out his stock of symbols and pictures with the abundant material of legend ; much less that he admits pagan myths to be valid analogies to the Christian Gospel. He is asserting the Christian faith in terms which deny a pagan travesty of it. The *true* mother of the incarnate Son of God is the messianic people—not Leto, nor any other goddess of pagan veneration. And the true Son of God is Christ, not Apollo ; it is Christ whose witness and warfare will result in the dragon's ultimate defeat—He and His loyal servants are the true actors in the great struggle between light and darkness. And if we still find difficulty in understanding how a Christian writer could refer so cursorily to the earthly ministry of Christ as John does in xii. 5 (' She gave birth to a son . . . her child was caught up to God and to his throne ') let us remember that the subject of the whole survey is strictly not the Messiah, but the messianic community and its future ordeal at the hands of

Antichrist.   John has this artistic peculiarity ; he deals rigidly with one subject at a time, and deliberately blots out from his canvas any details which might distract attention from the central figures. The picture of heaven in chap. iv. contains no suggestion of Christ ; that comes in chap. v. The silence after the breaking of the seventh seal deliberately withholds the information given by the ' loud voices ' and the Presbyters after the blowing of the seventh trumpet. The ' gap ' between the sealing of the martyrs and their appearance in heaven is filled later by the story of chap. xi. These are only a few of the more striking examples. Unless this characteristic of John's literary method is understood and properly applied, such passages as xii. 5 will always remain enigmatic, no matter what the ingenuities of source criticism may propose.

xii. 1–6 : The First Oracle : the Woman, the Messiah and the Dragon

1   And a great portent was seen in heaven, a woman clad in the sun—with the moon under her feet, and a tiara of twelve

2   stars on her head ; she was with child, *crying in the pangs*

3   *of travail, in anguish for her delivery*. Then another portent was seen in heaven! There was a huge red dragon, with seven heads and *ten horns* and seven diadems upon his

4   heads ; his tail swept away a third of *the stars of heaven and flung* them *to the earth*. And the dragon stood in front of the woman who was on the point of being delivered, to

5   devour her child as soon as it was born. *She gave birth to* a son, *a male child*, who is to *shepherd* all *the nations with an iron flail ;* her child was caught up to God and to his

6   throne, and she herself fled to the desert, where a place has been prepared for her by God, in which she is to be nourished for twelve hundred and sixty days.

1   **A woman**, a dragon : we have been introduced to the chief actors in John's new survey of the great conflict in the earth's

last years. Why, then, do we read that they were seen *in the sky* ? (For this is the sense of the Greek, rather than ' in heaven.') What have these portents on high to do with the sombre affairs of this world ? These two sketches, of the woman arrayed in solar brilliance, decked with the mysterious jewels of astrology, and of the nightmarish monster who succeeds her in John's vision, are nothing more nor less than what John calls them—portents. They are messages traced in the sky. The actual events of our story begin in the latter part of verse 4. Until then John has been occupied in showing us, by means of two successive ' sky-paintings,' that he is going to tell us about the fortunes of the messianic people and the activity of their enemy, the prince of evil. It is of some moment to be clear about this from the first. Otherwise we shall be caught in a web of our own weaving ; we shall ask how it is that these two beings seen in the sky are soon afterwards depicted in an earthly setting (verses 4 ff.). We shall do well to remember that the **woman clad in the sun** and the **huge red dragon** are portents of the same kind as the four horsemen (chap. vi.), and the five angels of chap. xiv. ; their purpose is to instruct. They are images projected on a screen where all may see them.

This is not all, however. The realities of which the two portentous figures form symbolical pictures were for other reasons appropriate to the heavens. Hebrew folk-lore found nothing anomalous in the presence at the Judgment Seat itself of the persecutor and accuser of men (see note on verse 10). And just as John can speak of the seven churches as having a celestial character—he can actually address them as ' angels ' —so he can speak of the messianic people ; their life on earth is the reflex of a brighter heavenly existence. At her first appearance in chap. xii. as a portent, the **woman** wears the glory of her heavenly character, as the ideal counterpart of the earthly messianic people. We need not pause long here over the mystical beliefs involved in John's picture. If we are to make the obvious inference from the procedure of chap. ii., where John exhorts, rebukes, and praises the ' angels ' of the churches exactly as if they were the churches themselves, we are also justified in believing that in his picture of the woman in the sky John is merely showing us the ' faithful remnant ' of Israel as an essentially spiritual community : no mere association of men bound together by such mundane ties as nationality or interest, but an honoured member of the great hierarchy of God's subjects, the earthly ambassadors of a divine king.

But how easy it is to lose the fire of John's words in these draughty, bare corridors of comment ! We have before us a glittering portent, a picture to stir wonder and courage in the hearts of martyrs. Time has much to answer for that its Lethean flow compels us analyse and argue. Yet we can do no other. It is only too easy to pursue in REVELATION :

> ' An *ignis fatuus* that bewitches
> And leads men into pools and ditches.'

Fortunately, however, it remains still in our power to recall to ourselves some at least of the restrained passion which memory and contemporary circumstances infuse into John's 2 words. **The woman . . . with child, crying in the pangs of travail, in anguish for her delivery** is the personified Sion of Hebrew prophecy, the ' poor, storm-tossed soul ' in whose pain and misery Isaiah discerned the earnest of untrammelled bliss in the future : ' for your husband is your Maker ' (Isa. liv. 1 ff.) The Messiah was the hope of a people trained by humiliation and adversity to seek deliverance from God ; her prophets taught her to see in present distress a necessary prelude to future glory. In these prophetic references to the pangs of Israel's travail, John detects the preparation of the messianic people for the coming of Christ. The **woman** is the true Israel in her pre-messianic agony of expectancy.

> ' Thou did'st make us, O Eternal,
> like a woman in her labour,
> near her time of travail,
> writhing in her pangs ;
> for we were labouring, writhing,
> and nothing came of it ;
> we could not make our country safe,
> or overcome the world.'
>
> (Isa. xxvi. 17, 18.)

They could not overcome the world ; no, only the Lamb was
' found worthy ' to break the seals of God's book of Doom.
Why then does Isaiah abruptly leave this lament and cry :

> ' O thou Eternal, thy dead shall live again,
> awakening from the dust
> with songs of joy ;
> for thy dew falls with light and life,
> till dead spirits arise ' ?
>
> (Isa. xxvi. 19.)

What fills the interval between the pangs of travail and the
consummation of joy ? John, we may be confident, saw in
this interval much more than Isaiah ; we may conjecture,
for example, that he saw some foreshadowing of the astonishing story told in his eleventh chapter. He certainly saw that
the woman in travail had borne her son—not unheralded by
the oracles of God : ' For a child has been born to us, a son
has been given to us ; the royal dignity he wears, and this the
title that he bears—" A wonder of a counsellor, a divine hero,
a father for all time, a peaceful prince ! " ' (Isa. ix. 6.) Such is
the character of the **son** born to the woman in REVELATION.
The true Israel had been granted her prayer of centuries ; no
longer was she a reproach for her barrenness. And, John adds,
though the prince of evil recognized in the child his deadly
enemy, he was powerless to snatch from the messianic people
the fruit of their years of ' patient endurance.' Shall we now
demand why John fails to say more about the **child**, who with 5
such apparent abruptness is **caught up to God and to his
throne?** Must he now amplify his narrative with an irrelevant credo ? Artistic economy forbade such a procedure.
The context is rich enough in allusion to leave us in no doubt.
Clearly, the **child** is not the Babe of Bethlehem. John's
thought does not even approach the metaphysical conceits of
later devotion, which saw the hosts of evil already recoiling
from ' the dredded Infant's hand ' :

> ' Our Babe, to shew his Godhead true,
> Can in his swadling bands controul the damnèd crew.'

When John tells us that **the dragon stood in front of the woman
. . . to devour her child as soon as it was born,** he has in mind

no thought of Herod's massacre of the Innocents. Such a historical event would have been regarded by him as the work, not of the dragon, but of his earthly representatives. The **son, a male child,** is Jesus *as Messiah,* and John's words are a reference to the occasion when the Lamb which seemed to have been slain actually won His messianic power, when He won the power of opening the scroll and its seven seals (chap. v.) ; when He conquered (iii. 21), and was therefore endowed with authority to **shepherd all the nations with an iron flail** (xii. 5 and ii. 27). This last quotation from the Second Psalm is interesting as an echo of the Jewish tradition which regarded the birth of the Messiah as His triumphant enthronement. John's conception has much in common ; he sees the ' birth ' of the Messiah in Christ's Crucifixion and Resurrection. This, we must hasten to add, does not imply that in John's theological scheme Christ's *divinity* was the outcome of His death ; far from it. What John did believe was that Christ, the origin of God's creation, achieved certain new powers in this victory over death—the judicial and punitive authority proper to the Messiah in His rôle as avenger and deliverer. John would probably have found little difficulty in interpreting the mysterious oracle of Isa. lxvi. 7 :

> ' Ere ever Sion travailed, she gave birth ;
> Ere ever her pangs came, she bore a son ! '

For, as is patent in the phrase ' the origin of God's creation,' the child who at last came to the true Israel after her pangs had come, was pre-existent, destined from the beginning to become incarnate among the chosen people. True, little is made of this conception in REVELATION. It is there, none the less, and the fact that John makes so little of it is in itself a comment on his deliberate omission at this point of any but implicit reference to Christ's earthly ministry, His Death, and Resurrection. He speaks of Christ in verse 4 as a fulfilment of prophecy ; as the full answer to centuries of loyalty, heroism, and yearning ; as the issue of a community which had long **been in travail, in anguish for her delivery ;** as the promised vindicator whom Satan, for all his power and vigilance and hatred, was unable to destroy; as the first 'conqueror' of the messianic community, the faithful martyr-witness, whose death (and that alone) had given Him the right to 'shepherd the nations' with such grim purpose. Let us remember that John was writing, not a theological tract, not a confession of the elements of the Faith, but an account of the decisive facts in the history of the messianic people.

We have called the **woman** *the true Israel* (that is, the 'faithful remnant' of prophecy) and the messianic people. But does not John plainly imply that she is also the Church of Christ? (See xii. 17.) Yet how, it has been asked, can the Church be said to give birth to Christ? Or, alternatively, how can the Jewish people be said to give birth to Christian martyrs— long years after Christ's ministry? To acknowledge this dilemma is to have missed the simplicity of John's thought. We must remember that metaphors illumine only a limited number of facets of any great truth; and when John speaks of the **woman** who **gave birth** to the Messiah, the metaphor should be translated into its simple literal equivalent: *the people amongst whom Christ was born;* the people, that is, who were fit, morally and religiously, to receive in their midst the incarnate Son of God. This same people *proved* their true quality by discerning and acknowledging Christ as soon as He came. So the Church and the true Israel are in one sense identical: they are the same messianic community at different times: then, **crying in the pangs of travail;** now, enriched with the achievements of the Messiah's earthly ministry. It was, indeed, as the messianic people rather than as the mystical Body of Christ that John regarded the Church. There existed a false Israel and the true Israel. The false Israel, long since doomed, as the prophets had plainly shown them, had sealed their rejection by a national refusal to acknowledge Christ when He came. More, John remembers, they had *impaled* him (i. 7). Yet amongst the loyal souls of Israel the Messiah had come, and found acknowledgment; they, and all who joined them in faith, of whatever 'tribe and tongue and people and nation' (v. 9; cf. St. John i. 11–13), were the latter-day embodiment of the true Israel of prophecy. It was they who had been made a realm of priests (i. 6) ; they who were the twelve tribes (chap. vii.), the earthly temple of God (xi. 1–2), the seven sacred lampstands (chap. i.), the inheritors of the hidden manna (ii. 17), the worshippers at the restored altar of incense (viii. 3–4), the possessors of the once-lost covenant (xi. 19), and tabernacle of testimony (xv. 5). The churches, in short, were the true Israel. The Lord of the messianic people had come, but their task was not yet done. They are still to know the **pangs of travail.** Christ is the first martyr-child of the woman. But, as we shall read, she has other ' offspring.'

This assumption of John's about the Church is fundamental ; it underlay all his reading of the prophets and all his thought about the future crisis. In recalling it, we may perhaps recognize in the figure of the **woman** yet another glancing polemic against ' those who style themselves Jews.' This, it is true, supplies only a subordinate element in the emotional content of the picture. It is present, none the less, and it is reinforced by the **tiara of twelve stars** on the woman's **head :** an obvious reference to the twelve tribes, of which the ideal Israel is composed. These twelve stars stand in relation to the twelve tribes of the ' sons of Israel ' in chap. vii. as the seven stars to the seven lampstands in chap. i. They are here depicted as communities with a heavenly allegiance and a heavenly character (cf. notes on i. 20). The symbolical **tiara** may have been suggested by ethnic usage or perhaps by the Isaianic oracle, in which Sion, the ' bride ' of the Eternal, sings :

> ' Loud shall be my joy in the Eternal,
> In my God will I rejoice ;
> He has clothed me with victory,
> arrayed me in a robe of triumph,
> like a bridegroom he bestows a tiara,
> and gives me jewels like a bride.'

(Isa. lxi. 10.)

John himself is responsible for the **twelve** jewels in this figurative crown. When he describes the messianic people in its last, most elaborate symbolism, that of the new Jerusalem, he once more lays great emphasis on the tribal divisions. They even determine the visionary shape of the eternal City. In fact, John's insistence on the twelvefold character of the Church has roots in deeper soil than polemic: it is his way of asserting eternal providence, of revealing the clear principle of the continuity of the divine plan in history, of showing to Christians the full measure of their wealth and of their responsibility.

We are often told by commentators that the **tiara** with its **twelve stars** is derived directly from astrological myths, and that it is thus of one pattern with the rest of the woman's appearance—the **sun,** her ' robe of triumph,' and **the moon under her feet.** That there is in John's picture a calculated allusion to popular myth has already been argued (see above, 'Introduction to Chapter XII.,' pp. 214 ff.). It was probably part of John's purpose to show that the glory of God's chosen people far outshone any fabled beauty. But it seems likely that the tiara of stars was John's triumphant discrimination of the personified messianic people from any pagan travesty current in mythology. There is, in fact, little that is really alien to Hebrew terminology in the description of the woman. In Genesis, for example, we find this very collocation of the sun, moon and twelve stars with the nation as a whole (in Joseph's dream : Gen. xxxvii.). That such symbolism, like that of the seven angels of the churches and much more in REVELATION, has its ultimate origin in astrological systems is undeniable. But it is not much to the point. For in any case John was as capable as Milton of saying categorically, ' Thus they relate, erring,' of traditions, or of the current interpretations of older material ; and the evidence is strong that he was ready enough with alternative interpretations.

The truth is that the portent of the **woman clad in the sun** is better to be understood from her place in REVELATION than from analogies in myth and astrological lore. She is intended to be seen in contrast to the other woman of REVELATION, the **great Harlot** (chap. xvii.). The one is to be the ' Bride ' of Christ—or, under another symbol, the new Jerusalem, the eternal City of God. The other is wedded to evil ; she is the city of the ' dark present,' the temporal city of doom. The appearance of the first woman bespeaks her heavenly origin and attributes ; of the second, her immersion in all the vice and arrogant pride of this world. The contrast of their outward appearance is complete, and it is supported by the contrast of circumstance. The first woman is menaced by a **red dragon** and preserved from his fury : the other is in alliance with (' seated on ') Antichrist, the **scarlet Beast,** the dragon's earthly replica, but is yet destined to be destroyed by him. The one is the mother of the stainless martyrs ; the other is ' the mother of harlots and of all abominations on earth.' The one gives birth to the Messiah and His servants; the other is ' drunk with the blood of the saints and the blood of the witnesses of Jesus.' (For further remarks on this contrast, see chap. xvii.)

3   The portent of the **huge red dragon**, which succeeds the picture of the woman in the sky, presents to the modern mind an aspect of oddity, almost of quaintness, rather than of horror— as of a creature in a fairy tale. So far as a more sceptical (if not more rational) age consents at all to a personification of the principle of evil, it visualizes some Byronic figure :

> ' His brow was like the deep when thunder toss'd,
> Fierce and unfathomable thoughts engraved
> Eternal wrath on his immortal face . . .'

or Milton's ' Arch Angel ruin'd,' heroic despite his Puritan creator. It is an ill-founded judgment which credits John with naïvety on the score of the monster's shape, however. Every detail in it is symbolical ; and no single symbolical detail takes its place fortuitously. The one verse occupied by this portent forms a sermon of commendable brevity—a sermon incalculably strengthened by memories of ' that great exemplar of apocalyptic,' the Book of Daniel. The seventh and eighth chapters of Daniel should be read as a commentary on the dragon in REVELATION, as well as on the Beast (chap. xiii.). The dragon and the Beast are essentially of one shape, alike in their three most striking characteristics, their **seven heads, ten horns,** and their colour. As we should infer after reading Daniel, such details are far from being merely decorative, or even crudely indicative of the single feature of horror.

The seven crowned heads indicate something like universal and complete power (a delegated power, of course) ; and similarly the ten horns indicate formidable and sinister strength ; they might be compared with the seven horns of the Lamb, which indicate *complete* strength. The dragon's colour suggests his malice and wickedness (cf. ' scarlet ' of sins, Isa. i. 18), and, as we shall try to show later, connects him with a central theme of REVELATION—Egypt. Now, why are the dragon and the Beast so much alike ? John tells us in chap. xvii. that the heads, horns, and colour of the Beast are visible phenomena connected with this world. The ' heads ' are emperors, the ' horns ' kings as yet uncrowned ; and the ' scarlet ' is of the vat in which the Harlot's robe is dyed. If the Beast's heads and horns are separate entities, what are the dragon's ? Are we to infer that in the symbol of the dragon we have a composite picture of the whole realm of evil spirits, united in power and will, under the leadership of one more potent? Perhaps ; but there is a more assured implication in the likeness of the two monsters. As men have fashioned their conceptions of God from what they have seen and heard and known of human nobility, so John's conception of the Devil derives its shape and colour from what a prophet has seen of earthly wickedness. Whether or not he is to be accused of seeing the Empire through jaundiced eyes, or through the spectacles of prejudice (the prejudice of an oppressed ' minority '), he saw enthroned there everything that was arrogant, vicious, cunning, and ruthless. That, he says, is what the Devil is like ; he is the pattern of what we see, and what worse things we are shortly destined to see. *That* is the ' shape ' of Satan. It is, then, only when the dragon is set side by side with his vicegerent, the Beast, that we appreciate what John has achieved ; he has given to a somewhat elusive conception a bold, concrete form. Grotesque though his picture is to our minds, it must have had an air of directness and simplicity to men inured to the flights of apocalyptic ; and since they were at home in a literary convention demanding awareness to implication, John's lesson probably found its mark.

We have already touched upon the theme of the dragon's

antecedents in myth and legend (see p. 215), and little more need be said. Apocalyptic as interpreted by John supplied the essential trait: that the Devil is the original of which the 4 representatives of earthly evil are a reflex. **The tail which swept away a third of the stars of heaven and flung them to the earth** is a characteristically syncretistic feature : for the suggestion of Satanic destruction of stars comes from Dan. viii. 10, but the **tail** belongs not to Daniel's beast, but to Python or the Egyptian ' Typhon huge, ending in snaky twine '—the Nile dragon of Isa. xxvii. 1. Perhaps we are to regard this mysterious detail merely as a visionary expression for the dragon's mighty strength. Or perhaps there is in John's mind some idea of the contrast between the security of the twelve stars in the woman's tiara (cf. the seven stars held securely in Christ's hand, i. 16, 20, ii. 1, iii. 1) and the seduction and despoilment of the disloyal. Or, again, John may be preserving the original meaning of Daniel : that the powers of evil formerly crushed the faithful. Or, on the other hand, we may have here some esoteric reference to Satan's seduction of angels (cf. ' his angels,' xii. 7, 9). It is impossible to tell which notion was in John's mind. But we shall lose little of importance if we take it as evidence only of the dragon's strength ; this corresponds with what John tells us in chap. ix. of the strength of dæmonic beings (cf. ix. 10, 19).

The interpretation of such details is, however, of comparatively small moment. Our chief care must be to see the whole portent in its proper light : not in isolation, but in its true relation to the main stream of the symbolism in REVELATION. One central thought colours a great part of the imagery from chaps. vi.–xvi. An old Jewish tradition preserved the belief that the second deliverance of the chosen people would be analagous to the first (cf. St. Matt. ii, 15). John uses this tradition in a remarkable way. For him the whole civilized world is Egypt, just as the Christian churches are the true Israel, pursued like the sojourners of Goshen long ago with the ' perfidious hatred ' of a latter-day Pharaoh. Such is the story told by the plagues of the trumpets ; and this is why the great City of xi. 8 is given the ' mystical name of Sodom and *Egypt.*' This is why the martyrs, ' those who came off conquerors from the Beast,' are described in chap. xv. as singing the song of Moses—of Moses and of the Lamb : the song of the *second* deliverance. And it is for this reason that we must see in the dragon some allusion to Typhon of Egyptian myth. That the allusion was conscious and deliberate must follow from the context ; for nowhere is the background of Egypt and the first deliverance more important than in chap. xii. Reference to Ezek. xxix. and xxxii. (where suggestions for chap. xvi. may also be discerned) reveals the sort of prophetic material out of which John's allegory was constructed. Ezekiel's oracular denunciation of Pharaoh as a great Nile dragon is universalized in REVELATION. ' Pharaoh, king of Egypt,' becomes the last Emperor to rule over the whole earth—Antichrist (xi. 7, the **Beast** that ascends from the abyss ; cf. xvi. 10 with context and Ezek. xxxii. 6-8). Thus the **dragon** is connected with the theme of Egypt in his kinship with the Beast.

Our preoccupation with the Egyptian colouring of the dragon has a very practical motive. We are confronted with one of the minor mysteries of REVELATION, the woman's flight to the desert : **she herself fled to the desert, where a place has** 6 **been prepared for her by God, in which she is to be nourished for twelve hundred and sixty days.** Are these words a mysterious relic of a source, no longer apposite to the main body of thought in REVELATION ? Do they refer to some historical event. What allegory lurks behind them ? Moreover, what is the connexion between these words and the **flight to the desert** mentioned in verse 14 ? The master key which unlocks all such mysteries in REVELATION is the realization that John was as conscious if not as elaborate an allegorist as Bunyan or Spenser. We must deal more adequately with the desert symbol in its proper place ; that is, in the third oracle of this series, verses 13-17. At this point we must be content to say that the **desert** to which the woman fled represents a quality of life ; a condition of *spiritual detachment* from the affairs and fortunes of the civilized world. Christ had enabled His people to flee from the ' world,' from the ' Egypt ' of the last

days ; now they need no longer fear its contamination or its
inevitable doom. They were in the desert. The Promised
Land was removed from them only by a brief, if distressful,
interval ; the **twelve hundred and sixty days** with their ' two
and forty months ' (xi. 2) correspond with the forty-two
stations of the original desert wanderings. As elsewhere, they
indicate a time of testing, and of the predominance of evil.
The first oracle ends on this note, with all its force of encouragement and warning : the process of deliverance was begun
with the ' birth ' of the Messiah, and it is about to enter into
its critical phase.

xii. 7–12 : THE SECOND ORACLE : ATONEMENT

7 And war broke out in heaven, *Michael* and his angels *fighting*
with the dragon ; the dragon and his angels also fought,
8 but they failed, and there was no place for them in heaven
9 any longer. So the huge dragon was thrown down—that
old *serpent* called *the Devil* and *Satan*, the seducer of the
whole world—thrown down to earth, and his angels
10 thrown down along with him. Then I heard a loud voice in
heaven saying, ' Now has it come, the salvation and power,
the reign of our God and the authority of his Christ!—for
the Accuser of our brothers is thrown down, who accused
11 them day and night before our God. But they have
conquered him by the blood of the Lamb and by the word
of their testimony ; they had to die for it, but they did not
12 cling to life. *Rejoice* for this, *O heavens* and ye that dwell
in them ! But woe to earth and sea ! The devil has
descended to you in fierce anger, knowing that his time is
short.'

7   **And war broke out in heaven** ! Here once more the reader
is tempted to cry out at John's naïvety. What place has this
uncouth monster of primitive fantasy within the pale of God's
dwelling ? And if the importunity of reason will not be
stayed without some attempt to trace evil to a transcendent

source, shall we not do better with Dante to imagine the Tenth
Heaven emptied of its rebels in the beginning of creation ?

> ' Ere one had counted twenty, e'en so soon
> Part of the angels fell '

nevermore to darken the Empyrean with any cloud of strife.
Alas, we can no longer solace our troubled minds in contemplating the serenity of a Ptolemaic heaven : the universe has
grown beyond our ken, and with it the mysteries of God's
dwelling. We have become more conscious of the shackles
chaining our thought to conditions of space and time, and for
all their frequent splendour the celestial courts of other ages
have on them the marks of archaism or of naïvety. And
yet, in REVELATION at least, we shall seldom fail to find
enduring truths within the strange, bright vesture of John's
symbols. It is all too easy to accept them for their mystery
alone, to be content with that, as if they belonged to some
Xanadu of drugged vision.

As we have already seen in the first oracle, **the huge dragon—
that old serpent called the Devil and Satan,** is no mere fairy-tale
beast. He is a much more subtle, much more terrible creature
than the monsters of legend and myth. For his malice is
intelligent, stretching out cruel tentacles everywhere among
mankind, through earthly institutions. On earth he is the
seducer of the whole world. And now, in this second oracle we
hear that his activities have reached into heaven itself, where
he is the Accuser, the ' prosecuting counsel ' at the heavenly
Assize. About this rôle of Satan in Hebrew thought we learn
more from the books of Job and Zechariah. In Job the
Adversary seems at first to be on terms almost of easy rivalry
with the Eternal ; a sceptic, whom the Eternal wishes by dint
of experiment to convince of human goodness. In Zechariah
he is more distinctively a type of malicious common informer,
and the angel of the Eternal is counsel for defence ; the two
contend forensically for the soul of the high-priest Joshua.
Here are strange notions of Divine Justice ! John does much
to mitigate them, however. True, the Adversary is still
imagined in the divine presence, accusing men **day and night**

before our God. But there is a change in emphasis. His presence may now be taken as an acknowledgment that an omniscient Judge knew the justice of the indictment of the human race—of even its finest souls. While there was yet **place . . . in heaven** for the Accuser and his angels, mankind was still frail, bound by sin, unredeemed. Although the conception itself is admittedly inadequate, the presence of Satan in heaven is essentially a vivid, objective statement of man's unfitness to consort with celestial beings. It represents the pre-messianic triumph of wrong in the universe. And this, obviously, is the ruling idea for John. For he mentions the **Accuser's** activity in heaven only in order to indicate the decisive victory won by Christ for human beings : the Accuser is mentioned only as he is **thrown down** after the messianic triumph.

The ejection of the dragon from heaven is, in fact, nothing less than a pictorial expression of the Atonement. John has hitherto used three familiar metaphors to indicate the outcome of Christ's death. He has told us that the sacrifice of the Faithful Witness *cleansed* men—or rather enabled men themselves to ' wash their robes ' ; that it ' *loosed* us from our sins.' These two metaphors, as John uses them, convey the direct moral consequences of Christ's death on men. Through it they are enabled to obtain forgiveness and power to lead new lives. Thirdly, he expresses a somewhat wider conception in his metaphor of redemption, or ransom : ' thou wast slain and by shedding of thy blood hast *ransomed* for God men from every tribe and tongue and people and nation ' (v. 9). That is, He has ' paid a price ' for them, and bought them a new status— made them ' kings and priests,' no longer thralls of this world. This metaphor has sometimes been worked out to grotesque conclusions by those desiring like John to indicate the extent of man's newly won liberation. John, however, has other weapons in his armoury. In his view, the crucial fact about the pre-messianic era was that mankind was disqualified by sin from entry to heaven—by their own sin, not merely by Satan's tendentious accusations. When Christ died and assumed the sceptre of Messiahship, He enabled others to live and die as He had done. He did actually enable men to live free of sin : and we must return in thought to the seven letters to see how rigidly John pressed this claim. What followed ? This : that the Accuser was now utterly discredited, his charges *proved false*. Therefore, because his accusations no longer were truthful, because he was discredited, the Accuser could be ejected and his angels with him : **there was no place 8 for them in heaven any longer.** But *was* the Accuser yet discredited ? After all, until Christians proved the practical efficacy of Christ's sacrifice, and showed conclusively by their conduct that they both chose to be loyal and had it in their power to remain loyal under whatever stress, were not Satan's accusations still unrefuted ? In other words, unless the churches availed themselves of the power to overcome temptation and if necessary to die for their faith, Christ's sacrifice had been in vain. But what words are these—in vain ? Never ! John was utterly confident that Christ's people would do their part. The Accuser, he said, *had already* been **thrown down to 9 earth.** And why ? Because the names of the Christian martyrs were already written in the book of destiny. ' Whoever is *destined* for captivity, to captivity he goes,' he said (xiii. 10). It did not require the accomplishment of the destined act to justify Satan's ejection. Heavenly prescience read the story of the ' stainless ' martyrs and the great Distress even now written on the thunder clouds of the future. All was destined, all was known. The **salvation and power** had come 10 with Christ's death, and with it **the reign of our God and the authority of his Christ** (that is, the authority over the nations (ii. 26), still usurped by Satan and his servants ; cf. xiii. 7). At any rate, **the reign of God** had come potentially. It is true that a sinister period of Satanic domination must precede its realization on earth. But it was inscribed in the scroll with the seven seals, and the Lamb had won the power of opening that scroll and putting into effect everything in it. It is not merely that the cry of the **loud voice in heaven** is proleptic, not merely the celebration of future events as if they were in the present. Time is but the handmaid of Destiny. In the heavenly records, the Messiah already reigned, the martyrs

had already **conquered**. Such is the story told in verses 10 and
11 11. **The Accuser of our brothers is thrown down** . . . **for** (the
Greek *kai* is better so translated, rather than as ' but ') **they
have conquered him by the blood of the Lamb and by the word
of their testimony ; they had to die for it, but they did not cling
to life**. The martyrs of the great Distress, purified and
sustained by Christ's sacrifice, were to be co-partners with their
Lord (cf. xi. 8 and context) in the task of casting the foundations of the holy City ; their sacrifice was to be the completion
of His sacrifice—so great did John conceive the responsibility
resting on Christians. And Satan was already **thrown down to
earth** on the score of their proof (already made in the mind of
God) of the efficacy of Christ's death in ennobling His people.

It is for such reasons that John sees heaven as a terrain of
supernal warfare. The Accuser had been proved wrong ;
there was now no place for him in heaven, and no bar to the
entry of God's people. Why, then, is it **Michael** instead of the
newly sceptred Messiah who leads the battle against the
dragon ? Is this, as many have imagined, a sign that John is
using a Jewish source ? On the contrary, it is one of the many
signs that he is composing freely. He wishes to show Christ's
work of redemption in a light quite different from that shed
by any celestial warrior, however glorious. It was a *moral*
disqualification which the Accuser had pleaded against
mankind. It was a *moral* victory which Christ had won on
their behalf. The expulsion of Satan was incidental upon this
far greater victory. The Devil did not, in John's view, withhold men forcibly from heaven ; they succumbed of their own
will to the temptations of the **seducer :** they withheld themselves from heaven, and must always have done so, unless they
had been morally freed by Christ's sacrifice. Therefore
Michael (the patron angel of Israel) was hitherto unable to
deal violently with his opponent : he could only cry out, as
the angel of the Eternal in Zech. iii. 2 : ' The Eternal rebuke
you, O Adversary ! '

The **loud voice in heaven** has been the subject of much
unnecessary discussion. Some (as, for example, Charles,
I.C.C., vol. i., p. 327) argue that they are the voices of martyrs,

since angels could not talk about human beings as 'our brothers' : as if the term conveyed nothing else but blood relationship ! The angels are fellow-servants of God (cf. xix. 10 : ' like yourself and your brothers the prophets '), and they are here rejoicing at the accomplishment, decreed in destiny, of their great martyrdom, with all its consequences in heaven and on earth. Their joy is unqualified ; the thought of the intenser persecution coming on the earth does not dim it, for they know that the fierce anger of the Devil, descending on the 12 earth in the knowledge that his time is short, must precede the realization in fact of the reign and authority they have just celebrated. The fierce anger of Satan can harm only those who fear it, and shrink from it ; not the Christian martyrs, for they are ' armed strong in honesty ' ; only the ' craven, the faithless the abominable ' (xxi. 8). ' Woe to earth and sea ! '—that is, woe to unregenerate mankind !

xii. 13-17 : THE THIRD ORACLE : THE CHURCH FLEES FROM VANITY FAIR, PROTECTED BY GOD AGAINST SATAN

And when the dragon found himself thrown down to earth, he 13 pursued the woman who had given birth to the male child ; but the woman was given the two wings of a great eagle for 14 her flight to the desert, to her appointed place, where she is nourished for *a Time, two Times, and half a Time,* safe from the serpent. Then from his mouth the serpent poured 15 water after the woman like a river, to sweep her away with a flood ; but the earth came to the rescue of the woman, the 16 earth opened its mouth and swallowed up the river that the dragon had poured out of his mouth. So, enraged at the 17 woman, the dragon went off to wage war on the rest of her offspring, on those who keep God's commandments and hold the testimony of Jesus.

We return now to the theme already touched upon in verse 13 6, the woman's flight to the desert. John gathers the threads of his narrative of earthly events, after the brief interlude of the second oracle, which describes heavenly warfare as a necessary prelude to the fierce strife on earth. We need not be puzzled at the recurrence of this theme, since the flight to the desert symbolizes a continuous process, begun at the inauguration of the Messiah ; that of spiritual dissociation from the affairs of the world. What this amounted to in sober fact may be deduced from the seven letters (see, for example, the notes on those to the churches at Pergamum and Laodicea). The symbolism is by no means difficult to follow. On earth, under the present régime, John saw two alternative spiritual homes. There was the great City—the civilized world, or what amounted to the same thing, the Empire ; this was the city of wickedness and doom, the city from which the saints must flee (xviii. 4)—' that great City whose mystical name is Sodom and Egypt ' (xi. 8) ; this was the City which drew its life from God's earthly enemy, the Beast (xvii. 3). Clearly, the faithful Christian could have no loyalties here. *This* was not his spiritual home on earth. Rather, he must choose

14 what was diametrically opposed to the City—the **desert**; not that the Christians of the seven churches should literally betake themselves into tents, and turn nomad, but that they should pay no allegiance to the present reign of evil. This condition of detachment from the world was as necessary a preparation for life in the new Jerusalem as were the desert wanderings of the Israelites for their establishment in Canaan. And these latter-day wanderings in the wilderness, begun for Christians on the ascension and triumph of their Lord, were made much more urgent by the newly sharpened enmity of the discredited and out-cast Accuser. The parallel between the forty-two months of this time of sojourning in the ' desert ' of holy life (**a Time, two Times and half a Time**—the symbolical three and a half years of persecution) and the forty-two stages of the original desert wanderings has already been noted. There are several other parallels ; not unnaturally, since the notion that the second deliverance should be like the first inspired some of the most eloquent songs of the Exile. The pursuit of the **woman** by the **dragon,** for example, is comparable to

15 Pharaoh's pursuit of the Israelites. The **water** gushing out of

the dragon's mouth (in REVELATION a symbol for the single fact of dæmonic hostility) is an allusion, shaped by the course of the narrative, to the Red Sea : the flood-tides of an autumn equinox returning with even greater menace than those of spring. John, reading Isaiah with eyes focused on the exigencies of the present, must necessarily have allegorized such assurances as ' rivers I will turn to dry land ' (Isa. xlii. 15) ; ' no rivers shall overflow you ' (Isa. xliii. 2) ; ' With one word of rebuke I dry the sea, I turn streams into desert land ' (l. 2). Since these Isaianic prophecies were not appropriate literally to his age, John, we may be quite sure, saw in them a figurative expression for divine assistance in overcoming evil. The river of destruction which pours out of the dragon's mouth has its heavenly antithesis in the ' river of the water of Life ' in the new Jerusalem (xxii. 1). As to the earth 16 which came to the rescue of the woman and swallowed up the river—mythology has been scanned in vain for any convincing parallel. Once more we must take it as a reference (cast in its present mould by John's allegorical story) to the channel of dry land through the Red Sea—the channel in which the Egyptian pursuit was engulfed. It is a loose enough reference, admittedly ; but we may be justified in seeking its origin, partly in the exigencies of the allegory, and partly in a recollection of a phrase from the Song of Moses (Exod. xv. : alluded to directly in Rev. xv. 2) ; ' Thou stretchedst forth thy right hand, the earth did swallow them.' Perhaps the most striking echo of the story of Exodus is John's symbol for the spiritual renewal and inspiration accorded to the ' fleeing ' Christians : the woman was given the two wings of a (literally ' the ') great eagle for her flight to the desert. This is a recollection of Exod. xix. 4, where the Eternal says : ' You have seen for yourselves what I did to the Egyptians, and how I bore you safe on eagle's wings, and brought you hither to myself ' (cf. Deut. xxxii. 11). The literal rendering in the R.V., ' *the* great eagle,' is perhaps preferable. John points his allusion. The eagle of which he speaks is a familiar symbol for divine strengthening and guidance—familiar from the acquaintance of Christians with the whole story of the first deliverance ; for such acquaintance is presupposed by several tacit allusions to the events described in Exodus.

We might conclude, then, with some certainty, both from the evidence afforded by allusions and from the nature of John's symbol of the great City, that the **desert** represented the Christian way of life, ' reserved and austere,' hedged off from the follies and vices of Babylon the great, so that the path to the new Jerusalem might always appear plainly. There is, however, strong confirmation for this view in a later reference to the desert (xvii. 3) : ' he bore me away rapt in the Spirit to the desert and [omit " there " : Dr. Moffatt's translation] I saw a woman sitting on a scarlet Beast.' Now clearly John did not see the woman (who represents the great City) situated in the desert. Far otherwise, the City is ' seated on peoples and hosts, nations and tongues.' She represents the busy world of civilization, which is hardly appropriate in desert surroundings. The ' desert ' into which the Spirit had carried John was a state of complete spiritual detachment from the confused and glittering scene of the world. In this condition alone could civilization be seen in its true colours. And it will be noted that the rest of chap. xvii. is precisely what one would expect— an analysis of the forces at work in the world from the distinctive point of view of the Christian.

This matter decided, we shall find none of the customary difficulty in appreciating the force of John's allegory. It is, without serious question, a free composition, and it is therefore not surprising that the combination of traits in it should not find any exact parallel in myth. The striking features of the allegory win their place chiefly by their allusive merit. **The wings of the great eagle,** for example, probably carry in them a double allusion ; direct allusion to Scriptural story, as has been shown above, and indirect, polemical allusion to the Leto myth (see, above, pp. 215 ff.)—to Boreas, who helped Leto to her island refuge. Nor is John's story enslaved to the alien circumstances of his allusions ; its general trend is decided by what he sees in his visionary survey of Christian experience.

That is why the **dragon** pursues the woman with so curious a
' sea of troubles.' It is not merely that this is the natural
weapon of a water dragon, for the Devil in REVELATION is
much more than any dinosaurian horror ; it is because John
wishes his readers to see a parallel between their experiences
and those of the fleeing Israelites long ago.

Here, then, in the third oracle of John's new survey, we are
given a glimpse of the consequences for Christians of Satan's
ejection from heaven. It was natural that the dragon, dis-
possessed and discredited, should attack the mediator of his
discomfort with all his venom. It was inevitable that she **who
had given birth to the male child** should be attacked by the
Messiah's deadliest enemy. Hostile he must be ; and since he
was discarnate (unlike the Beast of chap. xiii.) his weapons
were naturally spiritual. He pursued the woman with a **flood**
—of temptation, the sort of thing mentioned in the letter to
Pergamum (where Satan sits enthroned), and of spiritual
harassment, as is implied in the use of the term ' synagogue of
Satan ' for the Jews (letters to Smyrna and Philadelphia).
In the past he had been the would-be **seducer** of Christians,
on the whole decidedly unsuccessful ; the seven churches had
in fact survived, even though some had been stricken. But
John, probably arguing from the contemporary trend towards
intolerance (cf. the martyrdom of Antipas, letter to Pergamum), foresaw that the time was close at hand when seduction and harassment would be replaced by open persecution :
and this at the hands of the dragon's incarnate minister, the
Antichrist, the Beast of chap. xiii. Then, in the midst of
universal inquisition, the Church would still survive. God
had provided the means of her survival in the past : ' the
earth opened its mouth and swallowed up the river that the
dragon had poured out of his mouth.' And He would do no
less for His people in the future. As John wrote his book, the
woman had almost reached her figurative **appointed place,
where she is nourished for a Time, two Times and half a Time,
safe from the serpent.** The time of Antichrist had almost
come (see xvii. 10), and at this time John believed the nature
of the dragon's attack would change. He would give to an

earthly agent ' his own power and his own throne and great
authority' (xiii. 2), and instead of attempting the spiritual
17 destruction of the messianic people as a whole, he would **wage
war on the rest of her offspring** (her previous ' children ' had
been first Christ Himself, and afterwards the martyrs mentioned in vi. 10)—that is, the martyrs whose predestined
sacrifice had already resulted in the dragon's ejection from
heaven. The distinction between the woman and her *offspring* is simply that of the messianic community as a whole,
and the noblest of her sons—' the conquerors ' in the seven
letters. They bear the same relationship to the Church as
Christ Himself, though in humbler degree. Their birth is the
same—their witness is to be the same, ending in death and
resurrection (see chap. xi.). On these men, the ' witnesses,'
the dragon now bends his hostility, little knowing that the
realization in fact of their destined sacrifice is to turn his
former discomforture into his final defeat.

xiii. 1–4 : THE FOURTH ORACLE : THE EMERGENCE AND CHARACTER OF ANTICHRIST

1 Then, as I stood on the sand of the sea, I saw *a Beast rising out
of the sea* with *ten horns* and seven heads, ten diadems on
2 his horns, and blasphemous titles on his heads. *The Beast
I saw resembled a leopard,* his feet were *like a bear's,* and
his mouth *like a lion's.* To him the dragon gave his own
power and his own throne and great authority. One of his
3 heads looked as if it had been slain and killed, but the deadly
wound was healed, and the whole earth went after the
4 Beast in wonder, worshipping the dragon for having given
authority to the Beast, and worshipping the Beast with the
cry,

' Who is like the Beast ?
Who can fight with him ? '

It is broadly true that men get the rulers they deserve. King
Log is usually supplanted in the end by King Stork. And it is

this process which John foresees in the Empire. Into a world which worshipped ' dæmons and idols of gold and silver and brass,' a world which, in spite of all the death-dealing portents of the End, refused to ' repent of their murders, their magic spells, their sexual vice, their thefts,' a fitting monarch was about to emerge. He would occupy the Imperial throne in shape no different from that of his predecessors ; but to their evil intent would be added the full measure of sacrilegious power. As Christ was God incarnate, so this last of the Emperors would be the Devil incarnate, a being in whom all the arrogance and vice of previous emperors would be concentrated. Chap. xii. has prepared us, as was intended, for the understanding of this **Beast rising out of the sea.** The new 1 monster is almost a replica of the dragon in his appearance. The main difference between the two is that the dragon represents the ultimate unseen spiritual enemy, while the Beast is tangible, a force acting visibly on earth, even though its true spiritual home is the abyss (xi. 7). The fourth oracle of this series describes the emergence of the Beast into the world, and reveals his character and authority, his reception by the inhabitants of Babylon the great and his dealings with Christians. Before we proceed to a detailed analysis, we must be quite clear about one thing : this oracle, and indeed almost everything in chap. xiii. refers not to the past (as did most of chap. xii.) but to the future. As John writes, the Beast has not yet appeared among men : the vision is of the future (see xvii. 10 ff., notes). The Beast rising out of the sea is the last earthly opponent of the Messiah, the future executioner of the witnesses (xi. 8), the contriver of the great Distress.

His appearance is, of course, entirely symbolical, as was that of the dragon (xii. 3). We are not intended to visualize the **heads** and **horns**, and argue about the distribution of amphibian anatomy. What exactly presented itself to the inward eye of the visionary we cannot know. But of this we can be certain ; ecstatic experience left John in possession of *convictions*, and it is these convictions that he is reporting. Perhaps (it is unwise to dogmatize) the seer arrived at these convictions, as his readers must, through interpretation of dream-portents of polycephalic dragons and Beasts ; perhaps these nightmare shapes were natural to one whose literary diet was predominantly apocalyptic. It is, however, much more probable in this instance that a prophet's certainty about the future (a certainty derived, as he firmly believed, from Christ) found expression in terms of familiar visionary material. And in any case, it is the conviction, not its manner of arrival, which concerns us. The **ten horns** and **seven heads** of the Beast convey with suitable brevity the nature of his power and the fulness of his dæmonic character. The whole symbol is explained detail by detail in chap. xvii., but it is necessary to comment here on what must have been at once obvious to the more discerning of John's readers. It would be immediately clear to them that this Beast represented a power of this world ; the last world power, in fact, before the establishment of God's reign. Acquaintance with the Book of Daniel told them this : we must quote the apposite passage (Dan. vii. 2–8) :

> ' I saw in my vision during the night the four winds of heaven stirring up the great ocean. And out of the ocean up rose four Beasts, all of them different. The first was like a lion, and it had the wings of a vulture ; I watched till I saw the wings pulled off and the Beast forced to rise and stand erect upon the earth, on two feet like a man ; also, a human mind was given to it. Then came a second Beast, like a bear, with one of its paws raised to strike, and three ribs gripped between its fangs ; it was told to go and devour much flesh. After that I looked, and there was another Beast, like a leopard, with four wings of a bird upon its sides, and with four heads ; to it dominion was assigned ! After that I saw in my vision by night a fourth Beast, dire and dreadful, mightily strong, with huge iron fangs ; it devoured and tore its victims to pieces, stamping the rest down with its feet. . . . It had ten horns. . . .'

What these four Beasts meant for Daniel does not concern us here ; it is obvious, however, that John had his own

interpretation for them, and that he considered Daniel's vision
to be peculiarly directed towards his own later age. Of the
four Beasts which rise out of the ocean John makes one Beast.
This, he thinks, is the true meaning for later times of Daniel's
vision ; the seer was granted four glimpses of the same
ferocious monarch who was to oppress the world in the last
days. And so John depicts this monarch as like in character
to each of the three predatory animals mentioned by Daniel ;
The Beast I saw resembled a leopard, his feet were like a bear's, 2
and his mouth like a lion's. This composite Beast possesses
seven heads—as do the four in Daniel, when viewed collectively. And this trait inevitably commended itself to John,
for **seven** always indicates for him the notion of completeness.
So the seven heads announce that the Beast of the future possesses the character and powers of all preceding Emperors.
(It must, incidentally, be mentioned here that commentators
generally suppose that John had in mind a list of seven
Emperors, beginning with Augustus. The view taken here is
that the number is symbolical, as everywhere else in RE-
VELATION. (See chap. xvii.).) Finally, the fourth Beast in
Daniel's vision contributes to John's picture the **ten horns** ;
in REVELATION these ten horns represent earthly leaders, who
are to lend their services to Antichrist, and for a brief time to
exercise royal power, in the last battle, when the Messiah is to
lead His forces to victory. Here, then, is the main literary
source of John's picture of Antichrist. The reader of Daniel
had no difficulty in appreciating the simpler, composite picture
drawn by John, even though the meaning attached to individual details was markedly new. The parallels between the passages are too numerous and too striking to miss. Besides those
already noted, we should observe that John's Beast, like those
in Daniel, rises **out of the sea** (compare 'from the abyss,'
xi. 7 and xvii. 8 ; the sea, chaotic and hostile, traditionally represented the home of evil. Cf. also note on xxi. 1). In Daniel
it is explained that the ten horns on the fourth Beast represent
ten kings ; in REVELATION the **horns** are decorated with
emblems of kingship, **ten diadems.** The fourth Beast in Daniel
is associated with a king who has ' a mouth full of proud

words ' (Dan. vii. 8), who ' shall vaunt himself against the Most High ' (Dan. vii. 25, xi. 36) ; and this is precisely the meaning of the **blasphemous titles** on the Beast's seven heads— the Imperial arrogation of divine attributes (cf. verse 5 and xvii. 3). This monarch Daniel saw ' making war upon the saints and overcoming them.' And for John, too, the Beast's deadly persecution of the saints is the distinctive thing about him. It is this which marks him off from his predecessors on the Imperial throne ; or, rather, from all his predecessors except one—Nero : **he was allowed to wage war on the saints and conquer them.**

John's picture of the final earthly enemy of mankind is much more forceful and clear than Daniel's, and that for an excellent reason. The later prophet sketched his portrait, not only from the spectacle of unconsecrated earthly power, but also from the revelation of its heavenly antithesis. John's description of the Beast is decisively influenced by his belief about the Messiah. Thus, when John wishes to indicate the scope and nature of the Beast's power he uses terms pointedly reminiscent of those proper to Christ. Satan's gift to the last of the Emperors of **his own power and his own throne and great authority** recalls much that John has said about Christ : ' I will give him authority over the nations . . . as I myself have received authority from my Father ' (ii. 26) ; the Lamb stands ' in the midst of the throne ' (v. 6 ; cf. iii. 21) ; and as for the gift of **power,** if any reference is needed, we shall do well to remember the transference of the seven Spirits of God from their position before the throne (iv. 5) to the person of Christ (v. 6 ; cf. also iii. 1).

The most remarkable of these allusive definitions of the Beast's character, the most mysterious to us, and the most informative for John's first readers, is contained in the words :
3 **One of the heads seemed to have been slain and killed, but the deadly wound was healed.** . . . John's description of the Lamb, ' it seemed to have been slain, but it had seven horns and seven eyes ' (v. 6), occurs instantly to us ; a contrast is plainly intended, but without extraneous information it must appear somewhat arbitrary. The fact is that these words allude as

plainly as may be to a tradition which had arisen concerning the death of Nero. To counter murmured accusations of incendiarism this half-insane tyrant thrust the guilt of his alleged crime upon the Christian community in Rome, and set on foot a savage persecution. Not long afterwards he died in circumstances sufficiently mysterious to foster certain dark rumours. Some men, indeed, whispered that the monster had not died, but had contrived to flee to a refuge in the East, whence he would return to wreak mad vengeance on his enemies. Others, less incredulous of his death, still could not bring themselves to believe that the last had been seen of this arch-persecutor, and an apprehension assailed the minds of many that Nero would actually arise from the dead. Now, for John each of the Emperors in turn was a partial manifestation of one greater power of evil ; Antichrist, the last Emperor, differed from the others in that he was to be the complete manifestation of this power (see chap. xvii.). But of all the Emperors of the past, one had demonstrated most successfully the wanton savagery, the whole-hearted viciousness, the hatred of God's subjects, and (what was less comprehensible) the detestation of his own—all the qualities, in fact, which were to mark out Antichrist. This was Nero : Nero, who persecuted the saints (cf. vi. 9-11) ; Nero, whose temerity in setting hands on the Elect had brought on him the sword of God's anger ; Nero, who was to live again, **after being wounded by the sword** (xiii. 14 ; the allusion is probably twofold— primarily to the ' sharp sword with a double edge,' i. 16, symbolizing divine punishment, and secondarily, perhaps, to Nero's supposed suicide by the sword). The insistence on the theme of *Nero redivivus* (cf. xiii. 3, 12, 14, xvii. 8) incidentally illustrates how lofty were John's views on the work performed by martyrs. John believed that the death of martyrs was of cosmic importance : just as the great Distress was to encompass the downfall of civilization, so the Neronic distress had issued first in the death of its contriver, and then in a portentous period of bloodshed and excesses during the short reigns of Galba, Otho, and Vitellius. All this lies in the background of John's picture of the Beast with the head which looked as if it had been slain and killed (the emphasis is note-worthy—as if John were recalling a time when it seemed to Christians as if Antichrist had actually been destroyed), **but the deadly wound was healed.** The words carry with them both warning and encouragement : warning, that the enemy of the future will be supernatural, and will possess a scarcely imaginable capacity for malice and ingenious cruelty ; encouragement, in that martyrdom had once before proved to be God's irresistible weapon against his over-weening might.

Wonder is the first emotion stirred in the hearts of most men at the spectacle of the Beast. John mentions this again in chap. xvii. : ' and the dwellers on earth will wonder . . . when they see that the Beast was, is not, but is coming.' *Nero redivivus* was a miracle, demanding and receiving a bewildered reverence—from all but the saints, who were forewarned (cf. St. Matt. xxiv. 4). The Imperial cult becomes more fervent than ever before ; the **whole earth** become Emperor-worshippers. And, as John caustically remarks, in worshipping the Emperor they worship Satan, the source of his 4 authority. The wonder evoked by his first appearance gives way to another emotion, even less admirable. The cry now is,

> Who is like the Beast ?
> Who can fight with him ?

A sycophantic, timorous admiration of Antichrist for the abundance of his power—this is the final response of mankind ' in the hour of trial which is coming upon the whole world to test the dwellers on earth ' (iii. 10).

xiii. 5–10 : ANTICHRIST'S BRIEF REIGN HAS DIVINE SANCTION

5 He was allowed *to utter loud* and blasphemous *vaunts*, and
6 allowed *to exert* authority for two and forty months ; so he opened his mouth for blasphemies against God, to blaspheme his name and his dwelling (that is, the dwellers in heaven). He was allowed *to wage war on the saints and*
7

to conquer them, and also given authority over every tribe
and people and tongue and nation ; all dwellers on earth 8
will be his worshippers, everyone whose name has not been
written from the foundation of the world *in the book of
Life.** Let anyone who has an ear listen:— 9

> *Whoever is destined for captivity,* 10
>   *to captivity* he goes :
> *whoever* kills *with the sword,*
>   *by the sword* must he be killed.

This is what shows the patience and the faith of the saints.

* The words 'of the Lamb slain' (τοῦ ἀρνίου τοῦ ἐσφαγμένου) are probably
a gloss from xxi. 27. The book of Life elsewhere appears without any such
addition.

Repetition, one of the commonest devices in Hebrew
literature, takes a more modest place in the art of to-day ;
Flecknoe (so at least Dryden tells us) was the 'last great
prophet of tautology' in our language. The device, whether
used legitimately or not, is therefore unfamiliar. In verses
5 to 9 we have a characteristic example of John's use of repetition ; for this passage is, in the main, a slightly expanded
version of material in the first four verses. The critics who
suggest that this and similar passages are merely tautologous
have, however, missed the subtlety of John's style. The
general bearing of this section is quite different from what
precedes it. Previously the saints have been told what to
expect in Antichrist—his character, his reception by men.
Now they are told something new, and equally important ;
they are told that the Beast reigns by divine permission. He
is **allowed** to reign (note the threefold occurrence of this word 5
and cf. note on ix. 3-5) ; he is **given authority,** not by the
dragon, but by the supreme Disposer of authority. His
blasphemous claims to be divine, his odious fulminations
against the true God, against the Messiah and the heavenly
host, his slaughter of Christians, his seduction of the unworthy among mankind—all these things are ordained, a necessary part of God's eternal scheme. Therefore, the saints must
endure whatever befalls them without murmuring ; they must

suffer even martyrdom with brave resignation—nay, with something approaching joy, that Providence has so honoured them. The focal point of this section must be recognized in verse 10, an enjoinment on Christians of **patience** and **faith** in the face of the licensed predominance of evil.

Unless this crucial point is appreciated, the passage will have the appearance of inconsequential variation on themes already familiar. We have already heard, for example, of the **two and forty months** of Antichrist's reign (the three and a half years which symbolized a period when evil prevails; cf. xi. 2, etc.). The spectacle of the Beast's seven heads with their titles has already told us of his **loud and blasphemous vaunts**; we have had the opportunity of recollecting the similar conduct attributed to Daniel's satanic monarch, Antiochus Epiphanes (cf. Dan. vii. 25). Even the onslaught on the saints has been previously described in chap. xi., and is presupposed in the allusions to the Book of Daniel contained in the picture of the Beast. The whole force of this passage depends on our giving proper value to the word **allowed**. What could explain the martyrdom of God's people, but that the Beast **was allowed** to assail them? The saints are God's 6 **dwelling** on earth (cf. xi. 1), just as the angelic host are His dwelling in heaven (xiii. 6). His purposes in allowing their death must have been utterly inscrutable but for the revelations accorded to the prophets. John, indeed, knows why 7 Antichrist **was allowed to make war on the saints and to conquer them**. He explains that elsewhere (see notes, chap. xi.). Here he is concerned only with the fact of God's sanctioning of the event. We must do full justice to the vigour of a faith which saw in the very prevalence of evil the presiding wisdom and might of God.

Having seen the passage as a whole in its right proportions, we can permit ourselves to pause briefly over certain details. First, the **blasphemous vaunts**. Ever since Augustus, the Emperors had been venerated with greater or less fervour as beings with god-like attributes. The very name ˚Augustus carried with it the flavour of divinity. This monarch was worshipped as Apollo, the incarnate son of Zeus, and the apotheosis of the reigning Emperor was a process which continued, for it accorded well both with the religious temper of Asia Minor and with the Imperial policy. If the divine titles lavished on the Emperors had been merely the breath of flattery, the Christian need have viewed them with no greater emotion than disdain. But the cult of the Emperor-god apparently evoked sincere religious ardour, at any rate in the regions around the seven cities (see Introduction, p. xxxviii). John had every reason to take seriously the extravagant deification of Domitian and certain of his predecessors ; had not Antipas been martyred in Pergamum, the seat of the Imperial cult in Asia Minor ? These **blasphemies** uttered by Antichrist were not mere matters for more or less detached condemnation—as we, perhaps, should condemn the profanity of a roisterer or the excesses of anti-Christian statecraft in countries not our own. They were matters of life and death ; or rather, to the sincere Christian, of death—and then life. The blasphemies constituted the test of loyalty to the **name:** he who timorously acquiesced in them doomed himself to eternal excommunication : he who valiantly denied and rebuked the Imperial claims suffered martyrdom, but gained eternal life and untold privilege. John's elaboration of this theme, **he opened his mouth for blasphemies against God, to blaspheme his name and his dwelling,** illustrates how little he expected the impiety of a persecuting Emperor to be limited to self-deification. When Polycarp was later brought before the magistrate, it was demanded that he should curse the Christ ; active hostility of this sort towards everything the Christian held to be true and holy John attributes to the last and worst of Emperors.

It is well to keep firmly in mind as we read about Antichrist John's expression : ' until the words of God are fulfilled ' (xvii. 17). For although the aggressive policy of Domitian provided an urgent motive for John's predictions, Hebrew prophecy and apocalyptic, affected no doubt by Christian tradition, gave them shape. The course of earthly events,

8 John believed, was fixed in its main outline from the foundation of the world. It was for this reason that REVELATION thronged so thickly with quotations and echoes of the prophets. It was for this reason that John, and doubtless most of his readers, attached such immense importance to Daniel's prediction about the attack on the saints : he was allowed to wage war on the saints and to conquer them. (The word conquer, it should be observed, is ironical : the true conqueror is the martyr ; see the endings of the seven letters.) This quotation occurs in two of the most important parts of REVELATION : here and in xi. 7 ; where it is one of the many indications that the 'two witnesses' represent a substantial proportion of Christians. Evidently John relied for the effectiveness of his words on the acquaintance of his readers with the text of Daniel, and credited them with his own reverence for God's oracles. John's predestinarian creed, it must be admitted, gives rein to his least attractive qualities : a certain fanatical harshness, a lack of that humane hesitancy to judge his fellow-men, which the Christian holds to be essential in charity. It is true, of course, that the exile in Patmos had much better reason than Swift, exiled in an Irish deanery, to dismiss the bulk of mankind as 'Yahoos' ; persecution rarely evokes the cry : 'Forgive them, for they know not what they do.' Nevertheless, it is hardly possible not to feel distaste at John's statement of the predestined consignment of the non-Christian world to Beast-worship and its resultant eternal damnation (cf. xiv. 9–12). For his language is so deliberate. Antichrist is to be given authority over every tribe and people and tongue and nation. It is destined that all dwellers on earth will be his worshippers. And similarly it is destined that a certain number whose names have been written from the foundation of the world in the book of Life will be enabled to resist the otherwise irresistible seduction of the enemy. Even if it is argued that John saw the pagan world for what it was, and allowed no sentimental pretence to deter the drawing of terrible conclusions from what he saw (a view which will hardly commend itself wholly to the historian), so blunt a declaration of predestined damnation

and blessedness leaves little to commend in John's conception of the Creator-God.

It must be acknowledged, however, that John's predestinarian views do not blind him to the reality of the choice before Christians ; they do not preclude the possibility of shrinking from the ordeal of martyrdom, nor do they diminish the sense of responsibility felt by the Christian (cf. note on xii. 10-11). A man's name might be erased from **the book of Life** (iii. 5). Moreover, to give John his due, he contemplated Antichrist's seduction of mankind simultaneously with the activity of the witnesses (chap. xi.). During the three and a half years of terror, mankind would be confronted with ' an eternal gospel ' by Christian prophets. A plain choice would be presented to men : Christ or Antichrist, the things of God or the things of Satan. Each individual had it in him to recognize good for what it was and evil for what it was, and therefore he had only himself to blame if the witnesses were ' a torment ' (xi. 10) to him, rather than heralds of eternal life.

In verses 9 and 10, John points the moral of the Beast's divinely sanctioned activities. He emphasizes what he has to say with the traditional formula whereby the prophet demanded attention : **Let anyone who has an ear, listen.** Two 9 qualities are required above all others in the hour of trial : **patience** (that is, the quality of enduring bravely, without complaint) and **faith.** Courageous submission to the persecutor is certainly necessary when it is appreciated that God has decreed the activity of Antichrist and his servants :

> **Whoever is destined for captivity,** 10
> **to captivity he goes :**

But without **faith** in the ultimate downfall of the persecutors such patience would be motiveless. So the saints must also believe that

> **whoever kills with the sword,**
> **by the sword must he be killed.**

All those who wield the unhallowed sword of Imperial power

will be killed by the ' sharp sword with a double edge ' (i. 16), the sword of God's anger. John's demand is for two qualities : unquestioning submission to Providence and trust in the inevitability of ' the time for destroying the destroyers of the earth ' (xi. 18).

xiii. 11–15*a* : THE SERVANTS OF THE BEAST—PRIESTS OF THE IMPERIAL CULT, FALSE PROPHETS AND INQUISITORS

11 Then I saw another Beast rising from the land ; he had two
12 horns like a lamb, but he spoke like a dragon. He exerts the full authority of the first Beast in his presence, causing the earth and its inhabitants to worship the first Beast,
13 whose deadly wound was healed. He performs amazing miracles, even making fire descend from heaven on earth
14 in the sight of men, and by dint of the miracles he is allowed to perform in presence of the Beast, he seduces dwellers on earth ; he bids the dwellers on earth erect a statue to the Beast who lived after being wounded by the
15*a* sword, and to this statue of the Beast he was allowed to impart the breath of life, so that the statue of the Beast should actually speak.

(1) *Their Function as False Prophets*

REVELATION as a whole might almost be called an essay in contrasts. Some of them are striking and unmistakable, like those between the faithful and unfaithful among the seven churches, between ' the woman clad in the sun ' (chap. xii.) and ' the woman clad in purple and scarlet ' (chap. xvii.), or between the *slain* Lamb, who is to return as messianic conqueror (v. 12, xix. 11), and the Beast who lived after being wounded by the sword (xiii. 15)—the Beast who ' is not, but is to rise from the abyss—yet to perdition he shall go ' (xvii. 8). Some of these contrasts are less obvious, however ; and here, in the fifth oracle of this series, we meet with one which has generally eluded commentators. If the Messiah has His chosen and particular ' servants ' (that is, prophets) on earth, so also has the Beast. It is they who complete the contrast between the two greater actors in the final struggle. We have read of the Messiah's servants in chap. xi. They are the Christian prophets, the 'two witnesses' who 'prophesy,' proclaiming the Gospel of the risen and returning Christ. This new **Beast rising from the land** (and thus completing a 11 triumvirate of evil from air, sea, and land) symbolizes the priests of the Imperial cultus, proclaiming a false gospel of idolatry with every cunning appeal to credulity and all the persuasiveness of systematic inquisition.

We must spare no pains to discern the full force of the contrast. First of all we must note that both bodies of men are prophetic : the witnesses are true prophets, leading men with stern admonition to the true God : the new **Beast** is known 12 always elsewhere as ' the false Prophet ' (xvi. 13, xix. 20, xx. 10), leading men, by marvels and appeal to self-interest, to the worship of false gods, the Beast and the dragon. This essential trait of the false Prophet is recorded in the Book of Deuteronomy (chap. xiii. 1–3) : ' If a prophet or dreamer arises among you, offering you some proof or portent, and saying, "Let us follow other gods (gods that are strange to you) and let us worship them," even if the proof or portent comes true which he promised you, you must not listen to what that prophet or dreamer says ; it is the Eternal your God testing you. . . .' It is as well to keep in mind the bearing of this passage as we read of the miraculous powers of Antichrist's priests. In sober fact the **amazing miracles** they were to perform were 13– stock tricks of pagan magic ; **fire** produced by hidden devices, 15*a* so that it seemed to **descend from heaven,** images animated with an artificial **breath of life** and so bewitched by ventrilo-quists that they could **actually speak**—these are portents well within the powers of the magician. But Christians shared the general credulity of the times, abhorring such pagan marvels as the work of dæmons. John's description of these miracles has no trace of sceptical sarcasm in it. The **false Prophet** was false, not because of his trickery, but because he led men to false gods—much as did the Balaamites and followers of

Jezebel mentioned in the letters to Pergamum and Thyatira. The truth is that John, seeing in the priests of the Imperial cult the antithesis of Christian prophets, speaks of their powers of seduction in terms consciously reminiscent of the powers accorded to the witnesses. These men ' stand before the Lord of the earth' (xi. 4) and, as it were, ' exert the full authority of God in his presence ' : like Moses and Elijah of old, they are enabled to *perform miracles* (though not with the intent of winning credence) ; they are able even to consume their more active enemies with *fire* from heaven, until their task is complete. Similarly, ' the false Prophet ' **exerts the full authority of the first Beast in his presence,** and at least one of his ' amazing miracles ' glances discernibly at the story of Elijah's conflict with the priests of Baal : the priests of Antichrist are **allowed** greater power over supernatural fire than those discomforted protégés of Ahab and Jezebel. ' Do not marvel that the servants of Antichrist are allowed to perform signs and wonders,' John tells his readers. ' It is the Eternal your God testing you ' (cf. iii. 10).

12   We must note particularly the rather curious phrase, **in his presence.** It is curious, since John must have expected miracles to be performed by the priests of the Imperial cult almost everywhere except in the Beast's actual presence. These wonders were designed, after all, for the seduction of men throughout the whole civilized world. The phrase is used deliberately as many as three times ; twice in chap. xiii. (verses 12 and 14) and once on the last appearance of ' the false Prophet ' in REVELATION, as he is consigned with the Beast to the lake of fire (xix. 20). On this last occasion John takes the trouble to state expressly that it was the miracles performed in the presence of the Beast which seduced mankind. If this phrase is translated, ' *before* the Beast,' it is then seen to be the same as that used of the two witnesses, who stand ' before the Lord of the earth.' Elijah describes himself as standing before the Lord (1 Kings xvii. 1, xviii. 15) ; the two prophetic figures in Zechariah ' stand before the Lord of

all the earth ' (Zech. iv. 14). In short, the phrase is associated with prophetic readiness to do the bidding of God, and with the authority inalienable from divine communion. It is also associated with the performance of priestly functions (Deut. x. 8) ; the Christian witnesses stand before God because they are both ' priests ' (cf. i. 6 and v. 10) and prophets of Christ. And similarly the priests of Antichrist, false prophets, by virtue of this dual office are said to be *enopion tou theriou*—' before the Beast,' that is, constant and willing servants of his will.

Verses 12–15 enlarge upon the symbolic meaning of the second Beast's visionary shape (if so vague a picture as **he had two horns like a lamb but he spoke like a dragon** may be said to constitute a shape at all !). The **two horns like a lamb** probably possess several implications (cf. the interpretation of the Beast's seven heads, chap. xvii.). They indicate *power*, as do the seven horns of the Lamb of God, but apparently no terrifying show of power, since they are, after all, horns of a **lamb**—not even of the more formidable *ram*, with two horns, whose power and defeat Daniel celebrated (Dan. viii. 2 f.). It is tempting also to see in the expression some echo of the warning in the Sermon on the Mount : ' Beware of false prophets ; they come to you with the garb of sheep, but at heart they are ravenous wolves. You will know them by their fruit. . . .' The reason for the specific number, the **two** horns, is almost certainly to be sought in John's desire to make immediately clear the essential feature of the second Beast— the fact that it constitutes the antithesis of the two witnesses— ' the two lampstands and the two olive trees.' (A similar point of contrast is afforded by the Lamb's seven horns and Antichrist's seven heads.) When John says that the Beast **spoke like a dragon** he means to designate, not blustering fierceness, but Satanic powers of seduction ; it is the serpent's voice whose cunning whispers ' brought death into the world and all our woe.' The first argument of the Imperial priests is to be persuasion : only when this fails will the inquisition resort to force. **Amazing miracles** (a traditional indication to Christians of Antichrist's advent : cf. St. Matt. xxiv. 24 : ' for false

Christs and false prophets will rise and bring forward great signs and wonders . . . '; cf. also 2 Thess. ii. 9) will consolidate the ' wonder ' inspired in mankind by the Beast's supernatural resuscitation (xiii. 3, xvii. 8). Marvels were to be expected from the servants of him **who lived after being wounded by the sword** (for this expression, see note on xiii. 3). If the miraculous fire marked the Imperial priests as the Satanic rivals of the witnesses, their animation of the Beast's

14 statue was proof no less significant of diabolical thaumaturgy. It will be remembered that the final stage of the martyrs' testimony came after their death, when ' the breath of life *from God* ' revived them. This was the divine portent which at last convinced mankind, when by applauding the Beast's slaughter of the witnesses they had committed themselves eternally to the fate of murderers, that God's power was supreme. **The breath of life** is a phrase peculiarly associated with the properties of the Creator-God : and when the priests of Antichrist have thus animated their idol, they have acted a blasphemy exceeding that of all previous idolators ; this is the magician's most impious usurpation of God's power.

xiii. 15b–18 : (2) UNIVERSAL INQUISITION, PERFORMED BY THE PRIESTS OF ANTICHRIST

15b He has everyone put to death *who will not worship the statue*
16 of the Beast, and he obliges all men, low and high, rich and poor, freemen and slaves alike, to have a mark put upon
17 their right hand or their forehead, so that no one can buy or sell unless he bears the mark, that is, the name of the
18 Beast, or the cipher of his name. Now for the gift of interpretation! Let the discerning calculate the cipher of the Beast ; it is the cipher of a man, and the figures are six hundred and sixty-six.

John undoubtedly expected that the majority of mankind would succumb readily to the seduction of Antichrist, duped into a servile adoration at the sight of a resurrected Nero, and established in ungodly reverence by the miracles of his priests. The trial of mankind was to be of unexampled severity, however ; where magic was powerless to infatuate, the argument of force might prevail. **He has everyone put to death who will15ᵇ not worship the statue of the Beast.** Such enforcement of idolatry is, of course, strongly reminiscent of the Book of Daniel (chap. iii.), and John's prediction carries with it the sanction of an accepted authority. But use and tradition probably provided independent grounds for the notion. In Asia Minor, where the Imperial cult aroused strong religious fervour, the Emperor's statue was already venerated in many pagan temples, and to worship it was no doubt a common proof of loyalty. Moreover, one attempt had previously been made to enforce universal obeisance to this symbol of the Emperor's deity. Some half-century before John wrote, Caligula attempted to demand universal adoration, and pressed his claims even on the Jews, who were normally exempted from actual celebration of the Emperor's divinity, in accordance with the Roman policy of religious toleration towards subject nations. Their recusancy prompted the threat of sacrilegious reprisal. Caligula's death alone prevented him from erecting his statue, veritably an 'abomination of desolation' in the temple at Jerusalem. Memory of this scandalous Imperial aberration and all its circumstances naturally embedded itself in the apocalyptic beliefs of succeeding generations. It was in every way natural that John should expect the worship of the statue to be made the supreme test of loyalty to the Beast.

In John's mind the idolator is no better than a murderer (cf. xxi. 8). For the man who so blinds himself to reason and truth as to **worship the statue of the Beast** no fate is too horrible ; John adds to the eloquent denunciation of the Hebrew prophets the newer doctrine of everlasting torture (cf. xiv. 9 ff.). While we may perhaps deplore the belief, we can at least sympathize with the practical motive of John's vehemence. He wished his fellow-Christians to understand quite clearly that temporizing was impossible. To burn incense to the Beast's statue was to admit the validity of everything he stood for. A cowardly resort to formal observances implied a denial of Christ—complete apostasy. The normal early Christian attitude towards the State seems to have been one of submission and even co-operation (Rom. xiii. 1–7 ; 1 Pet. ii. 13–17) ; and some have been incredulous that John should have so far departed from this temper as to counsel defiance. But there was no question in the minds of those who respected Roman authority in secular matters of tolerating any interference with religious integrity. It was considered that the things of Cæsar were easily distinguishable from the things of God. John, too, urges nothing but submission to the State in its exercise of juridical decrees, however unjust they are : ' whoever is destined for captivity, to captivity he goes.' But to pay the tribute to Antichrist which is due to Christ—this is another matter. He is contemplating a time when the act of refusing to commit high treason against Christ will be interpreted as high treason against Antichrist, when, in other words, the mere fact of being a Christian will be a crime (see Introduction, p. xl.).

The inquisition is to be universal and inescapable in its 16 application : **he obliges all men, low and high, rich and poor, freemen and slaves alike** (cf. vi. 15) **to have a mark put upon** 17 **their right hand or their forehead, so that no one can buy or sell unless he bears the mark.** It is a matter of dispute whether John expected that this would be a literal brand or tattoo (in which case the metaphor would relate to the age-long practice of bearing signs to proclaim religious loyalties ; cf. Isa. xliv. 5), or whether his words rather imply the enforcement of explicit declarations of loyalty, and conduct to bear out such declarations. On the one hand it is argued that devotees of pagan cults, especially those of Asia Minor, delighted in the possession of religious emblems. On the other, it is noted that the seal on the foreheads of the martyrs is undoubtedly figurative (see note on vii. 3 ; cf. xiv. 1). It is a matter of small moment. The essential fact is that men are forced to pledge their loyalty in such a way as to deny all hope of escape to the recusants. If they contrive to escape denunciation by the priests, with its consequent sentence of death, they are faced with loss of livelihood through boycott. There is no escape; men must make up their minds, and espouse either truth or falsehood.

John's language undoubtedly seems here to foreshadow the death of every loyal Christian, and many have taken his words at their face value, concluding that he expected a universal martyrdom. Such an expectation conflicts, it is admitted, with certain expressions in the seven letters (cf. iii. 3, 11, etc.) and elsewhere (cf. notes on xiv. 1–5) ; but such inconsistencies are explained away on various literary hypotheses. The implication of the description of the risen martyrs, ' they are celibates ' (xiv. 4), for example, is brusquely swept aside by Dr. Charles as the blundering of a monkish interpolator. The same critic erects an elaborate theory to dispose of the inconsistency between the expectation in the seven letters that certain Christians would survive until the Messiah's advent, and the apparent expectation in chap. xiii. that the earth would be denuded of the righteous. These two expectations, it is asserted, belong to two different periods. The seven letters in their original form, without the promises to the conqueror, were previously composed in times of less severity ; and when they came to be incorporated in a longer tract for the Domitianic situation, the earlier eschatological beliefs were allowed to remain unrevised : John was martyred (so it is speculated) before he could cast his book into final shape. Such a theory is as arbitrary as it is unnecessary. John did not expect a universal martyrdom, in spite of his solemn words in chap. xiii.

For the real nature of his expectation, we must refer the reader to two passages : xi. 1–13 and xii. 17. The messianic community was to survive as a whole unharmed, divinely protected against the attacks of Satan and Antichrist. Her ' offspring,' those who, like her first ' son,' Christ, bear open testimony in the great city of civilization, are to be martyred ; and it is these heroic souls who occupy the first place in REVELATION. John is so anxious to forewarn and forearm them for their ordeal that he finds little occasion to reassure the others. After all, every Christian must be *prepared* for the ordeal : he would otherwise forfeit all claim to the protection described in xi. 1, xii. 6, and xii. 14. He would be in ' the court outside the temple,' and therefore ' given over to the Gentiles.' But how do we reconcile this notion with such words as ' he obliges *all* men, low and high, rich and poor, freemen and slave alike ' to bear his mark ? Does not John say unambiguously : ' He has *everyone* put to death who will not worship the statue of the Beast ' ? The force of such language is mitigated when we recollect the obviously hyperbolical nature of the earlier expression : ' and *the whole earth* went after the Beast in wonder ' (xiii. 3). John similarly excludes Christians from his usual phrase for humanity in general, ' the dwellers on earth ' (cf. ' the earth and its inhabitants,' xiii. 12). The truth is that in chap. xiii., as in vi. 15 (' the kings of the earth, the magnates, the generals, the rich, the strong, slaves and freemen every one of them '), John implicitly excludes from his categories of mankind the loyal souls who form the messianic community. The Beast and his servants operate in civilization ; the Church is ' in the desert ' (see note on xii. 14). Such an embargo as that predicted in verses 17 and 18 could not affect those who were ' to be nourished for a Time, two Times and half a Time ' in the desert : these were supernatural days, and Satanic onslaught was to be met with divine assistance. Somehow (John predicts no details, but is content to assert the principle) the people of God are to survive unmolested in their ' desert ' refuge, even as the Israelites of old, nourished and guided by the Eternal, until the promised reign of peace has been achieved ; all, that is, except the hundred and forty-four thousand destined to the greater glory of martyrdom. As we have said, it is to these men, the martyrs, as well as to those who are inclined as John is writing to remain in the outer courts of the faith (cf. notes on xi. 2), that the warning in verses 15-17 is addressed. For both the witnesses and the temporizers were destined to come under the heel of Antichrist ; the witnesses to suffer the first death (xx. 4-6), and to know the glory of the first resurrection ; the temporizers to be irretrievably corrupted, and condemned to the horror of the second death (xx. 15).

The mark of the Beast is said to be the name of the Beast or the cipher of his name (for the importance of *names*, see notes on ii. 17, iii. 12). John once more enables the discerning to enter into his beliefs about Antichrist. The interpretation 18 of his cipher will not be open to all ; only those who have the gift of ' wisdom ' will gather its inner meaning. All, however, will perceive that the Antichrist will come in human shape—as the Man of Sin in earlier writings ; for it is the cipher of a man. They will also perceive that he is some dreadful travesty of the divine fulness ; for three sixes have an obvious relation to the customary symbol in REVELATION for completeness, the figure seven. But it would need the discerning to explain to their less learned brothers (who were probably in the majority) that the cipher, transliterated, spelt ' Nero Cæsar.' For this meaning is carefully wrapped up, whether out of caution, lest its purport should meet the eye of sedition-hunters, or out of a natural love of mysterious symbols, in the concealment of the Hebrew alphabet.

(It should perhaps be added that this cipher, whereby the letters of the alphabet are indicated by numerical equivalents, has proved as alluring to subsequent critics as to John's readers. Many attempts have been made to solve it by application to the Greek alphabet ; many are the solutions offered, some of them completely absurd, and none as convincing as ' Nero Cæsar.' The point is one of secondary importance, in any case. Little would be lost if the cipher were insoluble. John's sketch of Antichrist's character is sufficiently vivid without this additional colour.)

xiv. 1–5 : THE SIXTH ORACLE : THE RISEN MARTYRS

Then I looked, and there was the Lamb standing on mount Sion,   1
and along with him a hundred and forty-four thousand
bearing his name and the name of his Father written *on*
their foreheads ! And I heard a voice from heaven, *like the*   2
sound of many waves and the sound of loud thunder ; the

3   voice I heard was like harpists playing on their harps ;
they were *singing a new song* before the throne and before
the four living Creatures and the Presbyters, a song that no
one could learn except the hundred and forty-four thousand
4   who had been ransomed from earth.   They have not been
defiled by intercourse with women—they are celibates ;
they follow the Lamb wherever he goes ; they have been
ransomed from among men, as the first to be reaped for
5   God and the Lamb.   And *on their lips no lie was ever
detected ;* they are stainless.

How will God answer the activities of Antichrist and his
servants ?   What is their appointed end ?   In this oracle
and in the seventh John shows what is to follow the three and
a half years of terror.   He shows first, the martyrs admitted
to the very presence of the throne, secure of eternal life, and
then, in terrible contrast, the doom of civilization.

The moving picture of the risen martyrs in heaven carries
us back to the ' great host whom no one could count ' in chap.
vii. ; and thence to the hundred and forty-four thousand who
were sealed ' with the seal of the living God ' upon their
foreheads.   That heavenly multitude was uncountable, by
mortal reckoning.   It is only now, when divine revelation has
enabled the prophet to see still more clearly across the mists of
time that he can say with certainty what he first suspected :
that every man to be sealed with God's seal, every man of that
great host drawn from the twelve tribes of the true Israel, has
loyally fulfilled his destiny, and has also known God's unfailing
power to rescue His servants from their enemies.   A hundred
and forty-four thousand were sealed, a hundred and forty-four
thousand were saved, still bearing the mystical impress of
God's name and the Lamb's name on their foreheads, the sign
that marked them as God's Elect.

1   But are they in heaven ?   John says, **on mount Sion.**   And
many have supposed that this represented, not the heavenly
scene of Christian hymnology, but the site of the restored
Jerusalem in Christ's millennium (chap. xx.)—or the new
Jerusalem which is to descend ' from God out of heaven ' on to

a new earth in the final reign of eternal peace (chap. xxi.). This
will not do, however. The martyrs are in heaven, whither they
rose in a cloud. We are beholding the heavenly **Sion,** the
celestial pattern of the once sacred site of Jerusalem ; and
much depends on our recognition of the fact. We have already
heard the echoes of that Jewish tradition which held that on
the rehabilitation of the chosen people, certain sacred objects,
lost or hidden away at the first fall of Jerusalem, would be
restored to the veneration of the faithful. We have seen how
John looked for the disclosure *in heaven* of these sacred objects
(or, rather, of their celestial archetypes), and how, on three
occasions when the End is portended in REVELATION, they
are indeed disclosed (viii. 3, xi. 19, xv. 5), to the accompaniment of ' peals of thunder, loud blasts, flashes of lightning, and
an earthquake ' portending doom on the unregenerate in the
world. Mount Sion had an equally important place in Jewish
eschatology, and John deals in a similar way with the tradition
in which it was central. Monolatry had bestowed on Palestine
a holiness far exceeding the glamour of patriotism, and this
devotion found its focus in the sacred city of Jerusalem. The
hill on which it stood became an ' ever-fixed mark ' in apocalyptic and post-exilic prophecy—indeed, literally the only hill
in the world re-created by God (Zech. xiv. 10) : on Sion the
Eternal would appear surrounded by His faithful servants ;
from Sion His scourge would fall far and wide on oppressor
nations. This day of the Eternal was to be a day of wrath :

> ' And then shall the Eternal punish
> the hosts of the high heaven above
> and kings on earth below,
> bundling them into a dungeon,
> penning them inside a prison,
> till their day of doom arrives ;
> the moon shall move under a veil,
> the sun shall pale,
> when the Eternal is enthroned on Sion,
> revealed in radiant splendour to his sheikhs.'

> (Isa. xxiv. 21-3.)

But it was also to be a day of blessedness, the beginning of the
Eternal's rule on earth :

> ' On that day, the Eternal promises,
> I will collect the stragglers . . .
> I will make the lame the nucleus of a nation,
> make the sick into a power,
> with the Eternal reigning over them on Sion hill,
> henceforth and for all time.'
>
> (Mic. iv. 6 f.)

Zechariah and Joel likewise paint a picture of the mingled terror and glory of this day of the Eternal ; against a background of cosmic disturbance—earthquakes, the dimming of sun and moon, the disappearance of mountains, warfare among men—Jerusalem is displayed, in the one as the centre from which the Eternal strikes His enemies in wrath (' On that day he shall set his feet on the mount of Olives ' : Zech. xiv. 4) ; in the other as the sole refuge on earth for the faithful remnant :

> ' But every worshipper of the Eternal shall be saved,
> for Sion hill shall hold those who escape, . . .
> and the fugitives whom the Eternal calls
> shall be inside Jerusalem.'
>
> (Joel ii. 32.)

In the later Jewish apocalyptic tradition, preserved in 2 Esdras xiii. 35 ff. the Messiah has taken the place of the Eternal, but the scene is fundamentally the same :

> ' But he shall stand upon the top of the mount Sion, and Sion shall come, and shall be showed to all men, being prepared and builded, like as thou sawest the mountain graven without hands. And this my Son shall rebuke the nations . . . and he shall destroy them without labour by the law. . . . And whereas thou sawest that he gathered unto himself another multitude that was peaceable ; these are the ten tribes. . . .'

There once again we have seen the day of salvation and the day of Wrath, with the divine saviour and avenger standing on Sion. John sees one essential thing in this tradition ; the *certainty* of divine action in defence of His people, and in confounding His enemies. His use of the term **Sion** to depict the scene before the Presbyters and the living Creatures and the throne conveys allusively the sure fulfilment of God's words

to His prophets.   All those glorious promises of security for the
righteous and the reversal of wickedness must be fulfilled ; but
it was to be no earthly hill on which the Messiah stood, no
earthly refuge to which His oppressed people fled.   The
martyrs are to rise in a cloud up to heaven (xi. 12) ; the
heavenly Sion is the refuge of the Elect, the witnesses in the
great city of wickedness, on the day of the Eternal's wrath.
On the day of wrath ! This, too, we must remember. As soon
as the hundred and forty-four thousand have ascended to
heaven to complete the number of the martyrs, then follows
the day of the Messiah's wrath.   Then the Beast and his
lieutenants and his followers, the ' low and high, rich and poor,
freemen and slaves alike', all who bear his mark, meet their
fate : the sharp sword with two edges sweeps over the crime-
stained earth.   It is in the seventh oracle of this series (xiv.
6 ff.) that John shows the reverse of his picture of heavenly
bliss : the revelation to mankind of the limitless power of God
(verse 7), the revelation of the certainty of doom on civilization
(verse 8) and on the Beast's worshippers (verses 9-12), and,
finally, the revelation of the great massacre of the unrighteous
(verses 14 ff.).

For the present, however, we are concerned with this
supreme fact ; the reference to Sion tells us that the loyalists
of the true Israel have been gathered to their home.   The
Messiah has appeared among them and claimed them as His
own ; the conqueror now has his reward : ' I will own him
openly before my Father and before his angels ' (iii. 5 ; cf.
xiv. 4).   The prophets spoke of the *Eternal's* appearance on
Sion : but John has shown us in chaps. i.-iii. how Christ has
been endowed with the Eternal's attributes.   The prophets
spoke of the faithful remnant of the Jews ; but John has
shown us in chap. vii. that the twelve tribes of the true Israel
are drawn from all nations on earth.   There they stand, the
Church, bearing the seal of the Lamb's **name** and God's **name,**
even as mankind displayed the sign of their loyalty in the mark
of the Antichrist—' the name of the Beast or the cipher of his
name,' standing no longer in the city of doom, but in the
Eternal City, which is to descend after the millennium upon a

newly created earth. And how glorious their lot ! These risen martyrs represent the first stage in the majestic performance of the divine promise to ' make all things new.' Creation is already beginning to slough its age-soiled vesture. The winter of old, unblessed things, is passing. And the noble army of martyrs sing their **new song.** For John, the **voice** of their triumphant praise drowns every cry of pain, every harsh command of bestial persecutors, every murmured counsel of discretion—all the shock of unparalleled discord in the nearer future. For the voice he hears is like the voice of the Eternal 2 and the voice of Christ (Ezek. xliii. 2 ; Rev. i. 15)—**like the sound of many waves** : it has in it an unspeakable solemnity— like the **loud thunder** of the divine voice, when its word of wrath is spoken against evil-doers : we are reminded that the great martyrdom has issued in the destruction of God's enemies. In chap. xv. the martyrs' song is of the second deliverance—' the song of Moses the servant of God and the song of the Lamb ' ; and it is the prelude to the second and final devastation of the mystical Egypt and its rulers. Finally, **it was like harpists playing on their harps** : in other words, it revealed that the martyrs had now joined the ranks of those who hymned the glories of the beatific vision. Like the Presbyters (chap. iv.), they now possess **harps of God** (xv. 3). The celestial harmony is now complete, ' the diapason closing full on man '—on *redeemed* man. Whereas it was the living Creatures and the Presbyters (angels of the Presence) who 3 sang the **new song** of Christ's triumph (chap. v.), it is now the martyrs who celebrate the inauguration of the new era of righteousness. They alone, **the hundred and forty-four thousand** who had been **ransomed from earth** (only they are admitted to God's presence until the day of Judgment), are privileged to sing this song. None but the martyrs can **learn** it, for it is a song whose deep mysteries are concealed from all except those who have known the pangs of the great Distress, and the rapture of subsequent triumph ; who, in short, have conquered as Christ conquered (cf. iii. 21).

' These are the people who have come out of the great Distress, who have washed their robes and made them white in the blood of the Lamb ' : so John was told in an earlier vision, when the vistas of the future had been only partially illumined by revelation (vii. 14). Now he can say more, for he knows that it is his *brothers the prophets* who are to win such honour. Essentially, we must recognize, they have been able to conquer death, because in life they were able to conquer sin—such was the force of Christ's sacrifice. And because they were **stainless, utterly sincere (on their lips no lie was ever detected)**, their death 5 was valid as a sacrifice to God. If we wish to recall the simple logic within this conception, we must refer to xii. 7–12 ; the sacrifice was made not to banish the frowns of a celestial Tyrant, but to demonstrate beyond question that redeemed man was capable of victory over the Enemy's last seduction. John's notion of sinlessness, however, is not one to commend itself to our own age ; nor, indeed, does it square with the true catholic ideal in any age. From the seven letters we might expect his standard to be severe. The conqueror, we learn there, with all his ' love and loyalty and service and patient endurance,' must possess an unbending sternness towards the lax. But this is not all. John seems to show quite clearly that in his view, to be completely **stainless**, a man must be **celibate**—' virgin,' as he puts it. Even within the bond of marriage—elsewhere in the New Testament always held sacred —coition is an act which defiles, and disqualifies a Christian from attaining the greatest honour of all. Such degradation of marriage by a Christian teacher in New Testament times is held by certain critics to be impossible. The desire to clear John from the stigma of holding views so unacceptable has led them into various attempts to explain away verse 4. The language is metaphorical (it is argued) : **They have not been** 4 **defiled by intercourse with women** is a realistic use of the figure used so often by the prophets for idolatry. Or, alternatively, John's words really refer to extra-marital intercourse : the word ' virgin ' (*celibates* in our translation) is shown to have been applied to widows, for example, who lived a life of purity and devotion. Or, again, since in any case John's words exclude women from the company of martyrs, the passage is to be regarded as a fatuous intrusion, the work of a monkish interpolator who braved the curse appended to REVELATION out of fanatical zeal for the cause of celibacy. But there is no valid reason whatever to suppose that John was incapable of holding the views literally stated in verse 4. They must be seen in their right proportion. Sexual intercourse outside the bond of marriage damned a man to all eternity (that is, of course, in the absence of timely repentance ; cf. ii. 16) : ' Begone, you dogs, you sorcerers, you *vicious creatures* [R.V., ' fornicators '], you murderers, you idolators, you who love and practise falsehood ' (xxii. 15)—' their lot is the lake that blazes with fire and brimstone, which is the second death.' (xxi. 8.) What John says here is that sexual intercourse *defiles* : detracts from the purity required for that sacrifice to God which is to be decisive in the affairs of the universe. He is speaking of a *sacrificial* purity. Such is the undoubted implication of the phrase : **the first to be reaped for God.** The Greek word *aparche*, here translated as **the first to be reaped** (i.e. the first-fruits), was used in the common spoken Greek of Asia Minor, and also frequently in the Septuagint, to mean simply ' sacrifice.' There are degrees of blessedness, and in John's opinion the married Christian is further from the godly ideal than the unmarried ; the celibate alone is fit to be the unblemished lamb of sacrifice. He will still find some who agree with him outright : he will find even more, perhaps, whose doctrine conflicts with their instinct. For when St. Augustine expressed his belief that there was something intrinsically impure in the sexual act he was stating boldly a prejudice from which the Church has never been able to free herself completely, despite the explicit doctrine of the sacrament of marriage. St. Paul sanctioned the principle of marriage—but chiefly as a concession to human frailty. It was better to be unmarried, he said. True, the main reason he gives for preferring celibacy lies in the imminence of the last days and the demands of evangelism. Nevertheless, there is in his thought more than a trace of the presumption that the greatest strength of spirit dwelt in celibacy : that marriage is a safeguard against worse things, to be applauded chiefly for that reason. Nor is it to be marvelled at. It is almost beyond human powers to be rid entirely of contemporary prejudice and to see beyond the distortions of environment. Even among the Jews, who as a people believed passionately in the holiness of marriage, misogynic heresies had arisen, whose ascetic doctrines probably had some influence even in the first century over individual Christian teachers. And what is more to the point, in their regard for marriage, the Jews distinguished themselves sharply from Hellenic peoples. ' In the popular religion of Phrygia there was a feeling, (expressed in the eunuchism, for example, of the priests at Hierapolis) that one came nearer to the divine life by annihilating the distinction of sex, while in the votive inscriptions of Asia Minor . . . marriage is not recognized as part of the divine or religious life ' (Moffatt, *op. cit.*, p. 436). This religious trait was encouraged by a morality which had few frowns for extra-marital sexual indulgence ; and it could hardly fail to follow that the prevalent immorality cast a shadow over the Christian attitude towards sexual life—especially over the attitude of a teacher like John, who foresaw the greatest of ordeals before Christians, and who held nothing of greater importance than the complete distinction of the Christian from the pagan practice. The pagan influence was twofold : imperceptible, since Christians were likely to absorb unconsciously the moral preconceptions in popular religion ; perceptible, since they were bound to recoil violently from the general looseness of life. It is not strange, therefore, that John places celibacy in his list of saintly virtues. Nor (if the point is to be prosaically insisted upon) can it be thought strange that John should exclude women, as he apparently does, from his hundred and forty-four thousand witnesses. If St. Paul could forbid women to preach, the writer of REVELATION could equally well regard them as lacking in strength for the task of proclaiming the Gospel in the ' realm of the Beast,' and of suffering the ignominies attached to imprisonment and death (cf. xi. 10). The witnesses were to be in the battle-line of God's army, and bitter strife was divinely enjoined on them ; there are military ordeals from which men instinctively exclude women—and there are military awards also which cannot be theirs.

When all is said, however, the crucial fact about the witnesses is not that they are **celibates,** but that they are **stainless,** and therefore fit to be a sacrifice to God. If we have discussed the matter at some length, our motive has not been to press the importance of verse 4 in the scheme of REVELATION —it is relatively unimportant. We have sought to show that the controverted passage, so far from being unauthentic, is entirely consistent with the prophet's temper. John's contribution to the record of early Christian thought and experience is more valuable than is sometimes recognized, but uncritical admiration of everything he wrote is more dangerous than its undiscerning condemnation. He lived in abnormal times ; he faced tangible perils and recognizable temptations with a lofty courage and unflinching directness of vision which has never been surpassed. He recognized evil for what it was ; no man was further from insincerity and cant. And, in spite of all, he recognized charity to be a paramount virtue for Christians (letter to church at Ephesus). But he would have been almost more than human if his zeal had not taken him to the verge of fanaticism. His picture of the **stainless** hundred and forty-four thousand might well be contrasted with another reflection on the Christian battle with sin :

' The soul of sin (for we have made sin immortal), the soul of sin is disobedience to thee ; and when one sin hath been dead in me, that soul hath passed into another sin. Our youth dies, and the sins of our youth with it ; some sins die a violent death, and some a natural ; poverty, penury, imprisonment, banishment, kill some sins in us, and some die of old age ; many ways we become unable to do that sin, but still the soul lives and passes into another sin ; and that that was licentiousness becomes ambition, and that comes to devotion and spiritual coldness : we have three lives in our state of sin, and where the sins of our youth expire, those of our middle years enter, and those of our age after them. This transmigration of sin in me, makes me afraid, O my God, of a relapse. . . .'

(JOHN DONNE : *Devotions.*)

He who cries ' perfection ' runs the risk of missing the humbler virtues which compose it.[1]

xiv. 6-13 : THE SEVENTH ORACLE : THE DAY OF WRATH (INTRODUCTORY)

The seventh oracle of this series is itself septiform. Seven angels portend, by speech or symbolical action, that the doom decreed on humanity by the supreme God of creation is to be complete and inescapable. That, briefly, is the gist of the oracle. And if this proves as dull and prosaic a comment to the general reader as it may prove contentious to the student of REVELATION, we must crave indulgence. Confessedly, it is largely a Bædeker function that the critic must perform. Let us not pretend that the comments of a guide can do more than hint at the ' pith and marrow ' of REVELATION. John's imagery tells its own story with incomparable force and splendour ; it is the language of a poet, of one who has seen further and felt more deeply than his fellows, and has the rare

---

[1] xiv. 1-5 has been called in some respects the most enigmatic passage in REVELATION. It has certainly given rise to some enigmatic exegesis. The difficulties have been : (1) To explain the relationship of the one hundred and forty-four thousand mentioned here with the one hundred and forty-four thousand who were sealed, and with the uncountable multitude in the heavenly scene of chap. vii. (2) To establish the locality of Mount Sion, whether on heaven or on earth. (3) To identify the unnamed ' voice ' which sings the new song. (4) To account for John's definition of the one hundred and forty-four thousand as celibates. We have stated our views in as great detail as we judge desirable in a commentary of this sort : and we must be content to say that the many erroneous conceptions of this passage take their birth largely from failure to recognize John's preoccupation with the theme of themes—martyrdom—and, secondly, from inadequate appreciation of John's literary method. The identification of the one hundred and forty-four thousand with the whole Church, for instance, makes it necessary to find grounds for the rejection of verse 4, and consequently grounds of a sort are discovered. The failure to see in the reference to Mount Sion some kinship with those to the restored furniture of the temple (viii. 3, xi. 19, xv. 5), and also to see its connexion with the Day of Wrath, has led to the placing of the whole visionary scene in the millenary period, and on earth. This in turn has led to an unnatural attribution of the new song to heavenly singers (the one hundred and forty-four thousand, it is said, are occupied in learning it). For John's literary method, see Introduction, p. xxvii.).

power of evoking in them his own passion, and stirring in them his own strong thought. Many critics have commented on the grandeur of John's imagery ; but it is one thing to pay lip service to a grandeur which is indeed hard to ignore, and another quite different thing to see that it is the product of a virile imagination—a concentrative and keen-sighted mental power, not to be put on and off like a cloak. Largely because this fact has been too little understood, certain errors have cast a pall of misunderstanding over the seven angels and their messages. Therefore, at the risk of seeming both obvious and dull, we must pause long enough to ask ourselves precisely what function these angels fulfil.

First and last, they are portents, and portents not for the bulk of mankind, but for John's readers. We are not to suppose for one moment that John expected the appearance over all ' the broad earth ' (xx. 9) of each of these angels, shouting messages and commands, and performing executioners' work. Consider the four horsemen : they also were portents—and how absurd to interpret them literally ! What is this mighty being, distinguished with the mark of sovereignty, bestriding a white horse, bearing a bow, and riding forth ' conquering and to conquer ' ? Was the earth actually to be trampled under the foot of some huge Pegasus of the last days, and was mankind actually to be transfixed with the arrows of some divinely armed Bellerophon ? Never ! Here is the portent of Parthian hordes, sweeping irresistibly in all their numbers over the whole civilized world. The horseman and his steed, one might almost say, assert an eschatological principle—that in these last days an invasion of unparalleled savagery must prove God's instrument of vengeance on evil-doers. The seven angels of chap. xiv. also assert that events which to the prophet and his readers in the interests of justice and righteousness *must* happen—will happen. That is their sole function. And when it is thoroughly understood that these angels (portents one and all) constitute a medium of revelation, not of divine action ; when it is recognized that the angels who **cried aloud** were not the unnecessary heralds of God's supremacy in creation, and of His power to punish, nor yet the extremely tardy bearers of a 'call to religion'; when it is recognized, moreover, that those bearing the sickles of harvest and vintage were in no way the actual performers of God's sentence on men—then every difficulty is dispersed—and the difficulties propounded by critics have proved more numerous than their solutions. Indeed, the alternative view to that proposed above is so beset with contrarieties that there is no entertaining it. For example, the fall of Babylon the great (the Empire—or, in other words, civilization) is to be the last of the seven last plagues, which ' complete the wrath of God.' As we shall soon read in chap. xvi., it is, in fact, accomplished or completed by an earthquake of unexampled severity. It is the culmination of God's punishment of mankind in general. Yet it is the **second** in our present series of angels who proclaims its fall ; if we are to be literal, the fall of civilization, of all the cities on earth, with all the consequent slaughter of men (cf. xi. 13, note), is described as preceding the final reaping of **earth's harvest** of wicked men, and the treading of the **winepress of God's wrath.** If we are to be literal, here are three separate events—each complete and conclusive ! This untenable notion is equalled in improbability by another : why should the **third angel** take the trouble to warn the worshippers of the Beast that they were in jeopardy of everlasting torture *after* they have pledged themselves to the Beast's service, and committed themselves to their punishment ? Is it for a moment to be considered that this angel, in his flight after the fall of the city, is acting the part of a superfluous announcer to men of the doom they have already incurred ? (Cf. notes on xi. 18 ff. and on xiii. 15 ff.) Is his purpose to aggravate, perhaps, their already unimaginable discomforture ? And even the first of our seven angels, regarded as a being who is actually to fly in **mid-heaven** as the end of the world approaches—is he not the fantasy of an infant in religion ? When God finally spoke in anger, He needed no angelic heralds to draw the moral ; men were amazed, ' awe-struck ' (xi. 13) and involuntarily ' gave glory to the God of heaven.' ' Fall upon us,' they cried to the mountains and the rocks, ' and hide us from the face of him who is seated on the throne and from the wrath of the Lamb ; for the great Day of their wrath is come, and who can abide it ? ' (vi. 16, 17). And the previous plagues, John believed, had displayed a moral no less plain, only to be ignored by men hardened in their wickedness, stubbornly determined not to repent (cf. ix. 20, 21). No, the supreme God of Creation had no need of an angelic expositor to make clear His meaning to mankind ; His actions spoke for themselves, clearly and universally. The plagues on the mystical Egypt, the civilized world, reached out to all men ; an angel's wings, and an angel's loud cry had power to reach a smaller circle—John's fellow-Christians. All in all, a literal view of the first angel is impossible.

Finally, before we leave these preliminary remarks, we must consider the angel described in verse 14 : **Then I looked, and there was a white cloud, and seated on the cloud One resembling a human being, a golden crown upon his head. . . .** At first sight it seems as if the **One resembling a human being** is Christ, and many commentators have decided that the matter is put out of all doubt by John's previous recollection of the famous passage in Daniel (see Dan. vii. 13 ff.) : ' Then in my vision by night I saw a figure in human form coming with the clouds of heaven' (cf. Rev. i. 13). Here, it is thought, is the fulfilment of that prediction : the Son of Man has returned to reap the earth ; and tread the winepress of God's wrath. Yes, but it is **another angel** who gathers in the vintage ; another angel, who, like the one resembling a human being, has a **sharp sickle** to **cull the clusters from the Vine of earth.** If the reaper is Christ, He does no more conclusive work than ' another angel ' : He does not even gather in the vintage— and John leaves no doubt what answer he gave to Isaiah's question :

> ' Who comes here, all crimsoned,
> his robes redder than the vintage ?
> Who is it, arrayed in splendour,
> striding in his strength ?
> radiant with victory,
> a mighty champion ?
> Why so red your robes,
> stained red like a vintager's ? '
>
> (Isa. lxiii. 1–2 ; cf. Rev. xix. 13.)

This particular Gordian knot has been cut by the sharp sickle of literary analysis : the harvesting scene is an interpolation, it is claimed, and the one resembling a human being was the vintager in John's original text (cf. Charles, *op. cit.*, vol. ii., p. 18). This is a desperate remedy—yet even though it were necessary, or critically defensible, it does not take us out of our difficulty. For two insuperable objections remain to the identification of the reaper-portent with Christ : first, he is *commanded* to perform his work by an angel, and, second, the picture of the one resembling a human being is quite different in quality from the other pictures of Christ. As to the first objection, it is beside the point to urge that traditionally the precise moment of the End was held to be determined by God alone, and kept secret by Him even from the Son (cf. St. Mark xiii. 32). For after His death the Lamb stood ' in the midst of the throne,' in communion with the Father so intimate that it is unseemly to contemplate the existence of angelic couriers between Father and Son. That the kingly Being depicted in chap. i., or the Redeemer in chap. v., adored by every hierarchy of angels, or the divine Warrior of chap. xix., should be submitted to the commands of an angel is on the face of it absurd. Nor is it the least help to say that John inherited his picture from a source, for then, surely, he would have adopted that source, with his customary freedom, and made the point clear. The baffling inconsistency still remains. It is almost inconceivable, too, in view of the previous passages in which Christ is described, that in the picture of the harvester He should appear with so little ceremony. To mention only one detail, the single **golden crown** is a distinction shared, not only by the twenty-four Presbyters, but also by the first of the four horsemen in chap. vi. ; in fact, even dæmon-locusts (chap. ix.) wear ' sort of crowns like gold ' ! The crown signifies power to prevail, or royal dignity—but not supremacy. On the Messiah's head are ' many diadems ' (xix. 12). He is not merely a prince, but KING OF KINGS AND LORD OF LORDS (xix. 16).

The phrase ' one resembling a human being ' (R.V., ' like a son of man '—the literal translation) in the process of time became exclusively associated with Christ. But it is a general term in apocalyptic for a heavenly being. In 1 Enoch, for example, where it is thought the term is first applied to the Messiah, angels are represented as men, and men as animals. The angelic figure at the end of Daniel, who swears the oath echoed by the strong angel in REVELATION (chap. x.), is ' a man.' It is hardly possible that a teacher as familiar with the terms of apocalyptic writings as John, one as convinced as he of their relevance to his own times, could have been uninfluenced by their commonest idioms ; it is surely almost as rash to suppose that any Christian at all versed in apocalpytic would have necessarily taken the expression, *one resembling a son of man*, to mean Christ and no other ' dweller in heaven.' After all, the literature of Jewish eschatology still exercised a lively influence on Christian thought : John's readers had no neatly bound New Testaments to decide their devotional terms and fix them rigidly. If we can judge by John's literary predilections, we must recognize that the time of REVELATION is one when ' he who reads aloud ' to the congregation (i. 3) and ' the hearer ' (xxii. 17) find in Jewish eschatological writings, both prophetic and apocalyptic, their main available devotional literature.

As to the phrase, **seated on a cloud**, said to be a reference to the messianic expression already quoted by John : ' Lo, he is coming on the clouds' (i. 7), this is far too slight a circumstance to indicate the reaper's identity. John dispenses entirely with Daniel's metaphor when he finally depicts the Messiah's advent :

> ' Then I saw heaven open wide—
> and there was a white horse !
> His rider is faithful and true. . . . '

In an allusion of this kind, moreover, pictorial identity is indispensable : there is every difference between the single motionless white cloud of John's vision, and the great surging masses of threatening storm-clouds, which were to chariot the Messiah. John has spoken before of cloud as an accompaniment of angelic appearance : the strong angel of chap. x. was ' clad in a cloud.' Again, we must remember how the witnesses

rise to heaven ' in a cloud.' The fact is that the reaper's position **on a cloud** simply corresponds with the flight **in mid-
heaven** of the angels who shout their messages to the world
in verses 6–12. His static position is dictated by the metaphor
of the sickle, sweeping with one final stroke through the ripe
corn of wickedness.

We conclude that the reaper was an angel, one of seven
portentous figures, who foreshadowed to John the inevitability and completeness of the earth's destined punishment.

xiv. 6–13 : The First Three Angels shout their Messages

Then I saw another angel flying in mid-heaven with an eternal 6
gospel for the inhabitants of earth, for every nation and
tribe and tongue and people ; he cried aloud, ' Fear God 7
and give him glory, for the hour of his judgment has come ;
worship him *who made heaven and earth, the sea* and the
fountains of water.' And another, a second angel, followed, 8
crying, ' *Fallen, fallen is Babylon the great, who made all
nations drink the wine* of the passion of her vice ! ' They 9
were followed by another, a third angel, crying aloud,
' Whoever worships the Beast and his statue, and lets his
forehead or hand be marked, *he shall drink the wine* of 10
God's passion, *poured out untempered in the cup of his anger,*
and shall be tortured with *fire and brimstone* before the holy
angels and before the Lamb: *the smoke* of their torture *rises* 11
for ever and ever, and they get no rest from it, day and night,
these worshippers of the Beast and his statue, and all who
are marked with his name.' This is what shows the 12
patience of the saints—those who keep God's commandments and the faith of Jesus.

Then I heard a voice from heaven saying, ' Write this : 13
" Blessed are the dead who die in the Lord from henceforth ! Even so—it is the voice of the Spirit ; let them rest
from their toils ; for what they have done goes with
them." '

6 The portent of the first angel (**another angel** : no distinction of importance is intended) asserts a principle already commented on (xi. 13), that when the End does come, it will be no longer possible for men to blind themselves to God's supreme power ; it will be forcibly borne home to the **inhabitants of earth** that the Creator-God is omnipotent. Every false heart pledged to idolatry and evil-doing must, with a flood of terror, recognize the irresistible majesty of God. In His presence, in the very awareness of His power to destroy,
7 a man must involuntarily **worship** : no unredeemed mortal could stifle the shuddering awe induced by consciousness of divine splendour. This theme is probably a development of the prophetic expectation that the Eternal's appearance in Sion must necessarily evoke universal homage to the true God and His people (for references, see notes on xi. 13). But John read such oracles unwarmed by any glow of optimism ; he did not believe in last-minute conversions. The angel's **eternal gospel** was not *good* news for the **inhabitants of earth,** at least, not for the great majority of them. It was not a last warning to the wicked. ' **The hour of his judgment has come,**' the angel shouts. And by this time human loyalties have been tested and pledged once and for all. The wicked have all received the mark of the Beast, and have associated themselves with the slaughter of the saints (xi. 10). They have already proclaimed evil to be their good. There is now no hope for them. Nevertheless, even their knees must bow : every created being must make its obeisance when the Creator reveals Himself in His mighty deeds, at that hour when the angelic choruses can at last cry out : ' The rule of the world has passed to our Lord and his Christ, and he shall reign for ever and ever ' (xi. 15). The Gospel is eternal because from the beginning of time creation has owed this homage to the Creator. ' **Fear God and give him the glory,**' cries the angel : after the ascension of the witnesses we see mankind filled with terror (xi. 11) ; and after the first disastrous shock of the great earthquake, their awe wrenches from them the admission of God's supremacy (xi. 13) : terror compels praise : ' The rest were awe-struck, and gave glory to the God of heaven.' They

at last understand that there is One greater than the Beast, whom they had formerly worshipped with the cry (a travesty of Old Testament hymns to God) :

> ' Who is like the Beast ?
> Who can fight with him ? ' (xiii. 4).

They now worship a God with greater power. They worship the God who has power over fourfold nature, over heaven, earth, sea, and fresh water ; who has power to shatter the heavens, to fold up the skies like a scroll, to dim and extinguish every star on high ; who has power to wrack the earth with upheaval, to drench it with blood and sear it with flame ; who has power to turn the sea into blood, and blast every living creature in it ; who has power to turn the fountains of water into loathsome wells of poison. They worship the God of heaven, **him who made heaven and earth, the sea and the fountains of water** ; they give glory to the God whose power over creation has been evinced in every conceivable admonitory plague (cf. viii. 6 ff.), hitherto unregarded, but finally intensified to such a pitch (chap. xvi.) that the moral is at last inescapable. Thus, in chap. xi., as in chap. vi. (where the unregenerate cower under mountains and rocks, praying for violent death that they may avoid the terrible spectacle of God's wrath), we have a picture of the fulfilment of the demand made in the first angel's cry.

It will readily be seen that the theme of the first portent is closely connected with that of the **second** and of the third. 8 For the fall of **Babylon the great** is the climax of all the plagues precipitated on the earth during Antichrist's reign. We have indeed seen that it is actually the first tremor of the final earthquake, with its devastation of the City and its decimation of mankind (chap. xi.), which drives men to **worship** out of sheer terror. And as to the **third** portent, with its prediction of everlasting torture for the Beast-worshippers, this is 9 the grim sequel to mankind's transference of allegiance in the last days. John recognizes that it will be made for no moral considerations, but through the flashing of God's ' sharp sword with a double edge.' Therefore, it will be idle for any man to hope that terrified remorse will be met by clemency. As a man sows, he reaps ; those who pay fealty to Antichrist must share the fate of Antichrist (cf. xix. 20 ff.). Yet here is the bitter irony of their lot : though they damn themselves eternally by their refusal to face the truth, one day they will be *forced* to face it. Sooner or later the **glory** they refuse to **give** the Creator willingly will be torn from them by the spectacle of His wrath. To worship the Beast is to commit the unforgivable sin ; but it is also the quintessence of folly. We must on no account allow the close logical connexion between the three portents to elude us, since, if we do, we are likely to carry away a totally false impression of the three angels and their purpose. Briefly, the first angel proclaims the all-compelling majesty of God the Creator, in whose awful presence all men must **fear** and **worship,** the loyal and rebellious alike. The second angel proclaims the occasion when this **fear** and **worship** must inevitably be aroused : that is, as the foundations of the civilized world crumble, at the fall of Babylon the great (the City in xi. 13—a passage which illuminates the connexion between the cries of the first and second angels). The third angel proclaims the sequel to this universal admission of God's supremacy : the eternal punishment inexorably decreed for those of God's subjects who have previously branded themselves with the negation of truth, and have worshipped a living blasphemy against righteousness. The connexion between the second and third oracles has also been signposted. Those in Babylon who have drunk the **wine of the passion of her vice** must also drink the **wine of God's passion, poured out untempered in the cup of his anger.**

It is unnecessary to say more at present about the fall of **Babylon the great,** since this subject recurs more prominently in xvi. 18 f. and chap. xviii. The cry of the second angel is indeed the theme of the great dirge over ruined civilization. Nor need we pause long over the words of the **third angel.** One could almost wish that their imagery admitted of some degree of doubt. This alone must be said about them : they are aimed at waverers in the Christian community, and so far from convicting John of gloating over the horrible fate of the condemned, they simply illustrate his consuming desire to drive into the understanding of the weak and wavering how great was the peril in which they stood. He spares nothing to bring out the contrast between the lot of the blessed (in verses 1–5) and the lot of the damned. Is any man in danger of succumbing to the enticements of the world—the ' world ' of the Roman Empire ? Is any Christian in danger of joining his fellow-townsmen in their besotted devotion to the things of Satan ? Let him beware ! If the Empire held out to men a cup overflowing with the **wine of the passion of her vice,** alluring, intoxicating, God, too, had a cup full of **wine :** the wine of destruction. It was a draught undiluted by the water of clemency—**poured out untempered.** Again, the reward of the ' conqueror ' was to be owned openly by the Lamb before the Father and before His angels (iii. 5). What infinite bliss the waverer stood in danger of losing ! What infinite pain, not only to be disowned but even **tortured with fire and brimstone before the holy angels and before the Lamb** ! Let no Christian be seduced by false teachers—those Nicolaitans (ii. 15) and Jezebels (ii. 20)—into idolatry. To receive the mark of the Beast was to approve the deeds of the Beast ; to **worship** him was to acclaim evil as good. For such a crime no punishment could be too severe. Few to-day will applaud John's conceptions of God's final dealing with sinners. Theology, like the law, has in recent years found little to commend in punishment which is merely retributive. The doom-songs of the Hebrew prophets, with their lurid pictures of enemy lands consumed with flames, desolated, smoking as an offering to the Lord of hosts, have in them a vengeful exaltation which we attribute to the crudity of the age. John's doctrine is even more terrible than theirs : where the prophets foresaw the smoke of ravaged countrysides rising to the heaven, and predicted the temporal destruction of God's enemies, John sees the **smoke of their torture** rising **for ever 11 and ever**—in the sight of the dwellers in heaven. This is the reflection of an age which saw in the juxtaposition of eternal bliss and eternal punishment a certain grim propriety : both conditions were enhanced. But it is a very incidental touch in John's picture, and it is questionable whether the phrase **before the holy angels and before the Lamb** was intended to be read literally. For John is attempting to show the contrast between the fate of the loyal and the renegade, and his picture is essentially nothing more than a picture of hell, to be seen side by side with previous pictures of heaven. Thus, whereas the conqueror is destined to be a pillar in the temple of God—' nevermore shall he leave it ' (iii. 12)—and is to be admitted to the presence of those who ' day and night ' sing the praises of God (iv. 8), the renegade is to pay a different kind of tribute **day and night** to Him whose power he once set at nought ; he is to dwell for ever and ever amidst flames **of fire and brimstone.** We might paraphrase the words of the third angel as follows : ' Let the waverer take thought ! The suffering he avoids on earth by cowardice and apostasy is immeasurably less than the punishment he will incur in after life.'

12   The comment in verse 12, **this is what shows the patience of the saints,** is a parenthetical reference to **the Beast and his statue** in the previous sentence. John wishes it to be clear beyond doubt that Antichrist's demand to be worshipped will be the fundamental test. The Christian's response to this claim will decide his future status. The response of the **saints** will be **patience**—uncomplaining, steadfast endurance of the suffering which their refusal to betray Christ will entail. These men **keep God's commandments,** not those of Satan ; the **faith of Jesus,** not that of Antichrist. (See note on xiii. 10.)

The messages of the seven angels in this oracle, we have claimed, are embodied in a form wholly designed to strike the imagination of John's readers. They are specifically messages of warning for the present ; by painting the inevitable doom of the wicked in his most sombre colours, John hopes to convey the folly of attempting to evade the responsibilities of a loyal Christian. He now pauses in verse 13 to deliver a message more obviously related to the present, and more obviously directed towards Christians. This welcome excursus (characteristic of

John's literary method) gives us the second of the seven ' beatitudes ' of REVELATION (see i. 3). **A voice from heaven** dictates 13 this message ; **' it is the voice of the Spirit,'** John is told—the prophetic Spirit of Jesus, whose utterances we have already heard in the promises to the conquerors of the seven churches (chaps. ii. and iii.). Having thus reminded his readers of the divine authenticity of what he is writing, and having impressed upon them its pressing importance, John formulates the positive motive for heroic loyalty—in striking contrast to the preceding verses, which formulate a negative motive. **' Blessed are the dead who die in the Lord from henceforth ! '** John is clearly speaking of the martyrs, of those who are to follow the example of ' faithful Antipas ' (ii. 13), in braving the Imperial sword. The time of intenser persecution is so near at hand that John can say—**from henceforth :** from the moment when he writes. What are the **toils** from which they are released ? We must remember the seven letters ; perhaps we should particularly remember the ' hard work ' of the Ephesian Christians. Their toils were directed against false apostles within the church. The struggle against ' the contagion of the world's slow stain ' is one which remains for less troubled ages ; John's fellow-Christians were subject to additional burdens of dissension within the ranks of their small communities, of exposing plausible pretenders to the authority of prophet and apostle, of meeting the rancour of Jewish opponents, of withstanding the pressure of enthusiasts of the emperor-cult ; and can we not say also, of witnessing under all these difficulties ? For John makes it clear in chap. xi. that the gospel of the End *must* be preached everywhere, before Babylon could be destroyed. These are the toils of a man who lives **in the Lord,** in close communion with His Spirit ; such toils are fitly consummated by the supreme glory of martyrdom. Christians who live and die nobly will have their reward. **What they have done goes with them.** This is true, indeed, of all men. For when the heavenly records are opened at the Day of Judgment, John says, the dead are judged ' by what was written in these books, *by what they have done* ' (xx. 12). One of the greatest rewards of the martyr is

that his holy living and dying assure to him the ' crown of
Life,' and absolve him from the ordeal of the Judgment day.
What he has done goes with him—he is rewarded immediately
according to what he has done. ' The conqueror shall not be
injured by the second death ' (ii. 11 ; see also xx. 4–15).

xiv. 14–20 : The ' Iron Flail ' of Retribution descends on the Unrighteous

14 Then *I looked, and there was* a white cloud, and seated *on the
   cloud One resembling a human being,* a golden crown upon
15 his head and a sharp sickle in his hand. And another angel
   came out of the temple shouting aloud to him who sat upon
   the cloud,
   ' *Thrust your sickle in* and reap,
      the time has come to reap,
         earth's harvest is now ripe and ready.'
16 So he who sat upon the cloud swung his sickle over the
17 earth, and the earth was reaped. Then another angel came
18 out of the temple, he too with a sharp sickle ; and another
   angel came from the altar—he who has power over fire—
   and called loudly to the one who had the sharp sickle,
   ' *Thrust your* sharp *sickle in,*
      cull the clusters from the Vine of earth,
      for its grapes are fully ripe.'
19 So the angel swung his sickle on the earth and culled the
   clusters from the Vine of earth, flinging the grapes into the
20 great winepress of God's wrath ; outside the City *was the
   winepress trodden,* and blood gushed out of the winepress as
   high as a horse's bridle for the space of two hundred miles.

We must now return for a moment to the theme of Mount
Sion, where the hundred and forty-four thousand stood with
their Redeemer. ' Mount Sion,' we showed, was wedded in
tradition to the notion of a rescued Israel and the chastisement of Israel's enemies. We have already quoted Joel's
description of Sion, the refuge of the faithful remnant (Joel
ii. 32) on ' that great and awful day ' of the Eternal. We are

now to see a complementary portent of the judgment executed
on the unrighteous, when—

> ' the Eternal thunders out of Sion,
> loudly from Jerusalem.'

John's twofold picture of the outpouring of divine wrath
recalls several familiar passages from prophetic books, but
its form is most obviously influenced by Joel iii. 13 :

> ' In with the sickle !—
> the harvest is ripe !
> Come tread the winepress, tread it,
> it is full,
> The troughs are overflowing with their wickedness.'

Joel's language, with its suggestion of both harvest and
vintage as a comprehensive description of God's mowing
down of the wicked (it is no more than a suggestion—' harvest '
is used of the gathering of grapes in Isa. xviii., and Joel is
using the one figure of vintage, first the culling of the grapes,
then the treading of the press), provides John with the sketch
for his picture. But the painting reveals a master hand.
Everything is ominous, majestic. We gaze first of all on a
still **white cloud**. Motionless, **seated** there, is a resplendent 14
figure **resembling a human being** : that is, according to the
apocalyptic use which John is echoing, a figure whose dazzling,
visionary appearance is that of a *celestial* being (see note,
p. 274). Like the ' strong angel ' of chap. x., this being reflects
the glory of the Lord of the harvest. (For Christ Himself
appeared in John's first vision, we shall remember, under this
very guise : ' like a son of man,' ' resembling a human being.')
In the appearance of this ' portent-angel,' John deliberately
reminds his readers of the messianic avenger whose dealings
with ' the nations ' could be read in the whole tale of destruction in the last days, in the great earthquake, the great hailstorm (xvi. 18 ff.), and even in the depredations of Antichrist
on his own subjects (xvii. 15 ff.). There is a wealth of grim
associations in the appearance of this cloud-borne portent ;
and yet, with them, an awful simplicity. Like the first of the
four horsemen (chap. vi.), the angel wears **a golden crown,**
a sign that none shall resist him : his **sharp sickle**, like the

sword of divine punishment, is tempered to mow down nations. The word of command is shouted. The Titanic figure stoops. His arm sweeps over the broad earth with one simple, telling gesture—**and the earth was reaped.** This air of majesty informs the whole scene, both reaping and vintage. John has found a fitting climax to the three preceding portents of the seventh oracle. The effect has been cumulative : one after another the angels have cried their messages of warning, command, triumph, each **shouting aloud**—' with a great voice.' Each angel appears in the eye of imagination clothed in the awful majesty of the message he shouts, or the symbolic action he performs. And their appearance grows successively more terrible, until finally the angel of vintage **culled the clusters from the Vine of earth, flinging the grapes into the great winepress of God's wrath** : here is a being who displays something of the fierce vengeful energy of Isaiah's vintager (Isa. lxiii. 1–6). Whether from motives of reverence or of artistic effect, John says nothing about the treader of the winepress. **Outside the City was the winepress trodden**—this is in the mysterious background of the picture. All that appears is a shoreless sea of blood.

Sermons on hell fire and divine anger have gone out of fashion. It is largely to satisfy a taste for the remote and curious that the plaster is pealed from mediæval wall-paintings of judgment scenes. Worship and morality born of fear, it is held, are of questionable value. But clearly enough, in John's view the recognition of God's dreadful power to punish was an indispensable part of religion. It was not necessarily that he sought, in his pictures of harvest and vintage, to terrify cowards into courage. What he was really trying to do for his fellow-believers was to clarify their thought, to get them to see things in their right proportions. Christians were to be confronted with tangible perils and concrete temptations —immediate and bitter penalties, perhaps, if they were loyal to their convictions, immediate respite if they were disloyal. The demands of Antichrist would be loud and insistent. Would they have power to deafen Christians to the demands of God ? For a man like John there could be no hesitation ;

a prophet was one who was able in this life to gaze in wonder at the throne, and see there the strong servants of the Almighty. After such a spectacle, the power of earthly monarchs, even though it stood menacing on every horizon, was seen for what it was—the veriest mirage. But John had enough knowledge of the churches to understand that all did not share his insight and confidence. He therefore tried with all the resources of a visionary, a poet and apocalyptist to make things unseen as vivid and real as things seen ; unseen peril as clear as that which appeared to the eyes of all ; unseen bliss as alluring as the subtle temptations of the world. He wished the doubters to appreciate that God's power was real and eternal ; that of Antichrist (in spite of its earthly show) unreal and transient. He wished them to see how vain and empty was the notion that a man could actually *save his life* by betraying Christ and succumbing to His enemy. Why, this was the one way of throwing away the only thing that mattered—the crown of eternal life ! He wished them, in short, to be true Christians, possessing the martyr's strength because they were clear-sighted—seeing and rejecting the shams of false religion, and despising the facade of ferocious power built up by Antichrist and his followers, What was the utmost they could do, these strong enemies of God ? They could kill the body ; but death was not the end for the loyal :

> ' Death, be not proud, though some have callèd thee
> Mighty and dreadful, for thou art not so :
> For those whom thou think'st thou dost overthrow
> Die not, poor Death. . . .'

Such was the lofty faith in the *redeeming* power of God, which John sought to foster. It was natural, in view of the contemporary situation, that he should stress side by side with it the supreme *punitive* power of God. For in refusing to brave the limited power of Antichrist, the renegade must in his folly brave the unlimited power of God. But, one may well ask, why should Christians be bludgeoned by pictures of blood and destruction into accepting the simple logic of such an argument ? Doubtless because clear sight is not the commonest of gifts ; because then, as now, a man's belief tended to be the dupe and thrall of his emotions. Few men are strangers to the subtle aggression of self-interest, and few of us to-day can claim to set our trial beside that which John foresaw confronting Christians. John saw it as his task to discredit and stultify the argument of self-interest. He spoke to Timorous and Mistrust as Bunyan did :

> ' Then, said Christian, You make me afraid, but whither shall I fly to be safe ? If I go back to mine own country, *that* is prepared for fire and brimstone, and I shall certainly perish there. If I can get to the Celestial City, I am sure to be in safety there. I must venture. To go back is nothing but death. To go forward is fear of death, and life everlasting beyond it. . . . '

' To go back is nothing but death.' The stern God of righteousness, who made all and has power over all, the God whose pure eyes abhor evil, whose strong arm must inevitably shatter the worshippers of evil—here is the true focus of self-interest ! ' Fear *Him* ! ' John cries. ' Fear *Him*, the supreme Judge, and no other. All worldly fear is to be heeded as the passing of a shadow. For whatever else may come, Judgment is certain.'

Before we concern ourselves with points of detail, let us make quite certain that we see the essential bearing of the harvesting and vintage scenes. Four angels portend, by speech and action, the ordering and execution of divine vengeance on evil-doers. There were two main implications for John's readers. First, there could be no escape for him who became an apostate through cowardice. If he refused to die the heroic death of the martyr, he must die the shameful death of a renegade. Death was bound to overtake him, for the earth was to be swept clear of the wicked. Such is the force of the two metaphors of harvest and vintage. The one reinforces the other. The fruits of a long era of wickedness were all to be gathered in, first the corn and then the grape, until evil was utterly destroyed. Some critics have imagined

that the reaper, swinging his sickle over the earth, is actually
garnering the ' good seed ' of the harvest in the parable, while
the vintager who swung his sickle on the earth is deputed to 16
punish the wicked—to gather the ' tares,' as it were.   Others,
with hardly greater justification, imagine the harvest to be
the general ingathering of both good and bad, corn and tares,
at the end of the world (cf. St. Matt. xiii. 39).   The vintage
scene, it is explained, is intended to amplify the first picture of
the End, in that it describes fully the fate of the wicked alone.
These divisions are false ; it is obvious enough that the sharp
sickle of the reaper is no less an instrument of punishment
than that of the vintager.   Besides (not to labour an obvious
point), we must consider that John has already told us how
the Elect have been gathered in—the preceding oracle deals
with them ; and this oracle deals specifically with the unredeemed.   Finally, as we hope to show later (see chap. xx. ; note
on the millennium and p. 259), John definitely did not expect
the whole Church to be martyred, nor did he expect the loyal
who survived Antichrist's activities to be mowed down by a
celestial reaper in order to be brought to judgment.   He
expected many Christians to enter into Christ's reign on earth
alive and unharmed.   The picture of slaughter in chap. xiv.
is a picture to warn the waverers of the retributive power of
God.   This is its first and main message.

   The second implication in the picture is a little more elusive.
John asked his fellow-believers to understand that all this
chastisement and destruction of the wicked was to follow from
the great martyrdom, when the number of those ' slain for
adhering to God's word and to the testimony which they bore '
was to be ' completed ' (vi. 9-11).   It is for this reason that
the angels are said to come from the temple and from the altar. 15-
In reality, of course, John thought of them as coming from 18
God's presence.   For in heaven, just as in the new Jerusalem
(xxi. 22), the ' temple is the Lord God almighty and the
Lamb.'   They come from the presence of the God of Creation,
for the command was His to give, and His alone (cf. Mark xiii.
32).   Why, then, does not John say ' from God's presence '
quite plainly ?   Are the temple and the altar mere figurative

variations ? And if so, could not John have said with equal, if not greater, aptness that the angels came from the throne—the symbol of supreme power ? John has given abundant evidence that the thought of the supremacy of the Creator-God is constantly in his mind (see iv. 11, x. 6 and xiv. 7 ; also the whole of viii. 6 ff., and chap. xvi.). Why then at this crucial point does he replace the symbol for absolute power in creation (as in chap. iv.) with the symbol for God's holiness (the temple) and with the symbol for His accessibility (as it were) to the prayers and the self-sacrifice of Christians (the altar) ? We must recognize at once in the allusion to the altar (the altar of incense, viii. 3 ; the altar under which the souls of earlier martyrs rested, until the completion of their number, vi. 9) a reference to that old tradition which connected the rehabilitation of the true Israel with the restoration of the temple furniture lost in the first fall of Jerusalem. John shows the fulfilment of this expectation in the disclosure of the heavenly archetypes of those sacred objects (cf. notes on pp. 72, 210). The heavenly temple plays a similar part in John's use of this tradition. The later Isaiah wrote in exile, after the desecration of the temple in Jerusalem (Isa. lxvi. 6) :

> ' Hark ! the city is in uproar !
> It is coming from the temple !
> 'Tis the Eternal dealing vengeance
> to the full upon his foes ! '

This, in Isaiah's mind, clearly meant that on the restoration of the earthly temple, God would send out destruction on evil-doers from His holy place. But there is no earthly temple for John—none, that is, except the Church (xi. 1). It should be noted that John expressly rejects the older expectation of a restored temple on a new earth (xxi. 22). It is from the heavenly temple that God's vengeance is dealt to the full on His enemies (xv. 5). And the fact that vengeance is said to come from the heavenly temple (as a symbol for God's presence) rather than from the heavenly throne, the ' great white throne ' of Judgment (equally a symbol for God's presence) is to be explained by John's desire to connect the outpouring of vengeance with the vindication of the true

Israel, with the presence of the martyrs in heaven, with the accomplishment of the ' great Distress '—the great sacrifice. This explains the triple allusion to **the temple** (verses 15, 17, and 18) ; it is a theme which recurs, and we must do it full justice (see notes on chaps. iv., viii., xi. and xv.). In short, it would leap at once to the eye of the discerning reader in the first century that John's picture of retribution assigned a decisive part to the martyrs in the devastation of the wicked on earth. This reader would no doubt quickly remember the promise to the conqueror of the Thyatiran church, the reward of ' authority over the nations ' (ii. 27) :

> ' Aye, he will shepherd them with an iron flail,
>   shattering them like a potter's jars.'

For this *is* the fulfilment of that terrible promise. The martyrs are now having their reward of retributive authority.

On this note our explanation of the chapter might fitly end, for we have already dealt with the fundamental messages in the scenes of harvest and vintage. And it can never be too greatly emphasized that John was wholly occupied with these general messages. He had no intention whatever of writing a detailed forecast of the future. We all have acquaintances who make a habit of scanning the international horizon and making sage predictions, partly, we suspect, in order to have the pleasure of saying, ' I told you so ! ' John was innocent of such a motive ; and though it may not seem altogether easy to avoid attributing to him something like the same habit, careful study shows that nothing is further from the truth. His outlook on the future was determined by faith and not by calculation ; and his picture of the future is correspondingly general in character. A final crisis was bound to come, he thought, because the ' Lord God of the spirits of the prophets ' (xxii. 6) had decreed it, and had revealed His decree to successive ages. The angel who cried, ' Fallen, fallen is Babylon the great ! ' (xiv. 8) was publishing a verdict long since passed on the corrupt world. Jeremiah had spoken of the ' harvesting ' of Babylon, as John himself might have done :

' For this is the sentence of the Lord of hosts,
  the God of Israel,
  Babylon to be trampled like a threshing-floor,
  Then trampled like the grain upon the floor ! '

(Jer. li. 33.)

The important thing for John is not *how* this sentence is to be executed, not the nature and order of its successive phases, nor the time and occasion of its consummation, but rather that it is certain to be executed. For that reason, the symbols of harvest and vintage are less misleading than some of John's other eschatological figures—the various hints he gives, for example, of future invasions, civil and international warfare, earthquakes, eclipses, hailstorms, and epidemics. How in plain fact (we are tempted to ask) did John expect the End to come ? What part was to be played in it by Antichrist and his captains ? *When* do they attack Babylon, ' lay her waste and strip her naked, devouring her flesh and burning her with fire ' (xvii. 16) ? *When* does John expect the earthquake (xvi. 18 ff.) to overturn the cities of earth—before or after the great battle of Harmagedon (xvi. 16 and xix. 17 ff.) ? Is there some special relation between the final earthquake of chap. xvi. and the harvest of chap. xiv., and does John wish us to understand a specific connexion between the treading of the 20 winepress **outside the City** and the ' feast of flesh ' at the battle of Harmagedon ? Such questions are really almost beside the point. Information of this kind could have little pastoral value—and that is John's concern. But once we have conceded the main point—that harvest and vintage scenes together assert in the most general terms the principle of divine retribution, terrifying and inescapable—we can permit ourselves to speculate upon the details of the eschatological preconceptions behind them.

There are, in fact, two outstanding occasions in John's eschatological scheme. The first is the fall of Babylon, when a voice from heaven cries : ' All is over ! ' (xvi. 17 ; cf. xi. 15). The second is the ' battle on the great Day of almighty God,' when the Messiah appears from heaven, to destroy His enemies (xvi. 12 ff. and xix. 11 ff.). The destruction of Babylon by

earthquake represents the fall of civilization ; there does seem
to be in John's mind some idea that the assembled hordes of
Antichrist, consisting as they do, in accordance with traditional expectations, of invaders from a far-off country, will
pillage and burn the stricken cities of the earth (xvii. 15 ff.).
The earthquake, with its attendant horrors, represents part of
the judgment on mankind ; and if we care to see in it some
correspondence with the reaping of the earth in chap. xiv.,
there is no obvious reason why we should not. For the fall of
civilization through universal earthquake is John's interpretation of all the prophetic pictures of doom on the cities and
peoples opposed to the Eternal—and Jerusalem is not the
least of the doomed cities. They are all included in the one
symbol, Babylon the great. All are to fall, and their inhabitants to die. The *battle* in which Antichrist and his invading
hordes are destroyed is a separate theme. It is best illustrated
by reference to the Book of Jeremiah (chap. xxv.) This
prophet, having acknowledged the complete justice of the
Eternal's punishment of Israel through the ravages of the
Babylonians, asserts that the invaders in their turn must be
punished for their evil-doing. ' Tell them this is what the
Lord of hosts, the God of Israel says : " Drink yourselves drunk
till you tumble in your vomit, never to rise again—under
the sword I am sending among you." And if they decline to
drink the cup you hand to them, tell them this is what the Lord
of hosts says : " Drink you must ! I begin by inflicting evil on
the city that belongs to me, and are you to get off unpunished ?
You shall not go unpunished, for I am summoning a sword to
fall on all the inhabitants of the world," says the Lord of
hosts ' (Jer. xxv. 27-9). We have quoted this passage because
it illustrates the general idea of John's distinction between the
punishment of the city (in Jeremiah, Jerusalem ; in REVELA-
TION, **Babylon**-Jerusalem, cf. xi. 8 and notes on pp. 184 ff.) and
the punishment of the city's despoilers. There are, of course,
several similar passages in the prophetic books. It was, in
fact, a general theme that an invader who acted the part of
God's scourge on the wickedness of Israel should himself be
smitten. But in the thought of some prophets this invader

was to be smitten in the vicinity of Jerusalem, while the holy City itself was to remain standing. John interprets such expectations in his own way. In his mind it is always the *heavenly* Sion which is inviolate. Yet there *was* an insistence in certain prophets of a massacre of invaders near Jerusalem. Joel, for example, summons the nations to the ' valley of the Verdict ' (Joel iii. 14)—apparently the scene of the ' treading of the winepress '; and this sombre valley is implicitly near Jerusalem. Zechariah speaks of the Mount of Olives as the scene of the Eternal's vengeance on the enemy. John uses the phrase **outside the City** in all probability with such notions in his mind. But as he uses it, the phrase implies that the City has already been devastated : now it is the turn of the invaders—the hosts of Antichrist. So we shall probably be

19 near enough to John's thought if we see in the treading of **the great winepress of God's wrath** a symbolical statement of punishment to be inflicted by the Messiah in the last battle, when the birds are summoned for the great ' banquet '—a banquet of flesh. This identification is supported by the fact

20 that John's expression : **the blood gushed . . . as high as a horse's bridle for the space of two hundred miles,** seems to be an echo of the battle scene described in the Book of Enoch : (Enoch c.) : ' From dawn till sunset they shall slay one another ; and the horse shall walk up to the breast in the blood of sinners, and the chariot will be submerged to its height.'

The phrase **outside the City** has given commentators some trouble. Which city ? Some have urged that it is the ' beloved city ' of the millennium, and that the scene is similar in effect to that indicated in chap. xx. ; others hold that the phrase is retained from traditional accounts of the End, and has no particular significance. Neither view will stand scrutiny. In its context the City means Babylon the great, the ' city ' of the world order. It has here a symbolical use, just as it had in xi. 8. The implication, as we have argued, is that ' the destroyers of the earth ' (xi. 18) are themselves destroyed in turn. But let us not pay disproportionate attention to a detail of secondary importance. The emphasis in John's picture is all on the spilling of the blood of men whose stubborn, deliberate wickedness puts them beyond redemption. It is the final gesture of God to a world which defied him. Like Isaiah, John believed that blood must be spilt in the interests of righteousness—God's righteousness. But, again like Isaiah, John saw in this purification of the earth a preparation for a kingdom of blessedness. The Eternal treads the winepress of the nations (Isa. lxiii. 1–6) because ' the time to free his folk had come.' And the Messiah in REVELATION does not destroy wantonly. **Blood . . . for the space of two hundred miles** (the number is symbolical, but, whatever it signifies, it is no small sea of blood!)—so much blood must be shed before the righteous can live in peace. John looks across this sea to the kingdom of God on earth.

THE LAST PLAGUES

(xv. 1–xvi. 21)

INTRODUCTION TO CHAPTERS XV. AND XVI.: THE PLAGUES WHICH COMPLETE THE WRATH OF GOD

THE reader who has manfully grappled with series after series of portents, all culminating in scenes symbolical of the annihilation of the wicked and the end of Satan's rule on earth, may now perhaps with some justice echo the query of Daniel's angel : ' How long shall it be to the end of these wonders ? ' The recurrence on three separate occasions hitherto of passages which delineate the End (viii. 5, xi. 19, xiv. 14–20) seems to leave little room for **seven angels with seven plagues—the last plagues, for they complete the wrath of God.** This is a feature calculated to puzzle the general reader of REVELATION as much as any other ; but he need not despair of his critical acumen, for there is an extraordinary lack of unanimity among the commentators themselves as to what John intended to convey in his successive cycles of portents—we say extraordinary, because when one simple fact is understood about John's general plan, controversy and doubt are completely banished. When Cortez first gazed from his peak in Darien at the Pacific, his first emotion, no doubt, was, as Keats says, a wild surmise. And he and his men can have had eyes for one thing alone—the silent ocean in the distance. Gradually, however, they surveyed the whole scene. Details of the foreground caught their eyes ; now the immediate foreground, now the middle distance claimed their attention. But time and again they looked further into the distance, straining to see more of that new coast and the sea beyond. Little by little, doubtless, fresh details became plain to them. John, too, has a great panorama before him. It is concealed from most men by the slowly receding mists of Time ; but John (so he most fervently believes) has been enabled by ' the Lord God of the spirits of the prophets ' (xxii. 6) to see beyond the present into the ultimate reign of blessedness. We are not to imagine that he sees the whole great scene of the future at one glance ; his visionary enlightenment is gradual. With each succeeding glimpse, he sees more, or sees more clearly. He does not recount his visionary experience as a geographer might describe the scene which confronted Cortez and his followers. He does not survey the tract of future events as a historian might, arranging events in neat chronological sequence— basing his plan on some mental time-chart. He does proceed methodically, but his method is that of a poet and teacher whose task is not to work out a thesis, but to convince his readers and nurture in them a living faith. He therefore writes *dramatically*, unfolding vision after vision as if they represented his own successive stages of enlightenment about the future—and indeed they may quite well have appeared to John in roughly the same order as he reports them. At first the impression of the End is quite general. The picture of destruction given in the allegory of the breaking of the seven seals shows a general view of cosmic disorder in the last days (chap vi.), a general view of those concerned in the great Distress (chap. vii.) and a general view of the End itself

(viii. 5). In the next series of portents, those connected with the blowing of the seven trumpets, several new details are added. To the picture of the affliction of earth and mankind, there is added the information that the plagues of the last days are to be like those on Egypt long ago. The whole framework of Nature is to be shaken, and mankind is not to escape direct affliction. To the picture of the ordeal before Christians is added the story of the great Distress in general outline—the task of the 'witnesses,' their rejection by men, their death in the mystical 'Sodom and Egypt,' their resurrection. And we are told more about the End—though this still remains quite general. The third survey is of a different order. In the seven oracles of chaps. xii–xiv. the salient events in that great struggle which entered its final stage with the Messiah's enthronement (cf. chap. v.) are reviewed and foreshadowed. We see now for the first time that the visible conflict on earth is the reflex of a mighty unseen conflict, between Satan and his servants on the one hand, and God and His servants on the other. The activities of Antichrist on earth are delineated, his power and authority defined, the circumstances of the great Distress are clarified: the nature of the ordeal and the principles involved in it are clearly set forth. Finally, the outcome of the struggle is described. For God and His servants —triumph (xiv. 1–5) ; for Antichrist and those who became his servants, whether through a predisposition for wickedness or (what was as bad) through a paltering cowardice—for them, death. It should be noted that the seventh oracle of this series, with its description of the day of wrath and all that was involved in the day of wrath, asserts the *general principle* of confusion for God's enemies without straying into distracting details. Like the other pictures of the End (viii. 5 and xi. 19) it is a purely general statement ; what detail there is wins its place by its effectiveness in convincing readers that God's vengeance will be complete and inescapable.

What remains to be told ? Certainly we need no more information about the preliminary chastisement of the world— such information as we received in the trumpets series, with the appended comment that these plagues were intended to warn mankind, but that mankind was heedless of all warning (see ix. 20). We have been told all that was necessary about admonitory plagues ; and John has already indicated as much, for, although he has heard the *seven thunders* (clearly another series like those of the seals and trumpets), he records only his consciousness of the divine injunction not to write their message (see x. 1–4). It is the End which must now be brought before our eyes. Two things remain to be told about the End, before John can allow his readers to contemplate the glories of the messianic reign on earth, and of the new Jerusalem. First, he must show how the plagues he has already described are finally intensified, until one decisive stroke destroys the whole fabric of civilization. Secondly, he must show explicitly, as a separate event, the scene in which Christ confronts Antichrist, the armies of God confront the armies of Satan—and the birds that fly in mid-heaven are summoned to glut themselves on the corpses of those unblessed hordes who have scourged the earth.

The new series of seven plagues, **the last plagues,** are to be understood as following the great Distress. They are an amplification of what has been said about the End in the portent following the opening of the seventh seal (viii. 1–5) and in that following the blowing of the seventh trumpet (xi. 15–19). On those two occasions God's wrath is displayed in brief but impressive terms ; we hear of loud peals of thunder, flashes of lightning, an earthquake, and (in chap. xi.) a hailstorm. These features appear afresh, as the seventh bowl of God's wrath is poured on the earth ; but there is now additional information about the extent and effect of the earthquake and hailstorm. And we are also told that although the earthquake and hailstorm end the death agony of civilization, they are accompanied or directly preceded by plagues of every kind, unexampled in their severity. Of the earthquake John says : **the like . . . never was since man lived on earth.** And it is so with the other plagues. Each in its kind is to be universal in its reach and unique in horror ; for John is remembering the words of many prophets about the horror of the Eternal's Day of wrath.

xv. 1–4 : The Courts of Heaven—after the Great
Distress

Then I saw another portent in heaven, great and marvellous : 1
seven angels with seven plagues—the last plagues, for they
complete the wrath of God. I saw what was like a sea of 2
glass mixed with fire, and, standing beside the sea of glass,
those who came off conquerors from the Beast and his
statue and the cipher of his name ; they had harps of God
and *they were singing the song of Moses the servant of God* 3
and the song of the Lamb—
' Great and *marvellous are thy deeds,*
Lord God almighty !
Just and true thy ways,
O King of nations !
Who shall not fear, O Lord, and *glorify thy name ?* 4
For thou alone art *holy.*
Yea, *all nations shall come and worship before thee,*
for thy judgments are disclosed.'

Before the portents of the seven seals were described, John 1
showed us the heavenly scene, the origin of the bloodshed and
chaos which was to fall upon earth. He showed us the scroll of
the last days, containing God's secret decrees for the future—
as yet sealed with seven seals ; and then he described how
Christ broke the seals, to release the flood of vengeance. The
same plan was followed in the next series of portents ; before
the seven trumpeters blew their blasts, they appeared silent
in heaven : they were associated with that scene when John
showed how the sacrifice of the martyrs and ' the prayers of all
the saints ' have power to call down the fire of retribution on
earth. (See viii. 1–5, notes.) Similarly the final series of
seven plagues is prefaced with a scene in heaven. Once again
the purpose is to drive home the lesson that God is the origin-
ator of the plagues on earth, and that they follow logically
from the great martyrdom of the Elect ; for that event, in

John's mind, was to prove finally the worth of redeemed man (see xii. 7–12) and establish once and for all the incorrigible wickedness of those who refused the witnesses' call to repentance (xi. 10 ff.). The introductory sentence of chap. xv. is something after the style of a heading for the whole of xv.–xvi. The angels are the chief actors in the play, and therefore they are mentioned first ; but they do not appear on the stage until verse 5. The intervening verses are by way of being a prologue to the dramatic representation of the End.

2 For the second time (cf. iv. 6) we are shown the **sea of glass** before the throne of God ; and now we are better able to discern its true significance. From the first it had the appearance of some symbol conveying God's ineffable, absolute holiness—holiness in its original sense of *separateness*. Could any man born of woman cross this ' sea of glass resembling crystal,' into the presence of the Creator ? As we read John's first vision of the heavenly court in chap. iv., we must have felt the utter impossibility of venturing near the haloed throne, whence issue ' flashes of lightning, and loud blasts and peals of thunder.' A shining ocean barred all approach. But in that vision there was no mention of Christ. It is not for ever that God is a monarch far removed from men by unnavigable seas ; there will arise those who, purified by their Lord's sacrifice and ennobled by their own sufferings, will reach the farther shore, the shore of the Presence. And here they stand, **those who came off conquerors from the Beast and his statue and the cipher of his name** (see xiii. 11–18). These **conquerors** are the inheritors of the sevenfold promise of reward, made in the seven letters (see ends of each, chaps. ii.–iii. ; cf. particularly iii. 5, and iii. 21). They stand beside the sea of glass ; but it is no longer limpid, untroubled—' resembling crystal.' It shines with a different kind of brilliance. It is now **mixed with fire.** This is an ominous hint of the day of approaching storm, for **fire** is always symbolical in REVELATION of God's punishment. A heavenly Red Sea ! We do not need the allusion

3-4 to the **song of Moses** (that hymn of praise and triumph sung on the seashore, after the pursuing armies of Pharaoh had been engulfed ; cf. Exod. xv.) to guide us to this conclusion : it is plain without further guidance. The ' sea ' has been forded by the martyrs. It is now about to submerge their foes.

John has previously alluded to the Red Sea in the symbol of the ' water ' with which Satan the dragon threatened to submerge the Church. All Christians must cross this earthly Red Sea, by God's help. Only so could they hope to remain within God's temple on earth (xi. 1) ; only so could they remain under the shadow of His Presence, within the pale of His care in the days of stress ahead of them. The **sea of glass** in heaven is infinitely more formidable than Satan's ' flood.' Its power to submerge and destroy the wicked is absolute : Satan's attempt to separate Christians from their God, and drown them in a flood of temptation (see xii. 15) may be resisted by all whose faith is stalwart and loyal. In fact, the **sea of glass** in heaven represents the only real separation of men from the presence of God, for it is a divinely willed separation. There will come a day when the sea **in heaven** (as well as on earth) will disappear : ' for the first heaven and the first earth had passed away, *and the sea is no more* ' (xxi. 1). In those days God will no longer be remote, for earth is no longer wicked. When the heavenly sea passes away the last barrier has disappeared. Henceforth, ' God's dwelling-place is with men.' But this is still to come. The sea still exists in heaven, to be crossed only by those who had the spiritual loftiness and courage of martyrs. God still dwells removed from most Christians, those who remain on earth ' in the desert ' (chap. xii.). His majesty now appears more terrible than ever before. For His wrath is about to descend in deluge upon the profligate cities of earth and the rulers of this world.

The **conquerors**, as we have shown, had a part in this dreadful work of retribution. They feel no impulse of terror in contemplating the throne with its lightning and peals of thunder. They burst into a song of praise :

> **Great and marvellous are thy deeds,**
> **Lord God almighty !**

John shows them to be no less a part of the choirs and orchestras of heaven than the Presbyters ; for the redeemed have **harps of God** (that is, harps befitting the increasing symphony of heavenly worship) and they, too, sing before the throne (cf. v. 8). They sing **the song of Moses the servant of God and the song of the Lamb.**

We must pause over this **song** (it is, of course, a single song, not two) for it has been the source of much controversy and misunderstanding.

It is difficult to conceive words fitting to this visionary occasion, the most solemn in the history of the human race. One can hardly imagine that a mortal could contemplate the throne and not fall into a stupefied silence. For men are commonly tricked into silence by mere size. A Grand Canyon hushes for a moment our tourist chatter ; a river falls over a cliff, and if the river is large and the cliff high, we feel it a profanity to enthuse over its splendour, like some Pontifex, celebrating the ' spiry pinnacles ' of Mont Blanc in a hotel visitors' book ! And when astronomers write their new books of Night Thoughts, a mere light-year drives us into mental immobility. What words can be imagined before the Creator of so many huge things ? What words, indeed, before Him who alone is **holy** ? When that loud voice from heaven summoned the martyrs to rise from the dust of death, they took on more than incorruptibility to enable them to venture at all into speech. The music of this company, prophetic heralds of a new creation, assuredly yielded nothing in splendour to that of the angel choirs who chanted the Nativity song :

> ' Such musick (as 'tis said)
> Before was never made,
>   But when of old the sons of morning sung,
> While the Creator Great
> His constellations set,
>   And the well-ballanc't world on hinges hung,
> And cast the dark foundations deep,
> And bid the weltring waves their oozy channel keep.'

Yes, when the martyrs sing it is like the sound of thunder, like the waves of the sea, like many harpists playing on their harps (xiv. 3). But when we come to read what apparently is intended to convey the glory of the song of Moses and the Lamb, we find words which an evening congregation might sing before the offertory. Are there no Davids among these harpists, to find words with the ring of fresh, personal feeling, to suit the unique wonder of their experience ? How are we to account for this hymn ?

The title of the song bears a very obvious allusion to the song of the first deliverance, sung by Moses and the Israelites on the shore of the Red Sea. (It is interesting to note that this song, according to Philo, had been already incorporated into the devotions of the Therapeutists, an Egyptian order of Jewish ascetics.) But it is the song of the *second* and *final* deliverance, and that is why it is ascribed to the Lamb as well as to Moses. The first song of deliverance (Exod. xv.) is a passionate ode to the warrior God, who flung Pharaoh and his chariots into the Red Sea ; the majestic Holy One, whose terrible deeds awed the nations ; the redeemer God, who brought Israel to a sanctuary. But there is no very great correspondence between the words of this song and John's hymn of the martyrs. The martyrs do not even make explicit reference to their own rescue, notable though it has been. Their song has earned from commentators the unflattering description of ' a collection of Old Testament phrases.' And so it is : it is culled from psalmist and prophet, owing little in its actual terms to the song of Moses and the Israelites (though it has discernible points of similarity), much less to original composition. To the casual eye, it might appear that John had despaired of equalling the occasion, and had fallen back on conventionalities.

But let us be wary of hastily concluding that John failed dismally, where elsewhere he succeeds magnificently. We may have to admit that his power over words, to breathe the breath of life into them, and make them true guides, did not desert him even here. His task was to translate something like the music of the spheres, not into a full score for a modern symphony orchestra, but into a few brief words. Words were his only material ; and we all know what baffling, tedious lying things words can be. A poet is like Plato's demiurge, in that the immortal patterns of his thought are printed on shifting, impermanent material—the quivering and trembling of the common air. A poet (a poet in the wider Sidnean sense) alone can make words speak truly for him. He can do what the magician sought to do in his incantations ; he can by words summon innumerable ghosts to his service. The ghosts are memories. Milton has only to write the word ' Fontarabia ' to conjure up the very spirit of ancient valour. Shakespeare makes homelier words do even greater service. Now John, too, is a poet, whose native tongue is the language of devotion. He has brooded long over these psalms and prophetic books from which he quotes, until they have become part of his mind, welded to his imagination. And if we are to admit that the song of Moses and the Lamb is ' a collection of old Testament phrases,' we will allow it only in the sense that certain passages of *Paradise Lost*, let us say, are a collection of classical names. It is commonly echoed that the appreciation of Milton is the last reward of consummated scholarship ; only the scholar possesses the skeleton key which unlocks all the gates of allusion. The writer of REVELATION, too, can be fully understood only by those who have tried to read as he read.

The substance of the martyr's hymn is an ascription of praise to God for His absolute power, wielded in justice. Holiness and justice are the fountains from which the punishments of the last days must spring ; and there must come a point in the infliction of these woes, when all nations must pay homage to the Holy One. The hymn is one in spirit with many of the Psalms, and some of its phrases are direct and recognizable quotations. The first phrase, **Great and marvellous are thy deeds**, is quoted freely from Ps. cxi. :

> ' With all my heart I thank the Eternal,
> in gatherings of good men for fellowship.
> Great are the Eternal's doings,
> to be studied by all who delight in them,
> splendid and glorious are his deeds;
> his victories know no end.'

But we are not to suppose that John treated this psalm as a

convenient literary quarry, filching a phrase to eke out his own stock of material—much as men wrenched hewn stone from derelict abbeys after the Reformation, to save themselves the expense of new quarrying. No, he had to quote only one phrase to recall the whole poem, as a man uttering any one of Christ's last words would recall to the minds of his hearers the whole scene of the Crucifixion. John's mind is filled with the whole psalm. He remembers that the Psalmist praises God because He is pitiful, holding to His compact with His people, fixing it for all time—and sending them *freedom*, dispossessing the heathen persecutor, and vindicating the oppressed. This indeed was a part of His eternal righteousness : ' faithfully he deals and justly '—or, as John says :

> Just and true are thy ways,
> O King of nations !

But because justice and truth were His attributes, assuring final vindication for the righteous, God must also rigorously punish those who are stubbornly unjust and untrue. The logic of this theme is a commonplace of the Psalms and the prophetic books ; almost inevitably the recognition of God's righteousness evoke thoughts of His hatred of evil, and the destined extermination of evil-doers. But if John had one passage in mind more certainly than another as he wrote these words, if he wished to recall to his readers any single passage rather than another, this must surely have been the great ' song of Moses ' in Deuteronomy (chap. xxxii.) :

> ' Hearken to my song, O heaven,
> let earth listen to my lips !
> May my message drop like rain,
> my speech distil as dew,
> like mists on the green growth,
> like showers upon the grass ;
> for I proclaim what the Eternal is—
> O praise him for his greatness !
> Steadfast—he rules aright,
> his methods all in order due,
> a God trusty and true,
> upright and honest ! '

305

What follows is a magnificent prophetic denunciation of those who refuse to pay the true homage of righteousness to the God of righteousness, and a vehement description of the peril in which they stand. For those who plunge into wickedness, scorning the laws of God, there can be no mercy and no escape. The plagues of REVELATION are here in miniature : plagues of arrows, famines, fevers, wild beasts to tear them, reptiles to poison them, death by the sword, volcanic eruption, celestial fire (cf. chaps. vi. and viii.) in short, the full wrath of God !

> ' I raise my hand to heaven
> and swear that (by my life eternal !)
> I will whet my flashing blade,
> gripping *justice* by the hilt,
> wreaking vengeance on my foes. . . .
> Hail his people, O ye pagans ;
> for he avenges the blood of his servants,
> wreaking vengeance on his foes,
> and purging his people's land.'
>
> (Deut. xxxii. 40–3.)

What are the **marvellous deeds** of the Almighty ? They are all deeds of justice and truth. The rescue of His people comes first ; and we must not forget John's picture in chap. xi. of how the martyrs were to be raised and rescued in the sight of their enemies. But there was their blood to be avenged, the land to be purged ; and these too are the marvellous deeds of God. After the martyrs have arisen, the great earthquake begins to rock the foundations of the world, men are killed, the rest are terrified into recognizing the supreme power of the true God—and after that, stained as they are in the martyrs' blood, they are killed.

The phrase, **O King of nations**, follows naturally from the thoughts in John's mind as he describes God's ways as **just and true** ; for it is His royal prerogative to punish those hordes of pagans who flouted His laws and persecuted His people. It is, in fact, a quotation from the book of Jeremiah, as is the question, **Who shall not fear. . . ?**

> ' O King of nations, who would not revere thee ?
> For reverence is thy due.'
>
> (Jer. x. 7.)

The allusion sets in motion another, but related, train of
thought. For the passage in Jeremiah introduces a scathing
attack on idolatry. To worship idols, to make supplication to
them and rely on their power, is unintelligible stupidity.
There is no ' breath of life ' in them : ' they break down when
the test arrives.' But as for God, the Creator and Lord of all
Nature, He is—

> ' a living God, an everlasting King ;
> earth trembles when he rages,
> no nation can endure his wrath.'
>
> (Jer. x. 10.)

This contrast between the real power of God and the delusive
power of the Beast and his statue is constantly in John's mind
(it is stated expressly in xiii. 11–18 and xiv. 1–12). When the
unregenerate attempt to take to themselves the power of false
gods, branding themselves with the name of the Beast and the
cipher of his name (xiii. 16–18 ; cf. iii. 12), they are committing
an act of stupidity which is credible only on the presumption
that they are blinded by their preference of evil to good.
These memories of Jeremiah's scornful indictment of idolatry
lend particularly appropriate colours to the song of the martyrs.
For they face the true, living (cf. xv. 7a) God in the moment
when He reveals Himself to the infatuated worshippers of the
Beast in all His terrible might, answering by His deeds the
blasphemous hymn :

> ' Who is like the Beast ?
> Who can fight with him ? '
>
> (xiii. 4.)

In acclaiming the Beast and his statue, the nations have committed treason to their true King, the living God. The martyrs,
patriots of ' the blest kingdoms meek of joy and love,' celebrate with swelling hearts the defeat and punishment of
Satanic treason.

The theme of idolatry, destined to be discredited and cast
down by the King of nations on the days of His wrath, leads
John to a thought already touched upon : the ' worship ' enforced by fear which the disillusioned idolators must give the
God of holiness. We recall that John has already given us a

picture of this 'conversion' of mankind in xi. 13. The martyrs are raised from the dead, to the terror of their enemies; and then, ' At that hour a great earthquake took place, a tenth of the City [i.e. Babylon—the Empire, or civilization] was destroyed, and seven thousand souls perished in the earthquake; *the rest were awe-struck, and gave glory to the God of heaven.'* They 'gave glory,' although they had already damned themselves by applauding the most sacrilegious deed of Antichrist, the murder of the saints ; they gave glory because (as the angel in xiv. 6 proclaims) all created things must bow down in fear and reverence, when God acts in His strength, redeeming and punishing. This is precisely the thought expressed in the martyrs' song :

> **Who shall not fear, O Lord, and glorify thy name ?**
> **For thou alone art holy.**

John uses the word **holy** to describe God's unapproachable splendour, His terrifying majesty. We shall understand his meaning best in recalling Ps. xcix. (R.V.) :

> ' The Lord is great in Zion;
> And he is high above all the peoples.
> Let them praise thy great and terrible name :
> Holy is he,'

We might compare Ps. cxi. 9, where God's freeing of His people is associated with this same awful majesty—divine holiness. Perhaps John's words may evoke some memory of that psalm (xxii.) which Jesus uttered on the Cross : ' My God, my God, why hast thou forsaken me ? '—the deepest cry of distress to the Holy One (verse 3), answered by a song of praise for His help, and the confident prediction :

> ' All the ends of the earth shall remember and turn unto the Lord :
> And all the kindreds of the nations shall worship before thee.'

It is in such soil that John's allusions are rooted. If we cannot ascribe them with complete certainty to one passage rather than another, this is merely testimony to the complexity of memories and emotion aroused by them. It goes almost without saying that John interpreted these passages in his own way. Thus, when he was confronted with a general expectation that the nations would finally **come and worship** before God, he does not echo the notion loosely, as a hyperbolical statement of what was to happen in the millennium, (as many commentators have assumed). He simply attaches a different value to the word **worship**. He had far too much reverence for the psalms and prophetic books from which he quotes to imagine that their predictions would be belied ; the words of God must be fulfilled—that was certain (cf. xvii. 17). But how ? For John was quite confident that the nations would cleave to Antichrist, and just as confident that this must earn for them the sentence of death (see chaps. xiii.–xiv.). How conceivably were the prophecies of universal worship of God to be fulfilled ? John shows us in xi. 13. Their worship is an act of homage, but it does not spring spontaneously out of a natural love of goodness, when it is displayed in the sight of all. It is an act of self-abasement, but not prompted by reverence for God's infinite purity. It has, in fact, a turncoat flavour. The Beast had been strong—' Who can fight with him ? '—so men gave him glory and worshipped him. Then God proved stronger—so men worshipped God. They were awed into homage by His might. This ' worship ' does not last longer than the first terrifying moments of the Day of Wrath. As the full measure of punishment is poured on them they once more blasphemed God (xvi. 21—this phrase must be read as a sequel to xi. 13), instead of acknowledging the complete justice of their sentence.

The conclusion of the song, **for thy judgments are disclosed,** derives its force not from allusion, but from the context in REVELATION. Once again, it is a reference to the events described in xi. 11–13. The disclosure of God's judgments begins with the resurrection of the martyrs. Almost simultaneously God deals His first devastating blow to the worshippers of the Beast ; and it is those two events together which wrench homage from the lips of the unregenerate. The martyrs are fresh from the scenes of their suffering and humiliation ; they see now the full vindication of their 'patience and faith' (see xiii. 10). And as we read their hymn of rejoicing for the consummation of their hopes, we must clothe it with all the intense drama of the occasion. They died in order that peace and righteousness and justice might prevail on earth ; and now at this moment they know that they died not in vain. They died in the faith that truth had its champion ; they live to see the humiliation of all who ' love and practise falsehood.' God's judgments are now disclosed. His reign begins.

xv. 5–8 : The Source of the Great Flood of Turmoil on Earth

5 After that* I looked, the temple of *the tabernacle of testimony* in
6 heaven was thrown open, and out of the temple came the seven angels with *the seven plagues, robed in* pure dazzling *linen,* their breasts encircled with golden belts.
7 Then one of the four living Creatures gave the seven angels seven golden bowls full of the wrath of God who lives for
8 ever and ever ; and *the temple was filled with smoke from the glory* of God and from his might, *nor could anyone enter* the temple till *the seven plagues* of the seven angels were over.

* That is, after the interlude of 2–4. The words always denote a fresh phase or stage of the vision.

The prologue to the representation of the final plagues is over. John now begins to sketch his vision of the day of Wrath, and he marks the beginning of his subject proper by
5 the words **after that**—a phrase which always marks a further stage in visionary experience. The scene disclosed is precisely the same as in xi. 19—naturally, since that too was a description of the source of the last plagues on earth : ' The temple of God in heaven was thrown open, and the ark of his covenant was seen inside his temple. . . .' The temple is now described as **the tabernacle of testimony** (**temple** and **tabernacle** are in apposition in the Greek) ; but this adds nothing of note to

the description of the ' temple of God ' in xi. 19, since the
temple is called the **tabernacle** by virtue of its housing the
ark of the covenant—the sacred record of the laws dictated
to Moses on Mount Sinai. We might be content to understand by this designation of the heavenly temple of testimony
that God discloses Himself, as it were, in all the majestic garb
of Justice—as the supreme Law-giver, about to execute His
sentences on all who have flouted His eternal laws. But, as
we have already shown (see notes on xiv. 14–20), the very conception of the heavenly temple is a visionary symbol for the
immediate presence of God, and John customarily connects
divine punishment with the **temple** rather than with the
throne, because it showed that the punishments of the last
days would fall in order that the people of God might be
finally vindicated, and that the new kingdom might be
established. The exilic expectation in Isaiah was that the
divine restoration of the temple would be accompanied by the
divine chastisement of Israel's enemies ; at one and the same
time, the faithful people were to be rehabilitated, with God
dwelling gloriously amongst them, and the wicked were to be
finally chastised. John's Sion of the last days—the Sion on
which the rescued loyalists of the true Israel were to stand
(xiv. 1)—and his temple, the source of God's final plagues,
are in heaven ; he sees the fulfilment of the old tradition, not
in the literal restoration of the temple and the rediscovery on
earth of its lost ark of the covenant and altar of incense, but
in the disclosure in heaven of their perfect celestial patterns.
Everything was now ready. The prayers of Christians had
a heavenly ' altar ' to bring them into God's presence. The
sacrifice of the martyrs had been presented on a heavenly
altar (cf. vi. 9 f. and viii. 3 ff.). Nor was there need for the
tablets of stone, on which the commandments of God were
written ; the loss of these things no longer constituted a
reproach (cf. Jer. iii. 16 ; 2 Macc. ii. 1–8), as if the faithful
did not possess proof of divine authenticity for the laws they
proclaimed and revered. God's righteousness was manifest in
His own Presence ; His demand for righteousness in men
needed no proof, admitted no evasion, for it was now disclosed

in the awful theophany of the End. For when John says **the temple of the tabernacle of testimony in heaven was thrown open,** he means that all men on earth, not only the dwellers in heaven, become conscious of God's overshadowing presence. (The verb **was thrown open** has already been used in the earlier description of the End (xi. 19) ; it is to be used again when the Messiah is disclosed in the sight of all (cf. i. 7) on the day of the last battle : ' Then I saw heaven *open wide . . .*'

6 (xix. 11).) Thus, when **the seven angels with the seven plagues** come out of the temple, this is the visionary equivalent of a theme which we must express in more prosaic and abstract terms : they portend the agencies whereby the sentences of the divine Lawgiver and Judge are to be executed ; they come from the presence of the Holy One, and in John's vision the presence is conveyed in a picture which asserts that the long-awaited time when righteousness must be vindicated and evil punished has now arrived. The most significant fact about the angels is that they come **from the temple of the tabernacle of testimony.** But their appearance and the drama in which they participate in the courts of the temple are also rich in meaning. It is not of any great importance to ask whether these seven portentous figures represent the seven angels of the presence (cf. note on viii. 2). But it is decidedly important to notice that they are high-girt, with **golden belts** encircling their breasts, just as Christ was portrayed in the first chapter—ready for their punitive mission. They are **robed in pure dazzling linen,** like that which (we are told in xix. 8) symbolizes the righteousness of the saints. In other words, their power to punish has the sanction of God's ulti- mate righteousness. It is characteristic of John's conception of God's utter holiness—His unapproachable majesty—that the angels receive their symbolical weapons of destruction from one of the four living Creatures, and not directly from the Almighty. The presence of these four about the throne and (as in this vision) within the temple conveys, more adequately than the threadbare language of exegesis can ever hope to do, this sense of God's holiness. They who chanted ' Holy, holy, holy, is the Lord God almighty, who was and is

and is coming ' have previously been connected with the
execution of God's decrees of punishment. They cry, ' Come ! '
to the plagues of invasion, civil war, famine, and pestilence
(vi. 1–8). And now one of them acts as mediator of the last
plagues. In the symbolical action of giving **seven bowls full** 7
of the wrath of God, he bestows on the angelic servants of
God the authority to release on civilization the bewildering
horrors of the End. The **golden bowls** containing these plagues
remind us of the golden bowls held by the Presbyters—containing the prayers of the saints (v. 8). An allusion is probably intended. In the parallel scene, after the breaking of
the seventh seal, an angel first presents the prayers of the
saints in a golden censer, then fills the same censer with fire
from the altar, which is poured on the earth (viii. 1–5). The
symbol of a ' container ' of God's wrath is, of course, simply
an elaboration of an almost inevitable metaphor. Punishment, like blessings, men have commonly said, are ' poured '
from on high. We might profitably remember what George
Herbert made of the metaphor :

> ' When God at first made man,
>   Having a glass of blessings standing by,
>   Let us, said He, pour on him all we can. . . .'

What is ' *poured* ' (xvi. 1) must also be ' contained.'

This scene in heaven is reminiscent of more than one Old
Testament passage, and it is helpful to be aware of them. It
is obviously analogous to Isaiah's vision in the temple
(Isa. vi.), when the awe-inspiring majesty of God's presence
filled the prophet with such terror and despair. The seraphs
in Isaiah's vision cry of the thrice holy God : ' His majestic
splendour fills the whole earth.' Now at last this is true, and
the living Creatures may amend their song of praise to the
Eternal who ' *is coming* ' (iv. 8) ; for He has come. In Isaiah's
vision, the holiness of God was brought home to the prophet
in the clouds of smoke which filled the temple ; John says,
smoke from the glory of God. That is to say, His Being is 8
obscured to the seer's gaze by the very intensity of His revealed
power and will to destroy evil—the ' fire ' of His wrath burning

vehemently, and surrounding His presence with a terror which cannot be contemplated. At this moment it was impossible for anyone to enter the temple till the seven plagues of the seven angels were over. We may recall the scene at the end of Exodus, where ' the glory of the Lord filled the tabernacle ' —the original tabernacle of testimony—and not even Moses could enter ; and the scene on Mount Sinai, when the Laws were first given to the Israelites, when God ' descended in fire ' upon the smoke-clad mountain, and denied Himself to the gaze of the trembling Israelites, even though (like the martyrs) they had consecrated themselves and ' washed their robes ' (cf. Rev. vii. 14). The terror of the presence when the Law was first given is exceeded by its terror when the penalities of the Law are finally inflicted.

xvi. 1–9 : THE LAST PLAGUES : CIVILIZATION IS PUNISHED THROUGH NATURAL CATASTROPHE

1 Then I heard a loud *voice from the temple* telling the seven angels, 'Go and *pour out* the seven bowls of *the wrath* of God *on earth.*'

2 The first went off and poured his bowl upon the land ; *and* noisome, painful *ulcers broke out on* those who bore the

3 mark of the Beast and worshipped his statue. The second poured out his bowl upon the sea ; it *turned blood* like the blood of a corpse, and every living thing *within the sea*

4 *perished*. The third poured out his bowl upon *the rivers*

5 and fountains of water, and *they turned blood*. Then I heard the angel of the waters cry, ' *O holy One, who art* and wast,

6 *just art thou* in this thy sentence. *They poured out* the *blood* of saints and prophets, and thou hast given *them*

7 *blood to drink !* As they deserve ! ' And I heard the altar cry,

' Even so, *Lord God almighty :*
true and *just thy sentences of doom !* '

8 The fourth angel poured out his bowl upon the sun ; and

the sun was allowed to scorch men with fire, till men,   9
scorched by the fierce heat, blasphemed the name of the
God who had control of these plagues ; yet they would not
repent and give him glory.

> ' Pour out thy wrath upon the heathen that know thee not,
> And upon the kingdoms that call not upon thy name.'

So the Psalmist cried (Ps. lxxix. 6), as he thought in anguish
of the sufferings of his people, and the apparent triumph of
the ungodly. Is it possible not to judge and condemn so harsh
a prayer ? Has this thirst for blood any part in true religion ?
It is our business not to condemn, but to understand. The
Psalmist could say :

> ' The dead bodies of thy servants have been given to be meat unto the
>   fowls of the heaven,
> The flesh of thy saints unto the beasts of the earth.
> Their blood have they shed like water round about Jerusalem ;
> And there was none to bury them.'

John, too, is contemplating a time in the future when the
Christian prophets, the witnesses, have been slain, and left
unburied in the streets of the great City (chap. xi.) ; when
men rejoiced because they imagined that the powers of evil
had finally triumphed. He has faith that God will now intervene, to answer the Psalmist's prayer : ' Render unto our
neighbours sevenfold into their bosom their reproach, wherewith they have reproached thee, O Lord.' The laws which
have been flouted and mocked must now be vindicated ; the
Creator, dishonoured by His creatures, can now do no other
than destroy them. The last series of seven punitive strokes,
foretold in Leviticus (xxvi. 24 ff.), is now to be inflicted ; the
lessons taught to heedless men by previous calamities is now
to be driven home with unsparing severity. God treats the
dwellers in ' the great City whose mystical name is Sodom
and Egypt ' much as He treated the Egyptians long ago.
Plague after plague He sends to demonstrate the folly of
resistance and the need for a change of heart—and the end is
stubborn impenitence, the condition recorded by John at the

end of the sixth trumpet plague (ix. 21). There is nothing to astonish or dismay John's religious sense in the thought that God will act without mercy, and inflict terrible wounds on mankind purely for punishment. If there is anything surprising at all, it is that He should hold His hand for so long ; that He should have allowed Pharaoh so long to condemn himself, and that He should now send the Beast and his adherents so many premonitory signs. John reads the story of the Egyptian plagues in the pages of later commentators. He owes something to the Book of Wisdom, for example. He would have agreed fully with the thought in the twelfth chapter of that book, that God judges ' by little and little, giving place for repentance ' (the impenitence of mankind is touched upon four times in the series of ' Egyptian ' plagues in REVELATION : ix. 20, xvi. 9, 11, 21). He would have agreed also that, although God in His mercy ' gives place ' for repentance, instead of sweeping away the wicked with one tempestuous stroke, it is by no means because He is ignorant that—

' their nature by birth was evil. . . .
And that their manner of thought would in no wise ever be changed.'
(Wisd. xii. 10.)

Not very logically, John similarly proclaims the justice of mankind's prolonged torture, by asserting their destined idolatry and their destined impenitence. He can only rejoice when in his vision he hears the loud voice from the temple (cf. notes on xv. 5) calling : ' Go and pour out the seven bowls of the wrath of God on earth.'

The general idea behind the first four plagues (verses 2–9) is that mankind must be punished through the universe they have dishonoured by their idolatry and corruption. It is a thought which is well expressed in the Book of Wisdom :

' He shall take his jealousy as complete armour,
And shall make the whole creation his weapons for vengeance on his enemies. . . .
And the world shall go forth with him to fight against his insensate foes.'
(Wisd. v. 17–20.)

Hence, earth, sea, fresh water, and the sun are depicted as

mediaries of pain and torture on men (cf. chap. viii.). The difference between this series of cosmic strokes and that recorded in chap. viii. is not to be sought in points of detail ; though, of course, small differences in detail do exist. The attack on the earth, for example, in chap. viii. took the form of supernatural hail and fire, destroying the means of life ; whereas this time the divine visitation results specifically and directly in the torture of human beings (cf. notes on chap. ix.). **Noisome, painful ulcers** (see Exod. ix.) **broke out on those who** 2 **bore the mark of the Beast and worshipped his statue** (that is, on all mankind except the faithful who were preserved ' in the desert ': see p. 238). In spite of this difference in form (the substitution of one Egyptian plague for another), the two attacks on the earth are essentially alike. The difference between them lies in their scope : the first is partial, the last universal. This is also true of the strokes falling on the **sea** 3 **and the rivers and fountains of water.** Previously, only a third 4 of the sea and the creatures in it have been affected. Now the **whole sea is turned blood, like the blood of a corpse, and every living thing within the sea perished.** Only a third of the fresh water had been tainted hitherto ; now all is turned into **blood,** and, like the Egyptians, the worshippers of the Beast must now face death by thirst (see Exod. vii. 19–21). The earlier attack on the heavenly luminaries, issuing in the plague of darkness affected only a part of mankind ; but the new terror from the sky (this time a direct, physical attack on men) prevails over the whole earth ; where previously darkness inspired terror in the hearts of many of unregenerate mankind, now **fire** inflicts mortal pain on all. There is no mechanical correspondence between the various parallel plagues in REVELATION, nor is there any attempt to reproduce those of Exodus systematically. The disorders and calamities of the last days are to be manifold and unique (affecting, as they must, the whole world). It is John's purpose to describe their fundamental character : God ' shall make the whole creation his weapons for vengeance on his enemies.'

All this is very remote, it must be admitted : perhaps it is fortunate that it is remote ; the modern reader would undoubtedly find it much more offensive, if it bore a closer resemblance to the manner in which he understands Providence actually to work. He is convinced that God does *not* send boils on men, nor does the Creator change sea and rivers into blood. Such periodic phenomena as the submarine convulsions which have stained parts of the Mediterranean red, and killed fish and vegetation, the modern reader sets down to the blind aberrations of Nature. A Lisbon earthquake may impress the believer with his utter incapacity to sound the depths of the mystery of pain and imperfection in the universe, but he will attribute it to anything but the direct intervention of God. It is inconceivable to him that God should so act. The disorders which overtake the social and economic structure of nations are on a different level ; for although the ' innocent ' still suffer with the ' guilty ' there is a certain community in wrong-doing. Few can claim to be completely guiltless in the matter of national and international wrongs ; potentially or actually, acquiescently or positively, the individuals in a nation create its sin. Therefore the Christian has no difficulty in believing that violent abrogations of justice, the deification of force, of greed or of luxury, the toleration of inhuman conditions—in short, the performance of any of those deeds, the existence of any of those conditions, which revolt the sense of right—are rewarded according to a simple law of retribution. The funereal train of sin is suffering : this is broadly true as it affects communities—and in REVELATION it is nations, not individuals, that fill John's canvas. If the innocent suffer on earth, he can say : ' Having borne a little chastening, they receive great good.' Suffering and death on this earth are not the end of the story for the innocent—they are the beginning. Nations, then, are his subject ; whole communities, who (except for the small minorities of despised and ill-treated Christians in their midst) have with one heart and will violated the simple law of humanity, and have denied goodness in their hearts. How are they to be rewarded ? History tells its sad story. There are no literal seas of blood in the records of history. But what limitless pages of agony and distress ! If we cannot see eye to eye with John over the means by which he imagined God would usher in a new reign of righteousness, if we cannot refrain from protesting that the Creator of men must cast aside His experiment without vengefulness, without taunting men with His omnipotence, without the clamour and demonstration of the seven last plagues, we can at least agree in part with the thought that lies behind the terrible cry of the **angel of the waters : ' O holy One . . . just art thou** 5 **in this thy sentence. They poured out the blood of saints** 6 **and prophets, and thou hast given them blood to drink ! ' As they deserve !** The underlying thought is that men are to receive punishment appropriate to their crime : experience has an abundant store of examples to prove to whatever nation cares to pay heed that communities do suffer proportionately to their crimes, and that often enough there is a grim and obvious aptness in the ill effect of an ill cause. (For comment on the **angel of the waters,** see p. 152.) This is a theme which recurs several times in the Book of Wisdom in connexion with idolatry. ' By what things a man sinneth, by these he is punished ' (Wisd. xi. 16). In the same chapter we find the probable source of this incident in REVELATION. For the author, in pointing out the contrast between the sufferings of the Israelites in the desert and the sufferings of the Egyptians, connects the plague of blood with the impious legislation of Pharaoh :

' When the enemy were troubled with clotted blood instead of a river's
    ever-flowing fountain,
To rebuke the decree for the slaying of babes,
Thou gavest them abundant water beyond all hope.'

(Wisd. xi. 6–7.)

Incidentally, one might find in such a recollection of the miraculous preservation of the Israelites in the desert an illuminating comment on John's words about the Christian community in these last days : they are to be ' kept safe ' and ' nourished ' in the desert. Their survival amidst the disintegration of the world is to be as miraculous as the punishments poured on the rest of men. We might, indeed, read the whole of the sixteenth chapter of the Book of Wisdom as a commentary on this rather puzzling question ; the conclusion we must draw is to be summarized in two brief verses :

' For the creation, ministering to thee its maker,
Straineth its force against the unrighteous, for punishment,
And slackeneth it in behalf of them that trust in thee, for beneficence.

.   .   .   .   .

That thy sons, whom thou lovedst, O Lord, might learn
That it is not the growth of the earth's fruits that nourisheth a man,
But that thy word preserveth them that trust thee.'

(Wisd. xvi. 24–6.)

7   The speaking **altar** (cf. ix. 13–14) merely reinforces the cry of the angel. For this association of truth, holiness, and justice with the judgments of God, see the note on the martyrs' song (xv. 3–4).

8
9   The result of this cosmic attack on mankind is what one might expect : men blasphemed the name of the God who **had control over these plagues ; yet they would not repent and give him glory.** This reference to mankind's impenitence must be taken together with that of verse 11, **blaspheming the God of heaven,** as a reference to the scene in xi. 13. There men forced by terror to acknowledge the Creator's supremacy : in spite of themselves and their crimes, for a moment they ' gave glory to the God of heaven.' This was a fulfilment of the old prophecies that in the last days, when God shone on the earth in splendour, the nations would be dazzled into homage and conversion. An ironical fulfilment ! For as soon as the first shock of the final earthquake is over, when the condemned are justly suffering for their sins, when God is executing His unalterable sentence on the crimes recorded in xi. 10 ff. and chap. xiii., mankind reverts to blasphemies. Now, however, they are the blasphemies of men who cannot close their eyes to God's supremacy :

For through the sufferings whereat they were indignant. . . .
They saw, and recognized as the true God him whom before they
    refused to know :
Wherefore also the last end of condemnation came upon them.'

(Wisd. xii. 27.)

xvi. 10–16: THE FIFTH AND SIXTH BOWLS: IMPERIAL ECLIPSE AND PARTHIAN INVASION

The fifth poured out his bowl upon the throne of the Beast; 10 his realm *was darkened*, and men gnawed their tongues in anguish, blaspheming *the God of heaven* for their pains and 11 their ulcers, but refusing to repent of their doings. The 12 sixth poured out his bowl on *the great river Euphrates*, and *its waters were dried up* to prepare the way for the kings *from the east*. Then I saw issuing from the mouth of the 13 dragon and from the mouth of the Beast and from the mouth of the false Prophet, three foul spirits like *frogs*— demon-spirits performing miracles, who come forth to 14 muster the kings of the whole world for battle on the great Day *of almighty God*. (Lo, I am coming like a thief; 15 blessed be he who keeps awake and holds his raiment fast, not to go naked and have the shame of exposure!)* They 16 were mustered at the spot called (in Hebrew) Harmagedon.

* Ver. 15 interrupts the sequence of thought; it is either a gloss or misplaced, perhaps from the third verse of the third chapter.

The throne of the Beast means, essentially, the power of 10 Antichrist (cf. iv. 2; also iii. 21, xx. 4). When the fifth angel pours his bowl over the throne of the Beast, so that **his realm was darkened,** we must not imagine that this is a prediction of a plague of darkness similar to that in viii. 12. The traditional pictures of the last days reiterate as a conventional feature the darkening of sun, moon and stars, as John depicts in chap. viii. But in chap. ix. (the plague following the fifth trumpet blast) it is a figurative shadow which falls over men; the shadow of pain brought by dæmonic visitants. And here the plague of the **fifth bowl** is again figuratively stated. Darkness falls over the Empire. But what sort of darkness follows a diminution of the tyrant's power? It is the darkness of civil strife, portended at the beginning of the three series of predictions, in the figure of the second horseman: he ' was allowed to take peace from earth and to make men slay each other.'

Such strife was also a stereotyped feature of eschatology ; it was the earthly reflection of chaos and catastrophe in the skies. But we can be sure that upon such traditional material there was superimposed in John's mind the memories and speculations of Nero's reign, and of the time which followed it. The Beast, *Nero redivivus*, would alienate his subjects once more ; and once more there would arise desperate revolts. This time, however, the old fear that Nero had found allies in the East among the deadly Parthians would be true. The shadow of civil war would be succeeded by the flames of invasion. But this is to anticipate a little ; before approaching this new subject, we must note how skilfully John preserves the unity of these last plagues. It is not merely in itself that the darkness over the Empire is an evil, though the majority of John's readers would have every reason to shudder at the memory or report of the confusion prevalent in the reigns of Galba, Otho, and Vitellius some twenty-five years previously. In the misery of civil disorders, the effects of the other plagues must necessarily be felt more acutely. John is constrained to
11 observe once again (cf. verse 9) that men would not **repent of their doings.** One might suppose this reiteration to be a little superfluous. But at this point it is really necessary. Literary arrangement decided that at the end of the fourth plague John should note the impenitence of men—in spite of the portentous behaviour of the fourfold universe. At the fifth plague, however, a portent of a different kind has been given. The Beast's end is foreshadowed in this eclipse of his power. And his subjects have risen against him. But this, John tells us, does not mean that they have adopted the cause of God : in spite of their revolt against Antichrist, they remain beyond hope in sin. If they had been really in earnest when they had ' given glory ' to **the God of heaven** (xi. 13) after the resurrection of the witnesses and the earthquake, they would now accept **pains and ulcers,** and all the miseries of the time, as a deserved punishment. But no, they recognize the existence of the true God only to blaspheme Him. Or perhaps more : for although they blaspheme the true God, whom they at last acknowledge as the Lord of power mightier than the

Beast, it is equally true that they can no longer worship their discredited monarch. Perhaps this, too, has something to do with the Beast's hostility towards his subjects (see xvii. 15 ff.).

The dark hint of civil war in the fifth portent is followed by an even darker, less defined hint of the invasion of the Empire in the sixth. Nothing is actually stated except the preparation 12 for the event—the drying of the **Euphrates . . . to prepare the way for the kings from the east.** But as we shall attempt to show, there is behind this simple statement a grim foreboding of universal bloodshed, pillage, and ruin. There are several references to the *burning* of Babylon the great (xvii. 16, xviii. 9–10, xix. 3) : the earthquake of which we are to hear in the next prediction finishes work already begun by the Parthians, in alliance with the vengeful Antichrist. The invasion and the mustering of **the kings of the whole world** have separate origins in eschatological tradition, and it will be as well to consider these sources before we proceed any further. For verses 12–16 there is such an extraordinary synthesis of familiar traditions, and so considerable a reinterpretation of them, that it is easy to lose one's way.

It is an exacting but informative exercise, preparatory to the 13–close study of REVELATION, to read as many of the prophetic 16 books as one suspects John of quoting, with the assumption always in mind : ' these are inspired oracles ; not mere records of contemporary beliefs and speculations, nor yet only partial glimpses of spiritual truths accorded to one generation or another, but prophecies which have only to be interpreted by the discerning mind to reveal themselves apposite in every detail to the historical situation in John's day.' (For this certainly seems to have been the assumption in John's mind as he read the Scriptures.) One is immediately struck by the incompatibility of some of the details in these different pictures. With our own habits of historical reference, it is almost impossible to attempt to do what John did—to collate the different pictures and by ingenious handling form them into a unity. Indeed, it is from most points of view an unprofitable task ; one thing alone we shall gain from it, and that is an understanding of some of the puzzling things in REVELATION. Let us think only of the main contradictions in this great synthetic picture of the End. A fair number of prophets say that the End will be connected with a siege of Jerusalem ; but some say that Jerusalem will be protected and saved (as it was once in the days of Isaiah) by the Eternal's hand ; while others say just as confidently that it will fall and be destroyed to the last stone—this appears to have been the confident expectation in the earlier part of the first century among Christians. How is it possible that both traditions should be right ? Which speaks most appealingly to John, as he writes somewhere in Asia Minor during Domitian's reign ? But still other prophets and apocalyptists connect the End much more definitely with the fall of some great world Power ; with the siege and destruction of Babylon, the downfall of Greece or Rome. True, it needs less guile to bring these traditions into line with those which speak of the siege of Jerusalem than to combine the contradictory traditions about the fate of Jerusalem and Judæa. Yet it is not so easy when one considers that Jerusalem had already fallen, and in sober reality was by now no longer in any way a religious or political centre of Christian eschatology. Again, the scene of the last great battle, which John places at the mysterious **Harmagedon,** varies considerably. Tradition was strong that it should take place somewhere in the Holy Land ; on the hills of Israel, Ezekiel says ; Daniel mentions the hills, too—between Jerusalem and the sea ; others speak of the vicinity of a besieged Jerusalem. But what geographical variety exists even within this tradition is much less difficult to cope with, in view of the great theatre of war provided by the Roman Empire, than the fact that there was no reason (save an unthinking respect for tradition) why Palestine *should* be regarded as the scene of the conflict. Why should all the nations march to Palestine ? It is easy to understand why, let us say, Joel or Zechariah should expect them to act in this way. The Holy Land was still holy to them. But had John any loyalties of this sort ? The evidence of his book gives us little encouragement to think so.

In spite of such difficulties, John took the inspiration of prophetic and apocalyptic eschatologies for granted ; he did not think of them as the fallible works of men, inspired in greater or less degree, mingling truth with error ; he thought of them as infallible oracles of God, whose meaning must often be sought allegorically. After all, these earlier pictures of the End have at least three fundamental qualities in common. One and all lay it down as inevitable that the Eternal will manifest himself in anger against His enemies, to put them finally to shame, and to establish a rule of justice. And for centuries it had been represented that this battle of the Eternal must be accompanied by unprecedented conditions in the universe ; the Creator fighting His enemies with the whole armoury of creation as His weapons. Again, all hold that the Eternal acts not only for the sake of His hatred of vice, for the integrity of His rule, but also for the sake of His faithful people, that remnant of Israel who remained loyal to Him :

> ' for he who touches you
> touches the apple of the Eternal's eye.'
>
> (Zech. ii. 8.)

These fundamental things in the earlier traditions are fundamental in REVELATION. John has an eye for the essential. And it is in some ways unfortunate that we must deal with certain detail at greater length than John's emphasis on it warrants. It is, however, of interest to see the true meaning of the last three plagues ; particularly as any misunderstanding of them will probably obscure the literary design and the purpose of later passages.

We must begin in our reconstruction of John's synthesis of different eschatological traditions at the point where he has decided that the Church is the true Israel, and that wherever the prophets promise protection and a glorious future to the faithful remnant of the Jews, they were really speaking of Christians. How, logically, must this belief affect John's views on the eschatological schemes which placed the final crisis in Palestine and spoke of Jerusalem as a focal point ? Regarded literally, they were pointless. For the fact is obvious

325

that the true Israel, scattered throughout the pagan cities of the world, has no earthly fatherland, no sacred soil, no allegiance to the stones of temple and home. To localize the conflict in Palestine was to disregard what we are coming to call ' realities.'

There can be little doubt that in reading the Scriptures, John interpreted ' Jerusalem ' in different ways, according to the context. Sometimes we must assume that he interpreted it as standing for the Christian churches : those who finally would form the community of the *new* Jerusalem. In this way he accounts for those prophecies which assert that Jerusalem will not fall, but will be preserved in the last days against the utmost power of the invader : an example of this will be found in Zechariah. But John himself does not use this particular symbol for the Elect ; where such prophets as Zechariah speak of ' Jerusalem,' John uses the symbol of the temple (cf. xi. 1–2). He had good reason for avoiding the former symbol, for he could not fail to see that other prophets speak of Jerusalem as the city of doom. Isaiah, for instance, compares Jerusalem to Sodom, and the synoptic Gospels ascribe similar denunciations to Christ Himself. The word must now mean primarily the Jews as a nation, claiming hereditary sanctity, yet doing everything to disinherit themselves. But this did not solve everything. It still remained true that there were certain prophets who wrote as if Judæa were the wide world ; as if the Creator had limited His interests largely to the one capital city, Jerusalem : as if, in short, *to the eye of the discerning*, Jerusalem was a pattern city of all earthly cities, an epitome of all that was evil in society. It was natural for John to put this interpretation on such prophetic oracles as admitted it, for few things are clearer in REVELATION than that God is now regarded no longer as partisan for a single race ; He is everywhere the Creator of all men, equally concerned with all men ; giving salvation to men from all nations for righteousness, and sentence of death to men from all nations for unrighteousness—without any respect whatsoever to race and nationality. The later Isaiah and Jeremiah both expressed a similar universality in their thought about the Creator ; but they

were Jews, writing for Jews, and therefore, judged specifically
as pictures of what is actually to happen at the end of the
world, their eschatologies display a preoccupation with Israel,
which to the thoughtful Christian at the end of the first
century must have called for some reflection. The problem
was fairly acute, for the synoptic apocalypses themselves
speak of Jerusalem and Judæa in this way. When, therefore,
John interprets the ' doomed Jerusalem ' of tradition to mean
the epitome of worldly wickedness, and hence a symbol for
condemned civilization, he has performed a remarkable piece
of exegesis. One result of this we have already met (xi. 8) :
the recognition that the great City in which the Christian
witnesses are to die is essentially the same as that in which
their Lord died. In other words, Christ's death is set to the
charge not of the Jews alone but of all civilization (cf. i. 7).
And it is all civilization which hastens its doom by slaughter-
ing the witnesses—or, to be exact, by rejoicing in their
slaughter. And this, also, is the stage for the wars of the last
days, the whole world ; Babylon the great, or the **cities of the
nations,** presided over by Rome.

This interpretation admirably reveals John's capacity for
seeing the essential spiritual truth in traditions which might
otherwise have been accepted at their face value, enigmatic
yet demanding respect, or much more probably, rejected out
of hand as inapposite to the age and stultified by the passing of
time. The tradition of a great invasion from a distant country
appears in several different forms in prophetic and apocalyptic
books. We might compare the form it takes in Isa. v. 25 ff.—
an attack on Israel by the Assyrians—with Jer. li. 11 ff.,
where it is Babylon which is the object of the attack and the
Medes who are to be the attackers. Whatever the names, the
essential fact in all such passages is that a generation of evil-
doers is to be punished by invasion ; and that the invaders
themselves will be destroyed by the hand of God. The drying
of the **Euphrates** is the signal in Revelation for this invasion.
The fierce Parthians are the foe, and the Empire their
objective. We must think of their invasion as accomplished
before the mighty earthquake mentioned by John in

the next portent. This is the punishment of *humanity* in general on those who have acquiesced in the Beast's rule, as opposed to the rulers of the earth. John always draws a distinction between Babylon—that is, civilization—and its rulers ; we must in the interests of clarity be aware of the distinction.

If the ruining of the Empire is the first object of the Beast and his fierce allies (see xvii. 12–18), their ultimate object is a more desperate conflict. Antichrist musters his forces for battle against Christ. The Parthian allies are not enough ; the kings of the whole world must be seduced to his aid. Seduction was necessary, for the kings of the world had mourned over the vanished glories of their cities, now smoking in ruins (cf. xviii. 9, 10), and had not shared that hostility towards the Empire which consumed the Beast. So Satan (called the Dragon here because he is the seducer), Antichrist (the Beast, who possesses the Dragon's shape and character—again chiefly, in this instance, the power of seduction) and the community of priests of the Imperial cult (called the false Prophet, again because seduction to evil was their purpose) send dæmon spirits to persuade the kings of the world to join forces with them. The loathsomeness of these spirits is conveyed in their shape. These frogs seem undoubtedly to belong to the various allusions in chap. xvi. to the Egyptian plague. But as we have said, the first plagues were remembered in conjunction with a host of later reflections on them, and there is every likelihood that John is alluding to a belief which had been assimilated into apocalyptic from an Iranian source : 'the frog was a special agent of Ahriman in the final contest' (Moffatt). However, the main allusion in the scene is to that belief expressed in several of the canonical books of the Old Testament, and in several extra-canonical apocalypses, that every nation in the world would be mustered against God's nation, would assemble and be annihilated by God in Palestine. John alludes to this belief, but alters it slightly. As we have seen, he has one punishment for the civil population of the world (if we may make the distinction in this way) and another for their rulers and for their Parthian executioners.

We should examine the tradition of the mustering of the nations with Jer. xxv. 17 ff. in mind. Here all the kings of the earth are warned individually of their doom (the wine-cup of God's wrath), which is, of course, a separate thing from the doom of Babylon. It is the kings (and their armed forces, no doubt) and not whole nations who move to Harmagedon, **for battle on the great Day of almighty God.**

We can perhaps justly reproach John for being not quite sufficiently explicit at this point. It is evident that in mentioning the preparation for the great invasion he wishes his readers to assume that the event occurs at once—before the great earthquake soon to be described : the barrier is down, and the Parthians immediately surge fiercely through the world. It is evident, too, that in mentioning the summoning of the kings of the earth, and the purpose of the infernal trinity to muster all their forces for battle, John wishes to imply that the event does occur. The armies are mustered, and before the earthquake gather at Harmagedon. These suppositions are necessary. We must be clear that the sixth plague shows the stage all set for the final act, the great climax of the Day of Wrath, when God acts in the **earthquake,** shattering what is left of the **cities of the nations,** and Christ appears from the heavens to put the hordes of Antichrist to confusion (xix. 11–21). For these two events must be regarded as simultaneous. When the **loud voice out of the temple of heaven from the throne** cries : ' **All is over !** ' it is to be understood quite literally, without any suspicion of prolepsis. And as to the literary *raison d'être* of chaps. xviii. and xix. (which seem superficially to imply that all was *not* over at the time of the earthquake), these chapters are merely an expansion, in John's customary style, of the details he leaves unexpressed in his description of the seven last plagues (see note on verses 17–21). When this is clear, we can proceed to discuss the mysterious Harmagedon.

Harmagedon is one of the notorious difficulties in REVELATION, though it must be said that many commentators have seen only the more obvious literal difficulty involved in it. John has pointed out to his readers that the word is a transliteration into Greek of a Hebrew word, and it is widely accepted that the original must have meant ' Mount Megiddo.' Commentators have noted, first, that there is no such mountain—for Megiddo, the scene of the battle celebrated in the Song of Deborah (Judges v. 19), is a plain ; secondly, that there was a tradition, exemplified in such passages as Ezek. xxxix. 1 ff. and Dan. xi. 45 that the final conflict was to be among the mountains of Israel. Some have assumed therefore that Mount Megiddo means the range of hills skirting the plain. We must cast aside such prosaic and literal notions. There is really no excuse for holding them, for John has told us as plainly as may be that the name is symbolical. We must pay attention to his words **in Hebrew :** when John writes a Hebrew word for his readers, who were mainly Greek-speaking, and who would therefore require oral explanation of it, he obviously has some esoteric message in mind. The Beast's cipher, 666, is based on the Hebrew alphabet : it is not difficult to guess why. And the mysterious allusion to the angel of the abyss (ix. 11 : Apollyon, the destroyer), is likewise given in Hebrew form, to point to a symbolical application : to identify him (we take it) with the Hebrew personification of destruction, Abaddon, to put him in contrast with the Creator and the Origin of God's creation. Similarly **Harmagedon** is intended to convey a secret message, a message which *perhaps* could not be more openly stated without the risk of falling foul of pertinacious Imperial loyalists, should it fall into their hands. For our purposes, it might be enough to be aware of the general meaning of the word : Móunt Megiddo means the ' hill of victory,' where the enemies of Israel and of the God of Israel are annihilated. It gains this meaning by its allusion to the earlier conflict described in Judges, when the stars in their courses fought against Sisera, and Sisera and his host were utterly vanquished. But there is no treason in talking about a hill of victory. Why, then, is the word pointedly given in Hebrew form ? The clue is to be found not, as certain critics suppose, in some apocalyptic myth which has not survived, but in the Book of Jeremiah. There (Jer. li. 25) Babylon is called a ' *destroying mountain*

. . . which destroys all the earth' (words to which John alludes in xviii. 21, and also in the portent of viii. 8). In other words, **Harmagedon** is the heart of the Empire, the city built on seven hills (xvii. 9), Rome. The all-conquering Parthian hordes, with their Satanic leader, have overrun the cities of the earth; and, with **the kings of the whole world,** they lodge themselves in Rome itself. Not unless we make this conclusion does the mustering of the forces of Antichrist antecedent to the final destruction of *Babylon the great* fall into line with John's eschatological scheme. This congregation is *his* version of the earlier Christian tradition in St. Luke (xix. 43 f.—of Jerusalem) : ' A time is coming for you when your enemies will throw up ramparts round you and encircle you and besiege you on every side and raze you and your children within you to the ground . . . and all because you would not understand when God was visiting you ' (cf. St. Luke xxi. 20). The collection of armies about the city is a sign that the End has come.

xvi. 17–21 : THE SEVENTH BOWL : ' ALL IS OVER ! '

The seventh angel poured out his bowl in the air; then came a 17 loud *voice out of the temple* of heaven from the throne, crying, ' All is over!'—followed by *flashes of lightning, loud blasts,* 18 *peals of thunder,* and a mighty earthquake, *the like of which never was since man lived on earth,* such a mighty earthquake it was ; the great City was shattered in three parts, 19 the cities of the nations fell, and God remembered to give *Babylon the great the cup of the wine of the passion* of his wrath. Every island fled away, the mountains disappeared, 20 *and huge hailstones* fell from heaven on men, till men blas- 21 phemed God for the plague of the hail—for *fearful* was the plague of it.

John has brought us now to that solemn and terrible moment when God consummates His destructive purposes. He has twice before reached this point in the earlier surveys

(viii. 5 and xi. 19) ; there, the portents of the End, thunder, lightning and an earthquake, are shown to be the sequel to the great Distress. Here, however, John is concerned to show the End in another light, as the great climax of an overpowering crescendo of plagues. It is worthy of note that the **voice** which proclaims that the End has come (this time the voice 17 of God : cf. xi. 15 ff.) comes **out of the temple of heaven from the throne.** Both the temple and throne of heaven are symbolical, the one of holiness, the other of authority and power. We have shown how the allusion to the **temple** in xv. 5 carried with it the association of the triumph of Israel. Now, however, the thought of Israel's triumph is subordinated to that of the all-holy, all-powerful God, acting once and for all against evil-doers with irresistible strength. God speaks : '**All is over !**' and, obedient to His word, the foundations of the world crumble.

The **earthquake** was a familiar feature of the traditional eschatological scheme. John stresses its effect on civilization : it is the last stroke, completing the havoc wrought by the invaders. It is unprecedented in its severity. As Daniel says of the ' time of trouble ' in the last days, as Joel says of the locust-horde which would herald the End, as Exodus says of the plagues of hail and locusts and the cry of the Egyptians at the plague of death, this is a calamity unprecedented in 18 human experience, **the like** of this earthquake **never was since man lived on earth.**

We shall at once recognize, as we read for the first time 19 the results of the great earthquake, that the **City,** the **cities of the nations** and **Babylon the great** are one and the same thing—civilization. John expresses the same idea in three different ways. His chief purpose in doing so is no doubt the simple one of emphasis and solemnity : the completeness of this judgment is conveyed thus most adequately. But it is also true that each clause tells a slightly different story. The **great City** is the term John used in connexion with the great Distress : the City in which the witnesses meet the same fate as their Lord (xi. 8). It is civilization in her character of the persecutor of the prophets. The term, **the cities of the nations,** gives us the wide picture of universal ruin. Incidentally, it might be held to explain John's symbol of ' the City '—if by this time it needed any explanation. Moreover, it is the **nations**—the great masses of irredeemable heathen, whose apparent strength in the present is so staunchly defied by John in ii. 26, where the ' conqueror ' in the tiny Thyatiran church is promised ' authority over the nations '—a large promise ! But John shows the enduring strength of the Christian whose cause belongs to God, and the pretentious insecurity and transience of the powers of this world. As for **Babylon the great,** here we are brought to think at once of the vice and insensate frivolity and corruption of civilization— the Roman civilization, which had seduced the whole world, and ' made all the nations drink the wine of the passion of her vice.' We think also of the doom already pronounced on the citizens of the world. The seventh ' bowl ' actually *is* **the great cup of the wine of the passion of God's wrath.** When John says, and **God remembered** to give Babylon the great the full measure of His passionate anger in return for her passionate wickedness, he is making no distinction between Babylon and the cities of the nations : he is merely asserting that God will remember to punish civilization proportionately to its sins.

We must not allow this threefold statement of the fall of civilization, with all its unimaginable carnage (cf. xi. 13 and xiv. 14–16), to overshadow the other results of the earthquake, and the accompanying storm of **huge hailstones.** For when we come to consider the disappearance of **mountains and 20 islands,** and the plague of hail on men, we shall be compelled to assign to them an importance equal to the fall of the City. But first we must remind ourselves of John's favourite literary device : he states a fact first cryptically and without detail, then later with as much amplification as he thinks necessary. We have noticed this device on many occasions, but for reference his treatment of the great Distress (chaps. viii., xi., and xiii.) provides as good an example as any. In the seventh of the last plagues we must detect still another resort to this device. The fall of the great City he describes more fully in the doom-song (chap. xviii.). But just as plainly the attendant circumstances of the earthquake are amplified in the description of the last battle in chap. xix. A moment's reflection will establish this fact : for in saying that **every island** and **the mountains** disappear, John is telling us that this earthquake is the equivalent of that described (for example) in Zech. xiv. 10, where it is said : ' The whole land shall be turned into a plain.' In other words, the earth is thus made ready for the messianic reign of the millennium. It may seem prosaic to insist on such a point, but it is at least worth remembering that among other mountains Harmagedon must disappear. This indeed is what is portended in chap. viii. where **what seemed like a mountain on fire** is hurled into the sea. When we read the description of the battle in chap. xix., we should have in mind the passage in which Zechariah describes the appearance of the Eternal on the Day of Wrath (Zech. xiv. 3 ff.) : The Eternal appears on the Mount of Olives (which in 2 Kings xxiii. 13 is called the mount of destruction ; cf. Jeremiah's description of Babylon, above) : and immediately this mountain is split in two ; implicitly, the earthquake results in the utter defeat of the hostile nations, for the messianic appearance plays its part, together with other plagues, in the defeat of the hostile nations. Other suggestions from Zechariah may have influenced John's thought at this point. In chap. iv. we find a brief oracle devoted to the victory of a messianic figure named Zerubbabel :

> ' " Not by fighting, not by force, but by my spirit ! "
> so the Lord of hosts declares.
> " What are you, O mighty mountain ?
> Be level ground before Zerubbabel ! " '

Again, there is a reference to Megiddo in Zech. xii. 11 : ' On that day the lamenting in Jerusalem shall be as mournful as the lamenting for Hadadrimmon in the valley of Megiddo.' We have already attempted to show that John called the city of doom (in Zechariah, Jerusalem) ' Babylon the great ' ; so Zechariah, speaking of the discomfiture of the Jews, probably provided John with the name for his hill of doom.

Whatever its remote origin, the eschatological hostility towards mountains is probably coloured by the prophetic denunciations of the ' high places,' the scene of heathen rites. It is not impossible, however, that John did not rationalize this hostility, thinking of mountains as places defiled by orgiastic ceremonies, or as barriers between nations and nations, or (with Isaiah) as obstacles to be removed from the path of the Eternal. He takes over the notion from earlier eschatologies, with whatever general associations come with it. But chiefly in *his* picture there is the parallel with the fall of the City ; the implication that their removal marks the completion of the process of divine wrath. That **islands** should be singled out also for seismic annihilation bears similar testimony to John's desire to portray a process which reaches over the whole earth, even into the kingdoms of the sea.

Finally, the **plague** of the **hail** : this belongs (perhaps quite 21 symbolically) to the scene of the great messianic battle, just as does the earthquake-stroke on the mountains. It is difficult to draw a line, and say what is symbolical and what is not in this scene. So much is figurative in REVELATION that it would be dangerous to say out of hand that this or that is literal. For example, the sharp sword with the two edges, which the Messiah wields at this battle, represents His power to *will* the deaths of wicked men : the power of the Law to prevail without weapons (cf. 2 Esdras xiii. 38). It is, indeed, well-nigh impossible to speak without metaphor of divine visitation, or of celestial power to engage in battle. And like as not the metaphor will fall sadly short of the mark : one has only to recall the ancient cannons invented desperately by the rebel angels in *Paradise Lost*. In this instance, the modern reader, particularly he who lives in a land where hailstones are marvelled at if they break the panes of a greenhouse, is not greatly impressed at a plague of hail as the last of the series of the seven last plagues. But hail in the East had long been regarded as one of the more terrible weapons in God's armoury : the visitation on the Egyptians provided a theme which recurred again and again in eschatological pictures.

It occurs, for example, in Ezekiel's description of the fate of the outlandish invaders, Gog and Magog (names which John interprets in chap. xx. as generic terms for barbarian hordes, similar to the Parthians from the East) : it is important to note that John models his account of the messianic battle (xix. 17 f.) largely on Ezek. xxxix. 17 ff. ; it is therefore not too much to suppose that Ezekiel's picture of the doom of the invader influenced that of REVELATION in this further point. The crucial passage is at the end of Ezek. xxxviii., where we find the great earthquake ' in the land of Israel ' (i.e., in REVELATION, the world), an earthquake which causes every created thing to recognize God as the supreme Lord of power (cf. Rev. xi. 13 and notes on xiv. 7) ; and side by side with this the Eternal (in REVELATION, Christ : cf. notes on the titles of Christ in the Seven Letters) reveals Himself in anger. The invading hosts of Gog and Magog are inflicted with overwhelming plagues, amongst which is the plague of hail.

It may appear too small a matter to argue about at length. What does it matter whether the hail is connected with this messianic conflict ? It would not matter at all, if it were generally agreed that the cry, ' All is over ! ' (verse 17), conveyed the finality of God's visitations on men, or that the seven **last plagues** were indeed the **last** plagues in John's mind ; that the messianic battle did not represent a further outbreak of divine wrath. But we must spend some time, whether we grudge it or not, on discerning the literary arrangement of REVELATION. Otherwise, we might well be content to note that God's enemies celebrate in the manner of their death the justice of God's sentence on them. They have recognized the supremacy of Him whose laws they have execrated by word and deed, but only to demonstrate their hopeless depravity. They acknowledged God—but then they **blasphemed God for the plague of the hail.** This is the conduct of the invaders, and of the kings of the world : the blasphemies noted in verses 9, 11 and 21 are those of the inhabitants of the great City.

THE FALL OF BABYLON THE GREAT
(xvii. 1–xix. 21)

PREFACE TO CHAPTERS XVII.–XIX.

Chaps. xvii., xviii., and xix. form a literary unit : their purpose is to explain adequately the final destruction of evil on earth. First the great City must be destroyed : the Empire must be ravaged by hordes of invaders from the East. When this is accomplished, the invaders in turn must be destroyed, since they, too, are unutterably evil. Their destruction, heralded by scenes of joy in heaven, is described in chap. xix.

Chap. xvii. is a kind of explanatory preface to the doom-song in chap. xviii. and the battle scene of chap. xix. ; the essential shape of the catastrophe to fall on the Empire is there described. Chap. xviii. is a song of triumph over the devastation of the seemingly invincible Empire. Its purpose seems to be fundamentally to warn Christians of the danger involved in compromising themselves with the sins of the Empire, for which so terrible and sure punishment is reserved. Chap. xix. describes the glorious outcome of the defeat of wrong on earth : it makes possible the union of faithful souls to their Lord. Then the scene changes from heaven to earth, and the final battle is briefly but passionately described.

Taken together, these three chapters glance back at the latter part of chap. xvi. They expand the story there briefly sketched of the fall of Rome and the defeat of Antichrist. But they also stand as a foil to the description of the Eternal City, in chaps. xxi.–xxii. We must not forget, as we read the story of the earth's last days, that John was not painting his terrible pictures for the joy of it. He had a severely practical purpose—to win his fellow-Christians to a true knowledge and a true evaluation of what was temporal, evil, doomed to destruction, and what was eternal, righteous, destined to glorious vindication hereafter. This pastoral purpose we must see in the closing chapters of REVELATION not a whit less clearly than in the letters to the seven churches.

xvii. 1–6 : Explanatory Notes on the Empire and Anti-christ : the Vision of the Woman seated on the Beast

1 Then came one of the seven angels with the seven plagues and
   spoke to me, saying, ' Come and I will show you the doom
2 of the great Harlot who is seated on *many waters, with
   whom the kings of earth have committed vice,* and the dwellers
3 on *earth have been drunk with the wine* of her vice.' So he
   bore me away rapt in the Spirit to the desert, and there I saw a
   woman sitting on *a* scarlet *Beast* covered with blasphemous
4 titles ; it had seven heads and *ten horns.* The woman was
   clad in purple and scarlet, her ornaments were of gold and
   precious stones and pearls, in her hand was *a golden cup*
5 full of all earth's abominations and impurities of vice, and
   on her forehead a name was written by way of symbol,
   ' Babylon the great, the mother of harlots and of all
   abominations on earth.'
6 I saw that the woman was drunk with the blood of the saints
   and the blood of the witnesses of Jesus ; and as I looked
   at her I marvelled greatly.

With the exception of the first five verses, chap. xvii. is
one of the least effective passages in REVELATION. It displays
most of the disadvantages of the apocalyptic style, and few
of its advantages. The reason is that its purpose is to explain
and not to inspire ; the language of apocalyptic is as ill suited
to a pedestrian venture of this sort, as, let us say, Shakespearian blank verse would be to the fashioning of a Shakespearian commentary. Nevertheless, the reader who has
taken the trouble to read similar explanatory passages in
other apocalyptic books (cf. 2 Esdras xii. 10 ff.) will perhaps
credit John with a comparative degree of clarity. When they
are properly understood, there are certain features in this
chapter which help us to appreciate the symbolism in the
rest of the book.

1–
3   The first thing that we must notice is that John has pointed
    with outstretched finger to the contrast between Babylon, the

city of doom, and the new Jerusalem, the eternal city, which forms the subject of the visions in chap. xxi. For in each scene John has an angelic guide ; and on each occasion he makes it clear that his guide is **one of the seven angels with the seven plagues** (cf. xxi. 9). In connexion with this, it must not be overlooked that these angels blowing trumpets of doom, or pouring bowls of wrath upon the earth are *portent* angels : John does not think of them, apparently, as the literal executors of the events of the last days. They act a changing pageant of revelation for the prophet and the churches. So it is not unnatural that two of the angels who previously have been associated purely with the revelation of punitive strokes to fall on the earth should perform the office of *ciceroni* to John and his readers. And since it is they, of all the angelic hosts, who perform this double task, we cannot avoid connecting the subjects of chap. xvii. and chap. xxi. There is another hint of contrast within chap. xvii. itself, however. John is conveyed **rapt in the Spirit to the desert.** Now we have already seen in chap xii. how the ' desert ' (in which the Church is to be miraculously preserved until the End) represents the perpetual condition of Christian detachment from the affairs of civilization : just as the Israelites of old cut themselves off from the grossness of Egypt, and chose to brave the hardships of a desert journey, so the true Israelites of the last days must detach themselves from the City of Destruction (called ' Sodom ' and ' Egypt ' : xi. 8) and venture on a figurative pilgrimage towards the Celestial City. Their path lay through **the desert.** It is from the ' desert ' that the Christian is able to view civilization clearly, as it really is. When John is conveyed on the wings of trance to the desert, here is the implication : *from* this desert he is able to see the whole elaborate structure of Roman civilization in an essential simplicity, as **the great Harlot.** He discerns the diabolical source of its power. And he sees that the glittering clothes of the Harlot, her **purple and scarlet,** her **ornaments** of **gold and precious stones and pearls,** are in reality the ' muddy vesture of decay ' ; that the very splendour of earthly institutions is a sign and proof of their corruption and destined fall.

' Come,' the angel cries, ' and I will show you the doom of the great Harlot. . . .' In spite of all that we read about the Beast in this chapter, the subject is the doom of the world-Empire ; it will help us very considerably if we keep this constantly in mind. When John gives us information about the Beast, it is closely connected with this central theme, and entirely subordinate to it. There are certain astonishing features in the attitude of the last of the Emperors, Antichrist, towards the dominions he governs, and these points he clarifies in verses 8–18. In this introductory section, verses 1–6, John shows that the basic principle on which the Empire rests is a formidable Satanic Power : **the Woman** (that is, the Empire ; Roman civilization) whom he sees in his trance is **sitting on a scarlet Beast covered with blasphemous titles.** We have learnt much about this Beast already (in chap. xiii. he forms the main theme) ; and we are to learn more later in this chapter. It is sufficient to observe here that the Beast in his present appearance represents what we may call the enduring reality underlying the political institutions of the Empire. Each successive Emperor (that is, each of the Beast's **seven heads**) constitutes a temporary manifestation of a constant force of evil : a force which may also take shape in other earthly rulers (the **ten horns** : see notes on verse 12). This Satanic power is no abstraction. He is a being with personality and mind, a creature fashioned in the shape of Satan to be the opponent of Christ, of His servants, and of His way of life. He claims from the citizens of the great City the loyalty and worship which is due to the Creator and to the Redeemer : the Beast is **covered with blasphemous titles.** Previously John has told us only of the blasphemous claims to divinity made by the Emperors (see xiii. 1 ; the ' titles ' are there on the Beast's heads). Now we see that in its entirety this evil Power is the full antithesis of God and Christ. Emperors come and go ; their ungodly claims are limited to their lifetime. But the force which they represent, of which they are the incarnate expression, is always there under the surface of events. One day, a day near at hand, this force will emerge in visible form. And meanwhile the dwellers in the great City are content to accept this basis for their society; they build their house on the insecure foundation of Satan's power.

For that reason, Roman civilization is doomed. When the angel calls the Empire **the great Harlot** he is asserting both her wickedness and her ordained downfall. For the term is an allusion to many prophetic passages, denouncing the profligacy and proclaiming the doom of great cities of the past. Nahum (iii. 4) denounces Nineveh in this way. She is a 'harlot' because of her evil ways, and also because her splendour bewitched other nations to share her vicious life—the life of a 'city soaked with blood.' In Isa. xxiii. 15, Tyre is called a harlot, because her sea trade enabled her to draw others into her profligacy : 'She shall play the harlot with all the kingdoms of the world upon the face of the earth '—a sentence which seems to be echoed in John's words : '**with whom the kings of earth have committed vice.**' Evidently the theme of seduction takes a prominent place in John's thought about the great City of his own day : 'Babylon ' is a **harlot** because her life has seduced and corrupted her countless citizens : **the dwellers on earth have been drunk with the wine of her vice.** John recollects Jer. li. 7 :

> 'Once Babylon was a golden cup,
> that made the whole world drunk ;
> the nations drank her wine,
> and lay before her helpless.'

Her downfall inevitably follows from her seductive viciousness :

'O thou that dwellest upon many waters, abundant in treasures, thine end is come.'

(Jer. li. 13, R.V.)

(For comment on **many waters,** see below, verse 15.)

But we must not forget that in Isaiah, Jeremiah, and Ezekiel it is pre-eminently Jerusalem who is the harlot-city. We have already seen (see excursus on chap. xi.) how John's picture of Babylon the great was fashioned with the thought constantly in mind of Jerusalem as the city of doom. It is therefore worth recalling some of those prophetic attacks on Jerusalem, and on the kingdoms of the North and the South, for it is largely from them that the emotional power of John's picture of Babylon is derived. ' How is the faithful city become a harlot ! ' Isaiah exclaims. He means, not a *seducer*, but an evil-doer ; her murders, her lust, civic corruption and oppression, all cry aloud that she has deserted and betrayed her God. Similarly, in Ezekiel (see chaps. xvi. and xxiii.) Jerusalem is a ' harlot ' because she resorts to the idolatry of alien religions, with all the immoral practices associated with them : she betrays and defiles her union with the Creator, her God. And this is the major reason why ' Babylon ' in REVELA-TION is called **the great Harlot, the mother of harlots.** For she, beyond all others, in her teeming profligacies, in her venerated iniquities (see ix. 20–21), has denied the Creator of men. Denied Him ? Yes, and betrayed His goodness, deliberately blinded herself to the claims of her Maker, deliberately ignored all His calls to repentance, execrated and cast aside His prophets. John shows us a picture of **the woman sitting on** that Power, which, when it emerges into the world, is to be recognized as Antichrist. There is a sinister implication here, only to be discerned in the light of Ezek. xvi. 36 ff. and xxiii. 22 ff., where it is predicted that because of Jerusalem's idolatry, and the evil she does in the service of idolatry, all her ' lovers ' are to be gathered against her—all the nations with whom she has prostituted herself. ' I will gather them all round you, and expose you to their gaze, baring your nakedness to them. . . . I will leave you to your lovers, and they shall pull down your shrines . . . stripping you of your clothes, robbing you of your fine jewels, and leaving you bare and naked ; they shall collect a crowd, to stone you and cut you to pieces with their swords. . . .' The Empire's ' lover ' (ironical word !) is the **Beast** on whom she is seated, and the **kings of the earth** with whom she has **committed vice.** It is they who, in John's view, are indeed to ruin her, as we shall read later in this chapter (see verses 15 ff. where the theme is developed at greater length).

At present, however, the **woman** still triumphs in her wickedness ; still enjoys her fatal union with the Beast ; still
4 flaunts her regal vesture of **purple and scarlet (scarlet :** the

colour of royal robes—and of sin ; cf. Isa. i. 18, and cf. the
scarlet of the Beast) ; still displays the meretricious **ornaments**
of her trafficking with mankind. She sits, the personification
of insidious vice, holding out to all men **a golden cup full of all
earth's abominations and impurities ;** a Circe, intoxicating,
alluring, stupefying and degrading mankind ; the pattern and
original of social corruption, wearing, like the prostitutes in
her streets, the sign of her depravity written boldly in the
name on her brow : **' Babylon the great, the mother of harlots** 5
and of all abominations on earth.' (The title in Greek is called
a ' mystery,' a term to be understood like ' Sodom and
Egypt,' xi. 8—allegorically. Dr. Moffatt's rendering, **by way of
symbol,** is admirable.)

Disloyalty to the ' God of heaven ' (see xi. 13 and xvi. 11 for
the significance of this term) and indulgence in every kind of
vicious practice have made the great City like Nineveh
(Nahum iii. 4) and like Jerusalem ' that killeth the prophets '
(cf. Ezek. xxii. 1 ff.) a city of blood. Her whole posture is
eloquent of impending doom. How can such flaunting
immorality escape punishment ? But it is her blood guiltiness
which completes the tale of her indictment. Discounting all
the rest, for one single crime she is sentenced beyond hope
of reprieve. **The woman was drunk with the blood of the** 6
saints and the blood of the witnesses of Jesus. (Saints and
witnesses do not signify two classes of martyrs : the terms
allude to the twofold task of the Christian prophets ; to preach
the Gospel, and to remain pure ; they correspond with the
description of the martyrs in xii. 17 : ' those who keep God's
commandments and hold the testimony of Jesus.') So closely
allied is the Harlot to the will of the Beast that she executes
his command to kill God's servants ; indeed, she is **drunk** with
their blood—she delights in her task. The picture is precisely
the same as in xi. 10 : ' and the dwellers on earth will gloat
over them and rejoice, sending presents to congratulate one
another—for these two prophets were a torment to the
dwellers on earth.' This is the crime of crimes ; there is
needed no further evidence of the woman's corruption. This
completes the contrast between the ' woman clad in the sun '

(xii. 1 f.) who 'gives birth' to Christ and His witnesses, and the **woman** clad in the proud robes of worldly magnificence, who slays them. Why does John tell us that he **marvelled greatly** at this portent ? His wonder is not merely conventional, nor is it evoked only by the strangeness of the vision. He marvelled at the sight of such unrelieved wickedness, at the revelation of the true nature of the Empire—and at the fact that this wickedness was allowed by God to exist. He marvelled that the woman was allowed by God to live, having identified herself in spirit with the Beast, even in the most ghastly crime he contemplated against God and His servants. The angel, noting John's wonder, proceeds to explain the symbol, and shows how the **doom of the great Harlot** is to be accomplished.

xvii. 7–14 : THE VISION IN THE DESERT EXPLAINED : THE SIGNIFICANCE OF THE BEAST

7 But the angel said to me, 'Why marvel ? I will explain to you the mystery of the woman, and of the Beast with the seven
8 heads and the ten horns who carries her. *The Beast* you have seen was, is not, but is to *rise from the abyss*—yet to perdition he shall go—and the dwellers on earth will wonder (all whose names have not been *written* from the foundation of the world *in the book of Life*), when they see
9 how the Beast was, is not, but is coming. Now for the interpretation of the discerning mind! The seven heads are
10 seven hills, on which the woman is seated : also, they are seven kings, of whom five have fallen, one is living, and the other has not arrived yet—and when he does arrive, he is
11 only to stay a little while. As for the Beast which was and is not, he is an eighth head : he belongs to the seven,
12 and to perdition he shall go. *As for the ten horns* you have seen, *they are ten kings* who have no royal power as yet, but receive royal authority for an hour along with the Beast ;
13 they are of one mind, and they confer their power and
14 authority upon the Beast. They shall wage war on the

Lamb, but the Lamb will conquer them because he is
Lord of lords and King of kings—the Lamb and the elect,
the chosen, the faithful who are with him.'

Before he can show how the Roman Empire is to fall, the
angel must explain the symbol of **the Beast**. This is necessary : 7
for the heart of the situation is that the Beast who **carries**
the Empire (supplies motive force and purpose) will also
destroy her. A paradoxical situation ! But as John unfolds
his belief about the Beast's character, his readers would not
be inclined to detect any great anomaly in the last Emperor's
hostility towards his Empire. For it is clear beyond doubt
that in the Beast which **was, is not, but is to rise from the abyss** 8
John is describing a *Nero redivivus* (see notes on xiii. 3, 12, 14).
According to enduring popular belief, Nero vented his rage on
Rome by burning her. Shortly after his slaughter of the Christians, he died—slain, as John has told us, by the sword of God
(see pp. 244 ff.). But a common dread persisted that he would
return, supernaturally revivified, to trouble the Empire once
again with his insane fury. This is the power who **was, is not,
but is to rise**. It is by virtue of this mysterious resurrection that
the Beast may be recognized by devout Christians, by **all whose
names have . . . been written from the foundation of the world
in the book of Life** (see notes on iii. 5 and xiii. 5–10), for what
he was—the Antichrist. For the Beast thus reveals himself
as the devilish antithesis of Him ' who is and was and is
coming ' (i. 8, etc.). The **dwellers on earth** (John's term for
the non-Christian world) will **wonder** at the Beast's supernatural origin. As John has shown in xiii. 2–4, they will
wonder, applaud and worship. Those who loyally recognize
Christ as their Lord will have no such temptation ; they will
contemplate the Beast's emergence into the world with horror
rather than wonder, for when he comes there will be no
mistaking his Satanic character.

The symbol of **the Beast** has to perform a function which is
really too complex for clarity. We become increasingly aware
of its inadequacy. The truth is that John's thought about
the structure of society and its underlying meaning has

outgrown its apocalyptic clothing. We are at once struck by an apparent inconsistency. How is it that the Empire can be seen in visionary form reclining on a Beast, which, according to verses 8 and 9, has existed on earth, at present does *not* exist on earth, but is destined to do so once again in the future ? Obviously there is some sort of a contradiction here. Yet it is only a verbal contradiction. The ruling thought is clear enough. For the Beast represents, not only one person who in the future is to emerge from the **abyss,** the underground dungeon of evil spirits, into the world of men : he represents also a Satanic being, who exercises a constant sway in the world through the successive Emperors. Each Emperor is, as it were, a partial incarnation of this evil Power : John expresses this idea by saying that the Beast had **seven heads,** and that the heads were **seven kings. Seven** is emblematic, as it always is in REVELATION, of completeness ; and it signifies the full number of Roman Emperors. The Emperor who had most nearly approximated to the formidable character of the Beast as a dæmonic entity was Nero—and Nero is variously represented in REVELATION as a ' head ' which was ' slain and killed ' (xiii. 3), or as the Beast himself, ' who lived after being wounded by the sword ' (xiii. 14), or as an ' **eighth** head,' who yet ' **belongs to the seven.**' He is thus diversely depicted according to the light in which John for the moment considers him : whether as one of a line of Emperors, or as the being who epitomizes the multifarious power of Satan in the world, who is to be Satan's vicegerent in the critical years ahead. When John speaks of the Beast who in the present **carries** the woman, he is thinking of the abiding principle of evil to which the Empire is devoted : or rather, to be less abstract, an enduring Power of evil, a being with shape and personality, capable of incarnate activity in visible form—the true object of the Empire's worship. But when he talks about the Beast who **was, is not, but is to rise,** he is thinking of this evil power specifically as it was incarnate in Nero, as it is to be incarnate in the Antichrist, the resurrected Nero.

One is sometimes tempted to ask whether John's readers really understood such a symbol as this. But assuredly they

had much less difficulty than the modern reader. For one
thing, John was writing of matters which had an acute
topical interest for Christians. He was probably not the only
one to see in an event like the martyrdom of Antipas (ii. 13)
a disquieting omen of worse times to come, and perhaps a
recrudescence of the now almost proverbial fury of Nero
against the Christian community. And it is also to be remembered that readers of apocalyptic literature were not unac-
customed to coping with fantastically involved symbols.
Nevertheless, it seems that John was conscious of a certain
difficulty in his thought. It is almost as if he set a challenge
to his readers : **Now for the interpretation of the discerning** 9
mind ! (cf. xiii. 18). The quality he appeals to is literally
' wisdom ' (*sophia*) : it is that aspect of the divine spirit of
active thought described in Wisd. viii. 8 :

' She knoweth the things of old, and divineth the things to come :
She understandeth subtilties of speeches and interpretations of dark
    sayings.'

One does indeed ask for a share of this quality in interpreting
the dark sayings of verses 10-12. The difficulties are prominent ; but let us not hastily conclude that they spring out
of a confused mind. As in verse 8, the oddities and anomalies
in this passage are really verbal. We had better first give a
paraphrase of this section, and then attempt to justify it.

' *The Antichrist, the Satanic Power to whom the Empire is
bound, is universal in reach, and is manifested in the whole line
of Roman Emperors. Most of these Emperors have passed : the
time quickly approaches when the Satanic Power will emerge in
its entirety. As to this Power (who has already lived on earth,
has died, and yet is to return again) in appearance he will
resemble his predecessors. He is at once distinct from them,
since in him Christians shall see the complete Being of whom
the Emperors were but partial manifestations ; and yet he is
one with them in the Imperial functions he performs and the
throne he occupies : in spite of his impressiveness, his doom is
certain. God has already ordained it.*'

The main difficulty lies in the apparent contradiction of
verses 9 and 10 : **The seven heads are seven hills, on which**

10 **the woman is seated : also, they are seven kings.** The habit of endowing a single symbol with more than one related meaning may not be entirely foreign to apocalyptic writers ; but here the two explanations given differ in kind—they are logically disparate. Everywhere in REVELATION the Beast represents a living being, with intelligence and personality. So much is certain : it holds good, whether John is considering the Beast as manifested in the whole line of Emperors—the constant dæmonic Power beneath the Empire's institutions ; or whether he considers him as the Neronic Antichrist who lived, died, and was to be resurrected to inspire the great ' trial which is coming upon the whole world, to test the dwellers on earth ' (iii. 10). These are merely two aspects of the same Power. How, then, can the **seven heads** of the Beast in any sense contain a purely geographical meaning ? How can they possibly represent the site of Rome ? *That* is no part of the Beast's personality ! It is, of course, the first thought that occurs to a modern reader ; especially one who remembers classical allusions to the seven hills on which Rome is built. But we have argued elsewhere that the woman (the great City ; see verse 18 ; cf. pp. 186 f.) does not represent Rome as a city, but is to be understood as the Empire, with all her far-reaching institutions. John takes the **seven hills** of Rome as suggestive of the world-wide domination exercised by the Roman order of things. **Seven** is used, in its inevitable sense in REVELATION, of completeness. But even understanding the symbol in this way, we are still left with the entirely anomalous attribution of a purely geographical meaning to what must logically stand for something personal. Whether the **seven hills** are here literally the hills of Rome, or something similar in kind, the whole civilized world, the puzzle remains.

We must begin our reinterpretation by asking what was John's general purpose in his description of the Beast. The answer is that he was attempting to define the Beast's *power* as it affected the Empire. Now, the only common-sense course in considering verses 9–10 is to assume that John is beginning this task by giving a comprehensive picture : in both verses he is saying something about the Beast's *power*.

In verse 9 he says that the Beast's power is universal, stretching as far as Roman institutions. And in verse 10 he says that this power is exercised in the successive Emperors. But, it may be objected, that is not what John says ; he says, as plainly as may be, **the seven heads are seven hills.** We can only reply that John had other means at his disposal for speaking of Rome or the Empire ; there was no necessity for him to attribute to part of his symbol for Antichrist a meaning which turned the whole thing into nonsense. The essence of the matter is the force of the number **seven.** John sees the Beast endowed with certain qualities which he describes in apocalyptic style under the allegorical figure of **seven heads.** What essential qualities has John already ascribed to the Beast in chap. xiii. ? His Imperial character is assumed throughout the chapter ; but the other note which is emphatically sounded is his universal dominion (see xiii. 2, 4, 8, 16). We conclude that the only legitimate approach to the interpretation of verses 9–10 is to seek personal attributes in both verses ; and taking them together, we understand the verses to refer to the *scope and nature* of the Beast's power.

Of the **seven kings,** John tells us, **five have fallen, one is living, and the other has not arrived yet.** We here stand on difficult ground. Most commentators would have us refer to a table of the Emperors, of whom the fifth (counting from Augustus) was Nero ; and the sixth (who would therefore be the reigning Emperor) was Vespasian. In order to arrive at this result, we must omit as mere pretenders the Emperors Galba, Otho, and Vitellius ; after all, Suetonius disposes of these three as summarily as may be desired—their brief reigns are ' *rebellio trium principum.*' So that the oracle we are considering is said to have been brought to birth in Vespasian's reign, with the Neronic troubles and the wars of the three pretenders still vivid in the memory of all. The argument proceeds to state that the oracle is ' brought up to date ' in Domitian's reign, by the addition of an **eighth head**—a procedure for which there is apocalyptic precedent. This, at all events, is one of the more adequate reconstructions of the passage ; there have been many other attempts to explain it,

11

349

based on this same assumption that John is using an older source, and that the material is only partially adequate to his purposes. None of these attempts is convincing. It is clear from the evidence of the rest of REVELATION that John was writing at a date towards the end of the first century, and most probably in Domitian's reign ; but it is not in the least clear that in reckoning the number of past Emperors he should omit Galba, Otho, and Vitellius. His point of view, like that of his readers, was not likely to have had much in common with that of a Roman historian. It seems in every way unlikely that John should have had to pause and ask himself whether his readers would really understand that he was beginning his count of seven Emperors from Augustus or from Julius Cæsar (as many did) ; or that he should tolerate an uncertainty as to whether his readers would agree with him that three men who had in fact occupied the Imperial throne were unworthy to be accounted Emperors. The fact is that those who seek in the reference to **seven kings** a list of seven individual monarchs must admit that the text is enigmatic beyond hope, and that a mere approximation to intelligibility is to be reached only by the arbitrary mutilation of the text, or the performance of extraordinary mental gymnastics. It is difficult, for example, to see how John could have imagined that he had brought this hypothetical Vespasianic source up to date by the mere addition of an eighth head to his Beast. By no obvious process of reasoning does this dispose of the plain statement : **five have fallen, one is living and the other has not arrived yet.**

No, the number **seven** has here its symbolical force—as always in REVELATION. It is used to convey the *complete number* of the Emperors—just as the seven churches represent the complete number of Christian communities ; just as the multifarious plagues of the End are neatly arranged in series of seven, to indicate that they will be complete. John tells us in his statement **five have fallen** that the line of Emperors was nearing its end. The time was at hand when Antichrist would appear : the king who is yet to arrive **is only to stay a little while.** John did not need the historical fact of Titus's brief reign to encourage him in this prophecy; it sprang directly out of his firm conviction that the times portended the imminence of the End. Whether there is beneath the surface of John's words some recollection of speculations current in Vespasian's reign, or in any other reign, we shall not attempt to decide. But we shall insist that in their present form his words admit of no exact historical reference: verse 10 is a general statement, and John's readers can have had no temptation to read it as anything else.[1]

The strange device of the Beast's **eighth head** bears striking testimony to the fact that some of John's descriptions of his spiritual experiences use the traditional language of dreams and visions to convey truths or convictions which may well have been arrived at through the normal processes of thought. It is impossible to visualize a Beast with seven heads, who may yet be described briefly as an eighth head. The oddity of the figure cannot conceal the very clear meaning which this eighth head conveys, however. John wishes his readers to understand that the emergent **Beast** (who like the returning Messiah has been previously incarnate, and has been subsequently endowed with supernatural powers: cf. chaps. v. and xiii.) is at once distinct from his predecessors, and similar to them. He is distinct from them, in that he possesses vast supernatural powers, granted him by Satan; he is distinct from them in his resuscitation, and in the final rôle he plays; he is distinct from them, because he comprehends them. But he is similar to them in that he takes the shape of an Emperor, fills the Imperial throne and directs the policy of the Empire. In this, he **belongs to the seven.** And just as the seven have played their earthly parts and disappeared from the society of men, so the Beast, for all his formidable powers and his miraculous rebirth, is destined to succumb to the decree of God: **to perdition he shall go.**

The **ten horns** are now described. They are **ten kings who 12 have no royal power as yet, but receive authority for an hour along with the Beast.** We are bound to ask the rather barren

---

[1] For a detailed examination of this question and the various attempts to deal with it, see I. C. Beckwith, *op. cit.*, pp. 704 ff.

question, ' Who are these kings ? '—though very plainly it cannot make any difference to the modern reader's appreciation of REVELATION, whether they are taken as provincial governors in the Roman Empire, or as Parthian satraps, or (as has been suggested) all the rulers in the world, described in characteristically symbolical style under the number **ten** : for in any case the number **ten** is to be taken not literally but figuratively. The evidence offered by REVELATION is inconclusive. All we can do is to point to the most probable solution. What does John tell us ? In the first place, they are specifically connected with the punishment of the **great City** ; that is the subject of the whole chapter, and the symbol is here explained with the object in view of introducing the crucial passage, verses 15–18. In the second place, they seem to be deliberately distinguished from those whom John calls the **kings of the earth.** If we glance at xviii. 9, we shall see that the ' kings of earth ' do not seem to be associated with the destruction of Babylon ; they weep and wail over her ruins. It is the **kings from the east** (xvi. 12) who are to destroy Babylon ; they lead the invading army of long-standing eschatological tradition (cf. the Medes of Jer. li., for example). ' The kings of the whole world ' (xvi. 14), in spite of the large way in which John talks of them, are really quite distinct from the invading kings from the east ; for they have to be seduced by evil spirits into joining the Beast and the Eastern powers for the ' battle on the great Day of almighty God ' ; apparently they have nothing to do with the attack on the Roman Empire, the source of their delight. And John has told us that these ' kings ' represented by the ten horns have, in the present, no royal status. That is to come through their association with Antichrist. Their **royal authority** is specifically designated as of the briefest duration. We must compare the symbolical ' **hour** ' of their reign with the symbolical ' three and a half years ' of Antichrist's authority over mankind (xiii. 5 ; cf. xi. 2, xii. 6). We are entitled to look for *proportion* in these symbolical indications of time, even though literal interpretation is out of the question. On the whole, the most reasonable course seems to be to think of them as Parthian leaders, whose powers the Neronic Antichrist employs in his destruction of the Empire. They are elevated to positions of kingship in the domains they ravage. But since their invasion marks the last stage before the End, they enjoy their kingship only for the shortest of times. In view of the traditional association of *Nero redivivus* with the Parthians, and in view of the task performed by the horns—the ruin of the Empire (xv. –xviii.), it seems almost certain that these ' kings ' are to be associated with the Parthian Satraps. The number **ten** is derived from Daniel (see Dan. vii.), as a cryptic designation of the associates of Antichrist. And the whole description is left purposely vague and mysterious—clear only in its essential bearing : Antichrist is to have allies, entirely united to him in purpose, and united to each other (having **one mind**) in subservience to 13 him. They seem to be inspired by the same Satanic impulse as the Beast himself ; like him personifying the principle of fierce ungodly power—they are the ' destroyers of the earth,' just as their master is the great Destroyer (cf. ix. 11 and xi. 18). And if their penultimate aim is the ravaging of the Empire (which they enable the Beast to perform, by conferring on him their **power and authority**), their ultimate hostility is aimed at God Himself, and the holy people. It is this ultimate hostility which John records in verse 14, before he proceeds to explain how these kings and the Beast together are to destroy the Empire. This reference to the messianic battle is strictly almost a digression from John's theme, which is **the doom of the great Harlot.** But it is a very natural digression. It would have been difficult for John to refrain from mentioning the peculiar significance of the **ten kings** to Christians, as he explained the sinister part to be played by the Beast's horns in the ruin of the Empire. Moreover, it is not quite so parenthetical as it seems. For in point of fact the identification of the Messiah's foes in the great battle of Harmagedon with the foes of the Empire is illuminating for John's readers. What he tells them in effect is that mankind, in accepting and worshipping the Beast (cf. xiii. 1–4 and xvii. 8*b*), is falling into a gross delusion, for which the appropriate punishment is death at the hands of the Beast himself, and his allies ; for it is the Messiah's

own antithesis whom they worship. Did they but know it, had they but sufficient moral perception to discover it, men must recognize their own foes in the Messiah's foes. John mentions the last battle only in passing, however. The victory
14 won by **the Lamb** and by **the elect, the chosen, the faithful who are with him** (that is, the 'conquerors,' the martyrs of the great Distress : cf. ii. 26) is described as a separate theme in xix. 17 ff. There we are shown more vividly how the **Beast** and his **ten kings** are taught that their opponent is **Lord of lords, and King of kings.** In chap. xvii. John is preoccupied with the fate of the great City ; he shows how that Satanic being who personifies everything that is loathsome in the ungodly powers prevalent in this world, who draws to himself and directs fierce, vengeful creatures from the east to do his will, who is the final enemy on earth of the Messiah, who is stupidly, fatally accepted and deified by the dwellers of earth—how *this* being, the Beast, is to be God's instrument of Judgment on the Harlot.

xvii. 15–18 : THE FALL OF THE EMPIRE

15 He told me, ' *The waters* you saw, on which the harlot is seated,
16 are peoples and hosts, nations and tongues. As for the ten horns you have seen, they and the Beast will hate the harlot, lay her waste, and strip her naked, devouring her flesh and
17 burning her with fire, for God has put it into their hearts to execute his purpose, by having one mind and by conferring their royal power upon the Beast, until the words of God are fulfilled. As for the woman you have seen, she is
18 the great City which reigns over *the kings of the earth.*'

Now at last we are shown why John has spent so large a proportion of this chapter, explicitly devoted as it is to the question of the Empire's ruin, in defining the symbol of the Beast. He shows that the Beast, whom all the dwellers on earth laud and worship on his supernatural advent (chap. xiii.),

is destined to turn and rend his worshippers. John's elucida-
tion of the Beast's character is designed to explain this curious
belief. When he depicts a resurrected Nero, and an alliance of
Parthian leaders almost dæmonic in their close association
with the Beast, the notion at once becomes credible and
natural for John's readers.

First, there is the question of the extent of the ruin to be
wrought by the Beast. John predicts that it is not to be
confined to the capital city of the world, Rome. For he shows
carefully that the Roman régime has been imposed on all
nations ; the dwellers on earth have drunk the strong wine of
Rome's vice : they share her life, they accept her institutions,
and therefore they are included in the fate of the great City.
It is worth pausing to consider the metaphorical language in
which John expresses this idea. The Harlot is **seated on many** 15
waters, he says ; this is an allusion to Jeremiah's description
of Babylon (see Jer. li. 13), which is translated by Dr. Moffatt,
' upon many a stream.' What seems to be more or less literal
in Jeremiah is taken over by John with a purely figurative
meaning. The ' many waters ' now symbolize the whole of
Mediterranean civilization. On this civilization the Empire
is seated. But this metaphor does not indicate an enforced
dominion, the tyranny of a world power ruthlessly forcing its
institutions on alien peoples. Compare the Harlot's ' seat ' on
the Beast (verse 3) or on the Beast's seven heads (i.e. his
universal power, verse 9), with her ' seat ' on the **many waters.**
The metaphor is the same : in both cases it means union, collaboration, or foundation—not dominion. The point is that
John's symbol of the **harlot** is not intended to mean Rome as a
single city which has a far-flung Empire ; it is intended to
mean Roman civilization, which embraces all **peoples and hosts,**
nations and tongues. To John, Pergamum is just as much
Rome as Rome itself: in Pergamum ' Satan dwells,' ' Satan sits
enthroned ' (see ii. 13). The wide walls of Rome included the
seven cities of Asia minor—they included all ' the cities of the
nations.' In one sense, of course, **the great City** exercises a
sovereign power over all her citizens, from the humblest slave
to **the kings of the earth.** It is the power of the community

over the individual ; or (more in accordance with John's point of view) the power of unhallowed civilization over those who have not embraced the Christian faith, who cannot escape into the ' desert ' of a nobler life (see above on verse 3). ' Babylon ' reigns over the kings of the earth because they have committed vice with her (cf. xviii. 9). It is not a reign enforced by the Roman legions that John has in mind, but a self-imposed slavery, the fruit of indulgence in voluntary abandonment to the harlot's vicious life. It is obviously a matter of some importance to establish the harlot's identity, for it affects our understanding of the eschatological picture which John draws in verses 16 and 17. He is there speaking not of the localized sacking and destruction of a capital city, but the ravaging of all the civilized world—the Empire is punished for her crimes and immorality.

A small difficulty which needs comment arises in the expression The waters you saw, on which the harlot is seated. John has not told us that he saw these figurative waters in his vision. Is not this an instance of intolerable literary carelessness ? The inconsistency arises directly out of the apocalyptic convention. When John ' sees ' a vision, he sees a truth, he arrives at an inspired conviction ; and this he clothes in the traditional language of visions, as apocalyptists were accustomed to do. This is not to say that his mental concepts were originally cast in the form of abstractions, which he mechanically transformed into symbolical pictures ; nor is it to deny that John's trances were essentially visionary in character. It is clear, however, that whatever the original character of his visions, John arranged and commented on his recollections of them, and that in recording them he brought out their significance in familiar apocalyptic terms. Now, what he actually saw in his vision of the Empire and Antichrist, if it is translated into our own more abstract language, was a civilization stretching to the four corners of the world, and allied to a Satanic Imperial Power, universal in reach. This is the heart of his vision ; this is what he saw. So when the angel says, ' The waters you saw,' what he means is that, in seeing the symbol of the Empire, John must understand that it stood for something universal, embracing **nations and hosts, peoples and tongues.** Fundamentally the words ' you saw ' are true. John did see, or apprehend, the truth of which the ' many waters ' form the symbol.

The doom of the great Harlot is described in terms reminiscent of Ezekiel's description of Jerusalem's fate (Ezek. xvi. 35 ff.). Jerusalem has been unfaithful to her God, and therefore she is to suffer the exposure, shame and death which the Law decreed for prostitutes. God will collect her lovers (those whose idols she has worshipped), armies will come upon her, to **lay her waste,** stripping her of all her splendour, leaving 16 her **naked,** cutting her to pieces with swords, and stoning her (thus **devouring her flesh**), and **burning** her houses **with fire.** It is probably these **words of God** which John expects to be 17 **fulfilled** in the Empire's destruction at the hand of the **Beast,** with his Parthian allies, **the ten horns.** For the picture is of the Idol crushing the idolators, the ' lover,' with whom mankind has been unfaithful to her Creator, turning to rend the harlot. Antichrist's three and half years' dominion over the world began with the slavish admiration of mankind, their seduction to worship evil and to participate in Satan's rancorous hatred of God and His servants (chap. xiii.). It closes with apt retribution : the Neronic Antichrist and his confederates **hate the harlot** and destroy her.[1]

Antony may not have been ' but a limb of Cæsar,' but this is precisely what John shows the kings from the east to be. The **royal power** they confer on the Beast, they gain through their association with him (verse 12). They are spiritually indivisible, joined to each other and joined to the Beast, in

---

[1] Dr. A. E. J. Rawlinson has made the interesting suggestion that in his reference to the final destruction of Rome by fire, John had in mind Nero's attempt to divert the blame for the conflagration in his reign from himself to the Christian Church : ' The fire in Nero's reign destroyed Rome only partially, and Christians were made chargeable with the crime. The returning Nero will complete his unfinished work, the tyrant city shall be consumed, and the kings of the earth, the merchants and the sea-folk shall wail as they witness " the smoke of her burning " ' (*Church Quarterly Review*, vol. xcii., no. clxxxiii., p. 146). The suggestion has the same value if, as we have argued, John's harlot is all the cities of the world.

a Satanic union comparable to the heavenly union of their opponents on the Day of God's wrath, ' the Lamb and the elect, the chosen, the faithful who are with him ' (verse 14). This fusion of the savage powers of the east with Antichrist, and the extraordinary unanimity of their hostility against the Empire, John shows to be inspired by God. When he says, **for God has put it into their hearts to execute his purpose,** John is echoing the thought of many prophets. Invading armies (little do they know it!) are the scourge of God ; but they themselves are already destined to destruction, as John has already said (cf. Jer. xxv. 12 ff.). Verses 17–18 constitute

18 John's reply to the question : ' How can **the great City,** the Empire which is so strong, so alluring, so irresistible to the dwellers on earth, be destroyed by the Satanic Power whom she worships ? ' This the prophets have foretold. But how is it to come to pass ? John briefly describes what he believes is the reality of the political situation ; and, having described the *manner* in which the doom of the great Harlot is to be encompassed, he proceeds in the next chapter to bring out the horror of her fate, its suddenness, its cause, and its finality.

xviii. 1–3 : The Doom-song on Babylon

1 After that I saw another angel descend from heaven, great in
2 might ; his radiance lit up the earth, and with a strong voice he shouted aloud,

> ' *Fallen, fallen is Babylon the great!*—
> *a haunt of demons* now,
> the den of all foul spirits,
> a cage for every foul and loathsome bird :
3 for *all nations have drunk the wine* of the passion of her
> vice,
> *the kings of earth have committed vice with her,*
> and by the wealth of her wantonness earth's traders have
> grown rich.'

The doom-song which celebrates the destined fall of Babylon displays John's powers of allusive composition at their best. The prophet has drawn into his service so many phrases and figures from the taunt-songs and dirges in Isaiah, Ezekiel, and Jeremiah that chap. xviii. has been described as a mosaic of quotation and allusion. Its very form is suggested by the exultant odes of the prophets. For that reason we cannot grasp anything like the full power of John's words unless we are familiar with the passages to which he alludes. The song in REVELATION is a resounding echo of the passionate faith and stormy exulting in the doom-songs of the great prophets. Let us read what Isaiah has written about Babylon ; and not Babylon alone, but all the wolfish nations, immersed in luxury and pride, who rejoiced at the misfortunes of Israel. We shall find that it is not merely a number of fortuitous phrases that John derives from Isaiah's songs ; it is the very spirit in which they were written. Let us read how Jeremiah and Ezekiel denounce the great cities of the world ; we shall find that John has remembered what they wrote, and that his words are charged with the emotion evoked by conscious recollection. What we must understand is that chap. xviii. is at once a ' new song ' in the sense that it has passed through the fire of the prophet's imagination, and also a summary of all prophetic oracles on the doom of unrighteous peoples. It is this second fact that is seldom appreciated as it should be. If we wish to savour the full effect of John's allusions in this chapter, we must be aware of the tacit belief about inspiration which underlies it. The Hebrew prophets announced that the end of the world, or of the existing world order, would follow the fall of Babylon ; and incidentally that the fall of the greatest Power would be preceded by or accompanied with the fall of every pagan nation. Babylon fell, the Persian Empire and the Greek fell ; the cities and nations of Isaiah's day experienced many of the woes predicted for them. But the end of the world did not come as the prophets had announced. Therefore, to John's mind, there could be but one conclusion : materially, the oracles of doom uttered by the prophets were still valid for the present and the future.

Babylon still stood, the type of earthly magnificence and vice. And when this Babylon did fall, then the rule of Satan would be at an end, and the rule of God complete. Babylon naturally bulked largest in the oracles of Isaiah, Jeremiah, and Ezekiel. But they did not forget to proclaim the doom of other nations and cities. Tyre, for example, is treated by all three much as Babylon is treated. And one section of John's dirge (verses 11–19) is inspired directly by Ezekiel's prediction of Tyre's downfall. As we inferred from the previous description of Babylon (the ' great City whose mystical name is Sodom and Egypt '), this symbol is designed to represent not only one city but all cities. When John read such passages as Ezek. xxvii., the song heralding the imminent fall of Tyre, he discerned a prophecy which bore upon his own world, the world of the Roman order. Tyre is less a city than a symbol : as John sees it, she stands for the complex sea traffic of the Empire. She is a part of the age-long Babylon, and therefore what Ezekiel wrote about her doom could appropriately mingle with what Isaiah and Jeremiah said about the doom of Babylon. In short, the eschatological picture in these prophets is of an earth utterly desolated. Nation after nation is named for destruction. And the instruments of destruction are also named : a terrible horde of invaders from a far-off land will deal the death-blow to Babylon : the king of Babylon himself is designated as the destroyer of some of the other nations. It is clear that such prophecies powerfully supported John's expectation of what was to befall the Empire, as he describes it in chap. xviii. The king of Babylon and his Parthian allies are to destroy Babylon—the whole Empire.

In verses 1–3 the theme of the doom-song is stated. An
1 **angel** resembling the impressive harbinger of chap. x., who brought tidings of the great Distress and its triumphant outcome for the Christian witnesses, shouts out the fate of Rome. He is magnificent in his robe of **radiance** (we might recollect Ezek. xliii. 2, where it is the radiance of God which lights up the earth) ; his glory is suited to his message. He is an angel **great in might,** and it is with a **strong voice** that he **shouts aloud** his message : in other words, he is a herald whom none

may ignore, and he proclaims an event which is stupefying in its magnitude : ' **Fallen, fallen is Babylon the great !** ' Such, 2 indeed, had been the cry of Isaiah (Isa. xxi. 9) to his down-trodden countrymen ; he too had cried, ' Babylon is fallen, fallen.' But had Babylon fallen ? Vanity Fair stood then, it stood as John was writing, and both Isaiah and John spoke as they did because they knew that God had written the decree of doom on Babylon. The span of God's almighty hand stretched from the present to the future ; the course of events was fixed ; Babylon *had* fallen. It is this vivid, unquestioning certainty that is responsible for a certain temporal inconsis-tency in chap. xviii. It comes as appropriately to him to say, ' Babylon is fallen,' as to say, ' She shall be burnt with fire,' or that the seafaring folk, her mourners, ' threw dust on their heads and cried as they wept and wailed :

' " Woe and alas, thou great city ! " '

A medley of tenses, present, future, perfect, preterite, testify to John's imaginative journeys from the present into a visionary future and back again.

At first we are taken far into the dark future. Whereas later in the song John describes the woe of the kings and merchants and seamen as they watch the smoke of burning cities, he now paints a scene of established ruin. Temple and tower have fallen ; the homes of men have crumbled in decay, and the cities formerly teeming with proud life are now **a haunt of demons** and **a cage for every foul and loathsome bird.** Several prophets depicted a ruined Babylon, haunted by pelicans, bitterns, owls, ravens, vampires, and ostriches, and by wild beasts and reptiles ; all of them creatures sym-bolizing defilement ; Isaiah peopled it also with **demons.** John's words are, in fact, an echo of Isa. xxxiv. 11-17, the climax of a terrible oracle wherein a universal massacre of the nations is predicted ; they shall fall by the sword of an invader, sent by God ; their blood shall drench the mountains and the whole country ; the very land shall be turned to pitch burning night and day, age after age, unquenchable. And none shall be left, of all the host of nations :

'Demons haunt the spot,
for the nobles now are gone ;
there no kingdom is proclaimed,
the princes are no more ! '

This is the scene of desolation to which John alludes.

John builds up his subject much as the composer of a symphony will construct the variations on a theme. The theme of this particular movement in the symphony of REVELATION has already been briefly anticipated. ' Fallen, fallen is Babylon the great ' was the cry of one of the seven angels in chap. xiv. (cf. xvi. 17–19). And the rest of the theme, the seduction of the nations and their rulers, this too we hear with ears already prepared : we remember particularly the first sounding of these notes in chap. xvii. Now the theme is stated fully and deliberately. Babylon is to fall—because 3 her immoral life now embraces all mankind. The **vice** of Roman institutions and manners has made the whole world drunk, besotted ; the **nations** are stricken with an insatiable craving for evil. The rulers of men, **the kings of the earth,** have identified themselves completely with everything that the Empire stands for. They are eager servants of her vicious ways. **Earth's traders** are now one with the Empire in guilt. Socially, politically, commercially, the whole earth stands condemned ; for the whole earth has become one in ungodly union with the great City. The universality of verse 3 is to be noted. It is **all nations,** the kings and traders of the whole **earth,** whom John names. In his mind there is the notion that God will not act until all men are committed one way or another. In chap. xi. he showed how the Gospel was to be preached to all nations, and he showed the response. Now he declares that as Babylon the great is ripe, fully ripe in sin, she shall at once be destroyed. Her seduction has reached its farthermost limits.

xviii. 4–8 : ' COME OUT OF HER, O MY PEOPLE '

And I heard another voice from heaven crying,	4
' *Come out of her, O my people,*	
that you share not her sins,	
that you partake not of her plagues :	
for *high as heaven* her sins are *heaped,*	5
and God calls her misdeeds to reckoning.	
Render to her what she rendered to others,	6
aye, double the doom *for all she has done ;*	
mix her the draught double	
in the cup she mixed for others.	
As she gloried and played the wanton,	7
so give her like measure of torture and tears.	
Since *in her heart she vaunts, " A queen I sit,*	
no widow I, tears I shall never know,"	
so shall her plagues *fall in a single day,*	8
pestilence, tears, and famine :	
she shall be burnt with fire—	
for *strong is God the Lord her judge.*	

> ' Come out of her, my people,
> save your lives, every man of you,
> from the Eternal's burning wrath.'
>
> (Jer. li. 45.)

This is the burden of the refrain in Jeremiah's great oracles on Babylon (cf. Jer. l. 8, li. 6). A savage invader comes to execute God's judgment on Babylon, whose ' doom rises up to heaven.' The faithful are warned to flee from the scene of impending carnage. ' Share not her doom,' Jeremiah implores them (li. 6) ; it is significant that John adds to this counsel that Christians must **share not her sins**. Perhaps there is some 4 recollection in his mind of Isaiah's similar warning (Isa. xlviii. 20 and lii. 11). It is not only from an imminent peril that the faithful must flee, but also from the ' things unclean ' of Babylon. St. Paul quotes this very passage (Isa. lii. 11) as he warns the Corinthians to shun the contamination of idols

(2 Cor. vi. 17). It is probable that John's words, ' **Come out of her, O my people,**' bear a double meaning, at once figurative and literal. For as we have shown in chap. xii., the Christian ' flight to the desert,' beginning with the Ascension of Christ and continuing in spite of Satanic wiles and persecution, can mean only a spiritual withdrawal from Vanity Fair. And John's book is written for the exhortation of Christians before they are faced with the severer ordeals of the last days. In these words the prophet might well be understood to reinforce his warning to such men as the Laodiceans, who obviously had not yet seen the need for leaving Vanity Fair. Such is the force of the warning, ' **that you share not her sins.**' At the same time, there is also the practical counsel to the survivors of the great Distress that, since Babylon is to pay the awful penalty for her sins, when the Parthians approach with Antichrist at their head, Christians must flee to a place of safety. It is an echo of the warnings in the synoptic Gospels. There, Jerusalem is the city of doom, whose fall heralds the end of the world. It is from Jerusalem and Judæa that the saints must flee when they perceive the signs of the End—the portents in the heavens, the wars and rumours of wars, the approach of armies, the activity of Antichrist in desecrating the temple. In REVELATION, the doomed City is all cities. All are to be ravaged by the invader, all are to be destroyed by earthquake. Christians must await the issue of the messianic battle (xix. 11–21) far away from the turbulence which accompanies the breakdown of all civilization. So John warns his charges in the seven churches of Asia Minor ; he warns all Christians in all churches, that they must hold themselves aloof ; they must shun the great City for two reasons :

> that you share not her sins,
> that you partake not of her plagues.

The heavenly **voice** sounding in the prophet's ears clinches this appeal and warning by reminding Christians that the downfall of the Empire is as certain as her wickedness is blatant. **High as heaven her sins are heaped** : the limit has been reached ;

the time for her destruction is ripe. God, who has for so long stayed His hand, is now about to act: at last He **calls her misdeeds to reckoning.**

From this appeal to Christians the heavenly **voice** (the voice of prophetic inspiration) turns to an impassioned prayer to God : ' **Render to her what she rendered to others. . . .** ' This is 6 a quotation of Jer. l. 29, where the prophet prays that an invasion of savage archers may requite Babylon to the full for her cruelty and insolence. She shall not go unpunished :

> ' Yes, Babylon shall fall, O slain of Israel,
> as slain men have fallen everywhere for Babylon.'
> (Jer. li. 49.)

The last iniquity of Babylon, that which precipitates her punishment, is her cruelty towards the people of God. And what held good in Jeremiah's thought holds good in John's, for it is the Empire's part in the great Distress (see xi. 8 ff.) which brings on her the full flood of God's anger.

On a superficial view, there seems to be no logical sequence in verses 4-8, with the appeal in verse 4, the prayer in verses 6-7, and finally the prophecy in verses 7-8. But we must consider carefully the essential purpose of the song in its setting in REVELATION. Fundamentally, chap. xviii. is designed to establish and confirm the loyalty of Christians ; to convince them that the self-denying and heroic is the sensible course—that severance from the affairs of the Empire is severance from a society whose wickedness will be demonstrated in her complete ruin. The whole point of describing a ruined Babylon lies in those simple words, ' **Come out of her, O my people.** ' The song in its entirety is balanced on that appeal and warning. And the picture of swift destruction, so vast, so dreadful that in contemplating it John's rapture seems to be tempered by a certain awe, almost regret—this picture has as its supreme purpose the enforcing of the urgent call to Christians. The importance of realizing this fact need not be laboured. It will be obvious that when the **voice from heaven** proceeds from a warning of Christians to a prayer for vengeance on Babylon, and a prediction of Babylon's approaching doom, there is no lack of logical connexion. It would not be fair to say that the prayer and prediction of verses 6–8 provide a *motive* for Christians' dissociation from the great City : the motive lay in perception of what was true, in loyalty to the Name of Christ. But John knew, as we see in the seven letters, that not all Christians felt the urgency of things as he did himself. John was far from believing that men could be terrified into faith and salvation : his predestinarian views preclude such a notion. But he did believe that the faithful themselves must be stirred into immediate and rigorous action. Their eyes must be opened to the exclusive claims of the Faith. And very clearly he hopes to achieve this end by asserting the hopeless corruption of Babylon, and (what in his mind followed inevitably from her corruption) her destined fall, with all the agonies of her dying convulsions.

' Ye have heard that it was said, An eye for an eye . . .' But the heavenly voice cries out for two eyes for every eye :

> ' **Mix her the draught double
> in the cup she mixed for others.** '

If John were accused of endorsing un-Christian sentiments in recording such words, if he were told that the persecuted Christian utterly failed when he surrounded the vengeful desires of his heart with the sanctity of heavenly approval, he might have urged that he foresaw a time when men delighted in malice for its own sake, worshipping power and reviling what was true and holy. In fact, John's belief was that when Antichrist returned, men would go about ' worshipping the dragon for having given authority to the Beast, and worshipping the Beast with the cry :

> Who is like the Beast ?
> Who can fight with him ? '

It is a picture of a society so hopelessly depraved that evil is acclaimed as good. Whatever its psychological origin, the exclamation in verse 6 is not the prayer of a Christian that his enemies may be persecuted, but the interpretation made by a

Christian of the heavenly response to cruelty, and the wickedness of irreclaimable evil-doers. John is here formulating not the victim's cry against the persecutor, but something like a judicial pronouncement on the sins of civilization, carried to their farthest limits; and the pronouncement is made by a **voice from heaven.**

The misery which is to fall on Babylon is to be measured by her immoral life and her heedless pride. As Isaiah said of the Babylon of his day, she thinks in her heart ' I am supreme ' (Isa. xlvii. 8) : it is this passage that John quotes, as he reveals the essential sin of the great City : she **vaunts** herself **a queen.** 7 She rejoices in her supremacy and enduring power. In other words, she denies her Creator. She claims to be self-sufficient, a law unto herself ; she is confident that no punishment can reach her. This towering pride puts her out of the reach of correction.

> **So shall her plagues fall in a single day,** 8
> **pestilence, tears and famine.**

Blind as she now is in her false security, she shall learn that One is stronger than she :

> **For strong is God the Lord her judge.**

In His hands lies the disposal of the **seven last plagues ;** at His direction the Parthians come from afar to burn the cities of earth **with fire.** And in the final cataclysm there will be no time for repentance. The wrath of God descends on earth **in a single day.**

xviii. 9–20 : Lament of the Kings, Merchants and Seafarers

And the kings of earth who committed vice **and wantoned** *with her* 9
shall weep and wail **over her, as they watch the smoke of her burning ; far off, for fear of her torture, shall they** 10 **stand, crying,**

> " Woe and alas, thou *great* city !
> *thou strong city of Babylon !*
> In one brief hour thy doom has come."

11 And the *traders* of earth shall *weep and wail* over her ; for now
12   there is none to buy their freights, freights of gold, silver,
    jewels, pearls, fine linen, purples, silk, scarlet stuff, all sorts
    of citron wood and ivory wares, all articles of costly wood,
13   of bronze, of iron and of marble, with cinnamon, balsam,
    spices, myrrh, frankincense, wines, olive-oil, fine flour and
    wheat, with cattle, sheep, horses, carriages, slaves, and *the*
15   *souls of men.** The *traders* in these wares, who made
    rich profits from her, shall stand far off for fear of her
    torture, *weeping and wailing :*

16   " Woe and alas, for the great city,
          robed in linen, in purple and scarlet,
          her ornaments of gold, of jewels and of pearl!
17   And all this splendour laid waste in a single hour !"

   And all *shipmasters* and seafaring folk, *sailors and all whose*
18   business lies *upon the sea, stood* far off as they watched the
    smoke of her burning, crying, *"What* city *was like* the great
19   City ?" *They threw dust on their heads and cried, as they*
    wept and wailed,

       " Woe and alas for the great City,
          where *all shipmen made rich profit by* her *treasures !*
          Gone, gone in a single hour ! "
20   *O heaven, rejoice* over her !
          Saints, apostles, prophets, rejoice !
          For God *has avenged* you on her now.'

    * Ver. 14 has been misplaced from its original position in ver. 23.

9   The stroke of Antichrist and his Parthian hosts has fallen
on the civilized world. The cities of the nations are aflame ;
their inhabitants have fled, all who have escaped the sword ;
but famine seizes them, famine and pestilence. Many ghastly
plagues have already fallen on the earth ; and now the blood
which God poured into the rivers and the sea runs free with the
blood of slaughtered men. Sores and ulcers have tormented

them, so that they writhed in anguish, cursing God. But
now their former miseries have swelled a hundredfold, for
the invading hordes of Antichrist sweep through the Empire,
invincible and ruthless. The End is at hand ; the cities are
in flames. Where are now the proud magnates of the Empire,
the rulers and the rich ? Fools, in their boasted strength !
They are now puny, helpless creatures, gazing horror-struck
on the ruins of their great City. They have fled. But **far off** 10–
for fear of her torture ... they stand, crying : 19

> **Woe and alas, thou great city !**
> **thou strong city of Babylon !**

Here are all **the kings of the earth** (all save those newly crowned
monarchs from the east), all **traders of earth, all shipmasters
and seafaring folk** : not one of all those multitudes engaged in
the world-wide traffic of the Empire but bewails her destruction. There is much more than a lament for the fall of one
capital city :

> ' Who list the Romane greatnes forth to figure
>   Him needeth not to seek for usage right
> Of line, or lead or rule or squaire, to measure
>   Her length, her breadth, her deepnes or her hight ;
> But him behooves to view in compasse round .
>   All that the Ocean graspes in his long armes ;
> Be it where the yerely starre doth scortch the ground,
>   Or where cold *Boreas* blowes his bitter stormes.
> *Rome* was th' whole world, and al the world was Rome.'

Rome was the whole world ; in John's vision, the whole
civilized world lies in ruins. The Empire's political system,
her commerce, her intricate communications, all have been
shattered. The kings lament, for there is nothing now for
them to rule. The merchants lament, for there is nothing for
them to sell, and no one to buy. The seafarers lament, for
their livelihood, their **rich profit,** is at an end. The Dark Ages
contracted to **a single day** have fallen on the Roman world.
The smoke from the funeral pyres of the world's cities clouds
the sky with its last gloom.

There is little that we need add to what John has said. His
words tell their own story. It is hardly necessary to linger

over the details of this lament; over the grouped list of commodities which represents the vast and fascinating wealth of the Empire; or over the refrain, which sounds like the sombre tolling of a bell:

> In one brief hour thy doom has come. . . .
> And all this splendour laid waste in a single hour! . . .
> Gone, gone in a single hour! . . .

John's threefold picture of the lamenting made by the strong and rich owes much to Ezekiel's prophecies over Tyre (Ezek. xxvii.): but it has a peculiar quality of its own. The desolation in men's souls speaks more eloquently than any objective description of the desolation on earth. Their grief and terror at the loss of power and luxury and rich profits is a more vivid argument for the Christian than the sober warning in the letters: ' I counsel you to buy from me gold refined in the fire, that you may be rich, white raiment to clothe you and prevent the shame of your nakedness from being seen, and salve to rub on your eyes, that you may see ' (iii. 18).

After he has finished his description of the lament made by the powerful and rich over the great City, John bursts out into a great cry of gladness. He remembers Jeremiah's words:

> ' Then heaven and earth and all their host shall exult over Babylon.'
> (Jer. li. 48.)

Whereas the kings, merchants and shipmen wailed and lamented, the saints, apostles, and prophets may now rejoice; for the fall of the earthly City makes way for the rise of the heavenly City. The community of the faithful now comes into its own. The solemnity and awe with which John contemplated the ruined Babylon is cast aside, in an access of irrepressible jubilation, which anticipates the heavenly rejoicing in chap. xix.

xviii. 21–24 : BABYLON IS HURLED DOWN : DESOLATION AND
SILENCE

Then a strong angel lifted *a boulder* like a huge millstone *and* 21
flung it into the sea, *crying,*
   ' So shall *the great* city, *Babylon,* be hurled down, hurtling,
    and never be seen any more :
   and the sound of harpists, *minstrels,* flute-players, and 22
      trumpeters
    shall never be heard in thee more :
   and craftsmen of any craft
    shall never be found in thee more :
   and the sound of the millstone
    shall never be heard in thee more :
   and the light of a lamp   23
    shall never be seen in thee more :
   and the voice of the bridegroom and bride
    shall never be heard in thee more.
   Vanished the ripe fruit of thy soul's desire!   14
   Perished thy luxury and splendour!—
    never again to be seen.
   For *the magnates of earth* were thy *traders ;*   23
   all nations were seduced *by thy magic spells.*
   And in her was found the blood of prophets and saints,   24
   of all who were slain upon earth.'

      ' O vaine world's glorie, and unstedfast state
      Of all that lives, on face of sinful earth.'
             (SPENSER : *Ruines of Time.*)

    Babylon's doom and desolation are proclaimed once again,
in the symbolic action and cry of another **strong angel.** The 21
picture is suggested by a passage in Jer. li. 63, where the
prophet, having given instructions to the chief chamberlain,
Seraiah, to read out in Babylon his predictions of woe and
ruin, gives instructions that his book is to be tied to a stone,
and cast into the Euphrates, as a sign that the city will be
utterly cast down. This passage has fallen into John's mind

like a seed ; it has lain there and germinated, to grow into a new, astonishing plant. The strong angel in John's vision we must visualize to resemble the mighty being in verse i, whose ' radiance lit up the earth,' or like that strong angel in chap. x., ' clad in a cloud, with a rainbow over his head, his face like the sun, his limbs like columns of fire. . . .' John does not need to say more of this angel than that he is **strong** (see notes, pp. 96, 168) ; for his appearance is suggested by that of his fellows. The angel's gesture is bold and simple. Deliberately he stoops, lifts a **boulder**—and how huge is this **huge millstone** of a boulder ! Then, poised like some Titanic athlete, he hurls the boulder into the sea. So sudden, so swift, so spectacular shall be the ruin of Babylon at the hand of God. It is a picture of quintessential simplicity, to equal that of the riders in chap. vi. or the reaper-angel in chap. xiv.

The angel's cry, like his action, is suggested by Jeremiah : ' I will banish from them the sound of mirth and gladness, the voice of the bridegroom and the bride, the sound of millstones and the light of a lamp '—so the Eternal told Jerusalem and the cities of Judah. The burden of these words recurs several times in Jeremiah's prophecies on the fate of his own people (vii. 34, xvi. 9, xxv. 10). It is significant, perhaps, for the purpose of a full understanding of what is implied in REVELATION, that finally ' the sound of mirth and gladness shall again be heard, the voice of bridegroom and bride,' in the streets of Jerusalem—the new Jerusalem under the steadfast rule of a Davidic king (Jer. xxxiii. 10-11). When Jeremiah prophesies about the earthly city of Jerusalem, which must suffer for the evil it has done, John feels free to discern in his words an oracular demonstration of the doom of Babylon—Vanity Fair. This city is accursed. Its ruins shall never be peopled again. But there shall arise on earth, and stand secure for many years, a community of Christian saints ; and these men, amongst whom the martyrs rule in highest honour, replace the community whose doom John now celebrates.

The passion of the earlier prophet has been transmuted to a more solemn mood. John lingers over every sign of desolation ;

there is awe in his eyes, as he contemplates all the activity of
the great City, the gaiety stirred by her hosts of musicians,
harpists, minstrels, flute-players, and trumpeters, the industry 22
of her **craftsmen,** fashioning the ornaments of her ease ; the
ceaseless turning of innumerable **millstones** ; the life of her
citizens, as they light the lamp in their homes, after their day's 23
toil ; the unending succession of marriages, with their promise
of new generations, and an enduring civilization. A secure,
preoccupied world ! Who but a prophet could read the letters
of its ruin ? All this multitudinous life is to be silenced. The
angel's great **boulder** hurtles into the sea. The sea leaps to the
clouds, and roars in tumult as the boulder is engulfed. But
soon silence, the deepest silence prevails. This is the silence
which spreads over the earth after the great City falls. All life
is suddenly, catastrophically stilled. The cities of the nations
become graveyards, where the whispering ghosts of sights and
sounds and doings serve only to deepen the grim desolation.
From Jeremiah John took a list of things nevermore to be
heard, or **found** or **seen** ; he adds a refrain, and in this way makes
us pause and become aware of the stillness in a ruined world.

John epitomizes this universal ruin in the misplaced verse
14 ; everything which is alluring and impressive, every
material possession which is held precious, is destined to
destruction. It is to be observed that in this verse John again
described the completeness of the Empire's ruin in terms of its
cause. The ruling feature of her life is a doting on the ' ripe 14
fruit ' of material prizes. **Luxury and splendour** are what she
holds most precious, and they are as evanescent as a summer's
day. John's picture of their perishing is inspired by the
thought of God's direct, catastrophic intervention in the world's
affairs. But even though the eschatological picture contains
misleading elements, it is none the less valuable. For not
many Christians can be said to have believed in their hearts,
without any reservation, that there is only one pearl of great
price, and that the glory of kingdoms, the pride of rank, the
privileges of wealth, the comfort and security of possessions
are ' shadows, not substantial things.' It is indeed a lesson
which hardly depends on any impulse which need be called

religious. The philosopher as much as the saint will observe
it ; the true philosopher will even act on it, as will the
Christian who values consistency. Habington read this lesson
in the stars :

> ' Thus those Celestiall fires,
>   Though seeming mute,
> The fallacie of our desires
>   And all the pride of life confute,

> ' For they have watched since first
>   The world had birth :
> And found sinne in itself accursed,
>   And nothing permanent on earth.'

For Habington and for us, this is the truth which Time has
revealed slowly, but more and more certainly with each succeeding age. John's REVELATION is a sort of cosmic drama in
which the ages are foreshortened, and the experience of countless centuries epitomized in the single day, the brief hour, of
Babylon's downfall.

Babylon has perished because the magnates of earth were
her traders : that is, her life was fashioned by men without
scruple or principle ; without any thought save for luxury
and splendour, and the exercise of a power which in the last
resort is shown to be Satanic in character. She has perished,
because like Babylon of old, she wielded her power to do evil ;
her intolerable vice and cruelty infected all nations with an
incurable plague. She has perished because it could be said
of her, ' Babylon, that killeth the prophets.' The climax of her
evil was reached in her treatment of Christians. But here
John looks into the future, towards the great Distress, in
which the Christian witnesses are to fall. He is reading in the
tendencies of his times the omens of a desperate attack on the
faithful, everywhere throughout the Empire ; not localized in
Rome, as it had been in Nero's day. It is this attack, still in
the future, which evokes the prophetic words : And in her was
found the blood of prophets and saints, of all who were slain
upon earth. It is this attack which calls down avenging fire
from heaven.

xix. 1–8 : Prothalamion

After that I heard what was like the shout of a great host in 1
    heaven, crying,
      '*Hallelujah!* salvation and glory and power are our God's !
      True and just are his sentences of doom ; 2
        he has doomed the great Harlot who destroyed earth
          with her vice,
      he has avenged on her the blood of his *servants.*'
    Again they repeated, 3
      '*Hallelujah! And the smoke of her goes up for ever and*
        ever ! '

Then the four and twenty Presbyters and the four living 4
    Creatures fell down and worshipped God who is *seated on*
    the throne, crying, ' So be it, *hallelujah ! '* And a voice 5
    came from the throne,
      '*Extol* our God, *all ye his servants,*
      ye who reverence him, low and high ! '

Then I heard a cry *like the shout of a* great *host* and the *sound of* 6
    many waves and the roar of heavy thunder—
    ' *Hallelujah!* now the Lord our *God almighty reigns!*
    Let us rejoice and triumph, 7
    let us give him the glory !
    For now comes the marriage of the Lamb,
    his bride has arrayed herself.
    Yea, she is allowed to put on fine linen, dazzling white ' 8
    (the white linen is the righteous conduct of the saints).

Shadow yields to light ; above the smoke clouds from the
ruined Babylon, a scene of ineffable brightness opens out.
The silence of the ruined city gives way to the shout and
thunder of eager rejoicing ; the ' Woe and alas ' of her
mourners is answered by the fourfold ' **Hallelujah !** ' of the 1
heavenly host. In such contrasts Revelation is prolific.

This new glimpse of the celestial courts should be studied
in relation to preceding descriptions. We hear the heavenly
choruses now for the last time, and the burden of their

rejoicing brings a long story to its conclusion. Let us briefly recollect what we have already learnt from John's visions of heaven. Chap. iv. conveys the remote majesty of the Creator in a heaven from which man, still unredeemed, is excluded. Chap. v. celebrates the conquest won by the Lamb, who made His servants ' kings and priests,' and unsealed the last pages of history. Through His death and Resurrection a new creation is assured : He has laid the foundation stones, as it were, of the blessed community of the new Jerusalem, which is to replace the accursed city of Babylon. And the Creator and Christ, ' the origin of God's creation,' are now hymned together. The next four scenes in heaven show the outcome of Christ's victory. In chap. vii. we are shown that martyrdom is a sure gate to salvation : the witnesses who fell in the great Distress appear clad in white robes and crying, ' Saved by our God who is seated on the throne, and by the Lamb ! ' In chap. xiv. the same host appears, this time numbered : we see that they are the full one hundred and forty-four thousand who were sealed. Their number is complete, and the cry of the martyrs beneath the altar (vi. 10) can now be answered by action from the heavenly Sion. In chap. xi. we were told that after the great Distress, and the miraculous resuscitation of the witnesses, the ' time has come for destroying the destroyer of the earth,' and in chap. xv. the connexion of the martyrs with the destruction of Babylon is more explicitly brought out. Hitherto the descriptions of heaven have all depicted the time immediately before the destruction of evil on earth : the rejoicing has been for a future guarantee by the unfailing will of God. But now at last the heavenly choruses can cry out in joy at the consummation of God's plan. Faith is now justified by fact ; for with the destruction of Babylon the earth has been disencumbered of a society intrinsically hostile to Christ and His community of faithful souls. The end to which all creation has been planned is now in sight. There is now a new note in the fervour of the heavenly praise and thanksgiving. **Hallelujah** four times repeated, recalls the liturgical thanksgiving in the Psalms ; its use in this way is unique in the New Testament. The **salvation** belonging to

God is the first motive of praise ; His **power** is exercised above
all to preserve and vindicate the loyal and righteous.   In this
care for His people He is glorious ; yet His **glory** is also terrible
(see xv. 8) ; in its presence evil is destroyed.   Because Roman
civilization proved corrupt, because ' the wine of her vice '
debased mankind (see xvii. 2 and xviii. 3), and because its
limitless depravity was testified beyond demur in the slaughter
of God's **servants** (see xi. 7–10 and xviii. 24), the supreme
Judge sentenced and destroyed her.   **He has avenged on her** 2–
the blood of his servants.   This is a celebration of a judicial 3
equity which fits the punishment to the crime, both in kind
and degree ; we might refer to xvi. 6–7 (where see notes) for
a similar expression of this idea.   The praise of God's **sentences**
as **true and just** (cf. xv. 3 and xvi. 7) is not evoked by this
thought only, however.   We must keep in mind the whole
situation on earth, as John expected it.   We should remember,
for example, the bearing of chaps. xi. and xiii. : to all nations
the Gospel was to be preached, to all men the choice between
God and Satan was to be clearly stated.   The sequel—the
universal worship of Antichrist, and the universal rejoicing in
the death of the witnesses—marked the pagan world not only
as guilty, but also as irreclaimable.   For present security, for
luxury or out of sheer inclination, the mass of men had sur-
rendered their souls to evil : they had committed that sin
which is unforgivable, because it hardens the heart for ever,
and stifles every breath of repentance.   Again, this earthly
society, pledged as it was to the service of Antichrist, consciously thwarting the designs of God, stood as an obstacle to
the new kingdom of justice.   A city built on ' large codes of
fraud and woe ' must make way for a city built on the eternal
rock of honour and love.   The rejoicing in heaven and the
ascription, at this point, of truth and justice to God's **sentences**
owe as much to the thought ' **now comes the marriage of
the Lamb** ' as to the thought that the **smoke** of Babylon
goes up for ever (i.e. her destruction is for all time ; from
Isa. xxxiv. 10).   Ostensibly it is on account of the obliteration
of Babylon that the Presbyters and living Creatures cry, ' **So** 4
be it, hallelujah ! '   But the God whom they honour by their

obeisance is the Creator (see chap. iv.), He who makes all things new ; their hallelujah rings out the old, but it also rings in the new.

Apparently from one of the four living Creatures, who previously uttered God's commands of doom on the earth, who are conceived, in fact, as the supreme agents of the 5 Omnipotent, and the closest of all created beings to the **throne** —there comes the cry : ' **Extol our God, all ye his servants.**' The command is fashioned out of echoes from the Psalms ; indeed, the whole scene of heavenly praise has as its background psalms of rejoicing as is plain from the **Hallelujah !** four times repeated. The implication of John's allusion is plain. The psalmists cried out in faith to a God whom they trusted to vindicate His cause, and the cause of righteous men : and now His cause was vindicated. ' Praise the Eternal, servants of the Eternal ! ' the Psalmist exclaimed : praise Him, because in faith you must see Him ' supreme over the nations, majestic over the heavens ' (Ps. cxiii.) ; praise Him, because you believe that He rules the mighty forces of Nature, and has power to destroy the wicked now as He destroyed Pharaoh and Og and Sihon ; because He is the true God whose cause will prevail mightily over that of idolators (Ps. cxxxv.) ; praise Him, because He rescues and vindicates the oppressed, ' raises poor men from the dust ' (Ps. cxiii.) ; because He, the Eternal, ' will right his people's wrongs ' (Ps. cxxxv.). The praises of the heavenly hosts celebrate the fulfilment of such hopes. The wrongs of the true Israel are righted now, God has asserted His sovereignty over the earth, the tempestuous forces over which He alone had power have been released against the wicked ; and the eye of faith no longer has to peer through a glass, darkly. Those **who reverence** (R.V.,' fear ') him, **low and high,** see their aspirations rewarded, and their troubles for ever banished. ' He will bless them that fear the Lord, both small and great ' (Ps. cxv. 13) ; this is a verse which John has already quoted, in a similar context (xi. 18). We might profitably recollect the rest of the psalm, which breathes the confidence that God will assuredly cast down evil and justify the righteous, because the purity of His Being requires it. The

pagan taunts of ' Where is that God of theirs ? '—fiery darts
once to be turned only by the stoutest shield of faith—now, in
John's vision of triumph, have lost all their power to distress ;
for now there is no need to ask where God is, no need to protest against unbelief that God is in His heaven : God has put
forth His strength, and none may now ignore Him. The day
has come when the dream of prophets and poets has come
true : **Now the Lord our God almighty reigns.** The very surface 6
of John's words flashes with brilliance of supernal joy : but
beneath the surface lie unfathomable depths of feeling. More
bitterly perhaps than most Christians to-day, John could say
with the Psalmist (Ps. cxviii.) that the pagans encompassed him
and his fellows like a swarm of bees, and blazed about them
like a fire among thorns. Perhaps more often than we, he
sighed for the sounding of the trumpets of doom and salvation.
The Psalmist's confidence is his ; he sees the strong right hand
of God exalted ; in his eyes there is the dawn of the eternal
day. He remembers the words :

> ' This is the day we owe to the Eternal ;
> Let us be glad and rejoice in it.'

Let us rejoice and triumph !   7

The marriage of the Lamb, the everlasting union of the
faithful to their Lord, is a theme which must be dealt with fully
in chap. xxi. It is necessary here to say only that this is the
ultimate bliss, and that the angelic chorus celebrates what still
lies in the visionary future, because they know that all
hindrances are now swept aside ; the new creation is within
sight over the serene space of the millennium. The battle of
Harmagedon ; then, after the thousand years' reign, a last
futile attack of Satan on the blessed community ; the Judgment—these three events intervene. But the martyrs, who
form the nucleus of the new Jerusalem (in effect, an alternative
metaphor for the Bride) are already safe, assured of their
reward. The two battles, the one with Antichrist and his
allies, the other with the hosts of Gog and Magog inspired by
Satan, are soon decided : there is no resisting the Messiah's
sharp sword with the two edges—the Law which consumes

evil-doers—and there is no evading the fire of divine anger. As to the Judgment, the martyrs have already undergone their 8 trial (see ii. 10) and already they are clothed in the **fine linen, dazzling white** which (as the rather prosaic gloss in verse 8 explains) symbolizes an inward purity (cf. vii. 9 and xiv. 4, 5). Christ's **bride has arrayed herself** long before the marriage, for her wedding robes are made out of **the righteous conduct of the saints**—imperishable, and tried for all time in the hour of trial which came over the whole world, to test the dwellers on earth (iii. 10).

xix. 9–10 : I<small>NTERLUDE</small>

9   Then I was told, ' Write this :—" Blessed are those who have been called to the marriage-banquet of the Lamb ! " ' The angel also told me, ' These are genuine words of God.'
10   Then I fell before his feet to worship him ; but he said to me, ' No, never that ! I am but a servant like yourself and your brothers, who hold the testimony of Jesus. Worship God ' (for the testimony borne by Jesus is the breath of all prophecy).

We are rather abruptly reminded that all the visions in chaps. xvii.–xix. are mediated by an angelic interpreter, who 9 was last heard of in xvii. 15. Of this angel we have by now almost lost sight : his part in the visions of chaps xviii. and xix. seems supererogatory—so much so, that we might feel justified in attributing his mediation rather to convention than to any urgent conviction in John's mind. It is easy to lose sight of the fact that the whole of John's apocalypse is said to be conveyed from God ' through his angel ' (i. 1) : apparently the prophet is enabled to hear even the words of Christ only through the medium of a ministering spirit. It makes little difference to our understanding of the book, of course ; but the inference which John seems to have drawn, that his ecstatic experiences and the visions which thronged in his mind owed something to the mediation of an angel, should help us to set aside our first feeling that there is something abrupt and strange in the transition from the scene of heavenly rejoicing in verses 1–8 to the precepts of the angelic interpreter in verses 9–10. The fervent contemporary respect for angels is mirrored in John's conduct : **Then I fell before his 10 feet to worship him.** There is obviously little likelihood that John's first readers would have been tempted to ask, ' Which angel ? ' as they read verse 9 : an interpreter-angel who also helped to portend the terrible plagues ' which complete the wrath of God ' was not one to be overlooked. It is necessary to say this, because it has been conjectured that at least part of verses 9–10 has strayed out of its original context, and might, for example, be more fittingly ascribed to the end of chap. xvii., where the interpreter-angel is still speaking, and where the context seems near enough to a kind of political speculation to call for the reassurance : ' **These are genuine words of God.**' However, these words fit their present context quite well. They can be taken either in a general sense, as applying to the subject matter of the visions in chaps. xvii.–xix., or to the underlying *motif* of all these visions—that the loyal Christian can face his earthly troubles with a stout heart and sturdy confidence, since his persecutors are already sentenced, and his own recompense is sure ; in which case the reassurance arises naturally out of the beatitude : **Blessed are those who have been called to the marriage-banquet of the Lamb !**

This, the fourth of the seven beatitudes in REVELATION (see i. 3), is, in its present context, remarkable evidence of the extent to which a strictly pastoral purpose lies beneath John's use of visionary material : even his sublimest visions are recorded for the one purpose of clarifying the minds of the faithful about the hard choice that lay before them. Having mentioned the ultimate glory of the Church as a whole—the Bride—he reminds Christians of their own part as individuals in this blessedness, symbolized now in the traditional metaphor of the **marriage-banquet.** There is some confusion in this juxtaposition of metaphors : the true Israel is the Bride as she is in Isaiah, for example ; but the individual Christian is a guest at the marriage-banquet as he is in the synoptic Gospels (see

St. Matt. xxvi. 29 ; St. Luke xxii. 30). A similar distinction between the community as a whole and individuals in the community is to be seen in chap. xii., where the woman is the Church, and Christ and His martyrs are her children. It is the essential meaning of metaphors which fills John's mind, often to the detriment of figurative consistency. The metaphors of the marriage of the Church, and of the admittance of individuals to the marriage-banquet have essentially the same point : and this is that the bliss of Christians will be consummated in a new degree of intimacy with their Lord. It is pertinent to recall the metaphors by which John represented the reward of the conquerors in the seven churches (chaps. ii.–iii.) ; diverse in character though they are, they have one fundamental purpose—to convey the different aspects of the final bliss, the new intimacy, with Christ, the attainment of security and immortality, in fact the possession of all those privileges and honours which a long prophetic, apocalyptic and rabbinic tradition had predicted for the faithful Israelite. Presence at the marriage-banquet assured to the loyal Christian every joy belonging to the future life.

It is not unnatural that when the angel in verse 9 solemnly pledges the divine authenticity of John's visions of doom and bliss, and assures him that the Christian may have complete confidence in these **genuine words of God,** the seer should be overcome by an impulse to worship so welcome and impressive a messenger. His prostration is the conventional response of an apocalyptist to the presence of a celestial being (cf. i. 17) ; and, as we might infer from the warning against angel-worship in the Epistle to the Colossians, Christians in Asia Minor would see nothing strange in John's conduct. That a tendency to angel-worship still continued seems clear from the fact that John twice prostrates himself—here, and in xxii. 8. It is equally clear that John felt himself inspired to rebuke the tendency to which his own conduct bears witness, for the two ' interpreter-angels ' who show John the ' doom of the harlot ' and the new Jerusalem both emphatically disclaim his attempts to worship them. They proclaim themselves fellow-servants of the Christian witnesses. In the service of God, redeemed man is in no way inferior to the celestial beings who already dwell in the presence of the throne. The Christian who holds the **testimony of Jesus** does no less than an angel : the angel proclaims the eternal truth of Christ's Gospel ; he comes from the Presence with messages to men. But the prophet also performs this task ; he also proclaims the mind of Christ ; **for the testimony borne by Jesus is the breath of all prophecy.** If John discourages angel-worship in these two passages, he does so not by abasing angels, but by exalting Christians (cf. Heb. i.-ii.).

xix. 11–16 : ' Lo, he is coming on the clouds, to be seen by every eye ' (i. 7)

> *Then I saw heaven open wide—*   11
> and there was a white horse!
> His rider is faithful and true,
> yea, *just are his judgments* and his **warfare** ;
> *his eyes are* a flame of *fire,*   12
> on his head are many diadems,
> he bears a written name which none knows but himself.
> He is clad in a robe dipped in blood   13
> (his name is called THE LOGOS OF GOD),
> and the troops of heaven follow him on white horses, 14
> arrayed in pure white linen.
> A sharp sword issues *from his lips,* **wherewith to** *smite the* 15
>   nations ;
> *he will shepherd them with an iron flail,*
> and *trample the winepress* of the passion of the wrath *of God almighty.*
> And on his robe, upon his thigh, his name is written,   16
> KING OF KINGS AND LORD OF LORDS.

The long-awaited moment has arrived. At last the glory of the heavenly court shines undimmed on the trembling earth ; John sees **heaven open wide** (cf. xi. 19 and xv. 5, 11 where the temple in heaven is opened wide—for the punishment of evil-doers) for the Messiah's descent to do battle against Antichrist and his hosts. It is not a *Lamb* that the prophet sees in his vision : the Lamb has been the symbol for the Redeemer of men, but now Christ appears as a warrior-prince. It is His steed, a **white horse** like that which symbolized the Parthian power to overrun the earth in chap. vi., that first catches John's eye. This white horse conveys the central idea in the portrait of the Messiah : He who shares the throne of almighty God is at last about to assert this unlimited authority in action. Practically everything else in the picture is a repetition, with small variations, of earlier touches. It was as the **faithful and true** witness that Christ appeared to the church at Laodicea : we remember the double implication—that Christ is the *genuine* Messiah, no matter what His opponents say, no matter how impressive the appearance of the Imperial usurper of His titles, and also that everything He reveals is *authentic*, His promises bound to be fulfilled. Again, we have heard many times those echoes of the psalms and prophets which speak of the justice of God's sentences of doom on men (cf. xv. 3–4, xvi. 7) : what is said in the Old Testament of the Eternal is characteristically repeated of Christ : **just are his judgments and his warfare.** It was with 12 flashing eyes, **a flame of fire,** that Christ appeared in John's first vision in Patmos ; and the Thyatiran church was confronted with One whose eyes saw into the innermost heart, to discover sins unperceived or uncensured by the worldly. The **many diadems** adorning His head (as contrasted with the single crown worn by the first of the four horsemen in vi. 2 and the reaper-angel in xiv. 14) proclaim Him ' the prince over kings of earth ' (i. 5), supreme with the Creator in His possession of ' power and wealth and wisdom and might and honour and glory and blessing ' (v. 12), infinitely more powerful than they 13 who on earth have usurped His rule. The **robe dipped in blood** reminds us that Christ is the Vintager, so awfully portrayed in Isa. lxiii. 1–6, who tramples the nations in His wrath, crushing them in His fury, spilling their blood on earth ; the sign of His mission appears in His robes, ' stained red like a vintager's ' :

384

His visionary appearance points forward to the function He is about to fulfil—the trampling of **the winepress of the passion of the wrath of God almighty.** But this theme has already been anticipated in xiv. 14-20 (see notes), where the Messiah is implicitly associated with all the punishments of the last days. The **sharp sword,** symbolizing Christ's punitive power 15 (see verse 21), was seen in the first vision in chap. i, and was held before the church at Pergamum. The **iron flail** to **shepherd the nations**—we have heard of this too : John has foreseen it in the hands both of Christ (xii. 5) and of His servants, the conquerors in the seven churches (ii. 27). And, finally, the reference to the **name** of Christ, the name which **none knows but himself,** is a recollection and expansion of what has already been said in the seven letters. To the churches at Pergamum and Philadelphia it was promised that the supreme privilege, that of knowing Christ's ' new name,' should belong to the martyr, and to him alone—just as the martyrs, and they alone of all created beings, are able to learn the ' new song ' (xiv. 3). In the ancient world it was very generally believed that to know the name of the Deity was to be enabled to come into His presence, to invoke His aid, and to avoid His displeasure. John's insistence on the Messiah's ' new name,' a name at present withheld from all men, is thus a hint at some mysterious reserve of power, some incalculable intensity of being, some secret majesty and holiness, which as yet is hidden from the eyes of men on earth. He tells us something about the significance of this new name : he says that it is **called the LOGOS OF GOD,** and that it means that Christ is **KING OF** 16 **KINGS AND LORD OF LORDS.** Many are puzzled by what they take to be an obvious inconsistency—the fact that John apparently names the name he has declared to be secret ; it has, in fact, been generally argued that the words **his name is called the LOGOS OF GOD** are interpolated. Such misunderstandings arise out of a failure to do full justice to John's cryptic and subtle style. He has told us that the name is secret, but he wishes also to indicate the extent of the power which is implied by this secret name. It might be enough to see behind the word **LOGOS** (literally, Word) some allusion to

God's power to destroy, deputed now to Christ ; John may have had in mind Wisd. xviii. 15 f. : 'Thine all-powerful word leaped from heaven out of the royal throne, a stern warrior, into the midst of the doomed land, bearing as a sharp sword thine unfeigned commandment.' But it is at least arguable that John was using the term in a sense perhaps not unfamiliar to the churches about Ephesus—in the sense in which it is used in the Fourth Gospel (see notes in this series on St. John i. 1 ff.). In calling Christ 'the origin of God's creation' (iii. 14) John has expressed 'the Logos idea without the name Logos' (Beyschlag). The Christ who speaks to the Laodiceans is one who derives His power to punish from His association with the very process of creation ; the Logos, through whom all things were made, possessed the power attributed by the prophets to the Creator Himself, of unmaking what had become evil. The general idea implicit in the term Logos of supremacy in Creation also suits the eschatological setting of REVELATION. *Because* He was the creative 'Word,' 'the origin of God's creation,' Christ was supreme not only over the heavenly hierarchies of angels (cf. Col. i. 15–17 ; ii. 9), but over the Satanic Powers whom He was about to confront and destroy. The blasphemous claims of the Beast are grimly answered by the faithful and true Lord, the Logos, who is KING OF KINGS AND LORD OF LORDS. In such thoughts we must seek the significance of the secret name.

This whole portrait of the Messiah should be compared with the earlier portrait in chap. i. They have many points in common, but the essential difference is that whereas in the first vision the figure of Christ stands waiting vigilantly amidst the seven golden lampstands, in the last vision He is about to leap into action. He is mounted, and at the head 14 of the **troops of heaven,** who also bestride **white horses.** The troops of heaven are the martyrs, who at last are about to assume the power promised them in ii. 26 ff. : 'They follow the Lamb wherever he goes' (xiv. 4)—they follow the Messiah as He rides out of the open gate of heaven, to do battle with Antichrist.

386

xix. 17–21 : HARMAGEDON

Then I saw an angel standing in the sun, who shouted aloud to 17
all birds that fly in mid-heaven, ' *Come, gather for the* great
banquet of God, *to devour* the flesh of *kings*, the flesh of 18
generals, *the flesh of the strong*, the flesh of *horses* and their
riders, the flesh of all men, free and slaves, low and high
alike.' And I saw the Beast and *the kings of earth* and their 19
troops *mustered* to wage war against him who was seated on
the horse and against his troops. But the Beast was seized, 20
he and the false Prophet who had performed in his presence
the miracles by means of which he seduced those who received the mark of the Beast and worshipped his statue ; both
of them were flung alive into the lake of fire that *blazes*
with brimstone, while the rest were killed by the sword 21
of him who is seated on the horse, by the sword that
issues from his lips. *And the birds were all glutted with*
their *flesh*.

' Blessed are those who have been persecuted for the sake 17
of goodness !—the Realm of heaven is theirs ' : or as John
says, theirs is the marriage-banquet of the Lamb. But for the
persecutors, the enemies of God and the saints, the hosts of
Antichrist, for them a different kind of banquet is prepared.
An angel of light summons all the birds that fly in mid-heaven
to a banquet of flesh at the mount of the messianic victory, 18
Harmagedon (see note on xvi. 16). This grim invitation takes
us back to Ezekiel's oracles on Gog (see Ezek. xxxviii.–xxxix. :
especially xxxix. 17–20 ; cf. also Rev. xx. 17 ff.). Ezekiel
prophesied that before the community of Israel was established
in final security and faithfulness to God, a host of invaders
from far-off, barbarous countries would ' sweep like a storm,
covering the country like a storm cloud.' They would come
to make war on the people of God, but would suffer an
overwhelming defeat which must convince all nations that the
Eternal was strong to uphold His honour. To the scene of

carnage birds and beasts are summoned, so that they may
' eat the flesh of heroes and drink the blood of the world's
princes ' (cf. Isa. lvi. 9). John's description of the last battle
is reticent, and derives its force largely from suggestive allusion to the scenes painted by Ezekiel. The dark anticipations
of the bloodshed at Harmagedon in xiv. 18 ff. and xvi. 12 ff.
are now flooded with a lurid light, but it is a light which shines
out of oracles uttered in a long past age.

The primary fact about the battle of Harmagedon is that
it constitutes the climax and conclusion of Antichrist's warfare against the Messiah *and His people*. The Parthian hosts
19 have been swollen, for to their ranks **the kings of earth** have
flocked after the ruin of the Empire : Antichrist has **mustered**
his utmost strength for the attack. It is the traditional scene
of eschatology, but with an important difference. The terrain
of the battle is no longer the mountains of Israel, as it was in
Ezekiel and Daniel, nor yet the vicinity of Jerusalem, as in
Zechariah : it is the spot symbolically entitled Harmagedon,
which one might roughly interpret, ' The Hill of Victory.'
And the faithful people of God, who along with their Lord
form the object of the attack, are no longer a single nation,
nor indeed are they an earthly community : they are represented by **the troops of heaven,** the martyrs. John's allusion
to Ezekiel's oracles on Gog and his host of invaders is interesting, for it reveals something of the freedom with which he
interpreted such ' words of God.' In Ezekiel, the invasion is
directed against a restored Jerusalem ; but after the great
slaughter on the mountains of Israel, after the corpses of the
invaders lay unburied—the worst shame and dishonour known
to the ancient mind—a new vista of blessedness opens out
for the restored Israel on earth ; the land is cleansed of defiling
corpses, and where blood has been spilt, vineyards flourish.
John finds place in his eschatological scheme for the attack
on the ' restored Jerusalem ' : it brings to a close the millennium, and is followed by the destruction of the old earth and
heaven, and the creation of a new universe, and an entirely
new Jerusalem. But at the same time there are obvious
features in Ezekiel's oracles which were inappropriate to the

Gog and Magog invasion in REVELATION : the laborious cleansing of the land, for example, as typifying the earlier prophet's forward look to a continuation of an untroubled reign of Israel on earth ; or more significantly, the general emphasis in Ezekiel, which gives the impression that the invasion of Gog and his armies of barbarians constitutes that great threat to Israel which provokes the Eternal's appearance on the Day of Wrath. John evidently took Ezekiel's prophecies in chaps. xxxviii.–xxxix. to foreshadow in a general way both Harmagedon (the last act of the Parthian invasion, headed by Antichrist) and the final attack on the ' beloved City,' described in chap. xx. But, of the two events, Harmagedon is, in his scheme, of infinitely greater significance. John was convinced that when the Messiah appeared on earth, unexpectedly (' like a thief '), clad in all the terrible glory of God's avenging anger, then the power of evil was at an end. The decisive, if not the final, stroke had been made. The corpses of **all men, free and slaves, low and high alike** must then lie unburied in a dishonour equal to that imposed on the martyrs (see xi. 9)—until the land was cleansed for the messianic reign on earth, and the establishment of ' the beloved City ' (cf. Ezek. xxxix. 11–16).

The battle is sketched in barest outline. **The Beast** (see 20 xiii. 1–4) is seized and committed at once to **the lake of fire** (see xx. 14) which awaits other evil-doers after the Judgment. A like fate awaits his bands of priestly adjutants, whose thaumaturgic powers of seduction earn for them the title of **the false Prophet** (see note on xiii. 11 ff.). They too do not enter hell through the portals of death : they are **flung alive** into their torments. As for **the rest,** they are slain by the 21 sword of the warring Messiah, **of him who is seated on the horse.** This is the word of command **that issues from his lips.** The Messiah in 2 Esdras xiii. held neither ' spear nor any instrument of war ' ; he slew his foes ' without labour by the law, which is likened unto fire.' The wicked are slain, as Isaiah said, ' by the breath of his lips ' (Isa. xi. 4) ; or in the words of the Book of Wisdom (xviii. 16), by the ' sharp sword ' of ' unfeigned commandment.' We are not told twice of that great sea of blood, which gushes out of the winepress of God's wrath (see xiv. 20). But a touch of subtler horror conveys the ghastliness of the scene : **the birds were all glutted with their flesh**.

THE MILLENNIUM
(xx. 1–10)

1 Then I saw an angel descend from heaven with the key of the
2 abyss and a huge chain in his hand ; he gripped the dragon, that old *serpent* (who is the *Devil* and *Satan*), and
3 bound him for a thousand years, flinging him into the abyss and shutting and sealing it on the top of him, to prevent him from seducing the nations again until the thousand years were completed—after which he has to be released
4 for a little while. And *I saw thrones* with people *sitting on them,* who *were allowed to judge*—saw the souls of those who had been beheaded for the testimony of Jesus and God's word, those who would not worship the Beast or his statue, and who would not receive his mark on their forehead or hand ; they came to life and reigned along with the Christ
5 for a thousand years. (As for the rest of the dead, they did not come to life until the thousand years were completed.)
6 This is the first resurrection. Blessed and holy is he who shares in the first resurrection ; over such the second death has no power, they shall be *priests of God* and Christ, and reign along with him during the thousand years.

7 But when the thousand years are over, Satan will be released
8 from his prison, and emerge to seduce the nations *at the four corners of the earth, even Gog and Magog,* mustering them for the fray. Their number was like the sand of the
9 sea, and they swarmed *over the broad earth,* encircling the leaguer of the saints and *the beloved* City ; *but fire descended*
10 *from heaven and consumed* them, and their seducer, the devil was flung into the lake of fire and brimstone, where the Beast and the false Prophet also lie, to be tortured day and night for ever and ever.

'Now the Lord our God almighty reigns!' A messianic kingdom of a thousand years is established on earth, and for a thousand years the Devil is restrained, lest he should trouble the serene life of the new Paradise. It is no bewitching sphere-born harmony, no arbitrary divine fiat which brings into being this Utopia of REVELATION, this earthly kingdom of God:

> 'Yea, Truth and Justice then
> Will down return to men,
> Th'enameld Arras of the Rain-bow wearing,
> And Mercy set between,
> Thron'd in Celestiall sheen,
> With radiant feet the tissued clouds down stearing. . . .'

It is a kingdom won by suffering, by the initial sacrifice of Christ, and by the sacrifice of His witnesses, who died **for the testimony of Jesus and God's word.** **4** Nevertheless, in spite of the moral impulse which underlies the prophet's dream, the whole of verses 1-10, with the chaining of the serpent, the temporary reign of God and Christ on earth, and the last futile recrudescence of pagan hostility against the people of God, bears a strangely remote appearance to readers of a later age. Sycorax imprisoned in a tree is as real as the serpent chained in the abyss ; Prospero has as sure a throne in the Imagination as these sharers in the first resurrection. What bliss is absent from the City in the new creation of the age to come, which must be fulfilled in the **beloved City** of the millennium ? Wherein lies the fitness in the Providential scheme of this interim between the destruction of Babylon and the appearance of the new Jerusalem ? There is no doubt whatever that John saw its fitness in the unique reward it gave to the martyrs. It was not enough that they should share in the general bliss of the new Jerusalem. As in this life their sufferings must be more bitter, and the proof of their loyalty surer, so in the messianic kingdom their status must be higher than that of the Christian who had been preserved in quietness of life during the reign of Antichrist (see below and note on xii. 14). Martyrdom is conceived to be the last act of a life utterly devoted to God ; and the reward of special authority is given to the martyr by virtue not merely of his death, but also of the unswerving devotion which inspired it.

It is, then, in the fifth of the seven beatitudes that we must seek the psychological clue to the understanding of John's
6 millennial expectations. **Blessed and holy is he who shares in the first resurrection :** the possessor, that is, of unique joy and honour—**holy** in its archaic sense of ' belonging to God.' Those who rise from the dead to participate in the messianic reign assuredly enjoy this surpassing privilege of being set apart as the most honoured of God's servants. For the **first resurrection** is awarded to the martyr alone (see xi. 11 ff.) :
5 **the rest of the dead** must forgo the millennium, and await the general resurrection before the Judgment. A dread awakening ! but the martyr rises secure from any fears of the Judgment. To the conqueror of the Church at Smyrna the promise was made of security against the **second death** (ii. 11) ; the martyr does not stand in peril of that last eternal exile from the presence of God, that fate which pales every fantasy painted by man on the blank canvas of death—of the first death, the death of the flesh on earth. He rises clad in the white robes of eternal life. Nor is this all : in chap. v. it is said that the redeemed are ' kings and priests for our God, and they shall reign on earth.' And this is repeated with
6 special reference to the martyrs : **priests** they are in their perpetual communion with **God and Christ,** and they **reign**— on earth—**along with Christ for a thousand years.** Over whom they reign, and in what direction their juridical authority is exercised, we are not told. The fact of pre-eminence is enough : John is concerned only to record the special distinction of martyrs. We recall once again the promises to the conquerors in the seven churches. The future martyrs of Thyatira and Laodicea in particular are promised a share in the power of Christ Himself : they are to share His punitive power over the nations (ii. 26-7), and resurrected to this end, martialled as the ' troops of heaven ' on white horses, they have already exercised this grim authority on the troops of Antichrist. It was promised that they should share Christ's throne, even as He through His conquest shared God's throne (iii. 21) ; and
4 here we see the **thrones with people sitting on them.** Those who were in this life judged (**beheaded**—executed as criminals

under the Roman law) are now **allowed to judge** ; and judgment is a divine prerogative. Behind this vision of the thrones lies the scene in Dan. vii. 9 ff., where ' thrones were placed ' at the great Assize of God, and the power previously in the unhallowed hands of world rulers is given to the true Israel. It is this prophecy which John sees fulfilled in his vision, in the exaltation of the martyrs. (John does not make a distinction between two classes of martyrs—those who were **beheaded for the testimony of Jesus and God's word** (compare vi. 9 and xii. 17) and those who fell in the great Distress—**who would not worship the Beast or his statue** . . . (see xii. 11 ff.). The two clauses are complimentary, and convey to John's readers what must be done and what must not be done, to gain the martyr's reward. This is not to exclude earlier Christian martyrs from the millennial thrones ; the Beast was a seven-headed monster, and his blasphemous claims had been the challenge to Christian loyalty in previous times. But in any case, John's words are uttered for those whose ordeal is still to come ; he mentions the great Distress of the future in order to press home the practical bearing of his vision of the millennium, for the Christians of the seven churches.)

The picture of the millennium is as remarkable for what it omits as for what it includes. Its historical antecedents are to be found in the earlier prophetic and apocalyptic writings, which looked beyond the Day of Wrath to a true Holy Land—purged of all evil, rid of all oppressors, inhabited by the faithful people of God whose sufferings in the past would be recompensed a hundredfold. We may recollect the eloquent descriptions of Isaiah, of an earth presided over by an Israel now wealthy in spiritual and material blessings—a nation of patriarchs :

> ' No babe shall die there any more in infancy,
> nor any old man who has not lived out
> his years of life ;
> he who dies youngest lives a hundred years ;
> anyone dying under a hundred years
> must be accursed by God.

They shall build houses and inhabit them,
they shall plant vineyards and enjoy the fruit;
the homes they build, others shall not inhabit,
what they plant, other men shall not enjoy.
My people shall live long as lives a tree. . . .'

(Isa. lxv. 20 ff.)

In this golden age the beasts of prey become gentle, and the peace of God falls upon the restless nations. ' On that day,' says Zechariah, ' the very bells on the horses shall be inscribed with "Sacred to the Eternal."' It was, indeed, a theme on which the fantasy of the apocalyptists could luxuriate. As years passed, the vineyards of the restored Holy Land became more fruitful in their visions, the harvests richer and the pastures greener : in the Apocalypse of Baruch we read of vines with a thousand branches, branches with a thousand clusters, clusters with a thousand grapes—' and each grape will produce a cor of wine ' : in 1 Enoch the grain yields a thousandfold, and the righteous ' beget thousands of children.' The spiritual renewal of mankind is equalled by a new miraculous vigour in Nature. John, however, mentions none of these blessings. The final glory, of which they are shadowy symbols, he describes in chaps. xxi.–xxii. in his visions of a newly created universe : his concern with the messianic reign is not to show its bliss, but to point to the special place of the martyrs in it. No doubt the early readers of the Apocalypse 9 were able themselves to fill the **beloved City** (so called from its association with the Messiah) with every blessing of peace and quiet simplicity of life. When we ourselves hear the word millennium, we have little doubt about what it means ; and when the churches of John's day heard of his vision of a thousand years' rule of the saints, there were doubtless those 6 to explain that this was the **thousand years**—in God's sight ' like the passing of yesterday '—which represented the cosmic sabbath at the end of the old creation : into such a conception the speculative piety of apocalyptists and rabbis had already adventured, influenced by Gen. ii. 2 and Ps. xc. 4. John leaves much unspoken in his account of the millennium, but legitimate inference can supply what is chiefly missing. He does not, for example, mention who else besides the martyrs

394

share in the messianic reign on earth. We are left to infer that the martyrs rise to partake in what the ordinary Christian inherits by virtue of being alive when his Lord comes ' like a thief ' into the world : against that time John has already warned the churches : they must be on the alert, and hold fast their raiment, ' not to have the shame of exposure ' (xvi. 15 ; cf. iii. 4, 18). But whatever hopes we assume to be implicit in John's account, whatever joys dwell in the beloved City, the capital of Christ's earthly kingdom, and the centre of a purified earth, death is as yet unbanished there, and the transcendent brilliance of the future in the new creation is seen out of the shadow of the Judgment throne ; so it is seen by all but the martyrs ; only they as yet can be called blessed and holy.

When the underlying religious motive of John's millennium is given its proper value, some of its strangeness is mitigated. Yet to the modern reader, whose acquaintance with the by-ways of eschatology is slight, chap. xx. must inevitably bear a somewhat factitious appearance. With the doubtful exception of 1 Cor. xv. 28 (see note in present series, p. 249; cf. also St. Matt. xix. 28, St. Luke xxii. 30), nothing like this temporary messianic reign on earth, with the special resurrection of martyrs to share in it, occurs in the Christian eschatology recorded elsewhere in the New Testament. Upon what authority did John build these expectations ? We must rid ourselves of any notion that John had some sort of system of reference, whereby he was enabled to pick up this or that shred of apocalyptic tradition at will, and incorporate it into an arbitrarily decided eschatology of his own fantasy. He made his claims to prophetic inspiration in all good faith ; the millennium, with all its strange concomitants, issued spontaneously out of a well-spring fed through many secret channels : deep in John's mind were mingled a great variety of eschatological conceptions, the sources of which, we may well suppose, he himself may often enough have been unable to name. It is therefore with some caution that we must set about finding such ' sources ' for the millennial interregnum in REVELATION. Precedents are to be found, not in any great number, but bearing clear witness to an inevitable tendency to reconcile two kinds of eschatological ideas : the earlier Jewish expectations of a divinely established theocracy (later becoming a messianic kingdom), wherein prosperity and righteousness should dwell side by side on a purified earth ; and subsequent expectations of the establishment of God's sovereignty in an entirely new creation. These two ideas, expressed with many idiosyncrasies and variations, existed side by side in the records of sacred writings, and it was only natural that some attempt at fusion should be made. In 4 Ezra, a work held to be approximately contemporaneous with REVELATION, but independent of it, we find a good example of the messianic reign on earth as a precursor to the reign of God in a new creation. It is worth quoting the relevant passage :

> ' And whosoever is delivered from the predicted evils, the same shall see my wonders. For my Son the Messiah shall be revealed, together with those that are with him, and shall rejoice the survivors four hundred years. And it shall be, after these years that my Son the Messiah shall die, and all in whom there is human breath. Then shall the world be turned into the primaeval silence seven days, like as at the first beginnings ; so that no man is left. And it shall be after seven days that the age which is not yet awake shall be roused, and that which is corruptible shall perish. And the earth shall restore those that sleep in her. . . . And the Most High shall be revealed on a throne of judgement. . . . ' (4 Ezra vii. 27 ff.).

Earlier examples of the messianic reign on earth, as an intermediate period between the destruction of the enemies of Israel and the ultimate establishment of God's sovereignty in a new creation are to be found in the Book of Enoch and the Apocalypse of Baruch. It is probable that the idea became a part of popular apocalyptic tradition. John clearly saw in it an inspired comment of those features in the eschatologies of prophecy and apocalyptic which were most disparate. It fell in with his own basic assumption about the prophets of past ages : that in spite of apparent contradictions, they told a consistent story about the divine plan for the future ; a consistent story, yet one nevertheless not by any means clear except to a prophet, in whose ears the voice of the Spirit sounded. If John had been asked why he supposed that his vision of a millennium were anything better than idle fantasy, he would probably have referred not to the Apocalypse of Baruch or the Book of Enoch as his authorities, but to certain passages in the Books of Isaiah and Ezekiel. In Isaiah, the bliss of the exalted Israel is described often in figurative terms, susceptible of spiritual interpretation : and the ' new heaven and new earth ' of which Isaiah spoke, supplied many of the colours for John's picture of a new creation. But at the same time there exist several passages in the later Isaiah which speak plainly and exclusively of a kingdom of God on earth ; in this kingdom premature or violent death is never known, but in the new Jerusalem of REVELATION ' death shall be no more ' (xxi. 4). John actually refers to that passage in Ezekiel which seems to him a direct allusion to his millennial inter-regnum (see Ezek. xxxviii.–xxxix.), and it is interesting to reconstruct his interpretation of it. Ezekiel foresaw a last desperate attack of heathen hordes on Jerusalem, under the leadership of a mysterious prince named **Gog** (' **and Magog** ': 8 John's addition is the result of a later misreading of Ezekiel's text : but the names in REVELATION are merely intended to connect the attack on the beloved City with the long-venerated oracle of Ezekiel). It was an attack on a restored Jerusalem, after Babylon had been destroyed, and after the faithful Israel had been many years established in their own land. So far Ezekiel's account fits the millennium very well : the ' warriors from Persia, Kush, and Put . . . all the hordes of the Cimmerians, all the hordes of Armenia in the far north . . .' these are the **nations at the four corners of the earth, even Gog and Magog** . . . **they swarm over the broad earth**, ' covering the 9 country like a storm cloud ' ; Ezekiel says that the attack is brought on by the Eternal, and John shows how God releases Satan for this sole purpose. But Ezekiel's account conflicts with John's in a very important respect. The sequel to the attack in Ezekiel is the destruction of the invading hordes and *the continued existence, in undisturbed peace, of the restored Jerusalem on earth.* For seven months Israelites are occupied in burying the bones of the defeated army, after the birds of prey have eaten their fill : but in REVELATION the Judgment follows, and the destruction of the old earth, and the creation of a new ; it is to the battle of Harmagedon that the birds of prey are summoned. It is fair to conclude that John had pondered seriously over these ' words of God ' (xvii. 17) in Ezekiel, and had finally seen in the oracles on ' Gog of the land of Magog ' predictions of the two invasions of the last days : the one partially successful in that it destroyed a city of evil men, Babylon ; but finally unsuccessful, since at Harmagedon it aimed its attack against the Messiah and the resurrected martyrs ; the other utterly unsuccessful, since it was directed solely against a City of righteous men, under God's protection.

1-8 Such exegesis of a prophetic oracle seems utterly pointless and misleading to our own generation ; it arises out of the same rabbinical method of reasoning about scriptural texts as prompted St. Paul's argument about Justification in Rom. iv. In REVELATION the actual process of reasoning lies hidden beneath an edifice of vision ; it is hidden and forgotten, probably by John as well as by his readers. A prophetic certainty dwells over the scene. This, like everything else in his book, was ' revealed ' to John, and he recorded what was revealed as ' genuine words of God.' In short, the vision of the millennium, no less than that of the risen Christ who spoke to the seven churches, is the child of devotion and ecstasy, not of invention and calculating erudition. This is true even of the most curious feature in chap. xx.—the chaining of the **serpent.** Persian and Egyptian eschatology furnish parallels for this capture of the Dragon, who personifies everything that is chaotic and evil : they are not exact parallels, but they bear witness to the sort of conceptions which may be presumed to have existed in popular eschatology. In the Book of Enoch the notion is found that the evil angels, with their leader

Azazel (a being resembling Satan), are to be bound and imprisoned as a preliminary punishment, and finally cast into a place of everlasting torture. An earlier example of such beliefs exists in a passage in Isaiah which John has used in other connections :

> ' And then shall the Eternal punish
> the hosts of the high heaven above
> and kings on earth below,
> bundling them into a dungeon,
> penning them inside a prison,
> till their day of doom arrives.   (Isa. xxiv. 21–2.)

The picture in REVELATION, in its external characteristics, savours strongly of myth. It is a **serpent** that is **chained** ; his prison is the **abyss**, a pit beneath the earth, a dwelling-place of evil (cf. chap. ix.) delved out of the macabre horrors of folklore. But the name used for the Devil, the cavernous lair in which he is sealed, the fantastic **key** held by the angel, in fact the picture conjured up by the whole scene—these things are words written in code. For the **serpent** is so called, not—at any rate primarily—because he represents the ancient Chaos, but because he is the seducer (cf. xii. 9) ; it is **to prevent him from seducing the nations** that he is restrained, and as the seducer of men that he finally re-emerges. The **abyss** is a colourful but incidental symbol for restraint—restraint for a purpose.

The **angel** with the **key** is, again, an incidental figure in a scene which asserts the theme of God's complete control over evil, after the decisive victory at Harmagedon : not God, nor yet Christ, but an unnamed servant of the throne flings the Devil into his prison. More obviously now than before, Satan's existence is subservient to a divine purpose ; for evil still has its part to play in the world. Once grant that there must be peace on earth so that the martyrs may enjoy their full reward, and grant too that Ezekiel's prophecy of an attack on the restored community of Israel is a divine oracle, literally true of some event in the last days of the world, then we have the motive for the serpent's confinement, and also for his release. Men are in themselves potentially good, and potentially evil; until they know the stress of trial their quality is 7- undiscovered. The **nations at the four corners of the earth** 10 enjoy the serenity of the millennium without desiring to erupt into the land ruled from the martyrs' thrones. Their virtue cannot withstand temptation, however; a last great trial is sent to test the dwellers on earth ; **Satan, the seducer, is released,** and the nations succumb to his persuasions : children of the flesh, they prove themselves evil, just as the martyrs, children of the Spirit, proved themselves righteous under trial. With the Devil's successful corruption of these nations of the millennium, and with their inevitable destruction **by fire from heaven** (the divine *word* of destruction) the old world comes to an end.

THE END OF THE WORLD AND THE JUDGMENT
(xx. 11–15)

11 *Then I saw* a great white *throne,*
    and **One who was** *seated* thereon ;
    from his presence earth **and sky** *fled, no more to be found.*
12 **And before the throne I saw the dead, high and low, standing,**
    and books were opened—
    also another book, **the book of Life, was opened**—
        and the dead were judged by what was written in these
        books, *by what they had done.*
13   The sea gave up its corpses.
    Death and Hades gave up their dead,
        and all were judged *by what each had done.*
14   **Then Death and Hades were flung into the lake of fire,**
15   **and** *whoever was not found enrolled in the book of Life*
        was flung into the lake of fire—
        which is the second death, the lake of fire.*

---

* Unless this line is to be omitted altogether, it must be placed thus after ver. 15, not after 14 (as in the ordinary text), since there is no question of a second death except for human beings.

What end is destined for the world ? Will primeval desolation steal back slowly, as ice encrusts more and more of the
earth and life dwindles to a wretched end ? Or will this planet
be wracked by unimaginable cataclysms, and destroyed with
the swiftness of thought ? Scientists are divided in their conjectures, but the later apocalyptists, arguing from moral
premisses, held that the end would be sudden and violent :
earth and sky must flee from the face of the Creator, **no more 11
to be found.** A vivid picture of this dissolution of the earth
is to be found in Isa. xxiv. 19–20 (held by scholars to be a
late apocalyptic insertion) :

> ' Earth breaks to pieces,
> earth is split in pieces,
> earth shakes to pieces,
> earth reels like a drunken man,
> earth rocks like a hammock ;
> under the weight of its wrong-doing
> earth falls down, to rise no more.'

What had been defiled beyond cleansing must be utterly
destroyed. ' Heaven and earth shall pass away . . .'—the
early Christian tradition follows that of contemporary Jewish
apocalyptic, which, in contrast to the earlier eschatological
notions, held that the physical universe was transitory and
doomed to annihilation. But this was not the end for mankind ; it was the beginning—the beginning of reward for the
righteous, and punishment for the oppressor, the beginning
of eternal life, whether in happiness or in torment ; the
resurrection brought men to a supreme court, where they
answered for the conduct of their lives on the earth now
vanished. 4 Ezra contains a passage which remarkably
illustrates the thought underlying John's vision. The Day of
Judgment is a time when all the *irrelevancies* of Nature are
banished, and the dead stand shown for what they are in the
' splendour of the brightness of the Most High ' :

> ' for thus shall the Day of Judgement be : A day whereon
> is neither sun, nor moon, nor stars ; neither cloud, nor
> thunder nor lightning ; neither wind nor rainstorm nor

cloud rack ; neither summer nor autumn nor winter, neither darkness nor evening nor morning ; neither heat nor frost nor cold ; neither hail nor rain nor dew ; neither moon nor night nor dawn ; neither shining nor brightness nor light, save only the splendour of the brightness of the Most High, whereby all shall be destined to see what has been determined for them.'

John's picture of the **great white throne** expresses the same idea with greater artistic economy. The Judgment seat is isolated, majestic, awful ; John mentions it first because it dominates everything. ' Judgment alone shall remain, truth shall stand,' Ezra wrote ; after everything else has passed away, the risen dead must gaze upon a light which is life, a light by which they may perceive their own darkness. For the **throne** is, of course, a symbol. It is necessary to state this simple fact, because it is sometimes remarked that the **great white throne** of Judgment differs from the throne in chap. iv. ; and that this is connected with the passing away of the ' first heaven ' (xxi. 1). This is to misunderstand the whole quality of John's style. The throne in chap. iv. and the throne in chap. xx. alike symbolize God's almightiness, His unchallenged, majestic power. These thrones stand for the supremacy of truth, and indeed of every divine attribute which John saw to be ignored or flouted by the pagan world about him. John does not name the One who is seated on the throne, as Isaiah did in his record of the vision in the temple (Isa. vi.). He does not need to do so, for the throne itself provides the apposite titles for Him who is **seated thereon**. If we must translate John's picture into more abstract terms, we shall say that the throne is **great** and **white** simply because it symbolizes the unique power of the Judge, and His absolute righteousness (for **white**, without stain or spot, represents probity and holiness in REVELATION : cf. iii. 4–5, vii. 14, xix. 8). But the full significance of the **great white throne** is not to be apprehended until we consciously recall the whole of chap. iv. : the Creator is now the Judge.

' Heaven and earth will pass away, but my words never ! '

We are inevitably reminded of these solemn words of Christ as we read John's account of the Judgment : ' the testimony of Jesus ' becomes now the measure of fitness and unfitness. It is, indeed, customary to remark at this point that Christ does not appear in John's vision. In Dan. vii. ' thrones are set ' at the great Assize, but in REVELATION there is only one throne, and only **One** seated thereon ; and this in spite of the fact that Christians customarily ascribed the Judgment of men to Christ, the Lord of the Harvest. In REVELATION it is said Christ judges and executes *living* mortals who transgress His commandments (see ii. 5, 16, 22, etc., and note on xiv. 14 ff.) ; but the last verdict on the risen dead is passed by God the Father. Such reflections, however, are little to the purpose, for it is clear beyond the need for argument that in John's mind the risen Christ shares the utmost power and authority of God. He conquered and rose to share His Father's throne (iii. 21) ; by virtue of His victory the Lamb is ' in the midst of the throne ' (v. 6). It is a great mistake to regard REVELATION as a *vade mecum* of early Christian doctrine, each vision to be isolated and minutely scrutinized for possible implications. The impulse of the book is moral, not intellectual, and that is true above all of the Judgment scene. Every irrelevance is cast aside, until the theme is stated in stark simplicity ; nothing is allowed to distract our eyes from the spectacle of the Judge, and the judged. It is John's rare power of laying bare an essential truth, without swerving aside into unnecessary qualification and expansion, that is responsible for the omission of Christ's figure in the last Assize.

The simplicity of John's picture is emphasized when one turns to other apocalypses. Where earlier writers speculate on the position of the throne (Enoch, for example, says that it is to be set up near Jerusalem) John is content to be silent. That is an irrelevance. Where the writer of 4 Ezra (as representative of the more powerful of later apocalyptists) could write : ' And compassion shall pass away, and pity be far off, and long suffering withdrawn,' again John is silent. Not that he would have questioned Ezra's words ; for, after all, it is implicit in his picture that truth and justice are now the only

12 arbiters, that men are judged once and for all by **what they had done** with their lives on earth ; that *deeds*, already committed, are the pitiless accusers of the damned. Nevertheless, to say such things outright would have been irrelevant, with the pointlessness of garrulity. The implication in John's words tells a far stronger story. For the prophet sees that **books were opened** ; these are the records of men's lives (cf. Dan. vii. 10 : these books of deeds appear in several apocalypses. In 2 Baruch xxiv. it is said that they are a record of ' the sins of all who have sinned.') And by the record of their actions **the dead, high and low,** are judged. The privileges of rank, wealth, reputation—even the privilege of faith, claimed by the Christian by virtue of his membership in the Church—all are set aside; and, as in a court of law, the evidence is allowed to decide. Here, however, the evidence is complete. There is this comfort : the quality which men call mercy is perhaps identical with justice, when justice sees and understands all. Much is said about the terror of the Judgment scene, much that reflects little trust in the Maker of men. And doubtless the prophet of REVELATION read in the flashing eyes of Christ, and the all-seeing gaze of the living Creatures about the throne, a message of little comfort to the mass of mankind. Yet it is also true, at least, that the fallacious verdicts of men will be reversed : if many who are confident will be dismayed, there may be many others, condemned on earth, who find vindication. Books are opened ; the name of Justice is no longer mocked, for God's eyes are pure eyes, and His witness is perfect witness. Whereas the **books** symbolize God's complete knowledge of men's actions, enabling judgment to be passed on the dead for **what they had done,** the **book of Life** symbolizes God's complete foreknowledge of those whose deeds win for them eternal blessedness. The names of the blessed are inscribed in it—none can be overlooked. Their names have been there since the foundation of the world (xiii. 8) ; only wilful sin can erase a man's name from this record (iii. 5). The figure of a divine register to preserve the name of every loyal soul is an ancient one. Originally (as in Isa. iv. 3, for example) it represented God's

record of the faithful Israelites who were to enjoy the bliss of
His reign on earth.   Later, in apocalyptic writings, it came to
represent the record of those who were to be admitted to the
blessings of the new creation.   This is what is implied in
REVELATION.   The mention of the **book of Life** is thus a passing
anticipation of what John has to tell us in chaps. xxi.–xxii.
about the reward of the righteous (cf. also Ps. lxix. 28 ; St.
Luke x. 20).

None can escape the Judgment—none is exempt, save
those who have proved themselves in life by self-immolation,
in full possession of all the virtues flowing from the death of
Jesus and the power of the risen Christ.   The **rest of the dead**
must answer before the throne, loyal and rebellious alike, the
subjects of the supreme King.   ' Let not thine imagination
assure thee that the grave is an asylum,' the rabbi Pirke Aboth
adjured his readers.   It is this thought, that there is no eluding
the last reckoning, which John expresses in the words,

> **The sea gave up its corpses,**   13
> **Death and Hades gave up their dead.**

The general meaning seems clear enough, but a literal and
unimaginative reading of the text exposes certain apparent
discrepancies.   For example, it has been said that heaven and
earth have fled from the presence of God : how then can the
sea give up its corpses ?   Again, are we not to infer from these
words a doctrine of physical resurrection, found nowhere else
in the New Testament ?   Thirdly (since it is apparent that
righteous and unrighteous alike are resurrected for judgment)
do the souls of the righteous dwell side by side with the
unrighteous in Hades ?   Does not John clearly think of Hades
(see verse 14) as the abode of the wicked alone ?   An elaborate
treatment of these supposed difficulties is to be found in
Dr. Charles' commentary on REVELATION (vol. ii., pp. 194 ff.),
and to this the curious reader may be referred.   The present
writer is of the opinion that the whole discussion is beside
the point.   John's words allude very freely to similar passages
in apocalyptic, which seek to indicate figuratively that the

resurrection before the Judgment will be complete ; it is wrong to demand of them scrupulous doctrinal precision. In 1 Enoch (where a physical resurrection is assumed—naturally, since the kingdom of the age to come is there situated on a purified earth) we hear that all who had been killed by wild beasts, by privation in the desert, and *by drowning in the sea*, were to be raised from the dead. John's memory of this phrase may have been affected by an ancient belief that the souls of the drowned were unable to reach the common dwelling-place of the dead. They visited the ' bottom of the monstrous world,' denied to the ' moist vows ' of those who mourned them. If such a conception dwelt in the suburbs of John's imagination, it certainly agreed with everything else that he says about the **sea**, which elsewhere in REVELATION symbolizes a power hostile to men, or a place in which evil is native. The Beast rises out of the sea (xiii. 1) : and the symbol of water as a dæmonic obstacle to the Christian is to be found in the ' flood ' poured from the Dragon's mouth (xii. 15). The sea in heaven corresponds mysteriously with the sea on earth, for it is represented as an obstacle in the way of man's approach to the throne of God (see chaps. iv. and xxi. 1-3). The ' sea ' which gives up its corpses is a personification of an undefined, sinister dwelling-place of the dead, holding souls and bodies in thrall until all such prisons are destroyed to make way for the Judgment. As to the objection that the sea ' no longer exists ' after the earth and sky have fled away (verse 11), this is to obscure John's text quite wilfully : for there is no shadow of justification for seeking chronological sequence in this account of the Judgment day. All that we are told is that as the earth and all material things vanish, the dead arise from whatever gloomy prison they occupy. John, we must remember, is recounting a vision ; the order of events is decided on dramatic grounds, not by a prosaic matter of chronological sequence. Similarly, it is far from his purpose to indicate in what shape the dead arise to stand before the throne. The urgent thought is simply that' they *do* rise : as we have said, the expression **the sea gave up its corpses** is figurative and allusive, and to insist that it implies a doctrine of physical resurrection is to show a complete misunderstanding of John's style. A literal treatment of John's references to those who have died robs them of their force, and turns the imaginative warmth of a poet into the speculative frigidity of an uninspired theologian.

Finally, there is the question of what John understands by **Hades**. This underworld of departed spirits corresponds to the Hebrew Sheol, where (as it was originally thought) the souls of men, righteous and unrighteous alike, dwelt for evermore. The later apocalyptists declared that Sheol must give up its souls for judgment. But some of these writers seem to imply that they believed the souls of the righteous to dwell not in Hades, or Sheol, but in ' treasuries,' whence they came to the Judgment throne already assured of their reward. It has been argued that because John says **Death and Hades were flung 14 into the lake of fire,** he clearly conceives Hades to be the evil abode of the wicked, and of them alone. One is reluctant to pause over so incidental and speculative matter, but it is perhaps worth mentioning, if only for the sake of bringing out the true emphasis in the Judgment scene. Like others of its kind, the argument is fostered by a desire to establish a correction of John's text (' sea ' is emended by Dr. Charles to ' treasuries ') ; it is both arbitrary and illogical. For obviously, if **Hades** is so evil that the righteous may not dwell there, **Death** also is so evil that the righteous may not die ; the two are wedded in one phrase. We must set ourselves against such absurdities : **Death** is the common fate of men, Christian and pagan together : and **Hades** is their common destination, until the Judgment day brings release. If there is any thought in John's mind of the ' treasuries ' holding the righteous souls, it is expressed in vi. 9 where the souls of the martyrs are said to dwell ' underneath the altar ' of heaven.

The verdict is passed : **all were judged by what each had done.** The wicked are consigned to punishment, and the righteous, whose names are in the **book of Life,** are rewarded ; 15 their rewards are to occupy the visions of the next two chapters. But before our eyes are allowed to rest on the new Jerusalem, they are bidden to rest for the last time on the fate of the damned. It is extraordinary how reticent John is on that subject, when his words are compared with those of other apocalyptists. In Enoch, for instance, the reward of the saints is completed by the spectacle of their enemies in torment, burning like straw and sinking like lead in water. John does not jubilate over the fate of the wicked, nor, happily, does he dwell on visions of celestial instruments and agents of torture. Where he cannot pity, he is silent. The **lake of fire**, a colourful and terrifying version of Gehenna appearing first in Enoch, is in REVELATION a symbol for spiritual rather than physical punishment. To be flung into this figurative lake is to suffer **the second death** ; and the second death is like the first, the death of the body on earth, in that it is a relinquishment of everything that a man holds precious. It is an exile into a fearful darkness : this time an exile from much more than the fleeting attachments of earth—an exile from the divine source of life, a deprivation of comfort, an unending awareness of loss, a sojourning in gloom as dark as the new Jerusalem is bright. There the wicked join Satan and Antichrist and the false Prophet, just as in heaven the righteous dwell in the presence of God and Christ. And in that lake the terrors of Death and Hades are banished, to dwell with the wicked. Literally, of course, John conceives death to have passed away completely : ' death shall be no more ' he says in xxi. 4 ; the damned (cf. xiv. 9–12) and the redeemed are destined to live for ever-more. In consigning the personified figures of **Death and Hades** into the lake of fire, he is saying that the **horrors** of both are for ever banished from the righteous, and for ever associated with the damned.

A word might be added about Dr. Moffatt's adoption of an emended order of the text. The formerly accepted text is as in the R.V. : ' And death and Hades were cast into the lake of fire. This is the second death, even the lake of fire.' ' Unless this line is to be omitted altogether,' Dr. Moffatt writes, ' it must be placed after verse 15, not after verse 14 (as in the ordinary text) since there is no question of a second death except for human beings.' But it is equally true that there is no question of *punishment* for Death and Hades ; nor is their consignment to the lake a poetic flourish ; at least, we have taken the view that *it is part of John's description of the lake of fire*. And this description is undertaken as a warning to the churches, whose errant members John never forgets. Can we not paraphrase the passage thus : 'Everything that men fear about death, all the terrors of death's mansions, will in the end be put far from the righteous ; they will be put in the dwelling-place of the damned. *That* is the second death ! Those are the terrors which await the disloyal. That is what the **lake of fire** means—eternal fear and darkness ' ? It is also true, of course, that to call the **lake of fire** (by an understandable ellipsis) **the second death,** is to emphasize its terrible finality for men.

THE HOLY CITY
(xxi. 1–27)

xxi. 1–4 : The New Heaven and the New Earth

Then I saw *the new heaven and the new earth,* **for the first heaven** 1
and the first earth had passed away ; and the sea is no
more. And I saw *the holy City,* **the new** *Jerusalem,* 2
descending from God out of heaven, all ready *like a bride*
arrayed **for her husband. And I heard a loud voice out of** 3
the throne, crying,
' *Lo,* **God's** *dwelling-place* **is with men,**
with men will he dwell ;
they shall be his people,
and God *will* **himself** *be with them :*
he shall wipe every tear from their eyes, 4
and death shall be no more—
no more *wailing,* **no more** *crying,* **no more pain,**
for *the former things* **have passed away.'**

The seer's gaze is now at last fixed on the furthest point of his vision ; his eye dwells on the perfection of a new creation, wherein God's agelong purposes are consummated, in the eternal bliss of the loyal. The old order has entirely vanished ; we must emphasize that it is essentially the old *order* of things, vitiated as it was by every conceivable evil, material and spiritual, which has disappeared. It is unnecessary and misleading to wander into speculations about the cosmic processes assumed by John in the summoning into being of a new order of things after the Judgment. For although a radical refashioning of the universe is undoubtedly in the background of his thought, it is spiritual rebirth which he tries to

1 describe. The passing of **the first heaven and the first earth,** the annihilation of the **sea,** the superseding of sun and moon, all testify to the final establishment of what is righteous and holy. And the imagery which John used to sketch the essential principles of the new order replacing the old is similarly designed to convey spiritual glories rather than material. We

2 might well have in mind as we read John's account of **the holy City** those lines in which Dante describes his visionary advent into the ultimate heaven (Canto xxx.) :

> ' Forth from the last corporeal are we come
> Into the heaven, that is unbodied light ;
> Light intellectual, replete with love ;
> Love of true happiness, replete with joy ;
> Joy, that transcends all sweetness of delight.'

The golden streets of the City of God gleam brightly ; but it is the gleam of the righteous, who reflect the glory of God. Light, love, happiness, joy—these are the architectural principles upon which the new City is constructed. It is true that John describes it in traditional cosmological terms, and that his picture is similar in all except an exuberant display of physical delights to other apocalyptic dreams of the future Paradise and the new Jerusalem ; yet it is also true that the embodied light in the buildings of his vision symbolizes the unbodied light of **the glory of God** (verse 11). The perfection of material things in the new creation is but a reflex of spiritual perfection ; and in John's vision, recounted as it is for the encouragement of the churches, the emphasis is all on this spiritual perfection. In other words, the picture of the new

Jerusalem is not a sort of lure or bribe ; it is a new challenge. None but the holy can ever aspire to dwell amidst this supernal holiness. None but the true Christian can dwell within walls whose foundations bear the twelve names of the twelve apostles of the Lamb (verse 14). Only those who long for communion with God can drink of the river of the water of Life (xxii. 1). Only the servants of God shall see His face (xxii. 4).

The first heaven and the first earth had passed away ; as John has told us (xx. 11), the old creation fled from the presence of One seated on a throne of Judgment. We can understand how John, in company with the later Jewish apocalyptists and his fellow-Christians of the first century felt that the old earth, drooping under the weight of its crimes, scarred by countless insurrections of the still active powers of Chaos, was a place totally unfit for the final establishment of God's reign. The earth must pass ; that is clear. And when John says **the sea is no more,** he is both recording the old earth's dissolution and giving its reason. For the sea personifies the very principle of disorder in the creation. In Persian thought that angry element is the dwelling of Tiamat, the Chaos spirit—as in REVELATION it is the symbolical lair of the seven-headed Beast. And the Egyptians also looked with fear and loathing on a monster who swallowed the sacred Nile—barrenness devouring fertility. In John's mind, no doubt, the abiding Semitic horror of the sea (the abode of Leviathan and Behemoth) was sharpened by such ethnic beliefs as these. When the sea vanishes we know that all the imperfections of the first creation have gone with it. But why should the **first heaven** also pass away ? What imperfections dwell in those heavenly courts where the throne stands, and the living Creatures around it continually cry ' Holy, holy, holy is the Lord God almighty ' ? There are no imperfections, but there are barriers and withdrawals. God is infinitely holy—that is, He is infinitely withdrawn from men. John has shown us several symbols for God's remoteness. The throne is isolated by a crystal sea, which the martyrs alone are finally able to cross. The presence of God is sometimes represented by a heavenly temple, in which the throne stands (viii. 3 ; xvi. 17) ;

and even the dwellers in heaven are unable to see the face of the Creator, when in wrath He destroys evil-doers, for ' the temple was filled with smoke from the glory of God and from his might ' (xv. 8). The temple represents God's remoteness from men ; but there is an altar. It is an altar on which the incense of prayer is burnt ; it is a channel through which the sighs of God's servants on earth may ascend to the presence of the majestic One. Within the temple are the tabernacle of testimony and the ark of the covenant—both essentially symbols for the enduring validity of God's righteous laws ; signs that the impiety and lust and cruelty of earth will be rebuked, that the truth will prevail and that the servants of truth will be vindicated. But now these symbols have vanished. God is no longer withdrawn from men, across an impassable sea ; in heaven as well as on earth, the sea is no more. Nor in the new order is there a temple (verse 22) ; sin has been vanquished, and evil-doers exiled for evermore ; God's tabernacle is now among men (verse 3). There is no more need for an altar—no need for any mediation of prayer, for the loyal now see God face to face (xxii. 4). The gates of the heavenly temple have long since opened wide to the terrified gaze of men (see chap. xv.) ; the laws of righteousness have been finally vindicated in the Judgment. So the **first heaven** as well as the **first earth** pass away, to be replaced by an eternal spring, a creation which is new, and ever renewed through the presence of the Creator.

It is not easy to speak of these ultimate things. They are almost beyond human imagination, as they are beyond human experience ; they are, as St. Paul said, ' What no eye has ever seen, what no ear has ever heard, what never entered the mind of man ' (I Cor. ii. 9). John's attempt to depict the new order is, however, extremely successful. He does not, on the one hand, present us with a mere list of abstractions ; his symbols give the imagination something to grasp and treasure. And on the other hand, the abstraction embodied in the symbol is conveyed with striking clarity. The reason lies partly in the fact that we cannot forget the 3 burden of that first **loud voice out of the throne** :

Lo, God's dwelling-place is with men,
with men will he dwell;
they shall be his people,
and God will himself be with them.

This is with John, as it was with Ezekiel, whose words he echoes (Ezek. xxxvii. 27), the supreme, immeasurable reward, embracing and overshadowing all others. In those words John has named the city of his vision as Ezekiel did : ' And the name of the city from that day shall be, The Lord is there ' (Ezek. xlviii. 35). This is the theme of chap. xxi. ; the rest consists of variations on the theme. The dwelling of God openly among His people implies, of course, the passing of all the imperfections and wrongs of the old world. **The sea is no more** (see above)—and **Death** has vanished, for that also was part of the original curse, the child and servant of sin (cf. xx. 13). Isaiah spoke more than once of the drying of tears, the silencing of **wailing** and **crying** ; perhaps John wishes us to **4** think particularly of that deepest misery which assailed the upright man in the past, the sense of abandonment by God ; we should not forget the bitter tears which he shed, when no one was found fit to open the scroll of the last days, so that redeemed man might join in the choruses of heaven (v. 4). John wept, because he saw no end to evil, and no hope for mankind. But despair is for ever silenced in the holy City where God dwells. The throb of **pain**—physical pain—is stilled, and the scars of the sufferer are healed : **the former things have passed away**—everything, that is, which testified to the cancerous evils of the old world, a world ravaged by the incalculable and hateful operations of sin.

But it is not only by the absence of grief and pain and death that John sketches the blessings of the reign of God ; the absence of accursed things is matched by a glorious fulfilment of everything that is good in human life, a positive bliss symbolized in the appearance of **the holy City, the new 2 Jerusalem, all ready like a bride arrayed for her husband.** Both of these metaphors, that of the **Bride** and that of the **City** represent the company of the loyal in their final state of bliss ;

and both metaphors are deeply rooted in the devotional reading of John's audiences. John has spoken of **the Bride** before this (xix. 7), and we have already remarked that it is a vivid term for the Church which is to be joined in ecstatic union with Christ. We may well assume that the Gospel tradition had familiarized the seven churches with the idea of Christ as a Bridegroom (cf. St. Mark ii. 19–20 ; St. Matt. xxv. 1 ; St. John iii. 29, Eph. v. 32, etc.). But in John's use of the term prophetic fire is fanned to a new blaze. The passionate faith and imaginative splendour of the later Isaiah live again in John's words. We are conscious once again of a God who yearns over His people, as a bridegroom yearns over his bride ; of worshippers who thrill at the sight of their Lord, as the bride thrills as she sees the bridegroom. In Isaiah, of course, it is the Eternal who is the ' husband ' of the faithful remnant ; it is the Creator in whose ' marriage ' the mourners are to be made joyful and the oppressed recompensed. But we have seen in chap. i. how in John's vision Christ appeared as the sharer of the Eternal's powers and titles (cf. chap v.). He who held the keys of Death and Hades is now the husband : His followers are to be joined to Him in an unending bond. In a sense, of course, this union is no new thing, for Christ formerly stood in the midst of the churches, guarding, and guiding His own people (i. 13). And again, the woman in the pangs of travail (xii. 2), the symbol for the true Israel into which Christ was born, already wore the signs of her destined glory ; the stars shed their light to be her jewels, the radiance of the sun was her garments, and the moon was beneath her feet. We must seek the realities beneath these symbols. The outward sign serves its turn when it conveys its own immediate truth, and then it must give way to some new figure, bearing a new shade of meaning. What John has previously said about the relation of the believer with Christ is not now diminished in force ; the metaphor of marriage conveys the thrill and joy of the believer in his new world ; a world dominated by ' the throne of God and the Lamb,' and resounding with the praises of the redeemed family of Christians.

The symbol of the Bride announces what is fundamentally

an individual blessedness ; though it may seem somewhat paradoxical to say that the consummation of the Church's bliss speaks so clearly of individual consciousness of joy. We shall, however, remember that promise to the conqueror of the Thyatiran church, which follows and transcends the assurance of a share in Christ's judicial powers : ' I will grant him the Morning-star.' It is Christ who is the ' bright star of the morning ' (xxii. 16) ; and the prospect of union with Him, nevermore to leave the holiness of His presence, answers the deep longing of a personal religion. But John does not let his listeners forget that the **Bride** is also a **City**. (Such figurative inconsistency bears witness to John's extreme familiarity with both terms ; it is only when a metaphor is in popular currency that its figurative associations can be ignored, and attention fixed on its essential meaning. We might compare xix. 7-9, where the Church is the Bride, and Christians are the wedding guests.) The collocation of a ' marriage ' to God, and of a holy City, in which the faithful dwell with their God, is one of the most striking features of the later Isaiah. But the new Jerusalem of Isaiah's dream is as spiritual a conception as John's holy City. Where is God to dwell ?—In buildings made by men ? Within walls made of rubies and gems (Isa. liv. 11-12) ? Yes, but we shall miss the whole spirit of Isaiah's vision if we forget those other words of his :

> ' Heaven is my throne, says the Eternal,
> my footstool is the earth.
> Where would you build a house for me,
> where would you rear me a home ? . . .
> What I care for are humble, broken creatures,
> who stand in awe of all I say.'   (Isa. lxvi. 1-2.)

John assuredly did not forget such words. God is to dwell among men, and if we wish to see to the heart of the symbol of the holy City, we must see a community of men there, rather than bejewelled walls and buildings. John speaks of jewels in profusion, as others had done before him ; but he is not describing a lapidary's paradise. He speaks of golden streets—but Mammon would have scorned such gold, as perhaps certain Laodiceans scorned the gold refined in the fire which Christ offered them (iii. 18). Let us be quite clear about what John really saw in his vision : it was not merely a set of buildings which he saw **descending from God out of heaven,** not the *shell* of a city, but the *soul* of a city ; a divine polity, the antithesis of the old civilization represented by Babylon. Or, if this is expressing it in too abstract and modern terms, it is the community of the faithful, upon whose garments of righteousness (xix. 8) the light of the Judgment throne still lingers radiantly ; it is the family of those who are called sons of God (v. 7) ; it is the family of men from ' every tribe and tongue and people and nation,' whom Christ has redeemed and made to inherit the ancient hope of Israel. It is a city which is a family. The ideal of perfect community, unrealizable on earth because of the curse of sin which vitiated the first creation, is now embodied in the redeemed from all nations.

The conception of a pre-existent divine City, springing out of the mind of God, the heavenly counterpart of the earthly Jerusalem, was a familiar one in John's age. It is this City which is described in 2 Esdras xiii. 36 :

> ' and Sion shall come, and shall be shewed to all men, being prepared and builded, like as thou sawest the mountain graven without hands.'

Esdras has described how he saw the Messiah deal destruction on the multitude of His enemies from this mountain hewn without hands, the heavenly Sion. After this, the heavenly City is manifested to another, a peaceable multitude, the holy people. It is not always easy to understand what is meant by such language, but we are helped by a suggestion in Heb. xi. 3 : ' It is by faith we understand that the world was fashioned by the word of God, and thus the visible was made out of the invisible.' This, then, is creation : the process of making visible what was invisible, of embodying thought in substance. The earthly Jerusalem—indeed, the whole created world—is an embodiment of a perfect pattern in the mind of God. Though the earth and all in it had been marred by sin, the perfect creation still remained treasured in the mind of the Creator, and eventually (so the apocalyptists and rabbis believed) those who were loyal to His laws would know this everlasting Paradise. But it was to be an apotheosis, not so much of the individual, as of the community in which he had proved himself loyal. It was impossible to conceive a state of bliss for the individual separate from the people. The blessed must form (as we have said) a family of souls, a transcendental extension of what was held most precious on earth. This was the *new* Jerusalem ; new in its manifestation among men, yet more ancient than the sun and the stars ; the future embodiment of a perfect order in a perfect creation. Towards this invisible City, to be made visible in a new act of creation, every blissful aspiration in the heart of pious apocalyptists arose. And the City remained to give shape to the hopes of Christians. ' We have no lasting city here below ; we seek the City to come,' says the author of Hebrews (xiii. 14). He sees in this glorious goal the motive for unstinting courage and endeavour ; in former times he says, terror moved men to obedience, but now Christians have before them a most splendid hope : ' You have come to mount Sion, the city of the living God, the heavenly Jerusalem, to myriads of angels in festal gathering, to the assembly of the first-born registered in heaven, to the God of all as judge, to the spirits of just men made perfect, to Jesus who mediates the new covenant . . .' (Heb. xii. 22-4). This ' assembly of the first-born ' is John's idea of the heavenly City, too ; and he too places his vision of it before the eyes of his fellow-Christians to spur them into new courage. Another facet of the same thought is presented by St. Paul (Gal. iv. 25-6), who contrasts ' Jerusalem on high ' with the earthly Jerusalem, representing the Jewish people. Christians already belong to this heavenly community—' she is our Mother.' To belong to her is to know the freedom of the redeemed heart, to belong indeed to the kingdom of heaven. Let us once more recall that John also thinks of Christians as belonging in this life to the heavenly City. He has told us so in that symbol of the woman clad in the sun (chap. xiv.)—bearing the splendour of her heavenly nature so

that all may see it. This woman gives birth to Christ and
the martyrs ; she represents the true messianic people, dwelling apart from the corrupt civilization of earth, in the ' desert '
of holy life. And she decks the bridal garments of joy when
at last God says : ' All is over,' when the sorrows of the first
creation have been banished for ever, and the glory which
anciently thrilled in the creation-song of the sons of the
morning shines now in the eyes of the redeemed ; when the
pattern of God's creation is seen in all its unspeakable and
deathless purity.

xxi. 5–8 : GOD SPEAKS TO THE CHURCHES

5 Then *he who was seated on the throne* said, '*Lo, I make* all *things
new.*' And he said, 'Write this : " these words are
6 trustworthy and genuine." ' Then he said, ' All is over !
I am the alpha and the omega, the beginning and the end.
I will let *the thirsty* drink of the fountain of *the water of
7 Life without price.* The conqueror shall obtain this, and
8 *I will be his God, and he shall be my son ;* but as for the
craven, the faithless, the abominable, as for murderers, the
immoral, sorcerers, idolaters, and liars of all kinds—their
lot is the lake that *blazes with fire and brimstone.* Which is
the second death.'

The Egyptians conceived the most high God to be voice-
less, ordering all things by the compulsive force of His will.
5 And similarly in REVELATION the Almighty, He who is **seated
on the throne** of absolute authority, has hitherto been silent
in John's visions ; His commands have been mediated by
servant-angels. He speaks now for the first and only time.
To whom does He speak ? Not to the dwellers in the visionary
City of the future—it was not they who could need the
encouragement and stern warning contained in His words.
He speaks to every soul in the seven churches, to the churches
throughout the world ; He speaks to men before whom the

great Distress lay, with all its opportunity for heroism and apostasy. The whole vision of the heavenly City is a kind of sermon in stones, and every period in it is fashioned by the immediate and pressing needs of the churches ; it speaks out of the future to the present. But the voice of God does not belong to that bright visionary future, but to the dark present. What He says is reported by John in this context to emphasize the fact that the visions of the new Jerusalem have been brought before the eyes of Christians for one purpose alone : to show that only the holy can dwell in the holy City, only the righteous can win the greatest blessing, of dwelling with the God of righteousness. We must not read these last visions in REVELATION as if they were intended to titillate an emotional piety, sundered (as no doubt it was in Sardis, for example) from moral rectitude ; the voice of One seated on the throne forbids us. John's pastoral mission is never more remarkably attested than in these verses, where he turns aside from his account of the new Jerusalem to report the unique utterance of the Almighty. John places every possible emphasis on it. First he tells us that it is the Creator Himself who speaks : ' **Lo, I make all things new** ' (cf. Isa. lxv. 17). And therefore the words which follow have an absolute validity, since they are spoken by Him who alone has power to build and maintain the holy City. Next he points the Creator's **words** with that traditional formula of emphatic assurance : ' **Write this** : " **these words are trustworthy and genuine.**" ' The passage is an interlude in appearance ; but in reality it carries the essential purport of all John's visions of the new creation.

A simple, direct contrast is made between the loyal and the disloyal, between the quality of life which assures possession of the ultimate reward, and that which excludes men for ever from possessing it. The force of this contrast lies less in the terms in which it is made (though they are powerful enough), than in the fact that it is made by One who can say : ' **All is over !** I am the alpha and the omega, the beginning and the end.' We might paraphrase these words as follows : ' God is sole arbiter, since He is the Creator and

6

all-comprehending Ruler. In His mind the End is decreed ;
in the chronicles of destiny, which He alone may dictate, *the
End is already written*. Therefore, though on earth the conflict
is still in front of men, its outcome is not in doubt : **All is
over** !—even now, before it has begun, the bitter strife of the
last days has ended, judgment has been done, righteousness
has been rewarded and evil banished to its own dwelling-place.'
This is not merely prolepsis. It contains the same implication as that in xii. 10, the cry of the angels : ' Now it has
come . . . the reign of our God and the authority of his
Christ . . .'—*now*, that is on the very Resurrection and Ascension of Christ. The events of this world, John believes, are
shaped in a matrix of eternal realities. God sees the processes of earthly affairs, not in sequence as they appear to
human beings, but as a whole, the end inseparable from the
beginning.

God speaks first to the **thirsty**, ' those who hunger and thirst
after righteousness ' (St. Matt. v. 6). And what memories
these words recall ! Of the Psalmist, who is ' athirst for God,
the living God,' *panting* for God, as the deer pants for a
stream' (Ps. xlii.) ; yearning and longing for God, ' like a
land without water, weary, dry.' We remember the promises
of Isaiah of water for this thirsty land (xliv. 3) ; and particularly must we recall that invitation already alluded to in
chap. iii. :

> ' Ah come, all ye that thirst, come to the waters !
> Come and eat, O fainting souls !
> Buy food for nothing,
> wine and milk without money ! '
>
> (Isa. lv. 1.)

Isaiah is speaking of food for the soul, not to be bought for
money : and so is John ; **the water of Life** is **without price**,
since it is in the gift of God alone. It is given freely and
generously, but only to those who, from the bottom of their
souls, are **thirsty** for it (cf. St. John iv. 14 and vii. 37–9).

7   It is this thirst after righteousness which makes the **conqueror** (see chaps. ii.–iii. ; ends of letters) ; it leads him to
account his martyrdom a blessing, since it assures to him
with unfailing certainty that his thirst shall be quenched in

the presence of God. To him who suffers death for the sake
of righteousness God makes the promise of a relationship with
Him in which all longing is assuaged, and the faithful servant
knows the blessing of content : **I will be his God, and he shall
be my son.** Others beside the martyr will thirst after God in
the tumult of the last days ; others will be loyal, and will find
satisfaction for their yearning. But only he who conquers by
death, the supreme test, is to ' share the throne ' of the first
Conqueror (iii. 21) ; to him alone the promise is made, ' I will
make him a pillar in the temple of my God (nevermore shall
he leave it) ' (iii. 12). And though the Christian Church in
general has been made ' a realm of priests,' ' kings and priests
for our God,' to the **conqueror** alone is made the promise of
a tenderer, more intimate relationship. It is a note sounded
but once in REVELATION. Elsewhere a certain austerity
tempers the high festival of the heavenly court. St. Paul
speaks more readily of the Fatherhood of God : all who for-
sake the impurities of pagan life become His sons and daughters
(2 Cor. vi. 18). But in REVELATION the **conqueror** must shed
his blood ; and a peculiar intimacy with God is the reward
of his fortitude and singleness of heart.

John's list of those who are for ever to be denied the
privilege and bliss of God's presence is influenced very plainly
by the time of stress which he foresaw for the Church. It is
not surprising that cowardice was the first disqualification
which came to his mind ; that, and the next sin of faithless-
ness (not disbelief so much as lack of trust : pure atheism was
not a foe which the first-century crusader met). These two
sins were the most subtle dangers which were likely to assail
the wavering Christian, and force him to commit apostasy—
the sin of all sins. Those who had it in their hearts to be **craven** 8
and **faithless** were to be faced with the supreme challenge :
were they willing to make a stand which involved loss of livelihood, threats of death, perhaps preceded by imprisonment and
torture—and perhaps the even more horrible threats against
friends and family, for it is hardly possible that this device is
peculiar to our modern Cæsar-worshippers? How many of us
will honestly claim a greater courage than the **craven,** and a

greater trust than the **faithless,** whom John imagines God to consign out of hand into eternal punishment ? How many of us would not seek to evade the trial by formal acknowledgment of Cæsar's divinity ? It is hard to say. For even the boldest of hearts can make but cold promises, until he actually feels the pull of the rack, ' Where men enforcèd do speak anything.' We may call John stern or harsh, according to our temper. But we must try to understand his motive in putting those who shrink from the test in so evil a company. To swerve into disloyalty through cowardice or lack of trust was not simply a temporary and insignificant sin. The time was short ; there was no recanting, for this was to be the final test. To utter the words of apostasy was to align oneself for ever with the enemies of God, with the heathen and their way of life ; to become ' a brother and companion ' of the **abominable, murderers, the immoral, sorcerers, idolators and liars of all kinds :** and it was not only a deadly blow against oneself ; it was a weakening and betrayal of those who still remained brothers and companions ' in the distress and realm and patient endurance which Jesus brings ' (i. 9). It was apostasy which assumed the guilt of untold crimes, the worst of which had still to be committed, since it pledged itself to acquiescence at least in the deeds of the Beast and his agents. John's list, which of course has many precursors in Old Testament and Christian writings, contains several terms which need a little comment. The **abominable :** this is probably a general term for all defiled by pagan cults. To worship any but the true God was in itself an abomination, but John was also convinced, not without reason, that the cults fostered or countenanced an evil way of life. The **immoral :** this term probably has more specific reference to sexual sin (but see the letters to Pergamum and Thyatira for the Christian temporizers at whom such words are aimed). **Sorcerers and idolators :** we shall understand what John had particularly in mind after recalling his prophecies in chap. xiii. Idolatry for him is essentially the worship of Satan, rather than the worship of senseless and meaningless objects, as in Isaiah and Jeremiah. The sorcerers of John's day put the breath of life into the

Beast's image. And as to these sorcerers, their other name is false prophets, Balaamites, who withdraw their fellow-men from the true God (see ii. 14). The self-styled Christian who did this did the work of the Beast who is called the false Prophet (xiii. 11 ff. and xix. 20). **Murderers :** this term alludes in all probability to something more general than sporadic crimes against pagan society—though we need not exclude actual murderers from John's meaning. It probably embraces that last onslaught on the people of God, described in chap. xi., where the whole world rejoices at the murder of the witnesses, and so shares the guilt of their death. This is John's preoccupation. In chap. xvii. he sees that vision of civilization personified. She is ' drunk with the blood of the saints and the blood of the witnesses of Jesus,' a murderess. And lastly, **liars of all kinds.** (Cf. xxii. 15 : those ' who love and practise falsehood ') : here, perhaps, is an acuter term, which pierces beneath evil deeds to the working of ' suffering souls that welcome wrongs.' The truth, John believed, was visible to all on whom the light of the heavens shone—to all on whom God's anger against society fell (see note on ix. 20). As in the Fourth Gospel, opposition to the Christian claims springs only out of deliberate falsity ; what a great teacher has called ' the only incurable sin—the lie in the soul.'

Into such a company the compromiser, the **craven**, or the **faithless** placed himself when he spoke—even though with his lips alone, not his heart—the fatal words of surrender : *Kurios Kæsar*—Cæsar is Lord. Who would not strain every nerve to be the **conqueror ?**

xxi. 9–14 : THE CITY

Then came one of the seven angels who had the seven bowls 9
    filled with the *seven* last *plagues ;* and he spoke to me thus,
    ' Come, I will show you the Bride, the wife of the Lamb.'
    So he carried me off, rapt in the Spirit, *to a* huge, *high* 10
    mountain, where he showed me *the City,* the holy *Jeru-*
    salem, descending from God out of heaven, *with the glory of* 11

12 *God*, the sheen of it resembling some rare jewel like jasper, clear as crystal ; it has a huge, high wall with twelve *gates*, twelve angels at the twelve gates, and *names* inscribed thereon which are the names *of the twelve tribes of the sons*

13 *of Israel, three gates on the east, three gates on the north, three gates on the south, and three gates on the west.*

14 And the wall of the City has twelve foundation-stones, bearing the twelve names of the twelve apostles of the Lamb.

9 John's guide is one of the seven angels who had the bowls filled with the seven last plagues : it springs at once to our minds that another of these angels has shown John the doom of the earthly city, Babylon the great Harlot (xvii. 1). Now he is to be shown Jerusalem the Bride. He is carried again in

10 a state of ecstasy, rapt in the spirit, to a huge, high mountain. The desert to which he was carried in chap. xvii. was symbolical, and this mountain (described as huge and high like the wall around the City) is also quasi-symbolical. For it is the visionary equivalent of the site of the City ; the only mountain on the new earth which John's eyes are now to survey. The seer doubtless mentions this as a literal feature of a future world shaped according to the notions of Semitic cosmology. But it is more than a mere physical protuberance. It represents to the reader of apocalypses the triumphant endurance and conservation of what was holy on earth. Other mountains pass (xvi. 20), but the mountain of God is seen once more in the new creation.

John states his theme with his customary incisive clarity. His vision is of the City, the holy Jerusalem—a city which comes from God out of heaven ; a city which wears a brightness of a different sort from that of earthly cities, no reflected

11 brilliance, but the very glory of God. From the first we perceive that John wishes to describe the intangible rather than the tangible ; the glory of God is more than a pictorial term ; it is an indication of God's active and indwelling presence, something to do with the very intensity of His being (see xv. 8).

There are many delusive side-tracks away from the main path of John's vision. Here, as so often in REVELATION, the student is as likely to wander away from the point as is the general reader. Much is obviously symbolical ; but the interpretations put on John's symbols are sometimes over-ingenious or eccentric. Yet other features seem to win their place for their poetical effect. Others, again, it is often said, are included out of regard for tradition—as the brown tree appeared in old landscape paintings, or as the fleur-de-lys lingered in the devices of English kings. So we find some critics who tell us that the jewels in the foundations of the wall are intended only to dazzle our eyes with the splendour of the City ; who tell us indeed that the City itself, although an unimaginable cube in shape, and traversed through inconceivable streets by a river which is undeniably figurative, is none the less a city in literal fact rather than a symbol for a new and perfect order. As to features conserved (rather inartistically, one might interpose) purely because they had been blessed by traditional use, we must particularly instance the **huge high wall,** and the 12 terms of verses 24–7. The latter we shall deal with as they arise ; but what are we to say about the **wall ?** Where is the need of a wall round a city which none may attack, since all evil is banished and shackled for ever ? Is not this a mere survival from traditional pictures of a Jerusalem which was to be gloriously rebuilt on earth ? Surely not. For even in Zechariah the new Jerusalem is to have no walls, though she is situated on earth. The presence of God is her protection (Zech. ii. 4). He hedges the sacred people about with a wall of fire—the fire of His power to destroy any rash and impious attackers. And, in fact, the wall is a highly significant feature of the new Jerusalem ; its foundations bear the charmed names of the twelve apostles, and its gates the names of the twelve tribes of the true Israel. We hear more about these foundations and gates than about any other part of the City. So it is hardly possible to dismiss the wall from further discussion with the too easy formula of ' traditional survival.' We must pause over it longer than that.

A wall round a city is not necessarily destroyed as soon as its original defensive purpose disappears. It may well remain, a solid demarcation of boundaries, a proud emblem of civic strength, and a reminder for those who care to consider it of present security after ' the former things have passed away.' It is not perhaps for precisely these reasons that an ancient city wall may survive. It may shelter the orchard of some wealthy citizen or the garden of an ancient Oxford college in one part, or form the fourth wall of newer buildings in another. Nevertheless, having survived, its walls and turrets lend to the city a distinction . not wholly picturesque or antiquarian. Let us consider the walls of the new Jerusalem in this light. There is, of course, no question of defence ; John's City needs no defence, for there is no active enemy. But, just as clearly, this visionary glimpse of a future, blessed order must in some way give to believers the impression of eternal security. What better symbol for this than a **huge high wall** ? (For the epithets, see note on verse 18). Let us be in no doubt about this : John was not performing an academic exercise in describing this community of the age to come ; he was showing those features of it which had peculiar interest to his own fellow-Christians in their present insecurity and peril. The City on earth (see chap. xi.) was not under God's protection ; the earth was overrun by the hordes of Satan ; the City was under the heel of the Gentiles, and the Christian community could survive in the defiled earthly city only because God protected them. And even so, the best of the believers were to be slain. But in the City to come—eternal security !

Security is not the only message of the wall, however. We must read the names on the gates and the foundations. The message of the gates is that Jerusalem lies open to loyal Christians : for it is Christians who form **the twelve tribes of the sons of Israel,** of the true Israel (see chap. vii.). The **angels** (with whom we must no doubt connect the ' twelve stars ' in the woman's coronet : xii. 1) are the Church's heavenly representatives, and the agents of God to guide and protect her on earth ; here they stand to welcome the wanderers in the desert of the world, as they reach their eternal home. The gates 13 stand on all four sides of the wall, **east, north, south** and **west**

426

(it is incidentally interesting to note that the peculiar order of the points of the compass here given seems to be a direct echo from Ezek. xlii. 15 ff.). We are again meant to understand that the entry is free to all loyal Christians—all the Elect, as St. Matthew says, ' from the four winds, from the verge of heaven to the verge of earth.' In such a way John appropriates to Christians the promises of salvation uttered by prophets and apocalyptists for the loyalists amongst the Jews ; in such a way he stresses the continuity of God's purposes, and the relevance to Christians of God's previous unfolding of these purposes. This, then, is John's claim : through the churches, in every part of the world (here twelve-fold but one, as in chaps. i.–iii. they were sevenfold but one), lies the entrance to the City of God.

The wall is a *sign* written in visionary skies (cf. notes on xii. 1 ff.), standing principally for limits within which the believer will be eternally safe ; limits beyond which he can only hope to pass through one of the twelve gates marked with the names which represent the messianic community on earth. It is no ordinary wall—it has no ordinary foundations. The most noteworthy point about the foundations is not so much their material (see below) as the inscriptions on them. As the gates are inscribed with the names of the twelve tribes, the foundations bear the names of the **twelve apostles of the Lamb.** Some 14 have seen in this number **twelve** a piece of anti-Pauline propaganda. Perverted ingenuity could go no further ; how inconceivable to have thirteen foundation stones, or fourteen, or any number except the sacred twelve ! It is hardly necessary to point out that in fact the **names of the twelve apostles** tell John's readers what he means by the **names of the twelve tribes ;** he is talking about the Christian Church, not the Jewish race. If we are to speculate at all, it would be more sensible, perhaps, to ask whether the word **apostle** did not have a wider meaning here than that given to it by our age— indicating a status and authority similar to what was falsely claimed by the ' apostles ' in the Ephesian church. For John's use of symbolical numbers amply excuses such a speculation. But these are secondary matters. The main point is that the symbol which indicates eternal security, and inclusion within the future kingdom, is intimately connected with the apostles of the Redeemer. (The word ' Lamb ' is used always when John has in mind Christ's redeeming power.) Again, the general inference to be drawn is that the believer's hopes of being included in the blessed community of the future lay in his fellowship with Christ's accredited representatives on earth ; His apostles, who wielded His authority and mediated His testimony. The new Jerusalem is the embodiment of holiness of life, and its boundaries are built of righteousness. The apostles are they who diffuse and attest the words of Christ which outlast heaven and earth ; the man who heeds and acts upon these words shall dwell within the wall of the City of God.

xxi. 15–17 : MEASUREMENTS OF THE CITY

15 He who talked with me had a golden *wand by way of a measuring-rod,* to measure the City and its gates and wall ;
16   the City lies *foursquare,* the length the same as the breadth, and he measured fifteen hundred miles with his rod for the City, for its breadth and length and height
17   alike ; *he made the measure of the wall* seventy-two yards, by human, that is, by angelic reckoning.

15   The measurement of the City is more obviously symbolical than some of the incidental details. To begin with, it is reminiscent of a previous scene in REVELATION—the measurement of the ' temple ' in chap. xi. There the notion was that what was holy must be protected against heathen malice ; and the measures taken by the reed in the prophet's hand were simply intended to convey that idea to the churches. The ' temple ' was measured, but the city of earth was expressly left unmeasured, and therefore doomed to utter destruction, since it had been defiled beyond hope by the heathen oppressor. Here, by way of contrast, the City (which

is perfect in holiness and therefore without a temple) is
measured ; obviously not for protection, but to convey its 16
eternal security to the minds of Christians—to convey also the
reason why it is eternal : its holiness, its perfection, its absolute
conformity to the ideal pattern of Creation. These ideas are
expressed in numerical and geometrical symbols. First, the
City is **foursquare.** The square was a Hellenic symbol of
perfection ; but we have only to recall Ezekiel's picture of the
holy City to understand how John had merely to utter these
words, **the City lies foursquare,** to convey the notion of divinely
wrought perfection. Hellenic and Semitic symbols here tell
the same story. We next learn something which surprises us :
the City is not only square, it is an exact cube, **its breadth and
length and height alike.** This symbol we shall better understand when we recollect that the sanctuary in 1 Kings vi. 20
was cubic. Perhaps John is even alluding directly to this very
notion : the Holy of holies in the old temple is replaced by a
creation in which God dwells among men, a city which is itself
the Holy of holies. Sixty cubits for the one is answered by the
fifteen hundred miles of the other. Such comment is in John's
style. But whether or not positive allusion is to be suspected,
the cube represents by its size and shape alike the perfection
of the new order. The size is purely symbolical, and for that
reason there is much to be said for the translation in the
Revised Version, where the measure of twelve thousand
furlongs is given for the twelve thousand Greek *stades*,
rendered by Dr. Moffatt as **fifteen hundred miles. Breadth and
length and height** are assessed in this huge multiple of twelve,
with its obvious associations. Similarly, the **measure of the
wall,** that is the height, or (as some have it) the breadth of
the wall, is in the Greek a hundred and forty-four cubits ; on the
whole, to translate this into the more conceivable measure of
seventy-two yards is to pay rather too much for a modern 17
dress ; for the approximate distance measured by a hundred
and forty-four cubits is of less importance than the symbolical
bearing of 12 x 12. The wild disproportion between the height
of the walls and city has often been noticed. Certainly the
numbers are symbolical, but there must be some proportion

even in numbers which do not pretend to be literal. One suggestion is that the seventy-two yards represents the thickness of the wall (the angel in Ezekiel's visions measures the thickness of the wall round the restored Jerusalem) : but does not this simply change disproportion into bad building ? One does not need to be an architect to see that seventy-two yards is not much of a width for a wall fifteen hundred miles high ! The problem becomes more acute when we acknowledge that the figures are very deliberately conceived by the seer to represent his visionary idea. He actually pauses over them to say the cryptic words: **by human, that is, by angelic reckoning.** Now it has been credibly suggested that these words contain a slight and incidental polemic against the contemporary tendency to venerate angels unduly (cf. note on xix. 10) : the idea is that in John's opinion comprehension of the future City is attainable just as much by men as by angels, since the symbolic measurements are stated in terms common to the understanding of both. Perhaps the reader will object that such a note of polemic comes ungraciously and inappositely in the midst of the description of the new Jerusalem, and he may prefer to think that John is saying something very strictly to the point. Is he not simply saying that ideas about the future order are being *comprehensibly elucidated by an angel to men* ? Whichever interpretation we care to put on his words, they certainly place some emphasis on the figures in question, the hundred and forty-four cubits of the wall. We must therefore ask another question. Is it not possible that John himself intended us to notice this vast disproportion between the wall and the City ? Is it not very clear that he wishes his readers to seek an inner meaning in the twelve thousand furlongs of the City's height ? This at any rate is certain : the notion of a city rising to enormous heights is not strange to the later Jewish elaborators of apocalyptic. We read in rabbinical writings of a City twelve miles high ; of a City which reaches the very throne of God in heaven. And in the Sibylline Oracles, too, we read that the City reaches to the clouds ; that it has a tower which touches the clouds, so that the righteous may see the glory of the invisible God. And does not John wish us to see this meaning in his measure of twelve thousand furlongs ? The City reaches heaven. The new heaven and the new earth are one. God does not dwell apart in heaven, but among men ; so that the distinction between heaven and earth has lost its point. The height of the City is not a matter of elevated buildings, but of the marriage of earth and heaven, of God and man, of the new order on earth with hosts of heaven. We need therefore no longer suppose that the wall is dwarfed.

xxi. 18–23 : THE MATERIALS OF THE CITY

The material of *the wall is jasper*, but the City is made of 18 pure gold, transparent like glass. *The foundation-stones* of 19 the city-wall are adorned with all manner of *precious stones*, the first foundation-stone being jasper, the second sapphire, the third agate, the fourth emerald, the fifth onyx, the sixth 20 sardius, the seventh chrysolite, the eighth beryl, the ninth topaz, the tenth chrysoprase, the eleventh jacinth, the twelfth amethyst. The twelve gates are twelve pearls, each 21 gate made of a single pearl ; and the streets of the City are pure gold, clear as crystal. But I saw no temple in the 22 City, for its temple is *the Lord God almighty* and the Lamb. And the City needs *no sun or moon to shine* upon it, 23 *for the glory of God illumines* it, and its radiance is the Lamb.

The precious stones and gold, clear as crystal, out of which 18 the City is composed are obviously intended to convey the splendour of the new order, to fashion out a picture of sparkling beauty, emblematic of a perfection beyond the power of thought. But when we have said this we have not finished, for there were in John's age, as no doubt in all ages, different ideas of celestial perfection, and John's purpose was not to dazzle, but to instruct his readers. It is as natural that a Christian teacher in Asia Minor should allude in passing to ethnic conceptions of the abode of the gods, as that he should allude to traditional apocalyptic assumptions. He does both ; not because he is at a loss for images, but because he wishes to correct or interpret current ideas.

It seems clear that the main outlines of John's description of the jewelled City were inspired by the Isaianic passage :

> ' Poor storm-tossed soul, disconsolate,
> I will build you up on jewels,
> and make sapphires your foundation ;
> I will make ramparts out of rubies,
> gates for you of crystals,
> and all your walls of gems.'
>
> (Isa. liv. 11–12.)

A passage in the Book of Tobit develops this theme, but we are not looking for a ' source,' which will leave no work to be done by John's searching imagination. That is not to be found. We are looking for the memories which stirred his imagination to creative action ; and we need not look beyond that book which inspired so much else in REVELATION. Isaiah's words form an admirable commentary on the emotional warmth in John's description. It is in its evocation of such memories that the power of REVELATION often lies. But there is little doubt that the incidental details in the picture are also allusive, though their vividness has been dimmed by the passing of time. The material of the wall, for example, is **jasper** ; the sheen of the City as a whole is that of **some rare jewel like jasper, clear as crystal** (verse 11) ; the One seated on the throne is said to resemble **jasper** and sardius. Is the **jasper** of the walls a purely ' poetical ' material, or is there an allusion to some ethnic notion derived from the Egyptians, whose Mansion of Life was said to be made of jasper ?—this mansion also had four walls, facing north, south, east and west. A connexion is not improbable ; if not with this, with some kindred belief. It is likely for two reasons. First, there is assuredly an inner and spiritual meaning in the **pure gold, transparent like glass**, with which the jasper wall is contrasted. At any rate, spiritual wealth has already been called **gold refined in the fire** (iii. 18) ; this, the Laodiceans were told, must be in the possession of those who wished to be owned by the Bridegroom and Messiah, who stands at the door and knocks. And here we are told that the holy City, the Bride, is built of this **pure gold** of righteousness (cf. the golden wand in verse 15, and contrast the 'reed like a rod' in xi. 1). Secondly, the gems in the foundations of the jasper wall seem almost certainly to have a curious and intricate connexion with the signs of the Zodiac, and therefore with astral *motifs* in pagan religions.

The **precious stones** which adorn the apostolic foundation [19-20] demand a paragraph to themselves. The Isaianic foundations of jewels have been given a rich diversity, which the general reader of REVELATION, who understandably might see no great literary merit in a mere list of precious stones, is likely to miss. To begin with, this list is an ancient one, as many of John's readers would naturally know. If we turn to Exodus xxviii. 17-20, we shall see them in the high priest's breast-plate (the Greek equivalent given by John for the Hebrew names of the jewels is different from that assumed by the translators of our Bible ; but this is natural, since the identification is often purely speculative). And if we turn to Ezek. xxviii. 13 we shall see the nucleus of the same list of jewels adorning the king of Tyre. These attributes of priestly and regal splendour are now set in the foundations of the City walls. Now Philo and Josephus both interpreted the twelve precious stones on the breastplate of the high priest as the signs of the Zodiac, and the connexion between these jewels and the Zodiac has been further established by the evidence of Egyptian and Arabian monuments. The precise correspondence between these signs and the jewels in John's list is best given in tabular form :

1. Jasper	The Fishes.
2. Sapphire	The Water-carrier.
3. Agate (chalcedon)	The Goat.
4. Emerald (smaragdus)	The Archer.
5. Onyx	The Scorpion.
6. Sardius	The Balance.
7. Chrysolite	The Virgin.
8. Beryl	The Lion.
9. Topaz	The Crab.
10. Chrysoprase	The Twins.
11. Jacinth	The Bull.
12. Amethyst	The Ram.

The extraordinary thing about this list is that it arranges the signs of the Zodiac in *exactly the reverse* of the usual order —that determined by the course of the sun through its various stations. If we follow the sun from his springtime station in the Ram, when he is high over the equator, we shall proceed next to the Bull, then to the Twins, and so on through the rest of the signs in the reverse of the order determined by John's list of stones. What inference are we to draw from this extraordinary fact ? (We call it extraordinary, but, after all, it exhibits much the same quality of mind as we have already seen in the composition of the cryptogram on Nero's name—and it demands a similar quality of enquiry in those who read it.) Dr. Charles has argued (and he seems to establish the point) that John is conscious of ethnic speculations about a ' city of the gods,' with which the signs of the Zodiac are connected in order to show a previous influence of this city of the Gods on Jewish apocalyptic ; he refers to certain passages in the Book of Enoch where we learn that there are ' twelve portals in heaven through which the sun, moon and stars go at different seasons,' and states his belief that this ancient conception of the city of the gods lived on to provide a polemical motive for the writer of REVELATION. His purpose in including a reversed zodiacal list of jewels was to dissociate the holy City from ethnic speculations in his own or other ages about this city of the gods. (See Charles, *I.C.C.*, ii., pp. 165 ff. : the argument is unnecessarily involved through an attempt to co-ordinate Rev. vii. 5–8, xxi. 13, and xxi. 19–20, and to account for John's alteration in the order of the jewels mentioned in Exod. xxviii. 17. If the identification of the jewels with the signs of the Zodiac can be relied on, there is no need to seek any farther for the explanation of the altered order.)

21   Finally, we have to discuss the gates of pearl : **The twelve gates are twelve pearls, each gate made of a single pearl.** A curious rabbinic story is sometimes quoted to show the kind of fancy which lay behind this description ; one version of it is referred to by Dr. V. Burch (*Anthropology and the Apocalypse*) : ' The *Pesikta rabbati* tells how the famous rabbi

Yohahan was expounding Isaiah liv. 12. And that he went on to declare that in the days to come Jahweh would make the temple gates of one precious stone. A hearer objected. Afterwards he was sailing in a vessel which sank. On the floor of the sea he saw angels at work with tools upon a single pearl. When he asked what they were fashioning, he was told the great gate of the temple.' Dr. Burch's comment on this is suggestive : ' The reason that satisfies, when we ask why John used those huge pearls, is that contemporary tales say such gems were to be put in the temple. John took them and used them in his new world, where there could be no temple.' We cannot be certain about this, however, for Dr. Charles quotes a variant of the same story : that this rabbi ' sat one day and preached : One day will the Holy One—blessed be He—bring precious stones and pearls thirty cubits long by thirty cubits broad, and excavate (openings) in them . . . and they shall stand in the gates of Jerusalem.' Perhaps it will be safer to conclude that John took over the pearls as he took over the inscriptions on the gates, from familiar Jewish pictures of the new Jerusalem, and showed them to his Christian audiences with the implication : ' These gates are yours, for you are the true Israel.'

The materials of the new Jerusalem, like its measurements, form a picture of a place of transcendent beauty, an absolute beauty, which nothing can rival. It is a place which will form a fitting dwelling for God ; or rather, less a place than a community amongst which God may fitly dwell. The jasper of its walls, the gems of the foundations, the huge inconceivable pearls which form the gates, all testify to John's desire to describe its spiritual qualities ; and so also do the streets of pure gold, clear as crystal. (We might add to our comment on verse 18 that ' Philo had already made gold emblematic of the divine nature diffused through all the world, owing to the metal's fusible qualities '—Moffatt, *Commentary, in loc.*) In short, we are prepared for the climax of John's description —his triumphant comment on his picture of materials and patterns : But I saw no temple in the City, for its temple is 22 the Lord God almighty and the Lamb. The temple is the

centre of other apocalyptic worlds ; whether they saw visions and told stories of a restored temple on a purified earth, or the manifestation of a heavenly temple (the divinely wrought counterpart of the earthly), the Jewish apocalyptists and rabbis felt that it was a temple which gave meaning to the heavenly city. On earth God must have His holy ground— holy, that is, ' set apart ' from what was profane ; but even in the future world from which evil was banished God must still dwell apart, His immediate presence held sacred, to be approached only by the privileged. But John claims for the whole of the new Jerusalem that absolute holiness which the temple represented. God dwells among men. They worship in His presence—**the temple** of the City **is the Lord God almighty and the Lamb.** Symbol has given place to reality— so we say, in our cold, abstract idiom. But John, we must repeat, was not simply making an innovation in apocalyptic theology. We must beware of imagining that he had in his mind merely some idea of winning people from Jewish ideas of the future world. We may say that this or that passage in REVELATION glances at Jewish hopes and appropriates them for Christians, or transforms them into something richer, distinctive of a new faith. And, indeed, it is true to say this ; but in saying it we must think of a man who is exalted far above the plains of controversy and debating ; one who stands ' on a huge high mountain,' and *sees* the holy City, and feels the life-giving warmth of its eternal Light beating upon him, burning in his heart. There are moments when John knows the incommunicable vision of the mystic ; and this is one of them. He has told us what he saw, so far as words have power to tell. What he did *not* see had the power to fill the minds of his hearers with awe and wonder and joy. But he still strives ; he has seen what they have not seen ; his rapture has taken him where they cannot tread. He has seen the
23 **glory of God** and the **radiance** of the **Lamb** shining freely on the countenances of men, the men who are the holy City. In this metaphor he attempts to convey the truth hinted at in the absence of a temple. What brightness is like God's brightness ? What radiance like the Lamb's ? The **sun and moon**

were divine—so the heathen believed, in their blind ignorance
of the true Light that lighteth every man. Kingly, queenly,
they lent their light to the world, and shone on that huge city
of earth, Babylon. But there was One who kindled their
brightness ; and there was the Lamb through whom creation
began. And the great City of the new heaven and earth knows
the incomparable joy of their presence : **the glory of God
illumines it, and its radiance is the Lamb.**

xxi. 24–27 : A NEW INTERPRETATION OF
ANCIENT PROPHECIES

By its light shall the nations walk ;   24
and *into it shall the kings of earth bring* **their** *glories*
(*the gates of it are never shut by day,*   25
and *night* **there shall be none**),
they shall bring **to it** *the glories* **and treasures** *of the nations.* 26
Nothing profane, **none who** *practises* **abomination or** 27
falsehood *shall ever enter,*
but those alone *whose names are written in the Lamb's book
of Life.*

Having depicted a new heaven and a new earth where evil 24
has no place, a **City** in which no shadow of darkness may fall,
a community of ' the spirits of just men made perfect,' John
proceeds to show that certain expectations about the future
city are to be interpreted not literally, but figuratively. As
we have done before, we must recall the assumption with
which John reads the psalmists and prophets of the Old
Testament : whatever apparent inconsistencies might dwell
in their words, however inapposite to a new age their predictions might appear, they had unquestionably preserved
God's oracles for the guidance of the messianic community.
Their words could not become out of date, their predictions
could not be falsified, for they were dictated by the voice
of God, whose words are trustworthy and genuine (cf. xvii.

17). But what was one to make of these seeming contradictions, and these prophecies which time seemed to have
falsified or rendered meaningless ? For example, to come at
once to the immediate difficulty, the Old Testament view of
the future reign of God for the most part does not rise above
this present earth, purified by God's intervention. Israel was
to become a theocracy, exalted by the care and might of the
Eternal to a supremacy over all other nations—and these
nations, the Gentiles, must acknowledge His might. Those
who avoided the fire of His anger on the day when He came
to Israel's rescue must become His subjects, and live according
to the ' light ' shed by His City. So of this earthly Jerusalem
it was quite appropriate to say :

> By its light shall the nations walk ;
> and into it shall the kings of earth bring their glories.

The notion of universal conversion of the heathen, induced
by the sight of Jahweh's irresistible championship of His
people, is to be found in the later Isaiah and several of the
Psalms (cf. Isa. lx. 1–3 and see notes on xi. 13, xv. 4). But it
did not agree with John's views of the future. The conversion
which he foresees is an exceedingly grim one ; he sees mankind
quailing at the sight of an angry God, perceiving and acknowledging His might—but in vain : they have squandered their
every hope. They die cursing their executioner, but acknowledging the might they have previously derided. Every knee
shall bow to God, Isaiah believed ; and John echoes the belief ;
the knees are bowed as the sword of God's wrath descends. It
was impossible that the new Jerusalem should give ' light ' to
the pagan nations, as Isaiah and the psalmists seemed to hope ;
there were no pagan nations, for the glory of the new Jerusalem was reserved for those whose names were written in
the Lamb's book of Life. Were such prophecies purely
illusory, then ? Had a lying spirit entered into the hearts of
those who uttered them ? No, it was possible to discern an
inner truth. Certainly the light of the new Jerusalem shall
be law to those who dwell within her walls ; these men shall

walk by her light—by their instant perception of righteousness, embodied in the new and perfect order. But who are
the nations ? Not the heathen, certainly. Not those who
joined Antichrist in the slaughter of the witnesses. The
nations are the redeemed, who belong spiritually but not
racially to the twelve tribes. Did not Christ redeem ' men
from every tribe and tongue and people and nation ' ? Very
well, *that* is how Christians must read these old prophecies :
they are the the nations. Similarly, the kings of earth are not
the old unblessed kings whom we saw weeping over the ruined
Babylon, nor the savage Parthian monarchs, crowned for a
day. These kings (so we must infer) are the martyr monarchs,
who reigned as the successors of the heathen rulers (cf. xx.
4–6) ; or perhaps all loyal Christians, of whom the heavenly
hosts cried out : they shall reign on earth (v. 10). If we care
to, we can dramatize the notion in John's mind. Let us
imagine the prophet speaking to the believers in one of the
seven churches about the new Jerusalem, as the Rabbi
Jochanan spoke about the gates of pearl. He paints a picture
of a transcendent city on a new earth, from which the pagan
oppressor is for ever banished. A hearer recollects familiar
verses in Isaiah :

> ' Ever shall your gates lie open,
> never shut by day or night,
> to let the nations pour their wealth in,
> headed by their kings.'
>
> (Isa. lx. 11.)

And he asks John what is the meaning of such words. They
must either be rejected or profoundly reinterpreted. John
reinterprets them. His argument is that the kingly treasures,
the blessings and wealth, of the messianic reign on earth, shall
be continued in the rich dower of the new Jerusalem. After
Harmagedon, he says, the Christian people inherited the
earth ; they were its new monarchs. And their state in the
holy City of the new creation shall be no less glorious. The
Isaianic prophecy is thus quite transformed. The gates are 25
always open : Isaiah says by day and night, but John's comment on this is : night there shall be none. Isaiah said that

439

26 it was to be the pagan kings who brought the glories and
treasures of the nations, but John's comment on this is :

27 Nothing profane, none who practises abomination or falsehood
   shall ever enter,
   but those alone whose names are written in the Lamb's book
   of Life.

Thus, verse 27 is an incisive comment on the three preceding
verses. John answers these prophecies from Isa. lx. by an
assertion frequently made in prophetic books, that in the
new Jerusalem no **profane** or unsanctified thing shall be found.
The gates are ever open, but only for righteous men. They
are never shut, because there is no night to fear, and no evil-
doers may approach the eternal radiance. Once more let us
ask : Who are the kings and the nations ? The redeemed,
John answers ; **those alone whose names are written in the
Lamb's book of Life ;** those whose realm and race are determined by their loyalty to Christ ; those brothers and companions ' in the distress and realm and patient endurance
which Jesus brings ' (i. 9 ; see also notes on xxii. 2).

A VISION OF EVERLASTING LIFE
(xxii. 1–5)

1 Then he showed me *the river of the water of Life,* bright as
   crystal, *flowing* from the throne of God and of the Lamb
2   *through* the streets of the City ; on both sides *of the river
   grew the tree of Life,* bearing twelve kinds of fruit, *each
   month having its own fruit ;* and *the leaves* served to *heal*
   the nations.
3   *None who is accursed shall be there ;*
        but the throne of God and the Lamb shall be within it,
        with the worship of his servants—
4   *they shall see his face,*
        and his name is to be on their foreheads.

Night there shall be none ;   5
they need no lamp or *sun to shine* upon them,
for *the Lord God will illumine* them ;
and they shall reign for ever and ever.

After Ezekiel had been shown the temple of the restored
Jerusalem, and had heard many instructions about the future
conduct of its worship, he was brought back to the temple
door (chap. xlvii.) to see a miraculous river. It flowed from
the temple down into the Dead Sea ; it turned brackish water
into fresh, it teemed with all manner of fish, and gave life to
groves of trees on its banks. In short, it was water which
represented a force of renewal in Nature, a divine removal of
the curse of barrenness, the pledge of a fruitful land where the
pardoned and restored Israelites might live and prosper.
Jerusalem was to become the centre of a second Eden.
Zechariah, too, had seen this water flowing from the Jerusalem
of the age to come ; flowing perpetually to the seas in the
east and west, making the whole land fertile. The river was
to spring into being when God descended on earth, setting
His feet on the Mount of Olives to deal death to His enemies
(Zech. xiv.). For John, these rivers meant something entirely
spiritual. A **river** flows **through the streets of the City** in his 1
vision ; it does not flow out of Jerusalem, for the City stands
for the whole order of redeemed humanity, the river is not one
which merely gives sustenance to Nature ; it is the **river of the
water of Life**—a stream of life-giving power from the intense
being of God, wherein the faithful may bathe, and find immortality ; of which they may drink, and find satisfaction for
their yearning souls. The source of this river is **the throne of
God and of the Lamb** : the power, that is, of the Creator and
the Redeemer. And the trees that grow on its banks similarly
represent to the readers of REVELATION a pledge of ceaseless
renewal. Here is John's comment on Ezekiel's vision : the
trees in the new Jerusalem are all of one kind—**the tree of Life.** 2
The term was a familiar one, and its appearance in other
apocalypses marks it as a symbol in common use. It was
the first promise made to the seven churches, that the

conqueror should eat of the tree of Life in the paradise of God (ii. 7). Few of John's readers would make the mistake of seeing in this a promise of material pleasure ; but if they had, there could be no mistaking John's meaning now. For the ' paradise of God ' (the garden-orchard which is also a City) is in REVELATION completely spiritual in the bliss it offers : everlasting life, unceasing worship in the presence of God and the Lamb—these are the rewards of loyalty. None but a religious man would desire such reward. There is no lure here except for those who in this life have known the exaltation of communion with God. Even the fruits of the tree of Life, **twelve kinds of fruit, each month having its own fruit,** carry no message for the sensual mind : they symbolize unfailing abundance of that food for the spirit which gives immortality. The **twelve,** of course, accords with the symmetry and aptness of everything in this paradise ; it is intended to remind us of the twelve tribes which symbolize the Christian Church, to show the fulness of provision made for them. A meagre and prosaic exegesis has fastened on John's references to the absence of the sun and moon (xxi. 23) to call into question his speaking of months. It is obvious, however, that in speaking of transcendental and eternal things one is bound to use the terms of men. Milton is more meticulous than John, in his—

> ' Nine times the Space that measures Day and Night
> To mortal men. . . .'

But no one was likely to misunderstand John's meaning. After all, the absence of sun and moon is not mentioned as a scientific curiosity ; it is mentioned purely to convey the sense of God's all-pervading presence, of His glory, which dims all our earthly notions of splendour and light. John is not a metaphysician, quarrelling with the intrusion of time into eternity ; he is a Christian teacher whose purpose is to show to his fellows the reward which was within their grasp.

In any case, his language is reminiscent. He asks the seven churches : ' Do you not know the priceless heritage set before you ? Remember what the prophets have said : their promises are God's words to you, the true Israel.' Ezekiel's picture of the river flowing out of the temple is before his eyes. ' On the bank of the stream, along both sides, every sort of food-tree shall grow ; their leaves shall not wither and their fruit shall never fail ; every month they shall bear fresh fruit, thanks to the water that flows from the sanctuary, and their fruit shall serve for food, their leaves for healing ' (Ezek. xlvii. 12) John's vision of these things is not to be regarded as second-hand, to put it bluntly. He did not use Ezekiel as we might use the *Encyclopædia Britannica*—a useful and authoritative source of miscellaneous information. He sees the river and the trees *afresh*. He sees what they stand for. And when he reports what he has seen in words already used by Ezekiel, he is actually authenticating the earlier revelation of God's will. He authenticates and interprets them. It is remarkable that he reverts to the ambiguous term, **the nations** (see notes on xxi. 24). In Ezekiel, the leaves serve *for healing* ; in REVELATION they serve **for healing the nations.** We need not ask again who the nations are, for John tells us in the next verse who they are *not*. **None who is accursed** 3 **shall be there,** he says ; and just as we saw the last verse of chap. xxi. as a comment on the three preceding verses, so here he tells us that the nations are *not* the accursed, even though the term were generally used to mean the heathen. He says, in fact, that the **leaves** of the tree of life shall **heal** the scars of those who had suffered for their faith ; in their undying bliss there shall be ample recompense for the hardships endured on earth.

None who is accursed shall be there : the literal translation of this expression is given in the R.V. : ' There shall be no curse any more.' It refers to things or people whose impurity invalidates worship. This, and the leading thought in verse 5, **night there shall be none,** are both reminiscences of familiar verses in Zech. xiv. In the first, Zechariah's thought is well interpreted by Dr. Moffatt : ' And there shall be no more curse of destruction,' Zechariah says—since Jerusalem is to stand eternally secure in the new age. Destruction had fallen on Jerusalem because accursed things were within her ; but in the new Jerusalem the meanest kitchen vessel was to be sacred (Zech. xiv. 21), and because there was no accursed thing she was to dwell secure. John fills this, and the conception of endless day, with the riches of his soaring vision. He has something positive to say about these two negatively described blessings, the absence of everything that defiles, and the disappearance of darkness. Where there is no defilement or impurity, no evil-doer, no evil thing, there can be unrestricted vision of God, and uninterrupted worship. Because Jerusalem is now a place of unsullied purity, the **throne of God and the Lamb shall be within it**—not far removed, out of the sight of men, in some inaccessible heaven. And those who are in the perfect likeness of God may come into the very holiness 4 of His presence—**they shall see his face**. They are **servants,** and they serve ; that implies nothing of servility, everything of privilege : redeemed man is no less and perhaps more than the angels who are also God's servants (see notes on xix. 10). Dr. Moffatt admirably brings out in his commentary the force of these reflections on the absence of the **accursed**. He reminds us of the thrill of horror which the Jews had felt when in A.D. 70 the temple in Jerusalem was defiled and pillaged. The temple of the Almighty ! That such unutterable impiety should be conceived, should be executed ! Truly, on earth, where not even the holiest place was free from the intrusion of the accursed, there was no security for the worshippers of God. The wise man could not avoid the conclusion : ' We have no lasting city here below ' (cf. Heb. xiii. 14). But in the City to come, worship is for ever free from the intrusion of the impious. There is no fear now of those who bore the name of the Beast on their foreheads ; for in this City there live only those who have God's **name** on their **foreheads** (cf. on iii. 12) ; the life-giving name, in itself a pledge of immortality and a sign of communion.

The last great apocalyptic theme which John develops is 5 that of the all-pervading glory of God : **night there shall be none**. We have called this a reminiscence of Zechariah's words : ' It will be one long day then . . . not a day and a night but light at eventide ' (Zech. xiv. 6–7). But such a thought was doubtless a common property of popular apocalyptic. It is reasonable to suppose that the ' hearer ' (xxii. 17) in the churches was as familiar with certain passages in Isaiah, Jeremiah, Ezekiel and Zechariah (to mention the four prophets to whom John most frequently alludes) as the modern Christian is with the parables. And just as some of us might hesitate before we assigned this or that version of a parable to its proper synoptic Gospel for example, they too might be perfectly aware of some apocalyptic idea, without being confident of its precise source. At all events, John takes the theme, and shows what it means to him. Zechariah's perpetual day becomes a perpetual day *of worship* ; as John said in xxi. 23, the glory of God and the radiance of the Lamb shine for ever on the redeemed. The ' true Light ' has superseded the uncertain luminaries of the old order. Once again we might say, symbol has given way to reality. And John's vision of the new order, of the City within whose wall heaven and earth were married for all eternity, ends with the thought of the supreme bliss of the redeemed, expressed in a metaphor which requires no comment : **the Lord God will illumine them.** Thus, the vision ends as it began : ' Lo, God's dwelling-place is with men.' *That* is the City, the holy Jerusalem.

One last word : John recollects that earlier cry of the heavenly host : ' they shall reign on earth '—a prophecy which he saw fulfilled in the reign of the thousand years. Now he can say : **they shall reign for ever and ever.** For the light of the living God shines upon them to give them life for ever, and in the presence of the King of kings and Lord of lords they are endowed with privileges beyond the dreams of earthly princes—their **reign** is eternal and real ; that of their oppressors was transient and shadowy.

EPILOGUE

(xxii. 6–15)

I John saw and heard all this ; and when I heard and saw it, I 8
    fell down to worship before the feet of the angel who had
    shown me it all. But he said to me, ' No, never that! I am 9

6 but a servant like yourself and your brothers the prophets, who lay to heart the words of this book. Worship God!' And he said to me, ' These words are trustworthy and genuine, for the Lord God of the spirits of the prophets has sent his angel to show his servants *what must* very soon *come to*

7 *pass. Lo, I am coming* very soon ; blessed is he who lays
10 to heart the words of the prophecy of this book!' He said to me, ' Do not *seal up* the words of the prophecy of *this book*, for *the time* is near :

11   Let the wicked still be wicked,
    let the filthy still be filthy,
    let the righteous still do right,
    let the holy still be holy !

14 Blessed are those who *wash their robes*,* that theirs may be the right to *the tree of Life*, the right to enter the gates of the
15 City. Begone, you dogs, you sorcerers, you vicious creatures, you murderers, you idolaters, you who love and practise falsehood, every one of you ! '

* Reading πλύνοντες τὰς στολὰς αὐτῶν.

A loud voice like a trumpet commanded : ' Write your vision in a book . . . ' (i. 11) ; and John obeyed. His book is now finished. He has recorded his deep convictions about the future in words which the discerning (xiii. 18, xvii. 9) at least will understand. He has garnered the rich harvest of his meditations on God's oracles, on the words of prophets, psalmists and apocalyptists. He has co-ordinated his new visionary enlightenment about what was and is and is to be with the tradition in which he lives : with the revelation of God's will in the old and new dispensations. And now he writes his epilogue, before sending his book, as he was bidden, to the seven churches in Asia Minor. These parting words are a summons to Christians, to ponder the new revelation as they value their hopes of future bliss. In verse after verse, John insists : ' These visions are authentic—genuine—true. They are the words of God who inspires the prophets ; of Christ, in whom your salvation dwells.' They come through a prophet
8 whom they know and acknowledge : ' I, John, saw and heard

all this.' They come from a Witness who is about to return to the world which crucified Him : soon, **very soon**, He is to come ! That is the second theme—the imminence of Christ's return ; this theme, too, recurs in verse after verse. And, thirdly, John repeatedly urges the necessity of the utmost purity of conduct. Towards this end, the whole of his book has been designed.

The accepted text of the epilogue has been rearranged by Dr. Moffatt, who (with other critics) has argued that the lack of cohesion in this section, as contrasted with the careful marshalling of material evident elsewhere in REVELATION, arises out of some ancient dislocation of the order—a common enough accident in old texts. The reader who wishes to know the grounds for this rearrangement (which is, of course, in the nature of things a tentative one) must be referred to Dr. Moffatt's *Introduction to the Literature of the New Testament* (pp. 495–7). The epilogue is ejaculatory in style ; its broken utterances are those of a man whose heart has swelled at the mystery and overwhelming bliss of the beatific vision. And it has been argued that we do wrong to seek in it the architectural symmetry of the apocalypse proper, whose septiform sections testify numerically to a revelation which is perfect. In any case, however, the order given in this translation conveniently groups the ejaculations and reflections of the epilogue, and we shall assume that John wrote it as it is here given.

A certain superficial difficulty arises over the identification of speakers in the epilogue. It is often difficult to decide whether John conceives the utterance to be that of Christ or of the angel who has been his guide, or whether, indeed, he intends us to understand that he himself voices some reflection. It is all one, however. Ultimately, it is the voice of Christ. The angel merely echoes the voice of his Master ; John, as a prophet, merely records it (cf. 2 Pet. i. 21).

The prophet has apparently felt all along that the revelation he has received owes much in some mysterious way to the mediation of angels : a trance did not in itself open the gate into heaven (iv. 1), or enlighten the freed soul about the trend of earthly affairs. ' Rapt in the spirit ' though he was, John was convinced that it was an angel who enabled him to see from his desert vantage the great city of earth (chap. xvii.) ; another angel who brought before his eyes the picture of the holy City (chap. xxi.). And throughout the whole of REVELATION, apparently, there stands by the prophet's side, guiding his pen, prompting his meditation, clarifying his dream-memories, an angel who seems deputed to this sole task of mediating Jesus Christ's testimony. God has sent Jesus Christ's Revelation ' through his angel ' (i. 1) ; and here again it is repeated, 6 **The Lord God of the spirits of the prophets has sent his angel** ... There is no doubt that John fervently believed he was supernaturally assisted, not only in his dreams and visions, but also in the very labour of recording them. The **angel** of whom we have just spoken, standing out of sight behind the whole of REVELATION, was no doubt the ' Genius ' who took counsel with ' the mortal instrument,' and guided the prophet's thought as he meditated on what he **saw**. This seems to be his proper function. But after John's eyes had left the new Jerusalem, he was more immediately conscious of the heavenly being who had shown him the bliss of the redeemed. His conception of these mediaries of Jesus Christ's testimony is august and resplendent. It is not merely that they are enormous, strong, dazzling, or that their voices resounded over land and sea : their impressiveness sprang less out of personal qualities than out of the fact that they represented God and Christ. The strong angel in chap. x., and the reaper angel in chap xiv. resemble most obviously the Lord whose ' testimony ' they are unfolding. But the angels who carry the bowls of the last plagues, one of whom John has already attempted to worship, also resemble Christ ; they were robed like the figure of Christ in chap. i. and like him bore a belt of gold round their breasts—they wear the 8 uniform of vicegerents. John's attempt to **worship** two of their number is prompted by his consciousness that they are representatives of the faithful Witness. It is what he **heard and saw** of heavenly things which makes him fall down to worship beings who brought such glories before his eyes. Both here and in the companion passage (xix. 8–10) the prophet has seen a vision of the Bride ; and he worships those who come in the name of the Bridegroom. There is, as we said before, undoubtedly some reflection here of contemporary tendency to worship angels : and undoubtedly such a practice is discouraged in the twice-uttered words : ' **No, never that !** . . . **Worship God !** ' It is not so clear, however, that such polemic is John's first motive. His main desire seems to be to put prophets, rather than angels, in their places. He wishes all to appreciate that he and his **brothers the prophets** are ambassadors of Christ no less than angels of testimony. They are equally **servants,** and the servant of a king carries the authority of his master. The term is one of high distinction, its religious use implying extreme intimacy with the counsels of God : Moses himself was the *servant of God*, and his name can be coupled naturally with that of the Lamb Himself, in the song of the martyrs (chap. xv.). John's purpose was no doubt twofold : first, and most urgently, to claim for his book the serious consideration which it deserved—since it was the work of one who had equal authority with an angel in mediating Christ's testimony ; and secondly, perhaps, to claim for his **brothers the prophets** a certain primacy in the affairs of the churches. The reason for the second motive has already appeared in chap. xi. It was not merely a question of Church government, for the time was too short to argue about ecclesiastical polity. It was a question of facing the three and a half years of stress, the great ' trial which is coming upon the whole world to test the dwellers on earth.' The Christian prophets were then to stand in the streets of ' Sodom and Egypt,' that great City. They were *witnesses*, and their task was to *prophesy*—to utter ' the testimony borne by Jesus ' (cf. xix. 10), to preach the gospel of the End : the sure triumph of justice, the speedy punishment of evil-doers. The angel's reply to John makes a most impressive claim for Christians on whom the spirit of prophecy fell : we recall that of each of these His servants on earth God says : ' I will be his God and he shall be my son.'

The arresting note on which REVELATION began is now

sounded again. We learn that the book is a record of the hidden purposes of God, who has sent **his angel** to disclose them in sounds and symbols to His servants. The voice of the risen Christ has spoken ! The Most High Himself has broken that majestic silence around His throne—here are His words ! 7 Certainly, **the words of the prophecy of this book** are to be laid to heart. These prophetic sentences have divine authenticity ; and what saint, listening through this apocalypse to the voice of God, and laying to heart what He says, can fail to be himself a prophet and himself proclaim the testimony of Jesus which is the breath of prophecy ?

We can pass quickly over the controverted phrase, **the Lord God of the spirits of the prophets.** What are ' the spirits of the prophets ' ? Does the phrase imply that primitive conception of the Holy Spirit seen in the guise of the seven Spirits of God (see iv. 5, v. 6) ? Or does it mean simply the souls of the prophets ? Or is John referring to angelic guides, as it were, who perform the same service for other prophets as the angel in i. 1 and xxii. 6 did for John ? The phrase is used several times in the Book of Enoch, but whether or not we can presume that the expression in REVELATION is remembered from that source, we cannot presume that the meaning attached to it by the two apocalyptists is identical. We are left uncertain. But after all, this is not an important matter. The fact that we must not miss or understress in the midst of such speculation is that John is again, as in verse 9, recording the most solemn attestation of his book. It is dictated by God, by the God who inspires the prophets : it comes through the angel of God. It is the very code word of prophecy, laying open all that had been ' sealed up ' in silence or expressed ambiguously in 6 ' mysteries ' by prophets in former times ; for it shows **what must come to pass** as no other book had yet done. This is John's belief, and his anxiety that others should appreciate the importance of Christ's great Revelation leads him to repeat several times the assurance of his book's divine origin. **These words are trustworthy and genuine**—they come from God, and John employs this traditional formula of assurance to emphasize the fact ; in xxi. 6 the expression is used by the

Almighty, and the words trustworthy and genuine (' faithful and true ') are used to describe the Witness who spoke to the Laodiceans (iii. 14). Next, we are told that the true prophet is one who will **lay to heart the words of the prophecy of this book.** Such a man is **blessed ;** the sixth of the seven beatitudes is devoted to him : **blessed is he who lays to heart the words of the prophecy of this book** (verse 7), for he at least will be prepared to meet his Master, when He comes on the clouds of heaven. And again John tells how he heard the command : ' **Do not seal up the words of the prophecy of this book** '—do 10 not hold secret this all-important revelation of the divine will. Isaiah (viii. 16) had been inspired to ' seal up ' his prophecies, because his countrymen slighted the truths he unfolded to them. And Daniel (xii. 4), it was related, had been commanded to ' seal up ' his book till the last days, since his visions spoke not of contemporary perils and rewards, but of those in a future age. John, however, has seen **what must come to pass very soon.** He lingers over this thought. He hears the assurance once again—that familiar verse from Daniel, to which he alludes in the first chapter of his book : ' Lo, he is coming on the clouds, to be seen by every eye ' (i. 7). An addition appears now : ' Lo, I am coming **very soon.'** This is John's preoccupation. His message is one of life and death, for **the time is near.** As he told the Laodicean Christians, Christ stands at the door and knocks. As he told the Christians of Sardis : ' I am coming like a thief ; you will not know at what hour I am coming upon you.' None but a fool will ignore a warning so often repeated.

And yet, John feared, there were those even within the fellowship of the churches who would scorn the very words of Christ, uttered though they were on the eve of His coming. What is to be said of them—and of the great mass of pagans whose depravity stifled all hopes of conversion in the mind of a clear-thinking man ?

> **Let the wicked still be wicked,**   11
> **let the filthy still be filthy,**

Their reward was near enough ! If any man were such a fool

as to imagine that he could escape the eyes of Him who was coming ' to requite everyone for what he has done '—why, let him continue in his ways. The grim irony in John's words springs out of a temper and conviction which he shares with other apocalyptists. They possessed no missionary zeal. The trial about to come on the world would result in no conversions ; it would group men clearly according to their good or evil characters ; there were sheep and there were goats— they must be separated. John believes that there are those whose names do not appear in the book of Life which we saw opened at the Judgment throne. Their ways are evil, their destiny decided; in the brief space before the End, they would merely demonstrate their incorrigible wickedness. He speaks rather to those whose names *are* in the book of Life ; he speaks to men whose names *may still be erased* from the book of Life (iii. 5). He speaks to those who may waver :

> **Let the righteous still do right,**
> **let the holy still be holy.**

The trial of their righteousness and holiness is about to come upon them. They must not falter.

The seventh and last beatitude (verse 14) asserts the supreme moral purpose of the whole book : insists on the profound necessity of repentance, of continued loyalty to Christ, to the commandments of God and the testimony of Jesus (xii. 14 17). **Blessed are those who wash their robes, that theirs may be the right to the tree of Life, the right to enter the gates of the City.** We see now, if we have not realized it before, how thoroughly practical in purpose John's picture of the new Jerusalem was. Only the holy may enter into this final holiness ; and therefore, **Blessed are those who wash their robes.** Most of the believers at Sardis, for example, had ' soiled their raiment.' They must repent, and wash their robes (as John expresses it in a metaphor which does not commend itself to everyone to-day) ' in the blood of the Lamb ' (vii. 14) : in other words, they must take to themselves that freedom from sin which Christ won through His death for all who wished to avail themselves of it. They must be clad in the pure white linen which is the righteous conduct of the saints (xix. 8). This was the condition of immortality, and participation in the life of the redeemed community in the age to come. None but those who have been made righteous by Christ can eat of the tree of Life (see verse 2) with its twelve fruits, or enter by those gates inscribed with the names of the twelve tribes of the true Israel (see xxi. 12–13). All others are *outside* the City. On the whole, we prefer to keep the R.V. rendering of the phrase translated here, ' **Begone, you** 15 **dogs. . . .**' Literally, it is ' Outside, the dogs, and the sorcerers, and the vicious creatures, and the murderers, and the idolators, and all who love and practise falsehood.' Dr. Moffat supplies an imperative verb, and excellently captures the vehemence of John's preaching. That must not be missed : the words burn with a fire of prophetic anger. But they probably speak of another sort of fire, too. Outside the city is the fire that burns for ever and ever, a place where the terrors of Death and Hades dwell, where the wicked are joined eternally to the dark Powers they worshipped on earth—joined in equal torture (xiv. 11, xx. 10, 14–15). For ever outside the gates through which the righteous enter, the evil-doers receive the reward of their crimes. John adds the term ' **dogs** ' to his list in xxi. 8 : he means contemptible, abhorrent creatures, probably those addicted to unnatural vices. The two passages, xxi. 8 and xxii. 15, are parallel ; and the threat in each is identical.

JESUS AUTHENTICATES THE BOOK

(xxii. 16–21)

' I Jesus have sent my angel to give you this testimony for the 16
  churches ; I am *the Scion* and offspring of David, the
  bright star of the morning.

13   I am the alpha and the omega,
      the First and the Last,
      the beginning and the end.

12   *Lo, I am coming* very soon, *with my reward,*
      to requite everyone for what he has done.'

17   ' Come,' say the Spirit and the Bride :
      let the hearer too say, ' Come ' ;
      and *let the thirsty come,*
      let anyone who desires it, take *the water of Life without*
      price.

18 [I adjure all who hear the words of the prophecy of this book :
   ' If anyone *adds to them,*
      God will add *to him the* plagues *described in this book ;*

19   and if anyone *takes away* any words written in this book,
      God will take away his share in *the tree of Life* and in the
      holy City described in this book.']

20 He who bears this testimony says, ' Even so : *I am coming* very
      soon.' Amen, Lord Jesus, come !

21 The grace of the Lord Jesus Christ be with all the saints.
      Amen.

   It has been commented that whenever John refers to
Christ's function as Revealer or Witness he uses the name
16 Jesus. He uses it here with great emphasis : **I Jesus have**
sent my angel : the Speaker is He who bore witness in His
life and death—He now bears witness in His glory. As the
historic Jesus He speaks to the prophets (**you** : the word
is plural in the Greek, and refers to John and **his brothers**
the prophets, verse 9) on behalf of Christians throughout the
world.

   He speaks next as the Davidic messiah, **the Scion and**
offspring of David (cf. v. 5), of whom Isaiah spoke (Isa. xi. 1) ;
the righteous deliverer, on whom every gracious virtue
rests ; the divine Champion of Israel—the new Israel, the
Church. He speaks as the inaugurator of a new era of
light, to succeed the darkness of this world ; **the bright star**
of the morning (cf. ii. 28)—a morning which is eternal, for

454

its light is the glory of God and the radiance of the Lamb (xxi. 23). (This is one of the many terms in REVELATION which has parallels in Babylonian and Egyptian theology ; we may perhaps suspect that the latter gave it currency in the cults of Asia Minor ; but primarily it is a late Jewish messianic term, whose source is to be sought in Num. xxiv. 17.)

He speaks as One who shares the attributes of the Most High : as One who is all-embracing—**the alpha and the omega ;** 13 as One who is eternal—**the first and the last ;** as One through whom Creation began (cf. iii. 14), and ultimately must reach its consummation (xxi. 6)—**the beginning and the end.** His words are those which Isaiah heard :

> ' Here is the word of the Eternal, King of Israel,
> Israel's deliverer, the Lord of hosts :
> " I am the first and I am the last,
> There is no God besides me." '
> (Isa. xliv. 6 ; cf. xli. 4 and xliii. 10. See also Rev. i. 18, etc.)

And, finally, Christ speaks as Judge, as we have heard Him speak before in the seven letters :

> ' Lo, I am coming very soon, with my reward,   12
> to requite everyone for what he has done.'

We have seen these words before in the shape of an ominous threat. The Son of God, whose eyes flash like fire, told the Thyatiran Christians that He would exterminate the evil-doers in their midst : ' So shall all the churches know that I am the searcher of the inmost heart ; I will requite each one of you according to what you have done' (ii. 23). The **reward** for the wicked is briefly hinted at in verse 15 ; that of the righteous in verse 14. It is almost unnecessary to repeat that the reward promised to the faithful is a spiritual one, and no bribe of sensual delights : it is a gift of holiness of life for those who desire it. And the deeds on which John is so insistent (' **what they have done** ') are the fruits of grace (cf. notes on xx. 11–15).

But for the loyal there is no terror in the coming of the Christ. He comes to right wrongs which they as His servants

abhor. Just as the four living Creatures one by one cry
17 'Come,' to the agencies of destruction which precede the
Messiah's advent, so cries the Church to her Lord—her Bridegroom. (For even on earth she is the Bride.) The prophets
cry, 'Come,'—it is they who are meant by **the Spirit** ; John
speaks of them collectively, personifying that gift which
distinguishes them from their fellows. There is an echo in
John's words of the liturgical worship in the churches : we
have heard in John's exordium of the 'reader' and the
'hearer' ; now we see the **hearer** encouraged to join in the
ecstatic response of the prophets. When Christ answers this
repeated 'Come,' as He will do soon, then **the thirsty** shall
find their yearning for God satisfied. This is the motive of
John's eagerness for the Parousia ; he sees all frustration of
soul for ever quenched by the **water of Life without price**
(xxi. 6, xxii. 1) ; therefore he bids the thirsty **come** even now,
to meet Him from whose power the living water flows.

Dr. Moffatt has bracketed verses 18–19 as an editorial note,
on the grounds that it forms an anticlimax, and that it is at
variance with the bold, prophetic spirit of the rest of the book.
He interprets the words as an instruction to copyists, modelled
on precedents, and really amounting to a 'stereotyped and
vehement form of claiming a canonicity equal to that of the
Old Testament.' This may well be the true explanation of
the passage ; if it is, we can spare ourselves Luther's indignation at its severity. On the other hand, Dr. Beckwith has
argued with considerable force (*op. cit.*, p. 778) that the writer
is addressing himself not to a copyist but to the same hearer
18– as in verse 17 : '**I adjure all who hear the words of the prophecy**
19 **of this book.**' It is one more warning that the truths in this
revelation must be heeded and faced, and not perverted. The
addition and subtraction refer to the mental attitude of the
hearer, or to the novelties and variations which the churches
might add, in their interpretation of the book, to suit their
own sophistries. Dr. Beckwith seeks the source of these words
in Deut. iv. 2, where Moses says to the Israelites : 'You shall
not add one word to my commands, nor take one word from
them.' John, similarly, was referring to the '*perversion* of

divine truth enjoined.' If this explanation is accepted, John is sternly facing an apprehension which assailed other apocalyptists. In the Ascension of Isaiah, for example, one of the signs of the Last Days is to be seen in the wilful perversion of divinely revealed truths : ' And they will make of none effect the prophecy of the prophets which were before me, and these my visions also will they make of none effect, in order to speak after the impulse of their own hearts.' Such evasion of the clear truths of REVELATION, such distortion of its message, could be only the work of someone like the Nicolaitans of Pergamum or the followers of Jezebel at Thyatira—someone who was lost to the call of repentance and devoted to works of mischief. Therefore, naturally, such a man must expect to lose all the privileges of a Christian, in this world and the next : the **plagues** from which Christians are sheltered (xi. 1–2) must fall on him, because he is of the world : in Babylon, not in the ' desert ' (see p. 238). He must also forgo the bliss of the redeemed community in the future age, as he put himself outside the pale of the Church in this age. His offence is against the voice of prophecy, which is the voice of God (cf. 2 Pet. i. 21).

If verses 18–19 *are* original, they are certainly out of place. For verse 20 skilfully resumes the thought and expression of verse 17. The Bride, the prophets, the hearer—all have said ' Come ' ; and now John, the bearer of **this testimony**, muses : 20 ' **Even so : I am coming very soon** ' ; he allows his thought to dwell on this promise of his Lord's ; it is so glorious to him that he cannot leave it, he must repeat it. And then he utters once more that liturgical **Amen,** and adds from the depth of his heart : **Lord Jesus, come !** He is repeating in Greek the watchword of the early Christians, the Aramaic *Maranatha* (cf. 1 Cor. xvi. 22).

The apocalypse closes in epistolary style, as it began (i. 4). It is John's valediction to his brothers and companions ' in the distress and realm and patient endurance which Jesus brings ' (i. 9). After the style of St. Paul, he prays that his readers will be given that **grace** which brings to birth good 21 deeds. We shall do well to remember that the whole of

REVELATION is a letter, illustrating the need for repentance, for continued faithfulness, new resolution and awareness of the trial which was to confront the churches; it illustrates and vividly enforces what is set out in normal epistolary style in the seven letters.

INDEX

459